MY MODERN MOVEMENT

Robert Dudley Best (1892–1984) was an industrial designer and manufacturer, noted for creating the Bestlite, the first iconic modern object in 1930s Britain. Born into a prosperous Birmingham family, he and his younger brother Frank had wanted to be music-hall entertainers but were derailed in their ambitions—first by their father, R.H. Best, who wanted them to join the family business, Best & Lloyd, and insisted that they study at Germany's best art school, in Düsseldorf, in preparation for this; and then by the First World War, which only Robert survived. Best was an early disciple of F.M. Alexander, the posture therapist and guru, and was politically active in Common Wealth, the alternative socialist group founded in 1942 by J.B. Priestley and Sir Richard Acland, among others. He wrote *Brass Chandelier* (1940), an appreciation of his father's business innovations, and a memoir of his early life, published posthumously by EnvelopeBooks as *From Bedales to the Boche* (2020).

Published in Great Britain in 2021
by Envelope Books, London

1 3 5 7 9 8 6 4 2

A CIP catalogue record is available from the British Library

ISBN 9781838172084

Cover and interior designed by Stephen Games | Booklaunch

Envelope Books
12 Wellfield Avenue
London N10 2EA
www.envelopebooks.co.uk

MY MODERN MOVEMENT

ROBERT DUDLEY BEST

ENVELOPE BOOKS

CONTENTS

INTRODUCTION
STEPHEN GAMES

Robert Dudley Best (1892–1984) should be better known than he is. He was the designer of the Bestlite,[1] the first recognisably 'Modern Movement' object to be made in Britain, hailed by the *Architect's Journal* in 1930 as a genuine 'manifestation' of the Bauhaus. It was no such thing, for reasons we shall see, but the Bestlite was unarguably the foremost modern icon of its time, and remains as loaded a symbol for household goods as Wells Coates's Isokon Building[2] was for architecture. It is instantly recognisable for its metal parabolic cone supported by a bent metal tube supported in turn by a straight metal tube rising from a circular metal base, and with its undisguised electric flex.

Coming from a less productive country, the Bestlite might have been enough to gain a little more celebrity for its creator. Not so in the UK, which requires more output and consistency to wreathe a designer in laurels. Best's misfortune—if it was a misfortune—was that no other well-known product is associated with his name, and he did nothing to publicise the products that he did design; in fact, he was reticent about them, for reasons we shall also see. To the extent that he is remembered at all in design circles, it is the Bestlite that defines him, but it is a definition that falls very wide of the mark.

---

[1] The Bestlite was first produced in 1930. It continues to be manufactured in several versions—a desk lamp, a standard lamp and a wall lamp. The original publicity image is catalogued in the RIBA Library at http://riba.sirsidynix.net.uk/uhtbin/cgisirsi/?ps=iL4lqoSDli/MAIN_CAT/X/9

[2] In Belsize Park, North-West London. Otherwise known as Lawn Road Flats, designed and developed between 1929 and 1932 and therefore exactly contemporary with the Bestlite, but not completed until 1934.

Best's shyness was matched by a measure of embarassment about some of the products his company made. Best & Lloyd had been started by his great-grandfather in Birmingham in 1840 and had by 1900 become the largest lighting manufacturer in the world. By the time he took the firm over from his father, it was supplying products from a massive back-catalogue, and while some of its goods went out of favour and others were introduced to catch new trends, it was nonetheless reliant on established sellers untouched by the recent influence of Walter Gropius. Its heyday, in fact, was the Belle Époque period, from about 1880 to 1914, when its goods bore the characteristics of sumptuous French decoration designed for the nouveau riche.

Best & Lloyd was set up to please its buyers, not challenge them, which pointed it in a very different direction from that of the Bauhaus workshops and more serious-minded enterprises committed to austerity and cultural improvement. Among its clients in the interwar years were the Odeon and Paramount cinema chains, which meant creating Americanised versions of Art-Deco drama and visual impact that would help its clients compete with other movie distribution franchises. It also provided lighting and other furniture (window frames and luggage racks) for Pullman carriages on the Orient Express, and fitted out the Royal Family's home on the Sandringham estate.

Best was brought into the family firm by his father, the charismatic Robert Hall ('R.H.') Best. Best Junior found the company's demands unwelcome at first, and resented its halting of his own childhood aspirations to become a music-hall entertainer with his younger brother Frank. But having become involved in the business and then taken it over, Best felt obliged to keep it going, not just to protect his own income stream and that of his many employees, but because there was no logic in upsetting a business that was successful and productive.

Best was committed, then, to keeping afloat a commercial operation with a range of bestsellers, which meant that, the Bestlite aside, Best & Lloyd's goods were by no means manifestations of the Bauhaus: in most cases, the very opposite.

Nor was Best such a manifestation—although, had he been ten years younger, he might have been. He had trained at art school —uniquely for a British industrialist—and, moreover, an overseas art school, and not just any overseas art school but the Kunstgewerbeschule (school of applied arts) in Düsseldorf. Rather than this being the school that Gropius had founded in Weimar in 1910, it was the school that the architect Peter Behrens (1868–1940) had run from 1903, restructuring it during his four years there and using it as the springboard for his creation of the Deutscher Werkbund[3] in Munich in 1907, the year he was also retained to transform Germany's leading electrical company, AEG. Best missed Behrens by four years—he attended the Kunstgewerbeschule from 1911 to 1912—but will have been aware of Behrens's reforms and benefited from them, as well as absorbing the collectivist atmosphere and the aesthetics that are familiar from the Werkbund and that his father admired. It was, indeed, to inculcate Best in this atmosphere that his father chose Düsseldorf for him, in preference to any other training ground his son could have visited.

Having immersed himself in German thinking for a year, Best then joined the atelier of a French artist-designer before becoming an apprentice in his father's workshop, where he was gently introduced to the theory and practice of design, making experimental castings and being mentored by the firm's senior staff in how to make them better. His tastes were educated, then, but not in the futuristic but financially impoverished climate of Weimar Germany into which the Bauhaus was born but in the richer, more generous climate of pre-war affluence, indulgence and political stability.

Because of his background, Best found himself torn, as he entered his forties in the 1930s, between what he recognised as the new Zeitgeist—the Central-European brand of modern

---

3 Behrens brought together Theodor Fischer, Josef Hoffmann, Hermann Muthesius, Joseph Maria Olbrich, Bruno Paul, Richard Riemerschmid, Fritz Schumacher and three others as founding members of the Werkbund, together with twelve companies.

minimalism that seemed to embody social and aesthetic progress—and his private and business commitment to the relative status quo in design and manufacturing. For these reasons—his personal tastes and upbringing, and his obligation to maintain the momentum at Best & Lloyd—he could not be an acolyte of the Modern Movement when it arrived in Britain. He shared some of its moral aims, not least its wish to give the public things that worked better, but in general he had not observed that Functionalist design was necessarily superior, nor that it had the capacity to elevate the public mind, nor that it deserved to be campaigned for. He also had strong reservations about those individuals and groups that did such campaigning, and about the techniques they used.

The main tool for promoting Functional design in the 1930s and 40s, other than books and the popular press, was the exhibition, and one of the most important was the 'Exhibition of British Industrial Art in Relation to the Home' held at Dorland Hall, off Lower Regent Street in London, in the summer of 1933. Two years earlier, an inspirational exhibition of Swedish goods had also been held at Dorland Hall, illustrating a standard of beauty and craftsmanship that caused some consternation in UK educated circles. The Swedish exhibition added fuel to the growing perception that Britain was lagging behind its overseas rivals and that its products looked clumsy and dated.

Best did not see this. His father had occasionally sent him abroad to sell—or, failing that, to assess interest in—the firm's products and he had travelled to Germany in 1923 to visit the first post-war trade fair, in Leipzig, to inspect new glassware. The feedback he got from buyers was that English design, though largely untouched by novel European trends, was valued—both for its enduring qualities and for its recognisable Englishness. He thought this gave the UK a different sort of competitive edge and one that should not be disregarded.

This dissenting voice—that there was sufficient merit in British household goods not to warrant apology—is not often found in accounts of the period, although he was not alone.

When the Gorell Committee[4] proposed that the government fund a permanent exhibition of good design to raise public standards, Parliament took the contrary view that design could be trusted to evolve at a more natural pace without the need for an expensive state-sanctioned showcase—although it did back the Committee's proposal for temporary exhibitions, local exhibitions and travelling exhibitions, at home and abroad.

Best's vested interest in Best & Lloyd partly explains his hesitancy about Functional design but has also to be seen side-by-side with his distaste for how Functionalism was being promoted. While modern design had an agenda of its own within art circles of the period, it had also become a modish preoccupation for individuals and groups with 'superior' or 'expensive' tastes. Best did not like anyone assuming the moral high ground to dictate standards and thought it divisive; others simply objected to who was doing the dictating.

To take a case in point, while most participants in the Dorland Hall exhibition in 1933 agreed that the mind of the public needed to be elevated, members of the Design and Industries Association—ostensibly the event's main sponsor—sat so uncomfortably with those recruited by the magazine *Country Life*[5] that they refused in the end to give the event their formal support. That run-in between supposedly 'authentic' Moderns (capital M) and 'bogus' modernists (small m and an -ist

---

4 The Committee on Art and Industry, set up in the wake of the Swedish exhibition by the Department of Trade and chaired by Lord Gorell (Ronald Barnes), a Liberal politician, poet, author and newspaper editor.

5 *Country Life* was better known for its coverage of country houses and antiques but it also took up the cause of modern architecture through the writings of its Architectural Editor Christopher Hussey, born and brought up at Scotney Castle in Kent (now owned by the National Trust). Hussey collaborated with his friend, the country-house architect and *décorateur-de-luxe* Oliver Hill (1887–1968), in generating support for the Dorland Hall exhibition, bringing in funds and further encouragement from philanthropists, industrialists and socialites including Sir Phillip Sassoon, St. John Hornby, Samuel Courtauld, Lord Aberconway, Lady Melchett, Viscountess Snowden and Lady Mount Temple, among others.

ending), or between intellectual fellow travellers and followers of high fashion, has been documented extensively, but does not represent Best's position. It was the authoritarianism that both sides were willing to engage in that he took issue with, and on this count he was largely alone.[6]

My Modern Movement documents Best's growing awareness of this distance between himself and those who claimed to speak for British design, as well as his opposition to the culture of imposition that they thought appropriate to their mission. As such, it is—or could have been, had it been published at the time —an important book, with a message similar to that of Karl Popper's *The Open Society and its Enemies. The Open Society*, which appeared at the end of the Second World War, is a defence of democracy in the face of totalitarian tendencies and ideas of historical inevitability that Popper traced back to Plato (in Volume 1) and to Hegel and Marx and others (in Volume 2). Best's study, far less grand, is mostly a memoir of his own life but increasingly broadens into an examination of how various contemporaries co-opted by the state engaged in an apparently benign economic campaign that had offensive political overtones.

My Modern Movement recognises that for people of 'advanced' tastes, Functional design was a welcome corrective to the debased aesthetics of the commercial world but cautions against the methods it used to make its case, for reasons that its propagandists found hard to understand (as Sir Charles Tennyson makes clear in his Foreword). If 'the few' knew better than 'the many', and had an obligation to elevate the less capable *whether they liked it or not*, was it not reasonable for 'the few' to impose their own standards from above? In the context of the times, with a centralised culture built around the B.B.C. and

---

[6] The issue of warring parties has been written about by Vanessa Vanden Berghe in a 2013 MPhil thesis that attempts to rehabilitate the society architect Oliver Hill from his reputation as too flexible, fashion-conscious and dextrous to be a true Modern.

growing cross-party acceptance of the need for a welfare state, such an idea did not seem problematic. If those with superior minds and educations did not intervene on behalf of the masses, they would have been betraying their own enlightenment and their obligation to elevate the less capable. But if they did intervene, where did this leave the democratic principles that our liberal society prides itself on?

Although raised in material comfort, Best was ill at ease with the privileges and entitlements enjoyed by the rich and the clever. In 1942 he worked with J.B. Priestley and others to set up 'Common Wealth', a left-wing grouping intended to counter the Labour Party and its suport for state control and to encourage cooperative ownership, decentralisation and syndicalism. *My Modern Movement* reveals the extension of these ideas into Best's thoughts on design, notably his aversion to exhibitions proposed by bodies like the Council of Industrial Design to promote modern manufacturing. Best argued that these events, however well meaning, were redolent of fascism. The selectors appointed themselves; did not hold themselves to account; did not see any need to make the reasons for their selections transparent; did not submit their selections to testing; and did not invite the participation on equal terms of those who supplied the products being exhibited or those they were meant to educate. Instead of leaving questions of merit open to debate, they made them subject to manipulation and ideology—as were exhibits at the Festival of Britain in 1951. Best called instead for collectivist exhibitions that gave equal weight to expert and public tastes, and left preference a matter of individual choice.

Design propagandists responded that the uneducated could not play an equal part in the discussion on design because they were too ill-informed—that they only acquired an opinion of any value once experts had trained them to a higher understanding —but the freedom of the ill-informed to make judgments is exactly how Western democracy works. We grant ultimate authority to those who appear least qualified to exercise it, not because we are convinced that each individual elector is part of a

Great Brain that collectively knows what none of its constituent parts knows independently, but because every other political system seems to us even more egregious—the so-called Winston Churchill defence.[7] This simple idea lay at the heart of Best's attack on the design establishment of his day. In his view, the sense of *noblesse oblige* that motivated such bodies as the Council of Industrial Design, set up in 1944 to improve the quality of British manufacturing and make it more saleable, saw no reason not to batter the public into giving up what it felt happy with in favour of more 'cultivated' alternatives.

Best was affronted by bullying. As a manufacturer he did not want to be dictated to by theorists and intellectuals; as someone without a university education he did not want to be dictated to by scholars; as a designer, he did not want to be dictated to by artists; and as a Brummie he did not want to be dictated to by Southerners. He recognised that he lacked sophistication and that his tastes were too conventional for the various smart sets, but he also saw that his vulnerability alerted him to the little abuses committed habitually by others and the tendency of the metropolis to ride roughshod over regional self-determination.

It was to exorcise his fears and prove his competence that he wrote the book that follows—to raise issues that more literate rivals were insensitive to while also confessing beguilingly to his limitations and humour. And behind all this stood his father.

Best's grasp of business—its commercial but also its moral imperative—was largely the product of his father's influence. R.H. Best (1843–1925) had taken personal responsibility for guiding his son's destiny, sending him to Bedales, the new, progressive boarding school that John Haden Badley (1865–1967) had started the year after Best was born, and demanding that he join him on trips to Germany that combined sightseeing with

---

[7] 'Many forms of Government have been tried, and will be tried in this world of sin and woe. No one pretends that democracy is perfect or all-wise. Indeed it has been said that democracy is the worst form of Government *except for all those other forms that have been tried from time to time* ... .' Winston Churchill, 11 November, 1947.

close examinations of his counterparts' innovations. Best later wrote, in Brass Chandelier, of his father's admiration for Joseph Chamberlain,[8] the radical one-time mayor of Birmingham, and of Chamberlain's emulation of German experimentation, which Best Senior carried over into his own studies of metallurgy and his proposals for educational reform.[9] It is not hard to speculate that Best Junior's various nervous ailments and his stammer resulted from his fears of not pleasing his father and, in his own words, of his becoming 'constipated' by his father's insistence that he emulate the accuracy and discipline of Ruskin rather than the 'ethereal smudge' of French Impressionism (pages 11–12).

Other charismatic adults also shaped Best's thinking, not least many whom his father had admired first. In one of the last chapters of Brass Chandelier, Best writes about the similarity of approach of his headmaster J.H. Badley and his father's friend Dr. Georg Kerschensteiner (1854–1932), director of education in Munich from 1895 to 1919. Both men believed in learning by doing. 'Both Badley and Kershensteiner set themselves to replace the old "book schools" with "work schools" [in which] physics and chemistry, instead of being a matter of memory, were taught in laboratories and became valuable not only as specialised knowledge, but as a method of work and observation [and in which] the artistic impulse was not confused with drawing of geometrical figures but related to the objects of the house, the workshop and the garden.'[10] According to Kerschen-

---

[8] Joseph Chamberlain (1836–1914) had made his fortune manufacturing screws, began his political career as a social reformer and worked tirelessly once in government to build alliances with Germany, the two goals coming together in, for example, his adaptation of Bismarck's system of compensation for injuries sustained at work. Starting out as a Liberal he moved to Liberal Unionism (in coalition with the Conservatives) and then to Conservatism itself. Best's father supported him politically and regarded him as a friend.

[9] R.D. Best, Brass Chandelier (London: George Allen Unwin, 1940).

[10] Brass Chandelier, 213.

steiner, these practical tasks were not introduced for the sake of manual skill alone but because 'work and not books is the means to culture, and work must be regardless of self in its service of mankind or of a great truth.'[11] Design as the product of doing makes Best a more genuine Functionalist than many of those who advocated Functionalism as an ideology, and made special sense in Birmingham, the centre of light industry in England and home to the first university department to study business at a scholarly level. Birmingham believed in the public and in the idea that behaviour and sentiment should be researched and understood, not disregarded or treated as inadequate.

A close friend and supporter of Robert Best was Philip Sargant Florence (1890–1982), the Cambridge-educated American economist who became the first Professor of Commerce at Birmingham in 1929 and who specialised in studies of factory conditions and fatigue. Reading about business management and industrial theory in technical manuals was a waste of time, Sargant Florence wrote in the Introduction to *Brass Chandelier*, because '[t]he difficulties inherent in materials and men are not realised by the reader, and everything seems too plain sailing.' What mattered were 'the particulars of a typical business, the big and little troubles that crop up continually due to the human nature of management ...'. Once these were studied, he added, 'the whole becomes a human-interest story where the attainment of efficiency appears as quite an exciting feat.'[12]

For Best, Birmingham embraced realities that London swept aside and he was sceptical and suspicious of personalities by whom he might otherwise have been merely overawed. On 17 January, 1935 he and his wife Mireille were invited to meet Gropius and his wife Ise, together with László Moholy-Nagy (1895–1946) and his wife Sibyl, at a supper given by the furniture

---

[11] Georg Kerschensteiner, *The Schools and the Nation*, trans. C.K. Ogden (London: Macmillan), 235; quoted in *Brass Chandelier*, 213.

[12] *Brass Chandelier*, 11.

entrepreneur Jack Pritchard (1899–1992) and his wife Molly in their flat in the Isokon Building (which Best & Lloyd had lit and which Pritchard had taken a display stand to promote at the Dorland Hall exhibition which Best & Lloyd had also lit). On that occasion, Best's 'admiration for [Gropius's] teaching and practical achievements ... [was mingled with] speculation regarding some of his theoretical principles,' including Gropius's contempt for snobbery on matters of taste, a trait that Best considered not only natural and excusable but something that designers should positively factor into their creations rather than condemning, along with 'style' and 'fashion'.

The Bests met the Gropiuses again later that year when they hosted a drinks party at their home in Handsworth, Birmingham, ahead of the annual dinner of the Design and Industries Association. On this occasion, Best felt more exposed. 'Gropius ... had warned us against the dangers that "modern" architecture would become fashionable and that snobbery would distort its fundamental truth and simplicity. But snobbery, I thought, may well, unfortunately, begin at home.' What might Gropius think of the Bests' electric candles or the 'charming antiques' that decorated their shelves or the 'pleasant chintzes' that might not be accepted as truthful and sincere—or, indeed, the electric Rippleray fire, with flame effect, that Best himself had designed? Had he not better hide it in the cellar? (See page 140.)

The fear that his household artefacts might label him a man of common tastes upset Best but did not ultimately undermine his judgment. Setting his fears about Gropius down on paper, 'these notions, I immediately realised on reading them, were childish and ridiculous, especially bearing in mind the tolerant and kindly attitude of my guest.' Best's generosity of spirit, and his recognition of this in others, usually saved him from more serious psychoses. He did, however, have a tendency to seek help from celebrity healers: in the 1920s from the French therapist Emile Coué (1857–1926), who created a sensation through his ideas on autosuggestion and self-improvement; and in the 1930s from the Australian posture guru Frederick Matthias (F.M.) Alexander (1869–1955), author of the Alexander Technique, whom Best first introduced to Birmingham, organising meetings for him and promoting him to prospective patients before finally denouncing him in an essay in 1941.

Best's disenchantment with Alexander's bullying parallels his disenchantment with the propagandists of the Modern Movement—the 'new Puritans', as he quotes Osbert Lancaster calling them—and rested on what he regarded as the use of methods, referred to above, that in politics would be reviled as dictatorial. Again, the paternal tyranny that his father exercised over him seems to explain his sensitivity to compulsion. Having foregone his own ambition to become a music-hall writer and entertainer, he was tormented that his younger brother's death as a fighter pilot in 1917 not only robbed him of his beloved writing partner but left him having to carry the burden of his father's expectations on his own when his brother might otherwise have shared it.

These experiences made Best acutely conscious of patterns of coercion and intimdation. He records in the pages that follow how he took to task Frank Pick (1878–1941), a man he otherwise admired as Chief Executive of the London Passenger Transport Board and as President of the Design and Industries Association and first Chairman of the Council for Art and Industry. Best accused Pick of misrepresenting to his own advantage the minutes of meetings they had sat in together to make it appear that the decisions Pick had wanted to push through were uncontested. Best also offers the first challenge to Nikolaus Pevsner (1902–1983), who had come to live in Birmingham after leaving Germany in late 1933, and whom Best had got to know and like well.

It was in fact Best's fascination with Pevsner and discomfort at some of his judgments that led him to write to me in 1983, shortly after Pevsner's death, offering to discuss their friendship and his misgivings. Out of that approach came my own affection for Best, my transcription of two First World War plays that he had written,[13] my publishing of his early memoirs (*From Bedales to the Boche*, 2020) and my transcribing of his later diaries (not yet published).[14]

Best was uncannily prescient about Pevsner. It was Sargant Florence who had nudged Pevsner from the sickly subject of Italian art history in the later sixteenth century towards the relevant and very Birmingham topic of discovering the social determinants of British domestic manufacturing in the modern day.[15]

This was an unusual piece of academic research, unlike anything Pevsner had done before, and led to *An Enquiry into Industrial Art in England* (1937), Pevsner's second book within four years of arriving in England. It was in this book that Best identified a tone of voice that he felt echoed the boot squads then making their presence known in Germany and that he found freakish, coming as it did from one of their victims:

> The manufacturer and the retailer who say that they are proud of not having any taste, that they are ready to supply anything which is asked for, and that educating the public is no business of theirs must be called public enemies plainly and bluntly. They must change their outlook, or sooner or later public enterprise will interfere and make life rather unpleasant for them.[16]

By any standards, that is a very intimidating threat and Best was right to call Pevsner out on it. He was also right to view Pevsner's contempt for public taste as snobbish, not in the 'unacceptable'

---

[13] The first, a Beckettian reflection on the boredom of life in the army mess; the other, a more John Buchan-type adventure, both based on experience.

[14] Among other things these refer to his remarriage, his first sales trip to America, his early lionising of F.M. Alexander and his involvement in Common Wealth.

[15] [Sargant Florence also commissioned Gropius to design a second Isokon building on land that he owned in Birmingham but the scheme was never realised, in common with most of Gropius's commissions in Britain.]

[16] Nikolaus Pevsner, *An Enquiry into Industrial Art in England* (Cambridge: Cambridge University Press, 1937), 231. See also page 179 et seq.

way that Gropius condemned as bourgeois but in the 'acceptable' way by which those of a progressive mentality preened their own tastes, and he identified Pevsner's habit of scapegoating as 'reminiscent of some race theories then achieving notoriety' (see pages 171–2). He called Eric Gill to account for the same reason: both had a habit of condemning public taste by making out that the public was the innocent dupe of commercial conspirators:

> In spite of his Christian faith, Eric Gill turned on businessmen in a way that recalls Hitler and his Race Theory. He cursed 'the monstrous filthiness of the man of business' who 'laid his evil hands on every corner of the earth' and who 'pandered to the lowest denominator of taste'. It was foul—worse than lechery and drunkenness. It was idolatory—destructive and desolating. The desire for money was the root of all evil. The businessman applied only one test: 'Does it pay?' Science and industry might be good things in themselves but they both led to the degradation of man and the isolation of the fine arts. The pages of his autobiography are scattered with variations on this theme. (See page 158.)

Best went on to level similar criticisms at the Council of Industrial Design, set up by the President of the Board of Trade in 1944 in the wake of the Gorell Committee's recommendations, and suggested in the book's final pages that his interventions had in fact won some concessions. In spite of that, he never quite forgives the CoID even though, as a syndicate, it is a form of collective that he has advocated for, whereas towards Gill, and especially Pevsner—individuals whom his politics ought to have made him more wary of—he is more emollient. 'In moral condemnation, Pevsner's bark was worse than his bite,' he comments. 'At the back of all this *vertu farouche* (ferocity) was much kindliness and common sense.' (See page 180).

BEST WAS A passionate and an earnest writer, sometimes a little gauche and whimsical when on uncertain ground, sometimes a little repetitive when at a loss for a more developed critical vocabulary, but with a level of insight and moral concern that is unsurpassed for its day.

What Best wants to air is the question that Pevsner addressed in *Enquiry*—what motivates design at a human level?—but he does so not by engaging in partisan research, as Pevsner did, but by quoting speculative writings by contemporary philosophers and social psychologists—Thorstein Veblen, Mary Follett, Rupert Crawshay-Williams, F.A. Hayek and Karen Horney.

He also expands the discussion beyond the limited terms of reference habituated by design critics, calling on his father's relationship with Charles Kay ('C.K.') Ogden (1889–1957), who co-authored with R.H. Best a 1914 book on 'continuation schools' (i.e. secondary schools for less scholarly pupils), and citing members of Ogden's circle at Cambridge including Ivor Armstrong ('I.A.') Richards (1893–1979) and the afore-mentioned Philip Sargant Florence, both of whom shared an interest in the interaction of meaning, language and thought, and in the idea of creating a Basic English for universal use.

Many of these references now read as stubbornly dated; especially problematic is Thomas Sturge Moore, a poet and artist who impressed Best while at Bedales but whose writing now reads as too self-indulgent and affected to be of any obvious value.

We are left with an archive that remains trapped in time—a document with no currency because it was not published when it might have been—but one that is revealing nonetheless. It brings to the fore names less prominent in standard histories of design: Best's tutors in Düsseldorf—the German painter Adolf Rudolf Hochreiter, the Austrian architect Max Benirschke (1880–1961) and the school's head, the architect Wilhelm Kreis (1873–1955); the French artist Georges Alexandre Lucien Boisselier (1876–1943); employees in the Best & Lloyd factory; leading figures in the Birmingham art world—Robert Catterson-Smith, who headed the Art School, his successor B.J. Fletcher, a friend of Sturge Moore, and Solomon Charles ('S.C.') Kaines-Smith (1876–1958), Keeper of the City Museum and Art Gallery; a number of French designers highlighted by Charles-Guillaume Janneau (1887–1981) at the 1925 Paris *Exposition des Arts Décoratifs et Industriels Modernes*, and their English counterparts, named by Harold Chalton Bradshaw CBE (1893–1943)[17]; contemporaries whom Best admired or worked with such as Herbert 'Bobbie' Simon, whom he credits with refreshing Best & Lloyd's approach to publicity, the architects Percy Morley Horder (1870–1944) and his partner Verner Rees (1886–1966), and the former Bauhaus teacher Naum Slutzky (1894–1965); his Birmingham University friends Sargant Florence, Cyril Batho (1885–1951), Professor of Civil Engineering; and his father's academic associates C.K. Ogden, I.A. Richards and Georg Kerschensteiner.

These are not the names that would normally populate a book on English design in the second quarter of the twentieth century; nor are the confessions that Best makes here about his own values and his liking for objects that his factory and others produced to please the masses and foreign buyers. Unfamiliar, also, are the criticisms Best levels at the design world's zealots, figures that conventional histories normally celebrate: the book designer Noel Carrington (1895–1989), 'high-priest of D.I.A.-ism' whom Best quotes for his accusations of treachery against those less hardline than himself; the—to Best—loathsome Australian philosophy lecturer Samuel Clement ('S.C.') Leslie (1898–1980), who became a British civil servant and was the Council of Industrial Design's first Director from 1945 to 1947; Lord Gorell of the Gorell Committee, whose report Pevsner hailed as 'the first official document to emphasise the vital importance of improvements in British industrial art and to confirm the urgent necessity of immediate action' but which Best condemned as an unaccountable dictatorship of design tsars; and craftsmen such as the potter Harold Stabler (1872–1945), the silversmith Edward Spencer (1872–1938) and the metalworker and jeweller John Paul

---

[17] Bradshaw was a Liverpool-born architect, recipient of the first Rome scholarship in Architecture (1913) and first Secretary of The Royal Fine Art Commission.

Cooper (1869–1933), whose work was unaffordable and, to Best's mind, illegitimate because it did not have to abide by the constraints of affordability.

In conclusion, *My Modern Movement* can be seen to be as much about political morality as about design, and I end this Introduction by noting the gap between Best's take on moral issues and that of various counter-propagandists, who have sailed under the false flag of morality to float ideas of their own about what is good for the public that are merely alternative versions of the views they oppose.[18]

IN MAKING THIS book available, I wish to record my thanks to Robert Best's son John, who entrusted to me his father's archive, and to John's executors for allowing me to bring his work to publication. Sam Woodward, who bought Best & Lloyd out of administration in 2002 and is now its managing director, has been helpful with background information about the firm. Magnus Englund, Director of the Isokon Gallery Trust, was also helpful. I thank in addition Derek Collett for his proofreading, Gareth Pugh for his final check, Christopher Dance for his indexing and the indefatigable Marshall Colman for his reading of the text and sensible editorial advice.

ROBERT BEST'S ARCHIVE is looking for a permanent home. It includes all the material covered in Best's three books, *Brass Chandelier*, *From Bedales to the Boche*, and *My Modern Movement*, the manuscripts of his two plays, the diary of his life (including his association with F.M. Alexander) and his notes on Common Wealth. All inquiries should be addressed to the publisher.

---

[18] I am of course thinking of the art historian David Watkin, whose *Morality and Architecture* I have battled with frequently before, and (among others) the late Gavin Stamp, whose treatment of this period was shaped by his outrageous snobbery.

I am very grateful to Bob Best for asking me to contribute a foreword to this book. He knows how heartily I disagree with a great deal of it and it is chivalrous of him to give me a chance of saying so.

I am quite confident that there are absolute standards of design and, in spite of what Mr. Best says, I believe that no one knows the difference between good and bad better than himself.

On the other hand I agree with him that passing fashion is too often made the test of merit. Designs which are not in the

---

[1] Sir Charles Tennyson (1879–1977) was a grandson of the poet Alfred Lord Tennyson, a civil servant and an industrialist with an interest in design. He was educated at Eton College and King's College, Cambridge, where he gained a first in Part I of the Law Tripos and was a Whewell Scholar in 1903. He served as an assistant legal adviser at the Colonial Office from 1911 to 1919. In 1928 he became Secretary of the Dunlop Rubber Company, a post he held until 1948. He was chairman of the Industrial Art Committee of the Federation of British Industry from its inception in 1921 until 1949. He was at various times a Fellow and Governor of the British Institute of Industrial Art, Chairman of the National Register of Designers and Chairman of the Board of Trade's Utility Furniture and Utility Furniture Production Committees. He served on the committee of the Council for Art and Industry's report *Design and the Designer in Industry*, set up in 1937, completed in 1940 but not published until 1944 because of the war. In 1944 he was appointed by Hugh Dalton, President of the Board of Trade, to serve on the Council of Industrial Design and chaired the CoID's Exhibition Committee. He was made a Companion of the Most Distinguished Order of St Michael and St George (CMG) in the 1915 New Year Honours and was knighted in 1945. Two of his three sons were killed in the Second World War.

current mode (or 'contemporary idiom') may be very good and designs which are in it, very bad, although I fancy that on the whole, artists of lively imagination are more likely to design well in the contemporary idiom than when asked to concoct some pastiche from the past.

What I think we have to attack is the far-too-common lethargy about design. Too few manufacturers have a definite design policy; far too many are content to go on making dull adaptations from their own past successes or the current successes of their competitors. If every British manufacturer regarded design as an important element of quality, and design as a technique requiring special abilities and training, Britain's productions might lead the world.

I have no sympathy with the man who laments that he has to sell bad design because the public wants it. I don't believe that anyone has ever proved that the customer who likes a particular style of design won't like a good example of it better than a bad one—especially if the producer is willing to put an equal amount of energy and thought into his efforts to sell the good.

Too often (and this is what I think annoys the spirited author of this book) the design enthusiast makes his attack on the wrong ground. He attacks what is sold on the grounds that it is not in the contemporary idiom whereas he ought to leave the choice of idiom to the producer who has to sell what he produces and attack only if and because the product is a bad example of the idiom chosen, which it much too often is.

As to the danger of centralisation, I agree that if there could be enlightened design organisations in all the chief industries and homogeneous industrial districts, this would be ideal, but the industrial epoch has been in existence for 200 years and more without this happy condition emerging, and the centralised organisation of the Council of Industrial Design has in my opinion done more to improve British design during the seven years of its existence than all the efforts of industrial and local organisations during the past two centuries.

The policy of the Council has always embraced a considerable measure of devolution and it is only the reluctance of industries to adopt this policy which has delayed its fulfilment. I hope that before long we may see some useful progress in that direction.

Meanwhile I commend my old friend's book as an entertaining and thought-provoking contribution to a controversy in which his knowledge and experience and dialectical ability entitle him to a benevolent hearing.

CHAPTER 1
THE GAP

Critic and manufacturer

Since the First World War, industrialists cannot fail to have noticed a growing volume of speculation about the nature of 'good' industrial design, much of it bound up with the so-called 'Functionalist' doctrine.

After 1934, when the Council for Art and Industry was formed,[1] the state became increasingly involved in design criticism and ten years later the Council of Industrial Design set itself to encourage a certain style—'the contemporary idiom'—by exhibitions, publications and other means.

There is now a whole school of individuals claiming expertise in these matters, which is not the same thing as distinguished performance. They are design critics and not designers, just as professional music critics are a different phenomenon from that of performers and composers.

In industrial design, one type of producer deserves special consideration. I refer to the person who has not only designed and manufactured goods but has taken around the results of his labours and sold them. His feelings about design are inclined to be coloured by his experience and his approach to criticism will be somewhat different from that of the individual who employs others to design and sell, and, in fact, from all those who know about the designer–customer relationship only at second-hand.

I have myself had this first-hand experience, chiefly in

---

[1] See Chapter 13.

connection with light fittings and architectural metalwork. The result has been a growing awareness of a gap between what the critics write and say about 'good' or 'bad' design and what is actually needed to enrich the flow of designed goods.

The critics and committee-men can no doubt play a useful part in this process of enrichment, but only if the gap between theory and practice is narrowed. In this essay I will discuss whether the gap is not being actually widened through attempts to simplify and provide ready-made rules for something which is, above all, mysterious and irrational; whether a source of confusion, peculiar not only to government councils but to art-school teaching, may not arise through trying to apply principles which are only appropriate to the fine arts; and whether the Kafka-like source of decrees on design might not be infallible because of its remoteness and ministerial imprimatur.

Lines of force

Industrial design seems to exist in a field of opposing forces. On the demand side we find the search for beauty, for satisfaction of the eye, sometimes mixed with the desire for influence and prestige (*snobbism*) and sometimes competing against it, as Veblen suggests.[2] Industrial design is sometimes opposed even to questions of utility.

On the supply side, the necessity to please a customer often conflicts with the urge to suit one's own fancy or to get something out of one's system—the need to 'express oneself' so strongly felt by the composer, poet or artist.[3]

It seems probable that, whatever the cash value of a great

---

[2] Thorstein Veblen, *The Theory of the Leisure Class* (New York: Macmillan, 1899), Chapter VI, 'Pecuniary Canons of Taste'.

[3] It might be argued that 'artistic integrity' is the result of an overwhelming need to expel some secretion, rather than the manifestation of moral conduct. If this aesthetic outflowing is appreciated by the public, so much the better for the artist's material standard of life. If not, he is prepared to suffer and even starve. Sometimes it looks as if he cannot help himself.

artist's work, it remains estimable in its own right. Not so with industrial design which, by definition, must be considered in relation to some market, even when the customer is a government department or, worse, a dictatorship. What sells well may not be 'good' design but all good design must sell, and at a price to cover the cost of production under conditions of reasonably good administration.

I referred to dictators. From behind the iron curtains of authoritarian governments there reach us ugly glimpses of power, backed by cruelty, being used against 'artistic integrity', such evil forces being answered in their turn by open rebellion or by sycophancy, mingled at times, thank God, with a form of satirical humour, guying the dictatorships.

But we should beware of assuming that the design and art world of democratic Great Britain is entirely free from these dark forces. The seeds of authoritarian government can be found in, let us say, the committee meeting of a suburban tennis club, with its dominant chairman or secretary and its faked skeleton agenda which effectively prevents members of the committee from preparing their thoughts before the meeting. And is not the desire for power, albeit in a mild form, to be recognised in some of Britain's aesthetic groups: the associations, academies and councils of the period under review?

The united front

There is obviously a special factor in the design of clothing, household appliances and furniture which scarcely exists in the fine arts. It is the functional. Unlike a painting or musical composition, good industrial design can in large respect be measured and graded objectively.

The doctrine of 'Fitness for Purpose' is, furthermore, a sound one. It is easy to see, therefore, how human beings, in their craving for simplicity and unification, should cling to this lifebelt when swimming in stormy aesthetic waters.

We must examine this, therefore, and see whether the very

simplicity of the functional criterion does not appeal to certain groups of critics as a foundation on which to build their own influence, because behind the functional standard, easy to explain superficially, a united front can be aligned.

If preferences in design matters are, like music and religion, largely personal, what, asks the man in the street, is the point of coteries that push good design? A good question. The real issues in this respect are not so much technical and aesthetic as those that concern human relationships or the exercise of power by groups—questions, that is to say, for investigation by the social psychologist.

The changing scale and new techniques of industrial output are leading to new forms of organisation and techniques. This is common knowledge. It is only to be expected that governmental groups should seek to extend industrial planning and *dirigisme* into the sphere of art and design.

But decentralisation, with devices for sharing power and responsibility, and for promoting two-way traffic in ideas, is as badly needed in the group activity we call 'design criticism' as in industrial units administered by the National Coal Board.

The Design Centre[4]

The opening of the Design Centre on 26 April, 1957 must have seemed an event of the greatest importance, a 'landmark for the Council of Industrial Design'.[5] It was the culmination of many years' patient work, the result of much propaganda, many reports and divers committee meetings in which official and unofficial bodies had been involved. As they entered No. 28 Haymarket, many felt a sense of relief and gratitude; but others, like myself, were uneasy about the way the landmark had been

---

4 [The four paragraphs that follow come from a 1957 revised text in which the author's thoughts of ten years earlier (and preserved in this edition) were rewritten in the past tense, as if to indicate that his battle had been lost.]

5 'A Royal Occasion', *Design*, May 1956, No. 89. Published by the Council of Industrial Design.

reached and doubtful as to its future.[6] This enquiry into the politics of industrial design is an attempt to trace the events leading up to such a notable occurrence and the causes of division. Since my own life has been very much mingled with these events, I have chosen the form of a memoir.

By trade I am a manufacturer, and through circumstances, education and character, industrial design has occupied my attention for many years. Although, at the beginning of the century, the foundations of my education were laid in the moralistic climate of Ruskin, most of the views expressed in the following pages were arrived at empirically.

In this biographical assessment I have set myself the task of determining within the limits of my experience whether there are absolute standards of design but the subject is complex. That is why 'design politics' in this country, from 1934 onwards, deserves the social psychologist's attention. Without it, much is likely to remain hidden or unnoticed unless, as in this essay, an attempt is made to uncover it and present it for discussion.[7]

---

[6] This uneasiness and doubt had existed for some years. In 1948, writing in the *Architectural Review*, Prof. Charles Madge, after suggesting that there is a sense in which all things are equally 'beautiful', depending on how you looked at them, admitted that there was something wrong, or perhaps odd, about the things which are liked by a large number of people today. He believed 'the malady to be by no means confined to speculative builders or humble art-school students who design wallpapers. The members of the Council of Industrial Design, for example, are (to judge from their own printed propaganda) sadly in need of therapy. Well-intentioned as they are, and beneficial as their efforts may prove in the long run, they are struggling not only with commercial mass taste but with their own psychological maladjustment.' 'Reflections from Aston Park', September, 1948.

[7] Whatever conclusions I have reached in the theory and practice of industrial design owe much to the influence of Thomas Sturge Moore, whose book *Armour for Aphrodite* will be freely quoted.

My earliest memories are of W.T. Stead's *Books for the Bairns*, cheap potted classics and fairy stories illustrated by Brinsley le Fanu.[1,2] His influence on my childish drawings was profound. Later, when in 1902 I entered Bedales School, I encountered followers of Aubrey Beardsley, William Morris, Phil May and many others. Working alongside Allan Gwynne-Jones and Ivon Hitchens, whose output even then showed distinction, I continued to turn out lamentable drawings in the manner of le Fanu, which nevertheless earned a disproportionate number of good marks from our drawing mistress. I was therefore encouraged to design in this style for that particular market, thereby carrying out a policy, sound enough for industry, but questionable in the fine arts.

The child-artist is in a difficult situation. Something inside him tells him to paint and draw things as he feels they are but he

---

[1] [An earlier draft of Chapter 2 began with the following paragraph, later deleted by RDB: 'If the conception of a force field is applicable to art instruction, then the position of the young person is indeed precarious. Unaware of what is going on, he is first pulled one way and then the other. That children are imitative is common experience, while, contrariwise, the freshness of much juvenile work is also widely recognised. Today children see about them 'modern' posters and in their books often look at pictures carried out in a free fashion, superficially rather like their own experimental efforts. These may, of course, be influencing the young people's style, but I cannot help feeling that, whatever may be the verdict of history on twentieth-century abstracts and distortions, their very primitive quality is more 'neutral' and therefore less distracting to the child than the sort of drawings which impressed my generation as children.']

[2] [Brinsley le Fanu (1854–1929), illustrator.]

will continually be tempted to depict them as he has been taught they should look on paper.[3] Unfortunately, there are plenty of well-meaning people ready to act as agents for this perverted demand.

The pattern makers

The student-designer of lighting fittings can probably learn most about workshop practice in the pattern-making shop. To my younger brother Frank and me, such practice soon became a centre of pleasure and interest. My father, R.H. Best, was fully alive to its potential attraction, for when we were no more than seven or eight years old, he would allow us to spend some of our holiday time with the pattern makers, the three Steventons and Ernie Warden, who helped us to carry out in wax, plaster and bismuth our primitive designs for lighting fittings, as well as toy engines, boats and machines.

We were taught always to start with a drawing. If, sometimes, it happened that we would draw on paper an article beyond our capacity to carry out, the drawing would then be taken away and in due course, amidst great excitement, the article itself would appear, always beautifully finished, smelling slightly of lacquer and wrapped in tissue paper.

Once I passed to my father, for factory production, a sketch of a thing like an eggcup intended as a trophy or cup or prize for a race in the playground of the school we attended. My drawing, with straggling handles of thin wire, was misunderstood, but so were those of the designer of the Kaiser Wilhelm Memorial Church in Berlin when they were shown to the late German Emperor. The Kaiser mistook an asterisk, or some dimensional

---

[3] The intelligent industrial designer studies his market but the young person is often the unconscious victim of it. It is interesting therefore to compare the paintings by Bedalian children reproduced in Herbert Read's *Education Through Art* (London: Faber & Faber, 1943) with those of my own generation.

sign above the spire, for an architectural feature and rather than show up his patron's mistake the architect altered the building accordingly!

I too had shown an asterisk on my drawing, with an arrow pointing to some technical instruction in the margin. I was astonished, therefore, to find this star and arrow engraved on the smooth surface of the cup.

But disappointment was quickly forgotten when I came to examine the workmanship, the faultless silver plating, the polish and the engraving of the signs themselves, for which I invented some imaginary significance when later, in the playground, the presentation was made.

This was my first experience of designing an article for others to produce. My second was for a toy pistol but this time I personally supervised the first stages of manufacture and in the evening, to my great pleasure, the finished article was unwrapped and handed to me. Made exactly as I had drawn it, with a barrel of half-inch brass tube, finished 'steel-bronze', a grip of varnished box wood and a spring operating a plunger within the barrel, it proved an effective weapon if charged with peas or pellets of blotting paper.

Ruskin, Bedales and J.H. Badley

Later, after the influence of Brinsley le Fanu, I was caught up in another powerful influence: Ruskin, as differently interpreted by two persons whom I greatly respected and admired. For my father, Ruskin meant careful work, mastery and 'Ars Longa stuff', as he put it; whereas, transmuted by J.H. Badley, the headmaster of Bedales, the teaching of the great Victorian critic emerged as something much softer in outline, much freer, less inhibiting.

My father made his influence felt even in the school studio. He had little liking for Impressionism or, indeed, for unorthodox work of any kind, which he would dismiss as slovenly or an 'ethereal smudge'. Since Ruskin stood for discipline, he insisted that I should carry out, as part of my schoolwork, nature studies in the manner of the master, by which he understood that they should be as accurate as a photograph and should show an understanding of plant life—to me an uninteresting subject. In a dutiful and over-conscientious mood I fell into line. As a result, my style, such as it was, became more constipated than ever.

Those who teach what the Germans call *Ruskinismus* widen the gap between their followers and the realities of present-day production. *Ruskinismus* has not much in common with a 'period style' or idiom. It is a backward-looking, nostalgic way of life. During a long and active life, Badley developed—and allowed himself to be influenced by—Modern ideas regarding architecture and industrial design. But when I first met him, as he admitted many years later in a letter (1949), he was 'an ardent devotee of Ruskin and started with the conviction that everything before the 14th century was right and everything after it wrong and that so far as possible there should be a return to simplicity in all arts and crafts. I still retain the latter part,' he continued,

> though I have long given up the former. In architecture, for instance, I am with the functionalists, and think that building likely to be the most satisfying which is best adapted to its purpose and relies on proportion, light and shade, and material rather than on any superimposed ornament. (Even the despised Gymnasium at Bedales seems to have its good points—though leprous flaking plaster is not one of them.)

This building (1917) had a flat roof and came in for some criticism because it was too plain and not thought to be in keeping with the other buildings.

Himself an able draughtsman, Badley made drawings for the main building and handed them to an architect to work out. The design of the Dining Hall was suggested by the large room at Bedales, the old Tudor house near Haywards Heath where the school started. Badley approved diversity. At different times as many as nine architects were employed on additional buildings and extensions. In 1911 an impressive barn-like hall was built by an old Bedalian to the drawings of Ernest Gimson, who also designed a fine Library, as an adjoining block. It was all very simple and substantial, with solid oak beams, copper nails and exposed brickwork. In building techniques, there were few concessions to modernity. Even the electric light pendants seemed to belong to a bygone age of primitive rural craftwork.[4]

Originally the furnishings for the main building had been selected and designed by Agnes Garett, Mrs Badley's cousin. They were of the simplest. For lectures and meals, we sat on deal benches varnished a dark green colour. Originally conceived for sitting back and listening, they were found to be too low for use at table and had to be altered accordingly. We took our treacle and ate our porridge from peasant pottery made at Farnham and slip-painted by hand in a free style. It was thought somehow fitting that local products should be used. We slept between blankets on wooden beds chosen for 'simplicity and comfort'. In all his life Badley never found a pattern he liked better. Instead of spring mattresses, there were wooden laths or slats which were liable to break in the hurly-burly of dormitory ragging.

Functional requirements may here have been at variance with the principle of pleasantness in use but the headmaster's intuition has been subsequently confirmed by the market; for metal beds, once popular enough, have for many years been out of favour except for certain institutions.[5,6]

The teaching of the arts and crafts was appropriate to the furnishing and architecture. There was much freehand drawing

---

4 [See R.D. Best, *From Bedales to the Boche* (London: Envelope Books, 2020) for more about life, design and moral values at Bedales in the 1900s.]

5 It is sad to think that, at a later date, the Bedales wooden beds were replaced by metal ones.

6 [RDB deleted the following paragraph from his manuscript, doubting its relevance to 'Ruskinismus'. 'Great care had been given to the design of the earth closets. In accordance with the conception of 'sanctity of labour', a party was detailed each week to scrape them and shovel the contents into wheelbarrows which were later emptied onto the land. The headmaster always took a hand in this duty. Unfortunately, a serious illness of two boys

and painting from nature, sometimes with coloured chalks on a
blackboard. Expeditions were encouraged, when we would
sketch or make architectural studies. It was all quite different
from the Pre-Raphaelite fiddling required by my father. Pottery,
basket-work and carpentry also found their place on the school
timetable and there is little doubt that the teaching was much in
advance of most schools of that period.

In this Ruskinian atmosphere Frank, fifteen months my
junior, began to blossom. Blessed with a sanguine and
uninhibited nature, his style was so free and imaginative that our
father thought it not good enough to merit special discipline and
left him alone. His later work was always original and high-
spirited—sometimes also surprisingly modern in conception.

Design dialectics

It must have been round about 1907, when I was fifteen, that I
began to discuss the question: 'What is good industrial design?'
It appears in my school essays and was taken up at home, where
unfortunately conditions were such as to increase my confusion,
for while I was lucky in receiving practical workshop training,
and in my father's shining example as a designer of functional
light fittings, on the aesthetic side I found much to perplex me. I
was caught between the Scylla of Ruskin and the Charybdis of
market requirements. In *Brass Chandelier* I have described my
father's attitude towards design problems as follows:

> Throughout all these changes in fashion and public demand, Best
> held to a certain outlook in regard to the design of the goods he was
> producing. Although his was an essentially practical viewpoint, he
> could not help being drawn into contemporary theory and
> speculation around the subjects of beauty and aesthetics. Best was

---

was attributed to the practice which, in consequence, came to be
performed by labourers. Later, the earth closets were replaced by WCs but
Badley was always sorry that it was held necessary to abandon them. He
thought they constituted the healthiest means of waste-products disposal.']

fully alive to the fundamental necessity of fitness for purpose, which he followed steadfastly in all his productions, and he was further influenced by what he understood to be the teaching of Ruskin; it was truth rather than pleasantness which he wished to embody in his designs. Work truthfully and honestly performed was, he believed, beautiful. A spiral scroll, for instance, which embellished the arm of a gas chandelier, justified itself if it formed a geometrically accurate figure. It must be a smooth-flowing curve and not broken by careless filing. Chasing must not be skimped and flat surfaces were required to be really flat, not made uneven by careless polishing. Questions of proportion, form and colour were never consciously recognised by him as bearing upon the success or otherwise of his designs. When questioned upon this point, he would quote the Latin motto *de gustibus non est disputandum*. In the family discussions which followed some confusion of thought would arise: the saying contains a half-truth in that dogmatic discussion on questions of taste is likely to be unprofitable, but the implication that proportion, form and colour are therefore so bound up with personal opinion as to be relatively unimportant led to misunderstandings and work which was needlessly ugly.[7]

It was small wonder that our arguments at times became fierce, so much so that during lunch one day, as I well remember, my mother burst into tears and implored us both to stop.

Roger Fry

In March 1910, while still at Bedales, I heard Roger Fry speak on Giotto and approached him immediately after his lecture. 'Giotto,' he had said, 'was the first artist since the time of the Greeks to imitate nature in figure drawing. But although he followed nature to a much greater extent than his predecessors, he was still far from the literal representation of everything as it is seen in real life. So it is not that quality which makes Giotto a great artist.'

Here, I thought, was more material for discussion at home. If

---

[7] R.D. Best, *Brass Chandelier* (London: George Allen Unwin, 1940), 122.

Roger Fry was right, was it necessary for me to continue this tiresome nature study, these conscientious but unnecessarily literal representations of plant life? Should I not be free to carry out my more imaginative book illustrations (still, unfortunately in the manner of le Fanu, though I did not realise it), which I so enjoyed?

Leading off with this personal problem, I wondered whether it applied to others in the chandelier trade. It was a question frequently thrashed out round the dinner table at home. For Fry had said, 'Besides the underlying idea behind the frescoes at Padua, the actual *workmanship* is so wonderful.' Was not this, perhaps—and one had to be fair—a point in support of my father's position: the chasing which must not be skimped, the spiral scrolls unbroken by careless filing, the flat surfaces not made uneven by poor polishing? Were not these examples of wonderful workmanship? On the whole, Fry thought not; for in answer to my question he replied, 'We must not confuse the workmanship of the great artists with "trade finish".'

At this distance in time I can well remember my impression of Fry's emotional attitude towards the manufacturer, whom he looked upon [in the words of Virginia Woolf, in her 1940 biography of him] as 'The Adversary, a compound of schoolboy bully, Pierpont Morgan,[8] the pseudo-artist and the British public', covering his products with an 'eczematous eruption', thanks to their employment of 'the pseudo-artist ... who professed to sell beauty as the prostitute professed to sell love.'[9]

There it was—the *gap*, the *hauteur*, the holier-than-thou attitude towards commercial men. Not far removed from the snobbishness sometimes to be found mingled with Bedalian *Ruskinismus*, it seemed to me completely negative and unhelpful. 'Trade finish' indeed ... .

---

[8] [John Pierpont Morgan (1837–1913), the American banker who dominated Wall Street in the late nineteenth century.]

[9] Virginia Woolf, *Roger Fry: A Biography* (London: The Hogarth Press, 1940), 184, 188, 189.

Fry's Omega workshops were not opened until 1913. It was, as he then said, an exciting adventure, and no doubt helped to move British industrial design onto a fresh track. But one cannot help noticing that perhaps a little more attention might have been given to 'trade finish' in his own products. As Virginia Woolf observes in her account, 'Chairs had to stand upon their legs; dyes must not fade, stuffs must not shrink. Sometimes there were failures. Cracks appeared. Legs came off. Varnish ran. He had to placate angry customers and to find new methods.'[10]

That short talk with Roger Fry made a deep impression. Kindly and enlightened, he still failed to understand or help the businessmen of that period who, though they 'roared with laughter at his suggestion that they should do business together' were 'quick to see how the designs could be copied and made agreeable to the public taste. Emasculated versions of the original Omega ideas appeared in the furniture shops and were more acceptable to the ordinary person than the original.'[11]

Fry was as ignorant of the materials and conditions of their trades as they were of a new attitude to art—the vision of Cézanne and Van Gogh—which he was trying to present to the public. My father's approach to industrial design, though imperfect and incomplete, came nearer the mark than that of Fry, who, like so many reformers, confused standards and objectives peculiar to the fine arts with those essential to industry.

I was thus made conscious of the wide gulf separating the artist-craftsman and critic from the manufacturer, and the need for easier communications between them. If the *hauteur* on the one side could be reduced, and the laughter on the other rendered less noisy, great benefit to industrial design would accrue. It is the question of two-way criticism and communications between groups which we must now consider.

---

[10] Woolf, *Roger Fry*, 196.
[11] Woolf, *Roger Fry*, 196.

Two-way traffic

During the period under review there was plenty of interplay between groups at Bedales. The personality of the headmaster, as was only natural, made itself felt throughout most of school life. A hierarchy of masters, mistresses, prefects and bosses formed a sort of ruling class, keeping order genially but with the help of fairly heavy physical sanctions.

There was nevertheless much intellectual and aesthetic liberty. I dare say that in no other school could be found such glorious debunking of authority, such questioning of every school institution or such caricaturing in the arts. Indeed, if criticism ever tended to be one-way, it was from below to above.

There was no censorship by the ruling class of the school magazine. It made lively reading. One of the most prolific contributors, representing the school intelligentsia, as it were, commented in Gilbertian verse on school institutions, classical poetry, plays, lectures, the drill instructor, sport and many other matters, all under the pseudonym 'Og'. But it is his 'Art Criticism à la Ruskin' verses which came closest to the heart of my subject and presented a point of view with which, more than ever, I find myself in sympathy. At the head of the poem is a quotation from Maurice Hewlett's *The Road in Tuscany*:

> The late Mr. Ruskin seldom left the pulpit; the late Mr. Grant Allen never left the schoolroom ... Our amateur, good easy man, pleasantly accepts them all [their dogmas] as binding, as having the force of law, and does his best to obey them ... . I declare that one of these days there will be mutiny. I shall join the banner of revolt.[12]

Then, after three verses of this sort of thing—

> While my temper's growing bellicose
> At works of Fra Angelico's
> (Who painted like a little child of two)

---

[12] Maurice Hewlett, *The Road in Tuscany* (London: Macmillan, 1904).

> Or some early Flemish horror
> A 'Destruction of Gomorrah'
> In the very crudest shades of red and blue

—he restates his case, referring in passing to the Baroque architecture of some Jesuit churches, which apparently did not appeal to him:

> Now I really don't see why
> We should not be left to try
> And discover what would naturally please us;
> I don't think there's any fear
> Of our coming to revere
> The style of the Society of Jesus.
>
> Our friends are very kind,
> But I venture to remind
> Them that Art is not a subject for dictation;
> And the public's not a fool,
> Nor a little boy at school—
> So I recommend another occupation.

'Two-way' criticism is something more than the liberty to pass comment on the foibles of the ruling class, to guy its musical and artistic preferences or discuss its standards. It is not something which takes place, as it were, in a vacuum. As a result, there must be some effects and modification of policy, however slight. The headmaster and his staff were sensitive enough to atmosphere. Criticism was effective and led to changes and reforms, even if these were gradual; changes, amongst others, in the sphere of architecture and industrial design.

J.H. Badley sums up

Shortly before the end of my last term I found myself in conversation with the headmaster. Once more the subject of industrial design came under review. Badley knew all about my business background and interest in design styles. He had even attended a lecture I had recently given to the Classical Society. Ostensibly on Renaissance styles, this rather feeble discourse had been actually, as I now realise, composed to justify the sort of period idiom we were then using at the factory in Birmingham.

'I am going into a manufacturing business,' I said to him, 'but in spite of all I have learned here I am still perplexed as to what constitutes good design. Before leaving, I should like you to sum up what you make of it all.' Taking up a poker from the hearth—we were standing in his study at the time—he said, 'Well, Best, consider this poker by way of example. It is designed, as you can see, to perform a special function. One end is thicker than the other because it is subjected to heat; while the handle is shaped thus in order to offer a good grip to the hand. And then, to show that the craftsman who made it took pleasure in his work, these chisel marks have been added. Or perhaps he might have given the handle an extra turn or twist.'

At the time this explanation seemed satisfactory enough. It was only after I had been working in the family business for some years that I began to wonder whether it quite went to the root of the matter; whether the forces working on the designer of that poker corresponded to those I found in operation at Cambray Works.[13]

The atmosphere still remained cloudy. In spite of Badley's advice, I failed to grasp that the functional and the aesthetic were two quite different factors in design and had nothing in common except that they were sometimes found together in the same article. I was so accustomed to associating beauty with utility or moral uplift that the idea of its being something to enjoy seemed too simple to be true.

Then again, the chisel marks on the poker may have indicated that the craftsman enjoyed his labours, and at the

---

13 The name of the Best & Lloyd workshop.

factory there were undoubtedly pleasant and interesting jobs. This, however, could not surely account for the decorative marks, the chasing, the polishing and plating, the wrought work and scrolls to be found on the patterns I was then handling in the business. They were there not primarily *as a result* of pleasure in creation but *to give* pleasure—to give pleasure to the customer.

Like many others, I placed the customer's pleasure in a separate compartment of thinking—as something slightly immoral. Because it sold, it could not be good design.

R.H. Best sums up

In the meantime, my father had been taking issue with Robert Catterson-Smith,[14] then head of the Birmingham School of Art. They had come into contact through my father's proposals for initiating part-time day continuation schools for boys in the brass trade. Father formed the impression that Catterson-Smith did not believe in training students to meet industrial requirements at all and he was partly right. Catterson-Smith, like William Morris, believed that 'As a condition of life, production by machinery is altogether an evil; as an instrument for forcing us on to better conditions of life, it has been, and for some time yet will be, indispensable.'[15]

But if the art master failed to appreciate the possibilities of modern materials and processes in industrial design, he nevertheless introduced a system of memory drawing from nature which had certain novel and notable features, and, indeed, brought into the school doves, fowl, rabbits and many other animals to be used as models. My father thought the animals were unnecessary when what was required by his trade

---

[14] Robert Catterson-Smith (1853–1938), artist, social reformer and propagandist in the West Midlands who became Principal of the Birmingham School of Art, and Director of Art Education for Birmingham.

[15] *The Revival of Handicrafts: Collected Works of William Morris*, Vol. 22 (London: Longman, Green & Co., 1910–15), 335.

at that time was a sound grounding in the decoration of period styles. After one of his visits to the School of Art he was heard to exclaim, 'I ask Catterson-Smith for Louis-Quinze and he hands me a rabbit!'[16]

Referring to this incident, Dr. Nikolaus Pevsner, in a lecture to the Royal Society of Arts, said:

Amongst other outcomes of Morris's doctrines was a new type of art school, first, I think, realised at Birmingham and then at the Central School of Arts and Crafts in London. They emphasised Arts and Crafts in their names because they wanted to teach equally the Fine Arts and what Lewis F. Day, one of the leading designers of the late nineteenth century, has called the Arts Not-Fine. But, and that is the drawback ... regarding the Morris reform, neither their art nor their craft was really in sympathy with industry. They helped their students a lot by fostering a freer, more imaginative draughtsmanship and a truer understanding of materials and processes of making (by hand, of course) but they would not listen to the needs of the manufacturer. To Morris he had been the enemy, and so he was still to them.[17]

And this is undoubtedly true. When my father asked for more Louis Quinze and less rabbit he was pointing to a lesson still unheeded by many who claim to teach industrial design: that the style or idiom which happens to be in demand at the time, or will be required in the near future, is an important factor and should not be neglected by those who wish to become professional designers. The methods of market research should, therefore, find a place in any art school with an industrial design department. In certain quarters the question of designing for your public as opposed to 'artistic integrity' is still treated with the same squeamishness as the Victorians were said to bring to bear on matters of sex.

---

[16] R.D. Best, *Brass Chandelier*, 223.

[17] Nikolaus Pevsner, 'Design in Relation to Industry through the Ages', *Journal of the Royal Society of Arts*, 31 December, 1948.

Only through frank discussion between central and peripheral design groups—between consumer and industrialist, between business executives and industrial designers—will these conflicts be resolved and any real progress in industrial design be achieved.

There is still room for the sort of free commentary which delighted the Bedales public. In no sphere are antidotes to 'the never-ending audacity of elected (and unelected) persons' more needed than in art and design criticism. It is to help the prophets and leaders in their difficult task, as much as the rest of the design community, that occasionally there should be heard clearly and loudly the soul-liberating retort, 'Sez you!'[18]

---

[18] See D.W. Brogan, *What is Democracy?* (London: National Peace Council, 1946).

CHAPTER 3
THE WORKSHOP AND THE DRAWING BOARD

Shortly after leaving Bedales I entered the arena of commercial design and production, where I remained until the outbreak of World War One. During these years I went through a period of training in the factory—'going through the shops, starting at the bottom'—according to a plan prescribed by many an industrialist for a son who was later to take his place in the family business. Again I found myself subject to conflicting influences such as manufacturing requirements, fashion, style and the appearance of things on paper.

My training was interrupted by an interval of some eighteen months abroad, first as a student at the Düsseldorf School of Industrial Art, then in Paris, where I spent much time in the atelier of a designer for interior decoration and furniture.

FACTORY EXPERIENCE 1910–11

My course at the factory, carefully prepared by my father, began in a special compartment, for owing to shortage of space in the foundry, he had caused to be constructed a cubicle adjoining it, just large enough to contain one brass caster 'tub' (a wooden trough in which the sand is moulded), a somewhat primitive gas radiator and myself. Here, under Bob Cowell, I began to practise the 'odd-side' process and to make 'false cores'.[1] Here too, as a student, I was expected to acquire a 'feeling for tools and materials'—a catchphrase we shall examine later.

---

[1] R.D. Best, *Brass Chandelier*, 107.

My father, a gifted designer, was nothing if not experimental. It would have been strange, therefore, if he had not suggested a number of practical tests for me to carry out. Casting sand was to be mixed with more clay than was good for it, or made too damp, or malletted excessively. The results, after the molten metal had solidified, were indeed remarkable. I can well remember the strange sponge-like or pock-marked objects which emerged from the sand when it was broken away.

But is this sort of experiment helpful to the designer or is it only of use to the student-technician? I do not believe there is any simple answer to these questions. At times, a quite haphazard occurrence will suggest something to the designer worth following up. Once, walking round a glass factory with Christian Barman,[2] we happened to notice a glass lampshade in a preliminary stage of manufacture; by cutting the piece in two, without completing the process originally intended for it, we formed an entirely different shape. This became a pleasing and popular design (and a good seller).

The amount of time available to students for workshop experience is, however, very limited and only the simplest and most essential techniques can thereby be acquired; most are lucky to get even these.

That said, whatever may be meant by 'a feeling for tools and materials', there are certain practical matters in every trade which must be thoroughly understood before anyone can even start to design. He who would design for foundry work must grasp the question of 'undercut' or 'leave'. If a casting is of such a shape that its cross-measurement is less (where the two sides of the sand mould come together) than elsewhere, then, obviously, sand will break away when one side is lifted clear. It is to overcome this difficulty that the small pads of sand or 'false cores' are made, since they can be removed after the two sides have been parted.

---

[2] Christian Barman (1898–1980), architect and writer, briefly editor of *The Architect's Journal* and *Architectural Review* in the early 1930s.

But the process, as I was soon to find out, was comparatively expensive. It is therefore desirable, other things being equal, to design your fluted shafts, necks or whatnot in such a way that they 'leave' the sand without necessitating false-core work.

Sometimes a fluted pattern is, as it were, 'faked': the flutes are waxed up on each side so that the sand does not drag, the necessary incisions being afterwards made with a chasing tool.

It is surprising, however, that designers of some experience will increase unnecessarily the cost of production through failure to attend to these rather elementary considerations; they are, after all, of wide application and must constantly be borne in mind when designing press-tools, spinning chucks, die-castings or moulded products.

Sometimes, however, false-core work is well worth the added cost; for in no other way is it possible to reproduce in metal the rich broken appearance of undercutting. Lying in the sand, some cunningly modelled garlands, wreaths and frames for lanterns compelled my admiration. There was also a ram's head, destined for application to sheet metal. Between the cheeks and the curly Assyrian beard there was a concave depression calling for a false core. Encased on each side by sand pads, the protuberant eyes of the ram still regarded the moulder in an appealing way, much as a patient looks at his dentist, from behind the mouthpiece of the gas apparatus.[3]

Bob Cowell was keen and skilful. By 'torching' the dry sand-mould over the smoke from burning resin, he produced not only a clean smooth surface but incidentally gave a beautiful iridescent colour to the metal. I have always regretted that this colour, being removed by subsequent processes, was quite wasted. It seemed, furthermore, impossible to imitate by other means, in spite of many experiments by my brother. An imaginative designer in the making, he quickly grasped that to find new colours and patinas was an important part of the job.

---

[3] [A reference to the metal mouthpiece through which dentists used to administer laughing gas.]

In our search for such colours and for knowledge of the existing processes, my brother and I were piloted by the foreman of the plating shop, William Passey:

> This erratic enthusiast could reproduce on brass by empirical methods the colour of almost any other metal, either in its polished state or as if changed by atmosphere and wear. ... Though resourceful in practice, his theoretical outlook was medieval; an artist in atmosphere, his manipulations of reagents suggested the control of powerful forces not recognized in the textbooks of Newth and Roscoe. Electrical instruments attracted him though he could not read them; he would estimate voltaic pressure from the size of the spark made by clean shorting the poles of his vats. If unable to transmute the base metals into gold, he frequently produced metallic wasps and beetles by coating these insects with electrolytic copper, which he would then finish out in gold or silver, suitably oxidized and relieved. Of Passey my father used to say, 'When his time comes to leave this world, he'll go off in a flash of flame!'[4]

Though he had little knowledge of drawing, William Passey was nevertheless a prominent member of the group of people responsible for developing industrial design within the company.

Having been, even as a child, in friendly technical relations with the pattern makers, I was glad to rejoin them during my apprenticeship training. They showed me how to turn and strike a thread on the lathe using a sort of toothed implement and how to make core stocks—the boxes in which sand cores are produced.

[These cores, unlike the false cores, are laid *inside* the depressions left by the patterns in the sand moulds; they represent the hollow space within a spindle, neck or vase, the metal flowing round them, between the inner core and the sand of the outside mould. After solidification of the metal the core is knocked out. But the core stocks are themselves of cast metal

---

[4] R.D. Best, *Brass Chandelier*, 112.

and the preparation of patterns for them was, in those days, an intricate operation involving moulding in plaster, laying thin strips of Plasticine on the inside, carving keys and so forth.][5]

Equally pleasurable and exciting was my term with the modellers and pattern chasers. Harry Vale, a tradesman of generous bulk, modelled scrolls on a framework of sheet brass, previously cut with a fretsaw to the correct profile. At his side was a Bunsen burner on which he heated his metal modelling tool or melted the wax.

His shopmate, T. Dahl, was a gifted Swede who advertised his German background and sympathies by his upturned Hohenzollern moustaches. He was probably the most skilful craftsman ever to work for the firm. Though employed chiefly as a designer and modeller, he once showed his ability as a sheet-metal worker by taking a halfpenny and raising on it by repoussé[6] the head of King Edward VII in such high relief that it appeared to be three-quarters round. But to make his self-imposed task more difficult, instead of following the profile as on the coin, he presented the royal likeness full face.[7] Many times he would show me how, when modelling, it is important to apply the wax bit by bit, building up the shape, instead of trying to carve away as if it were plaster of Paris. Sound enough advice, but in retrospect, I sometimes wonder how many of his own clever exploits really manifested a 'feeling for tools and materials'.

Together we covered many trade practices and under his friendly guidance I made two ashtrays and the Bedales badge (a Tudor rose) in sheet metal—simple exercises—as well as a bedroom door knocker of cast brass in the form of a wishbone, held with upraised arms by a tun-bellied imp—a family joke—to amuse my mother.

---

[5] [Sentences deleted by R.D.B.]

[6] Hammered into relief from the reverse side.

[7] Nikolaus Pevsner, *Pioneers of the Modern Movement, from William Morris to Walter Gropius* (London: Faber & Faber, 1936).

This gifted Swede also designed complete chandeliers, always a little heavy and Germanic in their lines and proportions. And though he could model wax or manipulate metal with the utmost delicacy, his drawings looked as if they had been executed with his pencil held like a chasing tool and followed over the paper with a hammer.

Production

The working drawing for each article was, at that time, traced by hand on linen and tacked to a wooden rod, round which it was rolled for storage. The quantity of those drawings then ran into many thousands. Each fitting was given a different number and a fresh series had to be started when electric lighting became common. In 1910 we had reached the 16,000s. Today (1949) a new design would be given a number in the 37,000s, indicating that some 500 new designs have been produced every year over the last forty years.

On receiving an order, the tracing would first be used to select patterns from the pattern stores; it would then be passed to the 'maker' or 'Brass Dressers' who were occupied in fabricating the complete article from the castings and other components. Over them presided a distinguished-looking foreman called Alf Wheeler. Tall, grey-haired and intelligent, he impressed me greatly when I came within his sphere of influence.

It was the custom amongst the men to give nicknames to some of the most popular chandeliers. There was the 'Angel Lamp' and the ''Arry Best' (Arabesque) fitting, and now it fell to my lot to produce a pendant in the Dutch style, called the 'Duck Lamp', on account of the birds' heads on the arms. My job was to turn up the cast spindles and necks on the lathe, 'striking' by hand the threads on the screwed portions (a skill not easy to acquire), filing, edging and brazing together the arms which were divided in two halves lengthwise. When it was finished, with some satisfaction, I took my handiwork to the viewer, who promptly rejected it on account of the poor fit of the threaded portions.

In my book *Brass Chandelier* I expressed doubt regarding the wisdom of setting a future manager to acquire experience under someone in the business whom he was later to direct. These observations were based on my father's trials and I still maintain that it is better that a son serve at least some of his apprenticeship training elsewhere. For myself, however, I have every reason to be grateful to the good people, the charge-hands and craftsmen, who showed me the ropes during these formative years.

The pattern stores

During my first year in the business, I was increasingly aware of the importance that style or idiom played in design, the mutability of fashion being brought home to me in the following way.

A most valuable asset of the company was (and is still) a collection of many thousands of casting patterns. Periodically I was given the job of arranging them in some sort of order. In the gloomy pattern stores were drawer upon drawer and rack upon rack of every shape used in the trade: necks, scrolls, pans, spindles, vases and cups—the components of a Victorian or Edwardian chandelier—in all sizes and in many styles. It was rather like some Tomb of the Kings, the 'Pickled Kings of Portugal', perhaps, lying, as I remember, in their court attire of different epochs, their faces seen through the glazed coffin lids, in various stages of decomposition.

In a like manner, the age of its style might be gauged by the thickness of the dust on each casting pattern.

And yet, such are the changes of fashion that some of the patterns would, as it were, miraculously come back to life. In a drawer of, let us say, Victorian Gothic chandelier bodies at least thirty years old, one would find several pieces quite free from dust and rubbed to a beautiful patina through contact with the caster's sand—designs recently revived, for no apparent reason.

Displaying their youth by freedom from dust and brightness of polish, the most recent arrivals to this collection were the work of a newcomer to the firm, a young designer named Mr.

Hamlyn. His shapely casting patterns contributed to some of the, to me, most pleasing designs the company has ever produced.[8] Marked by good proportions, smooth-flowing lines and a sort of eighteenth-century feeling, they have more than any other vintage stood the test of time. My father was most appreciative of Mr. Hamlyn's work and I, completely won over to this manifestation of the traditional style, thought that I had only to master some trick—the lines of the acanthus leaf perhaps —in order to be able to do likewise.

During sixty-odd years of accumulation, attempts had been made from time to time to classify and arrange the patterns systematically, a far from straightforward matter since it was not enough simply to number them serially as they were made. When a new design was produced, for the sake of economy, existing casting patterns were 'worked in' by the designer wherever possible. It was important, therefore, that he should be able to survey all patterns of similar kind or style and to know where they were to be found. These might then be combined with new patterns or with existing ones, but in new arrangements.

To meet this need, I adapted the Dewey Classified and Relative Index for arranging and cataloguing books (which I first encountered in the Bedales Library) by substituting trade categories for Dewey's classes, divisions and sections. 'Philology —Comparative—Prosody' thus became 'Knobs—Facetted—By Diameter' and so forth. It was therefore necessary to invent classes and divisions according to the surface treatment or decoration.

L'art nouveau

In one instance I experienced considerable difficulty. Named sometimes after a Paris shop and sometimes after a Munich publication, the then-waning Art Nouveau or *Jugendstil* was a style of decoration built up from long sinuous curves, 'reminiscent of stalks of lilies, of insects' feelers, of the filaments

---

[8] [Sentence deleted by R.D.B.]

of blossoms, and occasionally of slender flames'.[9] The examples of this idiom, carried out in brass, did not please me greatly and after reflection I invented the following name for the class: 'Art Nouveau—Palpable i.e. Squirms, Buds and Hunnish Motives'.

Nikolaus Pevsner, in his admirable book *Pioneers of the Modern Movement*, traces the origins of the Art Nouveau style through pictures and literature, and then goes on to suggest that it was primarily surface decoration and that it was bound to lose its value as soon as it was made by machinery. 'A genuine universal style could not therefore spring from it. Moreover,' he continues, 'it was incompatible with contemporary methods of production.'

The Art Nouveau style has certainly lost its value and now fails to please but I sometimes wonder whether the reasons for its waning in popularity were correctly identified by Dr. Pevsner. That many of its manifestations, though by no means all, were surface decoration seems clear enough but much of surface decoration was not at that time (nor, as far as one can judge, ever will be) specifically made by machinery. The cast surface of metal or ceramics, the pattern on wallpapers or textiles, of that time were no more 'incompatible with contemporary methods of production' than are many corresponding products in an idiom which would today be accepted as 'modern'.

And even if made by machinery, surface decoration does not necessarily lose its value on that score. Even in a machine age, part of the interior decorator's and industrial designer's job would have about the same relationship to machine production as might, for example, millinery or dress design.

Art Nouveau did not lose its value, as Nikolaus Pevsner suggests, because it came to be made by machinery. It lost its value and ceased to be saleable because, like many another style, it went out of fashion. There is no inherent reason why it should not be revived and I would not like to prophesy that modified forms of some of the South German designs would never again find their place amongst marketable textiles and wallpapers.

---

9 Pevsner, *Pioneers of the Modern Movement*.

The interplay of fashion, 'appearance values' and industrial requirements was particularly to be observed in the trade now under review; and as I came to survey the casting patterns now classified according to the Dewey–Best system, I had ample evidence that alongside my father's functional innovations in design, there had been changes which had nothing at all to do with construction or 'contemporary methods of production'.

I was nevertheless soon to find out that it was possible to pay insufficient attention to construction, function and methods of production. This seemed to be a defect of many of the Paris products at that time and to a lesser degree of the curriculum at the Düsseldorf School of Industrial Art. Such neglect may or may not produce unsatisfactory surface decoration. The two are interlocking but quite different factors in design.

THE DÜSSELDORF SCHOOL OF INDUSTRIAL ART AND THE DEUTSCHER WERKBUND 1911–12

When in the year 1911 I joined the Düsseldorf School of Industrial Art,[10] the Kunstgewerbeschule, I had already visited other German schools for training craftsmen and industrial designers, in the company of my father. He was at that time collecting material for two publications which were later to become widely read: *The Brassworkers of Berlin and Birmingham* and *The Problem of the Continuation School*. His visits brought us into contact with manufacturers—as a boy I had been conducted over the Beisswenger chandelier factory in Berlin—as well as design and designers for interior decoration. On the whole, this first-hand contact with German products impressed me greatly.

It was a period in history when, more than ever, the two countries were examining the other's institutions and products appraisingly. Two-way influences were at work, and in Germany

---

[10] Written about in more detail in R.D. Best, *From Bedales to the Boche* (London: EnvelopeBooks, 2020).

there was certainly much to be admired. Looking over German publications of that period (1907–14) I am still attracted by the style and quality of German furniture and fittings. Much of it was years in advance of anything to be found in British shops although, paradoxically, British designers such as Morris, Mackintosh, Ashbee and Voysey led the field in terms of influence felt overseas.

Whatever advantages these German products may have had over their English counterparts is very much a matter of opinion, but an industrialist cannot fail to find interest in these anticipations of certain tendencies later to arrive in Great Britain. In some way or other, fashions change and new ideas in design are always derivative, starting in one country and moving around until they have been widely adopted.

The most successful designers of one country are generally on the lookout for a fresh note from abroad, while, as we shall see, some continental designers looked with envy to the more conservative and stable English standards—the very opposite of the more familiar Arts and Crafts designers.

These movements of fashion are in themselves neither good nor bad. To dismiss them, however, as unimportant or deleterious is one of the signs of the fanatic and amateur.

The head of the Düsseldorf School of Industrial Art, Dr. Wilhelm Kreis, and several of his staff were members of the Deutscher Werkbund, which corresponded to the Design and Industries Association (D.I.A.) that would be launched in England in 1915. The Deutscher Werkbund was a society of firms and individuals accenting the standard of Fitness for Purpose and leaning towards a contemporary and functional rather than a classical or historical style. Founded five years previously it was in 1912 still in the first flush of reformist zeal and, in the manner of ginger groups, suffered at times from a certain dogmatism, much like the naive thinking of the English D.I.A. in the 1920s.

Kreis, like Catterson-Smith, was a man of original ideas but, unlike the head of the Birmingham School of Art, he had practical knowledge of manufacturing and industrial requirements for, besides being a distinguished architect, he had designed and supervised the production of furniture, lighting fittings, textiles, silverware and even the cabinet work for pianos. At that time it was quite customary for an architect to be invited by a client to design a whole interior, including furniture and fittings. With furniture manufacturers this form of cooperation was generally quite successful. But a peculiar difficulty arose when it came to lighting fittings, according to Herr Richard Schulz, an enlightened manufacturer of lighting fittings in the period when electricity was starting to replace gas. The architect would approach the task of designing a fitting exactly as if it were a piece of furniture and would fail to take into account the cost of new casting patterns or to leave enough freedom to the manufacturer to adapt existing ones. This difficulty is not unknown even today.

The analytical method of art instruction

To the student about to enter the Düsseldorf School, two courses were open: Three-dimensional design, including Architecture, Interior Decoration and Product Designing; and Commercial Art for Press Advertising, Posters and Commercial Literature. After a preliminary interview with the head, I chose the former and was posted to a preparatory drawing class under Herr Hochreiter. Here, just at first, I seemed to be going back to 'Nature Study' in England, with all its style-cramping associations; but I was soon to find that the method followed at this school was different and, had I but known it, was the first stage in what was then a comparatively new teaching technique.

On starting work, I found that my fellow students at the Kunstgewerbeschule used geometrical forms in their designs, whereas, still under the influence of Mr. Hamlyn, I naturally turned to classical motifs. In German public buildings and restaurants at the time, the walls were often divided into panels with, near the top, an oval plaque scalloped in a geometrical way around its rim. Spirals, diamonds, squares and rows of dots were also to be found in nearly every scheme. There was, furthermore, a noticeable difference between the preferences in the South and those of the Northern people. The exuberant Bavarians leaned towards artistic fantasy whereas the Prussians preferred less ornament. Throughout the country the influence of the *Jugendstil* was still apparent but in a simplified form and with less of the sinuous curves and floral effects.

According to an article published in *Kunst und Handwerk* (1907), the Düsseldorf method represented a new approach to the teaching of industrial design. It was in some ways a revulsion from the laborious method of building up a picture bit by bit from the natural object—a practice thought, quite naturally, to do the student more harm than good. 'The required results are best achieved if the picture is first broadly presented and the necessary details ... are added later.' This was known as the Analytical Method for Art and Art Instruction.

In the article quoted above, there was much talk of 'conceptional drawing', the student reproducing his total impression and then pulling out the details, enlarging them and drawing in the contours. Another aspect of the Analytical Method was called 'Splitting up the Difficulties', the application of colour being treated as an activity separate from the presentation of light and shade. To overcome the second difficulty the student was encouraged to draw in charcoal or chalk so as to grasp the principles underlying the shapes of shadows and light.

Dr. Kreis would himself take part in discussions with the students on these matters. One occasion particularly impressed itself on my memory. Prompted by a competition for some simple project, the students' renderings were so 'conceptional', so bold, so impressionistic—the difficulties of presentation having been 'split up' to such a degree—that my father, had he seen them, would have turned away in disgust.

The first exercises, under Herr Hochreiter, were then part of a general theory of instruction. The student was encouraged to treat his nature studies structurally, to observe accurately the complete form and the cohesion of parts, to make stylistic renderings and use them for ornament and then to design actual objects such as furniture, fittings and so forth. 'The shape of the whole article should be simple and geometrical, divided into clear, mathematical proportions, these being repeated in the shape of the principle parts, as also in the details.'

Whatever the merits of 'clear, mathematical proportions'— and we shall return to this question later—the student himself, as far as I remember, was never invited to try out different proportions and to find the combination which pleased him most.

I attended Herr Hochreiter's class for several months, alternating them with visits to the modelling class where I tried, unsuccessfully, to reproduce one of my own designs. The medium we were given, clay, was quite unsuited to the making of what we should now call a 'mock-up'. If there were any facilities for model-making in cardboard or wood I never found them. There were certainly no workshops where prototypes of the students' designs might be made by hand.

I was first told to draw the dried head of a poppy, not in meticulous detail but some ten times its full size, simplified, stylised, with a thick outline and coloured with flat washes of poster paint. This was a standard opening exercise. The student was then encouraged to enlarge sections of the plant, to pick out details in simple broad detail and later to depict light and shade as if the modelling were in layers, like contour lines.

At first my timid drawing was rightly condemned. '*Immer mehr kräftig!*' (make it stronger) was the watchword. At a later stage, Herr Hochreiter, whose manner was somehow appropriate to the style he advocated, suggested that I should adapt the shape of the plant to the design of a lantern or lighting fitting. Several of my suggestions he condemned as '*geschmacklos*' (tasteless) and on looking over these drawings I cannot but agree with him. They seem to lack everything which now pleases my eye.

In general, hard-and-fast categories such as 'ugly' and 'beautiful' only lead to confusion and misunderstanding but if ever the word 'ugly' might be rightly applied, it was to these early designs based on plant forms. The reasons for failure were not entirely inexperience or insensitivity. They arose partly from the assumption that natural shapes might, with impunity, be adapted to certain types of industrial products and partly because, forced to turn from the classical forms, I conceived the main objective in design to be originality. That the design was to give pleasure, either to the designer or customer, never even occurred to me.

Dr. Benirschke's class

Vaguely aware that this attempt to use natural forms was not yielding what I required, I applied to the Head for a change and was posted to the Department of Interior Architecture and Decoration. Under Dr. Max Benirschke, himself an architect and a distinguished member of the Deutscher Werkbund, I was allowed to go my own way.

With good grace, he provided me with the means to satisfy my appetite, fuelled by Mr. Hamlyn, for the antique and traditional. He furnished me with good reproductions of historical lighting appliances and at last I found myself moving towards a comprehensible objective: to master the sweep of the acanthus leaf and the general appearance of the old models, adapting them to modern requirements. In common with other students, I worked on coloured scale renderings, but never once, as far as I know, were full-sized constructional drawings prepared for the products we depicted in pretty colours.

Though Dr. Benirschke gave me scope to follow my own bent, it was always somewhat reluctantly, as if to suggest that sooner or later my own firm and English manufacturers in general would be compelled to work in a style more akin to what was then the vogue in Germany.

Although indifferent to these speculations as to the future, I could not help noticing the vagaries of contemporary fashion as, furnished with an elaborate portfolio of photographs, I occupied myself, during the holiday period of the Düsseldorf School, by calling on a few customers in the Rheinland on behalf of the firm. Here I found a marked difference between what the German buyers wanted from English suppliers and what they would buy from their own nationals. From German manufacturers they bought the sort of designs favoured by Dr. Benirschke and his school, whereas from us their requirements differed little from those of the home market. It was the *schöne einfachen englischen Formen*' (the beautiful simple English forms) they preferred, perhaps the most notable example of which, at that time, was Best & Lloyd's lantern No. 16060.[11]

Discussing, later, these market phenomena with members of the D.I.A. and other pundits of the design world, I found sympathy with the viewpoint of Dr. Benirschke. 'Yes,' they would say, 'we do not deny that at the moment [1912] this was and may still be the style that sells. But just wait: in ten or fifteen years, all that will be changed. Not only throughout Europe but in England itself, the demand for the lantern and in fact for all sorts of period fixtures will have given way to something more in keeping with the machine age in which we live.'

This prognosis has only partly been justified by subsequent events. It is true that in England, as elsewhere, changes in fashion and basic construction have taken place, so that many of the dreams of the reformers have materialised, but it is also true that those products in a classical style still seem to appeal to many, not only at home, but in all parts of the world—and not ten or fifteen but nearly forty years after my student year in the Düsseldorf School of Industrial Art.

Electric candles

As for my own trade, I noticed that a popular form of lighting fitting consisted of a number of light chains, or even naked electric wires, hanging from a ring some three-to-four feet in diameter on the ceiling. To the end of each would be attached

---

11 [No illustration of this lantern can be found in the Best & Lloyd archive.]

the lamp bulb covered by a glass or metal shade. In between the ring of light and the ceiling, the wires or chains would be drawn together slightly by sheet-metal hoops. Sometimes the whole arrangement would be based on a square, oblong or oval plan. This form of design was supposed to 'look electric', to answer to the new lighting medium, but by 1911 many were beginning to question whether its lines were actually dictated by anything other than fashion.

Living rooms were often lit from a silk shade in a dome of wicker work or light strips of metal, hung from the ceiling by a number of parallel chains. Strings of glass beads, cut crystals and plaques of sheet metal were used to decorate these and other forms and there was perhaps a tendency to strive overmuch for originality and effect. This at any rate was the opinion of the lighting manufacturer Richard Schulz. 'Unfortunately,' he wrote, 'this state of affairs [i.e. restless striving for effect] applies particularly to Germany. A harassed German manufacturer must feel envious of English firms when he notes that for decades on end, the same models are to be found in their catalogues—and even more when he is told that these models are as saleable now as ever. Do not let us suppose, however,' he continued, 'that the English have produced models which are worth copying. What they have done is to create and retain a wealth of typical shapes. They are on safe ground—ground on which they can build further without getting into difficulties.

'Today,' added Herr Schulz, 'we are familiar with the characteristic qualities of electricity and electric light. The novelty of it has worn off. It does not seem so important, therefore, that a lighting fitting should, under all circumstances, 'look electric'. Above all, let us see that it does not clash with the character of the room but enhances it. At the same time it should, in itself, be something worth having in a room. The fitting must naturally give light, but we must not imagine that its only object is to use electricity in the most efficient way.'

Referring then to the 'visible hanging wires in a thousand-and-one variations' which he thought restless, he continued,

The use of rings for carrying electric lamp bulbs seemed particularly appropriate to electric lighting and was widely adopted ... . The old shape of the Flemish candelabrum constitutes another model for the design of the centre lighting fittings. Its particular charm lies in the contrast between the static mass of the centre portion and the animated lines of the arms which carry the lights—a charm which has been approved too often for us now to discard.

Unfortunately one finds that much of the charm is lost if, to comply with practical requirements, one tries to alter its shape— perhaps by fitting lamps to shine in a downward direction in order to give more light or by eliminating the white candles and allowing the lamps, as it were, to grow out of the arms.

Furthermore, if the lamp bulbs are covered with glass shades or similar diffusers, the good proportions are destroyed, the light source being over-accentuated, and the dominating effect of the main body of the fitting is lost.

Bearing this in mind, one often decides to retain the traditional effect through the use of electric candles. This compromise, in spite of any theoretical opponents, has found wide acceptance.[12]

This eminently sensible essay was published in the 1912 Year Book of the Deutscher Werkbund. The writer, Schulz, was a leading member (*Vertrauungsmann*)[13] of the Werkbund, and also of his trade. His wide outlook and the tolerant attitude of the editor may serve well, even now, as an example to propagandists of 'good' industrial design.

Schulz's citing of the electric candle is a case in point. There are few articles about which more dogmatic nonsense has been uttered than the electric candle and its need for condemnation. I have made a careful study of the patrons of this accessory and find that they include art directors of repute, prominent

---

[12] Richard Schulz, 'Beleuchtungskörper', *Jahrbuch des Deutchen Werkbundes* (1912). The essay begins: 'It is a dubious pleasure to leaf through catalogues or to wander through sample warehouses in order to find good lighting fixtures for modern rooms. It is one orgy after the other, with the individual pieces competing to be "effective".'

[13] A trusted informant.

members of industrial art committees, Scandinavian 'modern' designers [considered worthy of inclusion in the *Architectural Review*][14] and distinguished architects with a reputation for designing in the 'contemporary idiom'. [The notion that experts always reject a design if it imitates something else is manifestly absurd. The experts do not agree.][15]

PARIS 1912–13

My father believed in keeping ahead of the times and in more than one letter to me expressed this conviction: 'We have always this problem of design to face—of keeping in front, of having good things which are not common to the ruck'.[16] In his search for new ideas he had found his way to the Paris atelier of an industrial designer and interior decorator named Boisselier and it was there, while still a boy, that I had first encountered the able draughtsmanship of this master of the Decorative Arts. During my stay in Paris, following my Düsseldorf year, I made up my mind, therefore, to go to him for special instruction. This decision met with my father's approval. 'I am glad you are going to visit Boisselier,' he wrote, and then, putting my future relations with the master in another light, he continued, 'We are open to buy designs—particularly suspensions[17]—you will let me know the result of your visit.'

A rather shy young man of twenty, obsessed not only by *pudeur Britannique* [British reserve] but also by *pudeur Bedalienne* (because at that co-educational school even smut had an innocent style of its own), I took my place amongst a racy group of some six or seven professional draughtsmen in Monsieur

---

[14] For example *Architectural Review*, Denmark—Special Number (November 1948): 25. [Phrase deleted by R.D.B.]

[15] [Sentence deleted by R.D.B.]

[16] 'Not common to the ruck': i.e. not usual with ordinary people.

[17] Light fittings suspended from the ceiling.

Boisselier's studio. Most of them seemed to be working on designs for complete interiors, rather in the manner of Dr. Benirschke's students, but with this great difference: without exception, they affected styles which would not have earned Dr. Benirschke's approval, being those peculiar to the reigns of the last three pre-revolutionary kings of France and the first emperor. The fluency of their pencil work was something quite beyond my powers ever to achieve, as I quickly realised: how they could dash in the swing of a Rococo scroll or the structural lines and silhouette of an acanthus leaf using a thumb or finger to indicate the modelling, almost as an afterthought. It was indeed the classical acanthus leaf—in contrast to the natural plant life of the initial exercises at the Düsseldorf School—which I was first taught to set out there. Beginning with the antique model, we worked through the various adaptations favoured by generations of French designers and craftsmen.

I did not find it easy. There was an awkward S curve in the upper frond, at the side, which had proved a stumbling block even in my Düsseldorf days, but as a moderate proficiency was achieved I felt a spurious sense of mastery which had no relationship to the actual importance of this newly acquired trick. The rest of my time in the atelier was occupied in copying from photographic reproductions. I was also encouraged to take my sketchbook round with me to palaces and museums. But of structural or production questions there was never a word; and I cannot help but feel that this was a symptom of the times.

Buying designs

That I was often fairly active as a sort of contact man or go-between is clear from my father's letters. His designer, Mr. Hamlyn, had recently left the company and had gone to a competitor. 'I hear Hamlyn is getting out some very good designs and it may be some time before we are able to find our right man. But for the present we are going along well with Morris and Osborne [two designers at the factory] and if we could find a few specialists—especially good—it would help very much. Let me know all about Boisselier.'

As I got into my stride, the relationship between the drawing board and the workshop was brought home to me in a number of different ways. Even as a boy, I had noticed a process of give and take in operation when my father, on previous occasions, had gone to the atelier for his designs. Following preliminary discussion, Monsieur Boisselier would rapidly make a number of small sketches and then, after a selection had been made, would set himself to draw them—full size on tracing paper—while we looked on. Using first a red pencil, he accepted suggestions from my father as he went along and when his client had finally approved the results he would go over the whole design in black lead.

Being both client and pupil I was placed in rather a difficult position. I was, even then, dimly aware that the quality of thought behind much of the work in the studio was two-dimensional; that is to say, it was more than anything concerned with the appearance of things on paper. Every time I approached Boisselier he would let himself go, expansively, in large scale, whereas what we wanted was more the sort of procedure I had seen at work some years before, when still a boy.

'I am afraid he is going to waste considerable time,' my father wrote to me in a letter, 'by doing his designs straight away in full size, because he should have details of construction, sizes and the general hang, so as to suit our market. He used to supply me with small sketches, about two inches long, to give me the idea —which I purchased—and from these we selected the most likely for detail and enlargement. However, if he likes to go about it full size, don't let him spend too much time on detail— until we approve the general hang of the fitting.'

How many times since then have I not experienced this same difficulty in working with freelance designers or architects.

In spite of my rawness, and perhaps because of the genial character of my drawing master, I satisfied the management at home, for my father wrote: 'You seem to be reaping the harvest.

George Vale [one of the directors of the firm] is going over the drawings and is sending those we like, with remarks on them. We will ask Boisselier to deliver the casting patterns, chased, of one of them, to see how they compare in practicability, style and cost, with our own methods. You can choose the one you would like to commence with. The one with the green parts is the simplest. I think those bands with olive glass crystals are beautiful. We also like your pick the best. But the question of construction, I expect, will have to be worked out and will delay commencing. Mr. Vale has written and has sent samples of wires, in order to assure that the wire ways are adequate.'

Design property

Since the formation of the Council for Art and Industry in 1934[18] there has been much talk about 'raising the status of the industrial designer', and his status is of course affected by the facilities available for protecting his designs.

But those employing designers also have a need to preserve a quasi-monopoly in the designs they buy. Without similar protection, it is difficult to see how they can pay adequately for good designs.

The registration for designs is one method, but in practice it has never proved very satisfactory. It is therefore only natural that manufacturers should be reluctant to make known the sources of their designs and it has always seemed evidence of cloudy thinking to recommend that the names of designers should be published by the firms who employ them. If designers, why not works- and sales-managers? My father had no illusions on this matter:

The question of secrecy is one for 'tack', as we call it at Cambray Works. We all think so much of [Boisselier's] drawings that we would like to keep the source of our supply to ourselves and keep

---

[18] See Chapter 13.

our competitors away, or, if Boissy designs for them, that he shall not put the Best & Lloyd touches and characteristics in. You must not give him any feeling of slyness, however. Just go as far as 'tack' will allow. It is better to send the drawings to the house. Then I can take the address off and it doesn't get all over the works. Generally speaking, keep your own matters to yourself as far as possible. A quiet tongue makes a wise head.

Monsieur Boisselier's designs were actually registered but at least one was copied by a competitor who was nevertheless persuaded, without going to law, to take the model off the market.

The Adam style

In correspondence with my father, the question of style was continually under discussion. 'We are open to buy "Adam" designs. Do you think Boisselier could do something good in that line?' he asked in the early stages of these negotiations, and I soon found that, although designed and decorated in a manner reminiscent of the period immediately prior to the French Revolution, Monsieur Boisselier's designs would almost certainly answer to my father's requirements.

He wanted Adam—the style of Robert Adam, the Scottish architect and designer who worked in London from around 1760 —and went to France for it, whereas the originator of this notable and exotic style studied Diocletian's palace at Spalato in the company of the famous French architect Clérisseau. Like Doctor Kreis, he was intimately concerned with the furniture and fittings as well as the form, decoration and construction of a building.

An Adam drawing room is to English what a Louis Seize room is to French art and it was French influence which led him to develop painted furniture with inlays of different woods. It was indeed characteristic of the free influence of one country's design on another that in eighteenth-century England so many changes in French fashion were reflected in the work of the most famous furniture manufacturers in this country.

In spite of the attempts by associations and governmental bodies to promote a 'modern' school of British design, it may well be that the real centre of influence will be found in some quite different part of the world.

Passed through the creative mind of Robert Adam, these foreign ideas emerged in a changed form of unsurpassed grace and delicacy. His wreaths, paterae, honeysuckles and fan ornaments have delighted generations and an Adam house is essentially English. Monsieur Boisselier's ideas, according to my father, were also to be transformed: 'The drawings duly arrived and though I have not seen them yet, Mr. Vale writes that they are very nice—perhaps a bit too Frenchy for English "*Adams*", but if so we can easily "Anglicise" them.' And 'Anglicise' them we certainly did.

Reference will be made below to certain criticisms of my company's products in this style, and it is arguable that only by working in a style more akin to the machine age shall we recover the creative ability of the gifted Adam brothers. This I believe to be a mistaken view. There is, in this country if not in the company under review, much creative ability. In what degree it exists or is desired by the consuming public has, however, no more to do with any particular style today than when Robert Adam was making his studies of classical architecture in Dalmatia.

My father was delighted with the form of collaboration I had developed and with the Parisian designer I had selected as a teacher:

> Yes, the 'Boissy' is a marvel. I've never met his equal. I've had some of his designs put into shape for him to work up in detail ... . Don't let him interfere with your studies with him. You should get him to take you round and show you some 'chic' furniture and brass work, so as to give you a general notion of French work.

Modernistic design

Because Monsieur Boisselier's clients turned to him for designs in a historical style, it would be a mistake to suppose that other styles of design and decoration were not at that time conspicuous. At the *Salons d'Automne* and the *Salons de la Société des Artistes Décorateurs* I found, during those years immediately prior to the First World War, similar influences at work as in Germany. Designers turned to nature for decorative motifs and forms: there were the same stylised versions of plant and marine life, the same shapes and constructions for lighting fittings.

There was, furthermore, a general interest in German designs, which were often to be seen at the exhibitions. In both countries the Art Nouveau or *Jugendstil*, with its sinuous curves, was giving place to anticipations of the work exhibited at the Paris Exhibition of 1925. Designed in a style not very different from that of his exhibits thirteen years later, the glassware of Réné Lalique was much in evidence. Already there were to be seen the *Directoire* chairs and sofas (New Style), as seen in the suite for a French Embassy (1925), the ribbed table legs narrowing suddenly towards the top in a voluptuous curve, the iron work of Edgar Brandt and the designs of Paul Follot. Baskets of flowers, rosebuds, leaves, birds, fishes and animals all had found their way into the decorative schemes but in a politely cubist form. The influence of Léon Bakst and the Russian Ballet was apparent in many of these designs, as were suggestions that were even now beginning to appear of the radiating lines—like the light beams from a rising sun—adapted later in the form of triangular plates of rises for lighting, which were later to sweep across England like an epidemic.

It may still be necessary to remind ourselves that design is not just something to be applied but something that concerns the whole structure of an object, just as it is desirable to remember that design does not end with considerations of structure and function and that there is no fundamental reason why decoration should not be applied.

Amongst Parisian designers and their customers in 1912, it was the first of these propositions which needed proclaiming most loudly. The cult of decoration, to the exclusion of functional and structural considerations, was then such as to make the most moderate member of the Deutscher Werkbund raise his eyebrows.

In 1911 the French Society for the Encouragement of Art and Industry, formed originally for the students of Paris and provincial schools, had already been in existence for twenty years and in the Autumn of that year held a competition, the twenty-first, for the decoration of a panel to go above the door of a study or library. There were 229 entrants and in the report of the results of the competition, it was said that the Society had never before presented such a complex subject to its young people.

'Up to now,' the report continued, 'the competitions have been centred on designs for fountains, clocks, mirrors and lanterns; whereas the "panel above a door", requiring, as it does, much advanced theoretical knowledge of scale, accessory motifs and atmosphere, offered definite difficulties which stopped many from entering.'[19]

Reflecting on the implications of this report one cannot but be surprised at the comparison between the designing of fountains, clocks, mirrors and lanterns, on the one hand, and a decorative fresco on the other. Both require 'theoretical knowledge of scale', to say nothing of many other things. Is it not possible that the real nature of three-dimensional product design was being swamped by too much *Arts Décoratifs* and that there was in fact too much of the drawing board and too little of the workshop?

Design for a market

Throughout this Paris episode I was still unaware of any principle or principles underlying the work I was doing. I was trying to acquire technical mastery and I was following the requirements of the market—on the whole, quite blindly. But he who blindly supplies what the market requires, without some

---

[19] Emily Lévy, *Art et Décoration* (Paris: Librairée Centrale des Beaux Arts, 1911).

regard for his own preferences, may lay himself open to the charge of prostituting his gifts.

'Good' designing, I suspect, consists in blending or reconciling the two, rather than in conforming to any absolute or objective standards.

It would be rash to say, however, that there are no standards. There is, for example, a kind of design depicting *private and personal experiences* which invariably gives the spectator, at first glance, a shock of embarrassment. But at that time I was doubtful about its value.[20]

I recall one such occasion, as my course of study was drawing to a close, when I was shown some startling water colours, in large scale and lovingly portrayed, of *brute facts with which, whether we like them or not, we have to come to terms.*[21] Had they been funny, I should have stood on common ground with the artist. They were not. I must have expressed scandalised disapproval for I was told —somewhat hastily, as if it were in some way a justification— that these drawings were for the German market.

News of this episode must have spread round the quarter, for a week or two later, visiting a small employer who was supplying the firm with casting patterns, I was asked to accept, as a parting gift, an example of die-sinking. Apparently a five-franc piece, it displayed on the obverse side what struck me then as obscenity reduced to its most simple terms. I took the gift and later threw it down the nearest street grating. Some account of this incident evidently reached home for, a short time before my return, I received from my father the following summing up:

> I am thankful that you have come through your *Wanderjahre* safely and have got your experience in contact with all sorts and

---

[20] [In his manuscript, R.D.B. deleted the words from 'It would be rash ...' to '... a peculiar' and substituted 'But at that time I was doubtful about a certain'. This appears, however, to be a sanitising of his thinking.]

[21] [Evidently a sexual image that Best's '*pudeur Britannique*' stopped him from articulating.]

conditions without getting soiled—and that you are able to put the smut down the sewer while assimilating the good. Folk are, as a rule, very decent. If they know you don't appreciate that sort of humour, they soon suit themselves to you and try to give what they know you do like—and it is quite easy to convey it without jumping on them. That is one of the things you have learned in Paris, I fancy.

Whether I did in fact learn anything of the sort seems, in retrospect, extremely doubtful. It is certain, however, that at the time, I shared with my fellow countrymen a widely held but erroneous opinion that somehow the French in general, and the Parisians in particular, were more smutty than the English, just as the Parisian designer suggested that his immodest pictures were best suited to the German consumer. Such generalisations seem as futile as the comment of an eminent design critic—a high official of the Council of Industrial Design (CoID)—who, on being told that certain designs that he found displeasing had sold well in Switzerland, said, 'Oh, but the Swiss were always known to have bad taste.'[22]

THE DRAWING OFFICE AT BEST & LLOYD 1913

Returning home in 1913 I wasted no time in setting up my trestle and board in the drawing office at the factory. My father was encouraging and uncritical but George Vale, his co-director, examined my work carefully and, by his comments, showed an understanding of practical and commercial requirements which merited closer attention than I gave them.

He was, at the time, occupied in a campaign for more practical construction. Some neat-looking arms of quarter-inch hexagon tube were to be increased to five-sixteenths of an inch, to allow easy wiring, while other designs were being modified to facilitate replacement of glass and lamps.

---

[22] [In his manuscript, R.D.B. deleted his reference to the CoID and changed 'Switzerland' to the more fanciful 'Ruritania'.]

Designers at work

Amongst my fellow draughtsmen were different types and I soon found that their relationship with the firm repaid careful study. Mr. Hamlyn had left behind a number of fine designs, some of which came under George Vale's critical eye for structural alterations. Mr. Hamlyn had never been at a loss for ideas but he did not show the same facility with the pencil and brush as had Monsieur Boisselier. His coloured renderings were in fact sometimes quite perfunctory. They nevertheless revealed a fanciful quality which occasionally surprised me greatly. A ring or bowl, hanging on elegant chains, would be depicted with the chains not pulled out straight under the weight of the bowl but forming graceful parabolic curves. When challenged on this point he had replied that the designer, as well as the poet, was entitled to licence in such matters. In spite of this free fantasy in illustration, the actual articles were often better looking, or so I thought, than his drawings.

Mr. Osborne was quite different in temperament. His wash drawings were extremely competent but his inspiration was intermittent and unreliable. He could stand for long intervals, balanced on one leg, sorrowfully surveying his drawing board. Some even thought that at times he might have fallen asleep. If so, he retained an intuitive sense of the status of anyone entering the office. In the case of juniors he remained motionless but George Vale had only to approach the door from outside and he was instantly alert and occupied.

Though not above looking through the catalogues of other firms for ideas, Mr. Osborne generally favoured a style of his own. His fittings often consisted of sheet-metal scrolls made by slitting a rectangular piece in two places longitudinally, turning the two outside members backwards and curving the middle section forwards. These arms were then arranged round rings of metal to carry the wires and lamp-holders. The general effect was pleasant if somewhat arty-crafty, and it seemed to appeal to architects who accepted them for 'Georgian' interiors such as the White Horse hotel in Birmingham. I considered that, unlike Mr. Hamlyn's creations, the finished products were sometimes disappointing when compared with the attractive coloured drawings.

Mr. William Morris—not the famous William Morris—who was later to become one of the company's leading designers, seemed to caress the paper lovingly with his pencil, while Mr. Frank Cashmore, a future designer-director of the firm, was already showing signs of the feverish energy which has ever marked his work. Both were producing promising designs. There were five other draughtsmen, including a veteran Mr. Cowley who specialised in fittings in which electricity was combined with gas, so that the latter might be brought into use in case of breakdown. The construction of them was somewhat complicated.

Pendants and brackets were still, for the most part, essentially gas fittings, except for the bowls which were made from alabaster. This material, adapted for lighting, had been seen by Mr. Vale while travelling in Italy on the firm's business. Bowls fashioned from alabaster were the first successful departure from the older lighting materials and designs. By 1913 alabaster had been used by the company for about three years.

My own designs were unimpressive but one, according to my father, seems to have had some success. 'We were counting over those two-light bedroom pendants you designed—over six dozen have been sold. That's very good, *nicht wahr*?' I was also engaged in redesigning an adjustable table lamp which could alternatively be hung on the wall as a bracket. The original model seemed to me capable of improvement. Its base was unshapely. Composed of rounded cheek-like surfaces it had been given an anatomical nickname by the men; I felt, moreover, that the position of the switch in the original was hardly satisfactory, and this led to a simpler shape. I mention this project not because my design was particularly attractive but as an example of the experimental process, of recognising mistakes and trying to go one better, recommended by Thomas Sturge Moore and discussed in the next chapter.

During this brief period of designing I began to realise that the craft of putting pencil to paper, so useful if not indispensable to the designer and attractive for its own sake, can also prove a source of frustration. [Twenty-five years later, while trying to draft a report for the Council of Art and Industry, I was able to summarise this difficulty as I had found it in the drawing office at Best & Lloyd:

> A saying sometimes used by architects is that such and such a design 'drips drawing board', meaning that the designer has shown more interest in pictorial effects than in the happy solution of practical and structural problems. This is the great danger of all art instruction related to industry.[23]][24]

A feeling for tools and materials

Reference has already been made to the phrase 'a feeling for tools and materials' and we have considered some practical considerations which must be thoroughly understood before starting to design for brass-foundry. The meaning of this phrase nevertheless remains somewhat obscure and I have yet to meet a designer in the trade who could give a satisfactory explanation of it or point to examples which either showed or did not show evidence of this 'feeling'.

Sometimes reference to the feeling is artificially generated as a sort of ban to discourage a student from attempting to make some material resemble something else: a plastic product that looks like a wood carving, an electric lamp that looks like a wax candle and so forth. The sooner the design field is cleared of such pedantries, the better for all concerned. One has only to

---

[23] R.D. Best, 'Design and the Designer in the Light Metal Trades: Report of a committee set up to consider how to give practical effect in the light metal and allied trades to the recommendations' in *Design and the Designer in Industry* (London: Board of Trade, H.M.S.O., 1944). [This report by a committee of the Council for Art and Industry was completed in May 1940. Publication was delayed by the war.]

[24] [Deleted by R.D.B.]

examine the homes of people of acknowledged artistic taste and judgment, if there is such a thing, to realise the futility of using a slogan to cramp the style of a designer or consumer. Whatever catchwords are used, the designer and his customer will, in the long run, have their heads.

But is the conception of 'a feeling for tools and materials' entirely without objective significance to people in industry? It can best be understood in terms of economy of effort and cost. The old saying of the classical economist—'the greatest effect with the least means'—should be continually in the minds of all concerned with design.[25] It should not be confused with cheese-paring or 'designing at so much an ounce'. 'Feeling' of this sort is capable of objective measurement and has nothing to do with the superficial dogmas of the amateur design critic.

During my last apprenticeship year, along with interest in pictorial effects, I found plenty of examples of the right sort of awareness of cost and effect. There is a continual search for more economical methods of production and this is part of the process known sometimes by the high-sounding name of 'design research'. Another factor is the quest for new materials—not necessarily because they give a better effect in proportion to the cost but simply because they are new and are likely to appeal to the public.

Whenever the directors discussed 'design policy' they were almost invariably considering which way the cat of fashion was going to jump and whether perhaps they could make it jump the way they wanted. The enthusiastic search for functional improvements such as resulted in my father's 'Surprise Pendant' was accepted as an obvious necessity, but speculation regarding the course of fashion took place in the same atmosphere of wonder, with perhaps a touch of mysticism, as farmers talk about future meteorological trends.

---

[25] Walter Gropius, *Bauhausbücher*, No. 12 (Munich: Albert Langer Verlag, 1930), 8. [Adapted frequently by the designer Abram Games as 'maximum meaning, minimum means'.]

When Gilbert Scott, the Victorian architect, altered the style of the new government offices in Whitehall to suit the predilections of Lord Palmerston, he was only acting like any sensible manufacturer or designer. I have never been able to understand why such behaviour should be looked upon as 'profound artistic dishonesty'.[26] If the building fails to please now, is it not the result of Scott's peculiar sense of proportion rather than the particular style which he eventually adopted to suit his client?

1914–18

The First World War interrupted any further training and experience and, reviewing my part in it, I can remember only two instances in which the questions and problems associated with industrial design were brought to my attention.

The first was a peculiar device for attracting the attention of a pupil-passenger in an aeroplane. During machine-gun practice in the air it would often be necessary to check the pupil from committing some gross indiscretion such as releasing a stream of empty cartridge cases through the propellor in the rear (I was flying a pusher[27]).

My design consisted of an arm with an axe-like head of wood. When his instructor pulled a toggle, the pupil received a sharp dig in the ribs and, looking down, was exhorted, by means of a notice on the wooden head, to turn round his own [head]. Complying, he was confronted by a sort of ship's telegraph, on which were certain instructions as to the appropriate handling of the gun.

But industrial design, in the sense we are giving to it, cannot be said to exist unless appearance values are studied, and it may be asked in what way this gear was relevant to our subject. Its

---

[26] Pevsner, *Pioneers of the Modern Movement*, 20.

[27] [During the First World War, R.D.B. gained experience in the Royal Flying Corps flying unequal-span Maurice Farman biplanes, known as pushers.]

appearance was indeed carefully, though perhaps unsuccessfully, 'styled', not only in the shape of the axe-head but also in the strong colouring and lettering.

The second example was an attractive piece of furniture designed by my brother. He was killed in 1917.[28] Some nine months later I found myself near his old squadron in France and visited it. In the anteroom, still used, was his cabinet for the storing of gramophone records, with an elaborate system of codes and signals for separating and classifying the different sorts of music—sacred, sentimental, humorous and so forth: another derivation from the Dewey decimal system which had impressed us both in the Bedales library.

---

[28] [See R.D. Best, *From Bedales to the Boche* (London: EnvelopeBooks, 2020).]

CHAPTER 4
THOMAS STURGE MOORE

At the 1921 Bedales reunion I met Thomas Sturge Moore, the poet and wood-engraver. He was a follower of Charles Ricketts and some of the works of both pupil and master were to be seen at Hillcroft, the house he and his wife had taken near the school.

Meeting him was a turning point in my life. Whatever conclusions I have reached in the theory and practice of industrial design owe much to Sturge Moore's influence. His fine head and white beard still remain in my mind's eye. His voice was pleasant. His eyes twinkled. And if, at this first meeting, I felt that his ideals and manner of expressing them were somewhat above my head, I also had the impression that we both might well have been members of some friendly club. He seemed to enjoy talking about art and design to the inexperienced, and some years later he gave a series of lectures on aesthetics to the Bedalians that were afterwards published under the title *Armour for Aphrodite*.[1]

'"Taste and see" is the whole business,' he said, and every subsequent year confirmed to me the poet's precept as to the importance of experiment. But there were nevertheless some loose ends in the doctrine. 'Taste and see' is indeed the whole business—but by whom and for whom? To the individual working or buying for himself, the matter is as simple as relishing milk or honey; the development of taste is undoubtedly like training the palate to distinguish the flavours of teas, coffees and wines; but what are the implications of these analogies when extended to the manufacturer and his public?

---

[1] Thomas Sturge Moore, *Armour for Aphrodite* (London: Grant Richards, 1929).

I put some of my perplexities before him.[2] (Before continuing, however, I feel I should acknowledge that in looking back on our conversations from a distance, Sturge Moore's mode of speech strikes me as more abstract than I remember it at the time. Like all charismatic men, his impact lay to a considerable degree in his presence; if the reader feels that the words that so greatly influenced my younger years are now impenetrable, I invite that reader to miss this chapter out and advance swiftly to Go.)

I led off with the doctrine of 'fitness for purpose'. His view was that 'fitness for purpose' was a narrow and insufficient standard. Many objects might do a perfectly good job but fail to compete with those addressed to refined senses and a finely balanced soul.

Refined? Balanced? Perhaps the war years had put me out of touch but these were not words I had heard used in recent debate. Were not sound workmanship and 'a feeling for tools and materials' the crux of the matter today? He disagreed. Skill, he felt, consisted in the capacity to wed certain shapes and masses to the promptings of the imagination or emotion.[3]

Were there no general characteristics that could be used in, say, the design of lighting fittings? His opinion was that 'Beauty is never beauty for a general reason but always for one that applies in no other case.' There had to be shared properties. 'A severely simple vase cannot be compared aesthetically to a Rococo one. You may prefer a Burgundy to a Hock, but scarcely

---

[2] Many of these thoughts are taken from *Armour for Aphrodite* and *Albert* [sic] *Dürer* (London: Duckworth, 1905).

[3] I have simplified greatly. Sturge Moore's actual words, as I have them, were: 'The exploitation of opportunities latent in the material is the last trench of the puritan aesthete, the "one-thing-necessary" man. But opportunities native to the skilled use of his materials consist in their capacity for wedding certain shapes, certain masses, which can be effectively juxtaposed and combined; and that becomes insensibly their capacity for yielding to the promptings of the imagination, emotion or idea in this or that direction.'

aesthetically. The real gourmet distinguishes between diverse vintages of the same wine. General preferences are, as a rule, wholly a matter of prejudice or sentimentality.'

I asked, then, if we could not give serious attention to the idea of 'building in truth'? Moore did not think so and challenged me to explain how, if that were the case, many Italian Gothic churches have a façade that is practically a screen set up to hide the building and create an anomaly in its construction? 'Not infrequently such churches are more beautiful than others which conform far better to the theory,' he said.

'Then it would seem pretty hopeless trying to define beauty at all,' I said. That was his belief, that beauty could not be defined. 'Things are beautiful for a woman's reason: because they are beautiful.' What he meant is that there is a difference between analysis and enjoyment, and that women are better able to enjoy. 'Some art lovers like to distinguish, then jump to the conclusion that what they have distinguished is what they like. But it is quite a different thing to be pleased at sorting and naming wild flowers, and to love and gaze at them and admire their forms, growth and characters. The one pleasure in no degree implies the other; the first is scientific, the second purely aesthetic.'

It was the capacity to appreciate that Sturge Moore thought needed to be developed: the training of the aesthetic palate. 'People think there is some abstruse science about it but it is the sense of proportion within a design which is employed to stimulate and delight the eyes. Taste and see.' And he had a suggestion. 'Begin in the corner of a room and order everything therein according to your taste. Admit nothing that does not fascinate your gaze. The corner may very well end by comprising your whole home.'

I doubted whether that was possible because my wife and I did not share the same tastes, and she had already established the character of our home. But perhaps when we moved into a new home, we could each have rooms of our own. I would want to give support to contemporary workers and would have furniture by Edward Barnsley and curtains from Heal's. In other rooms, my wife could have her antiques and furnishings in the eighteenth-century manner: derivative period reproductions. She likes our rooms to be lit with electric candles mounted in sconces of Georgian design.

To my surprise, Sturge Moore defended her taste. 'To dismiss designs for furniture or works of art as derivative, as it is fashionable to do, is to fall into error. All design, all art, all poetry is derivative. Early stone temples were copies of preceding wooden ones. The earliest Egyptian stone jars imitate the baskets they replaced, being meant for the far-future use of the dead, while esparto [grass] served the living.'

Did he not agree, then, with those who condemned the electric candle? He did not. He did not think that mimicry aimed to deceive, and he respected any genuine liking, as long as one had not been guyed by advertising, something one needed constantly to be alert to. One test, he thought, was whether one gravitated to the costly. 'You will never believe what beautiful things can be had almost for nothing; but if you heed the guide of fashion you may have to pay through the nose.'

'But if we could probe beneath the surface, many preferences would be found to be the result of fashion,' I said. He warned me to be wary of fashion. 'The world and fashion generally acclaim the wrong works first and loudest,' he said. 'A marked approach to truth, beauty and goodness needs not and rarely does go hand in hand with success as the world judges of it.' Beauty, in his view, was intrinsic in the object. It belonged to the whole and was largely a matter of proportion. It must be so, he said, because all normal men tended to admire the same objects.

To me that seemed to make it rather a poor lookout for the manufacturer who wishes to improve his designs, because his first duty as an industrialist was to make his business pay, just as it was the first duty of the state to protect itself from foreign enemies, and in the matter of design the manufacturer was limited by public taste.

Sturge Moore thought, however, that what limited the

manufacturer was a hesitancy to grant more freedom to his employees. 'I am willing to accept your meaning and allow that your object is laudable,' he said. 'But employers who leave no room or leisure for the craftsman to be his own designer degrade the world for their personal advantage. The history of our cottage-ware well demonstrates how taste which is acted upon may benefit the world.'

We had craftsmen, of course, but I could call to mind no product of our factory that could be compared in any way with craft-made 'cottage-ware'. I asked him not to expect too much in his relations with manufacturers like myself, and for my own part my conscience was clear.

Discussions of this sort continued for many years, but the immediate effects of our first conversation were recorded in a letter I wrote on my return home:

> Since my talk with you I've come to the conclusion that I must hitherto have been putting up with a lot of things which, rightly or wrongly, I did not really like. And this goes not only for the factory products but also for the things to be found in my house. Our catalogues and advertisements leave much to be desired. And yet there were founts of decent type at the printers waiting to be used. Lettering based on Edward Johnston's book that I first saw written by Allan Gwynne-Jones, while still at Bedales, is, I find, to be seen on some commercial advertisements. It doesn't cost more than the other stuff. Our letterhead on this stationery is not nearly as nice as that of, say, the Napier Motor Car Company. To me it all seems a matter of comparison and selection. Until I can find someone to do the job, I can only experiment and choose the things I like the best. It seems selfish and I would willingly relinquish the work to anyone in the firm who had strong likes and dislikes, but at the present I cannot find him.

In retrospect, this seems a fair appreciation of the situation at Best & Lloyd, for there was little of the cottage-ware type of experimentation which the poet had advocated. Indeed, the most helpful aspect of his teaching was the glimpse he gave of the way a designer should go to work. The arrival of the idea, brooding over it while subsidiary notions flock around—the holding back, the need for docility or willingness to learn—all answered more and more to actual experiences.

'Imagine a workshop,' he wrote, 'lined with shelves, pigeon-holes and drawers, all crowded with the jumbled parts of watches and clocks ... . Picture a skilful clock-maker sorting them till at last he can fit together a clock and then a watch, till he has there one, there another, steadily ticking. Such is the creative artist, only his shop is infinitely more abundant and confused and could rival that Garden of Eden in which the first Creator put together so many diverse types of plant and animal, and at last mankind.'

A poet's preferences

In the Autumn of that year, Thomas Sturge Moore visited the London showrooms of Best & Lloyd, which were then at 11 Bartletts Buildings, an eighteenth-century house near Holborn Circus. His criticisms and comments may be compared with illustrations of the articles he saw there.

> Dear Best,
> I enjoyed going over your show rooms and seeing the fine Adam's [sic] ceiling in the first-floor room ... . I think you are tackling the problem in the right way and spirit. Attention to all the things that you yourself feel to be wrong and the gradual weeding out of what you consider bad designs is the true way to begin. There are many quite decent and tolerable patterns you can keep while you are looking round and making up your mind for and against this or that. Your own taste and its development are the most important problems for you and if it is once active and determined not to stop soon, it will find plenty of friends and food in this world.

There followed suggestions about ways in which we might modify some of our designs. Not many were actually made, but something of the principles he advocated could not fail to get across. We tried, by experiment, in the new designs to make more shapely the links of chains, to alter the scale of some decorative features so that their appearance was neater, to clean up the lines of lanterns and to work out alternative versions whenever an occasion presented itself.

Dynamic symmetry

Remembering the recommendation of the Düsseldorf School to use 'clear mathematical proportions', I became interested in a book called *Dynamic Symmetry* by Jay Hambridge[4] in which the author said that the secret of beauty in Greek vases and old master pictures was to be discovered by means of geometry. The poet did not agree with these theories and questioned whether it might not be possible to make an ugly vase with dynamic proportions? It was in his view that it was only by taste that the Greeks chose, out of so many possibilities, those that would be effective, and he cautioned, 'Theory is always preferred to taste by the intellectual, for having little taste he wants to decide by some rule instead of by liking.'

Sturge Moore was right in declaring that distinguishing is not the same thing as liking. The wine- and tea-taster must put his own preferences in the background; so must the manufacturer. And yet I suspect that somehow or other the most fertile, happy and successful industrialists *do blend* their own tastes with those of their customers. Otherwise the result would be so distasteful to the manufacturer that sooner or later something would have to go wrong in the business. In any case, industrialists and designers should be using their artistic palates as sensitive instruments to detect the finer points of their customers' predilections.

In suggesting that Ricketts's taste might be better than and therefore sometimes different from his own, Sturge Moore also laid himself open to the question, how would he have proceeded

---

4 Jay Hambidge, *Dynamic Symmetry—The Greek Vase* (New Haven, CT.: Yale University Press, 1920).

if his creative output depended on Charles Ricketts's approval? And as for the notion that all normal men tend to admire the same objects, until some way has been discovered to estimate what 'normal' means, the question must remain an open one. Disagreement amongst music and art critics is such as to make one doubtful. But in the meantime, a survey of taste and furnishings in the homes of individual members of the Council of Industrial Design might provide some useful data.

And what about agreement between the employer and the designer in industry? I had been recommended to develop my own taste but I soon had to ask myself how far I was justified in interfering with the work of my fellow designers in the business when we disagreed. These seemed to me most difficult questions, to which *Armour for Aphrodite* provided no simple answer.

CHAPTER 5
THREE MEN

Amongst the many by-products of this first encounter with Thomas Sturge Moore were a recommendation to read [Havelock Ellis's *The Dance of Life*,[1]],[2] membership of the Design and Industries Association and an introduction to Moore's friend, Mr. B.J. Fletcher, then head of the Birmingham School of Art.

[*The Dance of Life* opens with the words 'It has always been difficult for Man to realise that his life is an art.' Difficult it may be, but the conception, though surprising, is an attractive one, above all to the designer; and especially to one who would free himself from dogma; for if 'the morals of a community at one time or place were never the same as that of another or even the same community at another time or place,' was it likely that any hard and fast standards, or 'general characters' could be found for the design of objects produced to please the eyes of human beings?][3]

Sturge Moore did not approve of artistic coteries; still less, as we have seen, did he believe in the doctrine of 'fitness for purpose', which was then one of the main planks in the D.I.A. platform. It may be doubted whether he ever took the Association very seriously but was probably drawn towards the

---

[1] Havelock Ellis, *The Dance of Life* (London: Constable & Co Ltd, 1923). [Ellis (1859–1939) was a pioneer in the study of human sexuality and promoted greater openness about sexual practices, needs and modes of gratification. He wrote a medical textbook about homosexuality and formulated ideas about narcissism and autoeroticism taken up later by Freud. He was also a Vice-President of the Eugenics Society from 1909 to 1912.]

[2] [Deleted by R.D.B.]

[3] [Deleted by R.D.B.]

sincerity of its members in their search for better design. It was he, at any rate, who first told me about this body and in the year 1921 I was duly admitted to its ranks. I am still a member.

B.J. Fletcher: Lessons from Coalbrookdale

B.J. Fletcher[4] was, with Harry Peach of Dryad Furniture, a co-founder of the Design and Industries Association and had come to the Birmingham School of Art in 1920, from Leicester, whence his influence had radiated gently in many directions. A few art-school masters, like Catterson-Smith, learn fine handicrafts from such men of genius as Morris; Dr. Kreis, of the Düsseldorf School, had experience of designing for industry; but Mr. Fletcher had actually been in it, for when young he had worked at the famous Coalbrookdale iron foundry in Shropshire.

Not many receive such a good training as he for the teaching of product design; a number get caught up in a circular process, returning, after some years of training in schools, to their starting point: a school. Though he had studied drawing and painting at the local art school, he chose to follow on with the City and Guilds course in Foundry Work rather than take an art teacher's diploma. He was a gifted draughtsman but distrusted draughtsmanship when it came to making things. Events continually reminded him that industrial products had to be *made* and the drawing was, at best, only a means to that end, while at the worst a good-looking drawing might well result in a badly designed article. If a design were simple and natural to make, with given tools and materials, that design generally gave him, personally, more pleasure than a technically difficult and showy example.

While still a boy, Mr. Fletcher could not help noticing several poor, impracticable designs at 'The Dale'. One particularly

---

4 [Benjamin J. Fletcher (1868–1951), teacher at Coalbrookdale School of Art, 1885, Deputy Head at Leicester Municipal School of Art, 1888, Headmaster from 1900, Principal of Birmingham School of Art, 1920–1934.]

struck him. It was a cast-iron gate, designed by an architect. On clearing away the sand from the top half of the mould, a panel dropped clean away, owing to the unequal cooling of the metal— inevitable, as it turned out, with this particular design. On the second pouring, precautions were taken to secure a different result and at first all seemed to go well; but in the dressing shop (then under Mr. Fletcher's uncle), at the first touch of the mallet, the panel again parted company with the frame and eventually had to be rivetted in position. The architect should have known better.

'The pencil continually proposes something alien to the job,' he would say, 'and the foundryman and metal worker is ever being frustrated by difficulties created by the inexperienced draftsman.'

As another example of what to avoid, he offered a 'well-known work in cast iron ... called *The Eagle Slayer* by John Bell, now standing outside Bethnal Green Museum. It has its limbs spread and precise; the modelling is sharp and detailed.' But B.J. Fletcher did not like it.[5] He knew, furthermore, that while it was being cast at Coalbrookdale, the whole works had held its breath until the metal came out of the expensive mould.

But by contrast, his eyes had been soothed and delighted by the rounded and simple forms of some sugar pans produced at The Dale for export to the West Indies. The shape seemed admirably suited to the upper and lower moulds of sand; the gentle curves were, he thought, almost inevitable [so that when later he noticed that two Chinese figures of cast-metal at the Victoria and Albert Museum were of a similar shape and equally suited to the process of casting, he was altogether delighted. To him they seemed beautiful].[6]

---

[5] B.J. Fletcher, *The Artistic Treatment of Cast Iron*. A paper written for and delivered to the National Foundryman's Association in London at its Annual Meeting the year Mr. Sydney Gimson was its President. The paper was later read to the Leicester Association of Engineers on 23 January, 1914.
[6] [Deleted by R.D.B.]

He would give example after example of products going wrong, because the designer knew more about drawing than about the job of making. A design for printed fabrics by William Morris, for instance: the lines were too thin for reproduction in the wooden blocks; brass strips had therefore to be used. The result, in Mr. Fletcher's estimation, was unsatisfactory. They were not as nice as the drawing.

Some damask, linens and textiles by Walter Crane came in for criticism. All seemed to suffer from the same defect. They were too complicated. What was the use of making a pattern for damask out of children dancing? he asked. He thought them charming but not easily readable as a design in two tints of white; something more in the nature of a silhouette was wanted. The designs of Joshua Reynolds and Burne-Jones for stained glass were often poor, he considered, because, for the artists, they started and ended on paper.

Many of the historical examples published by the Worshipful Company of Goldsmiths—especially those by Paul Lamerie—earned his condemnation for the same reason. 'The more prolific the ornamental draftsmanship, the worse it is ...' and 'objects like the famous salt cellar by Benvenuto Cellini have done as much harm to the public taste as the Chantry Bequest ...' and 'directly a man feels dominant over his material, he is done.'

When it came to furniture, his patience had been sorely tried by the poor craftsmanship he had seen at Roger Fry's Omega workshops. They might just as well have been put together with tin-tacks and painted up. The designers seemed to have been selected because they liked making things rather than because they had any ability in furniture production.

Lettering

Most noticeable was his influence on the lettering of signboards, shopfronts and fascias in Leicester. He had first noticed some lettering prepared by Eric Gill for W.H. Smith & Son and had written to St. John Hornby for permission to use it as a sample for his signwriting class.[7] Eric Gill was then drawing his inspiration from the distinguished calligrapher Edward Johnston and had taken a shed near the latter's house in order to study from the master. Both gave lectures at the Leicester College, greatly influencing Mr. Fletcher and through him the students and business people in the city. But what impressed him most about Johnston's work was his finding the right *tool*—the broad quill. With that tool, the whole art of writing was rediscovered.

So important, in Johnston's estimation, was the tool that now and again he would take a whole class-hour while he showed a student how to cut a pen; and so well had Mr. Fletcher learned this lesson that he even perfected the tool Johnston was using for his blackboard demonstrations by causing to be made square pieces of chalk instead of the customary round sticks Johnston had always used.

'Dryad' furniture

Fletcher liked practical people. While at Leicester, an employee of Dryad, which made basket, cane and willow products, came to him for drawing lessons and, at the student's own request, designed a cane chair. The art master suggested that he might like to make the actual article and this was duly carried out by the man himself in his kitchen. The chair was then 'quizzed up and down'; they would agree, after discussion, to remove this or that feature since it served no useful purpose and certainly did not improve the appearance, until finally an excellent article emerged. Out of this man's skill and Fletcher's influence the Dryad chair industry eventually grew.

But although the Dryad cane chair became a famous and eminently saleable product, Fletcher never seems to have recognised that the market was, in a way, part of the raw material of industrial design. This may have been partly due to an

---

[7] [C.H. St. John Hornby (1867–1946), founding partner of W.H. Smith. He had an interest in fine printing and founded the Ashendene Press.]

unfortunate interview with a buyer in one of the large London furnishing stores. This man refused point blank to interest himself in the new line of cane chairs and seems to have dismissed him with some rudeness. It was apparent that he knew little about well-designed furniture and, so Fletcher suspected, was surrounded at home by articles as displeasing as the ones to be seen in the shop in question. The buyer was obviously not fit for the job and would have benefited from a practical course in furniture making. 'Inspiration will come out of the doing,' he would say.

Those businessmen

Birmingham manufacturers had not taken as much interest in the work of the School as Fletcher was justified in expecting. Few had visited the Annual Exhibition of the students at the Art Gallery and, as a group, they seemed to be tarred with the same brush as the London buyer. 'But this is what sells,' they would repeat, when challenged, and Fletcher, as if in reply, would often ask himself, 'Does this mean that for themselves they would select something different? If so, where are the examples of these lovely things? Where is the little choice collection, possibly near the office or works entrance, of the "best" that the firm had made, or the "best" that could be found from the past-masters of the trade?' None of them seemed to take the attitude 'This is what I have to sell but that is what I would choose for myself!'

In France, on the other hand, he had seen such collections of choice goods selected by the trade and had noticed furthermore that the exhibits were freely discussed by people in the industry. In England it was the fine-arts man—'the "artist" in his own right'—who got the credit. Was this perhaps because, when the Technical Education Act was first passed, the tradesman of that time feared that the 'mysteries' of their crafts would be revealed, and objected to the teaching of any 'practical' work, thus closing the most fruitful source—through the workshop—of designs? At all events, a draughtsman seemed to be preferred to a craftsman and the drawing office to the bench.[8]

Soft-voiced criticism

Thus would B.J. Fletcher speculate on the unfortunate state of affairs in Birmingham; and since he believed that a teacher should come down pretty severely on a student—his own kindly master having once said to him, 'You young fool, you'll never see anything beautiful,' because he was missing the point—it was not surprising that indications of his displeasure should occasionally come through his mild manner, especially when one of his few industrialist disciples—amongst whom I counted myself—failed to reach the root of the matter. And yet his voice was never raised.

Voices always affected his friend Edward Johnston and gentle voices especially drew him. 'I remember,' he wrote, 'my first evening in Leicester' [with the Fletchers]. 'It reminded me of a doves' house with some (rather than filled with) doves and pigeons.'

For myself the voice of this art master had always suggested a murmuring background for the strings, with now and then a slightly astringent passage for woodwind or muted horns. It was all piano, if not pianissimo, but pointed, like his neat beard. He was small in stature and everything about him—his clothes, the colour of his hair and, above all, his voice—was quiet.

I found him an excellent critic of any new designs that might be in preparation. 'The loveliest thing about brass is brass,' he would say, 'but the more you tie it up with linear qualities [by which he meant complications], the worse it is,' and as if to give practical evidence of these principles, he himself designed two wall-brackets for the company which were actually made and put

---

[8] From a lecture by Sir William Kendrick to the National Association of the Motor Industry in Birmingham, 1890, delivered at the London School of Economics, 14 January, 1925.

on the market. But above all, it was his practical attitude to design criticism which most affected his disciples at that time. From him, we learned to 'quiz' our products and it was from him that I first heard that word used in this connection. Oft-times were we brought from our aesthetic beds by the sound of his horn—*en sourdine*,[9] of course—to hunt for what he called 'that added loveliness'.

General characteristics

Sturge Moore and Mr. Fletcher were friends. They liked and respected each other; but although I never heard the one criticise the other, it must be abundantly clear to the reader that there was some disagreement between them regarding artistic principles. The poet had rejected the idea that 'the exploitation of opportunities latent in the material' had any bearing on the question of good design; on the contrary, he held that this was 'the last trench of the puritan aesthete, the "one-thing-necessary" man'.[10]

B.J. Fletcher would have been the first to agree that many imponderable factors entered into industrial design but maintained that 'every material has its appropriate range: strained outside that range, it shows to disadvantage; used within its range even the most unpromising material shows surprisingly pleasant qualities.' They should therefore be selected for emphasis and made much of. 'We recognise these special qualities and limitations,' he continued, 'by writing music for particular instruments, and know that a work composed for one kind of instrument cannot be rendered, without loss, on another kind.'[11]

---

9 Muted.

10 See Chapter 4, footnote 3.

11 B.J. Fletcher, *Right Making, Being a Lecture on the Principles of Design* (London: The Design and Industries Association, 1927). Delivered at the London School of Economics, Aldwych, 14 January, 1925.

When, some twenty years later, my first and only orchestral composition was tried over by the Birmingham School of Music Orchestra, I was often met by more than one player pushing the instrumental part, as it were, under my nose and asking me how I thought he was going to play certain notes when his instrument only went up (or down) to so-and-so. Few would deny the need for this sort of regard for tools and materials; but when it comes to the settings, the transcriptions, whether a piano work is 'pianistic' and so forth, we are on much more difficult ground and we shall later have occasion to return to a consideration of design principles in music—if such exist.

However much Sturge Moore might decry the notion that artistic value attaches to a general character which, he maintained, belong to both good and bad design, Mr. Fletcher, as we have seen, stood for certain principles. These he upheld uncompromisingly. He was a school-of-art master and so I suspect, from experience, that in dealing with the young people, manufacturers and designers of Leicester and Birmingham, it would not do to be too vague, too much up in the clouds, to leave it all to 'conscience'. Neither the School nor the evangelical D.I.A. would get very far on that sort of thing ... and as for imitations of one material by another—'paper made to look like cambric, tiles or terracotta made to look like stone or marble, iron made to look like bronze, cotton to look like silk,' the stupidity of these, he urged, 'needed no comment [because] art is never artifice.' He would stand no nonsense—especially when it came to electric candles.

Nor was his disapproval confined to the products of recent centuries. Even the ancient Egyptians would have done better, he maintained, if they had held to sound D.I.A. principles. While Tutankhamen's lion proclaimed the hardness of the basalt from which it was carved and was a notably beautiful work, 'the alabaster jars ... show such disregard for the brittleness of the material that they must have given Mr. Carter much anxiety in handling them; their elaborate handles, like loops of macaroni, violate ... the quality of the material, fitness and beauty. Here the

craftsman is showing off and has lost respect for his material …
In short, the article is eloquent of the situation in the
workshop.'[12]

Herbert 'Bobbie' Simon: the master printer

At that time, until his death in 1925, my father took little active
part in the management of the business, except when appealed
to, contenting himself, as he put it, with 'a bit of pottering about
in any little detail' that did not encroach on my direction. He
nevertheless retained his old zest for design; his presence,
furthermore, heartened and encouraged the members of the
firm during the difficult times of the first post-war depression.

One day, on coming into the office, I found him talking to a
youthful figure, stooping a little, with his back turned towards
me. My father was explaining to him the principles of the slide
rule; but although the visitor seemed deeply absorbed in this
instrument of calculation, I found later that his interests lay in
other directions. This was my first meeting with the printer
Herbert 'Bobbie' Simon, then manager of the Kynoch Press, who
had come to Birmingham in 1922 after a period of training in
America. Later I met his brother Oliver and Harold Curwen of
the Curwen Press.

I listened with interest to Bobbie Simon's manner of
speaking and was at once attracted by the inflections of his
voice, though my colleagues afterwards wondered what he had
been getting at. They agreed that he had created about him a
somewhat rarified atmosphere, mingled with a feeling of
business capacity; he also soon showed a practical knowledge of
ball games such as fives and cricket—but not golf.

On this occasion he had been invited to discuss the
production of some good commercial printing for my company;
for at last I had found a catalogue—it had been carried out by his
firm for Henry Hope and Son—printed in exactly the way I

---

[12] Fletcher, *Right Making*.

wanted. The type-forms, margins, spacing, arrangement of the blocks and even the touches of red seemed just right, in a way which brooked no argument.

Bobbie Simon greatly respected Mr. Fletcher, who had absorbed, and seemed to radiate, something from the great craftsmen of the nineteenth-century revival. Mr. Fletcher was a link with Ernest Gimson, Sydney Barnsley, Emery Walker and even William Morris. Bobbie Simon thought he was aiming to do good work as a contribution to the betterment of social life and to the realisation of England as a Green and Pleasant Land.

Although sympathetic I was not fully converted to the faith and shared my father's distrust of high-falutin' principles when what was required was teaching that accorded to trade conditions.

Some years later I accompanied Bobbie Simon on a pilgrimage to Kelmscott, the home, near Lechlade, of William Morris; here we were received by his daughter, May Morris, and shown the lovely old house and its contents. I could feel the rising pressure of admiration, mingled with awe, as my friend's attention was caught by the Kelmscott *Chaucer* lying open on the bed. Throughout the visit, I was depressed by a sense of inferiority; I admired the fine brass chandelier in the entrance hall but had to admit to myself that it was designed for real candles rather than electric ones. Thus do we lose touch with the 'divineness of liking' and allow our tastes to become entangled by irrelevant factors.

Design standards in printing

In spite of Monotype and Linotype machinery, the essential gear of printing has remained sufficiently stable for long enough for a classical standard to have taken shape and become generally accepted. 'Typography is an art in which violent revolutionaries, in the nature of things, cannot hope to be successful.'[13] The

---

[13] Oliver Simon and Julius Rodenberg, *Printing of Today* (London: Peter Davies Ltd, 1928).

letters on the Trajan column did not greatly differ from those of the Henry Hope catalogue. The book on the bed at Kelmscott would have caused no great shock of surprise to Caxton; but there was a profound difference between the old candelabrum in the entrance hall and the electrical appliances already beginning to appear at the time of our visit. In the design of light fittings no standards have even now become widely acknowledged.

But even though there may be a 'right' and 'wrong', are there no 'general characters' in printing to which artistic value attaches? The mind recoils from the jumble of words and meanings suggested by the question. Consider, for instance, the functional standard. Tests for legibility may be conducted as easily as with an optician's chart, but do they get us very far? Surely what the individual has been accustomed to must affect the ease with which he can pick up the printed word.

And for what purpose must the printing be fit? We have heard of 'a rather eccentric German typographical reformer, for whom legibility is the great enemy [and for whom] the infamous thing must at all costs be crushed'. We read, he argues, too easily. 'Our eyes slide over the words and the words, in consequence, mean nothing to us. An illegible type makes us take trouble. It compels us to dwell on each separate word; we have time, while we are deciphering it, to suck out its full significance. Putting this theory into practice, this reformer had designed a set of letters strangely unlike those with which the typographical practice of generations has made us familiar ... .'[14] Clearly the functional standard may lead us anywhere—or nowhere.

Turn to 'the exploitation of opportunities latent in the tools' and we seem to be on equally insecure ground. The tool may have enabled Edward Johnston to rediscover the art of writing but Gutenberg, as a good industrial designer, studied his market and, ignoring the 'press-tool' quality of type, took instead the thick and thin strokes of the pen-made letter as his model. Most printers have followed his example.

---

[14] Simon and Rodenberg, *Printing of Today.*

Printing for business

At the time of this first contact with good commercial printing, I was not in the least disturbed by theoretical speculation. It was just an exciting experience. Wanting, somehow, to be 'in the movement' and with my appetite whetted by such an edifying manual as Joseph Thorp's *Printing for Business*,[15] I was soon absorbed in the art of layout for advertisements and other printed matter. The pages of the *Kynoch Type Specimens* became well thumbed, but none seemed so well proportioned and in every way so excellent as Caslon Old Face. I became a purist and a little intolerant. The old hearty commercial catalogues, with their innumerable letterforms, jumbled up together, made me wince.

Compared with previous publications, the first catalogue ever printed for the company by the Kynoch Press seems, even now, highly satisfactory but in the year 1933 the excellence of the presentation only served to heighten my vague dissatisfaction with the goods shown therein. There was nothing wrong with them, certainly—at any rate, not by ordinary commercial standards —but then, were many of the articles wholly 'right', in the sense that the typography seemed right? Did they conform to the exacting standards of our leader in the D.I.A., Mr. Fletcher? Were they, as Thomas Sturge Moore would have had it, 'addressed to refined senses and a finely balanced soul?' I was doubtful.

Commercial disaster

But it was not before I discovered that Bobbie Simon suffered from similar doubts and misgivings regarding his own work; and indeed, in this Pilgrim's Progress, he plays a peculiar part, for at certain times he has been a veritable Mr. Great-Heart of Design while on other occasions he would appear as a sort of gleeful

---

[15] Joseph Thorp, *Printing for Business, a Manual of Printing Practice in Non-Technical Idiom* (London: John Hogg, 1919).

Giant Despair, relishing keenly not only mishaps in the products of his own firm and mine but the whole rich complex of commercial disaster.

Looking through the glossary of his book *Printing Explained*,[16] I can almost sense his enjoyment of 'Printer's Pie'—'an accident in which lines of type become a mass of disorderly confusion'. This and other technical misfortunes had their counterparts in the brass trade. Nothing could be so final, so irretrievable, as the completely spilly casting; and the porous casting riddled with fine holes, too small to be seen with the naked eye, can, in the final stages of manufacture, also give results as disturbing as 'pie', for an unsightly series of blotches, like some childish complaint, sometimes appears days or even weeks after the metal has been finished and lacquered. Badly fitting glass might be compared with the half-tone block, unhappily appearing upside-down on an otherwise faultless page. The cloudy effect of the 'vignetted'[17] background, due, the printers say, to the age of the block and not to defective 'make-ready', suggested the 'runs' or streaks in the cellulose lacquer of finished brassware.

If he was fully alive to 'Fletcher Values' he never had any illusions that the market, sales or what he called 'the Chart' were not important factors in design for industry. They were as much a part of the creation of fine commercial printing or high-class light fittings as ploughing the fields is an act of husbandry. We were as sensitive as Mr. Fletcher to rebuffs, in this sphere, but we accepted them as one of the conditions of our work. Bobbie Simon insisted that some of my products must be eminently saleable, even if others were designed to appeal to the sectarian members of the D.I.A. It might even be necessary to make some pot-boilers—of the best kind:

---

[16] Herbert Simon and Harry Carter, *Printing Explained* (Leicester: The Dryad Press, 1931).

[17] The article as reproduced is not enclosed in a definite border, nor does it meet the virgin paper in a sharp outline. It is surrounded by vague cloud, gradually shading off.

You must prepare a 'cute' domestic range. Just half a dozen of each would set the ball rolling. Put them in cold storage; and as for the trade name, how would 'THE COMFILITE' do? But engineering principles must prevail and any tendency towards disintegration in use, or failure to allow easy replacement of glass without splinterage, should be resolutely eschewed ...

The commandos

The 8:40 train for London became a sort of commando raid; whereas, returning on the evening train in the company of many other businessmen, we were an army in retreat. Our weapons were our sales-satchels or briefcases filled with catalogues and leaflets. Bobbie Simon was well informed on railway matters and while sitting opposite to me would comment freely on the design of the rolling stock, the equipment of the breakfast-car, the square teapots and all the rest of it. Even the L.M.S.[18] kippers were appraised. They had pictorial qualities, he maintained.

The designs most pleasing to him had always been those associated with the Industrial Revolution, all this period being, in his eyes, touched with a romantic quality. His imagination was never so lively as when some old engine, machine or building suggested what he called 'the general backcloth of industrial history'. The names of distinguished engineers and inventors were frequently invoked and while I was working on *Brass Chandelier* he would put forward, invitingly, any little titbit he might have come across while reading.

'What do you think of this little cameo?' he would say. 'Charming, my dear Sir, is it not? Of course it is a little before "our period" but, Guedalla-like,[19] one can almost hear the drums beating their frenzied welcome to Arkwright, Naysmith and James Brindley ...'

I would pass to him photographs or drawings of new designs

---

[18] [The London, Midland and Scottish Railway Company.]
[19] [Philip Guedalla (1889–1944), a popular writer, wit and epigrammatist.]

and, after some fanciful preamble, he would mingle practical suggestions with references to 'his period':

> ... and what about introducing some colour in the main space and framework? An orange vermillion might be a good finish and give even more dash to the notion you have put forward. There is something of the Matthew Boulton about your design. He would undoubtedly have discussed sales possibilities with Mr. Fothergill.

Two or three hours in his company, whether inside the L.M.S. breakfast-car, on-board the *Isle de Beauté* bound for Corsica or walking alongside a canal in the Midlands, was like assisting at some peculiar film premiere. His thoughts seemed to project themselves in a series of visual images. It was not a silent film, though there would be plenty of captions.

He liked to find the appropriate trade name or brand to stand for wider categories and issues. All clothing, whether or not ready-made, he called his 'Montague Burton's';[20] 'Lapsang-Souchong', sometimes rather dilute, stood for the colour of my complexion and, by implication, health in general; 'Daimler Hire' represented all automobile services paid for by the hour and could even be applied to the more expensive forms of public transport.

Without the key, these captions sometimes led to unfortunate and expensive misunderstandings. Then, when his private film show was speeding up towards some kaleidoscopic climax—when his favourite characters of the Industrial Revolution were overlapping contemporary figures in the world of sport, industry and design—the recurring theme of commercial or bodily mishap would introduce itself, generally to be followed by a proposal of further holidays together:

> I have come to the conclusion that even a good weekend, charged with sport and good fellowship, cannot be enjoyed without NEMESIS. All business, my dear Bob, is at a standstill and the

---

[20] England's first mass retailer of ready-made men's suits.

famous SPOUT, up which we must ascend, is once more discernible. What could be more shattering than the downward twist and spiral of the Chart? But how about another weekend in the country of Arkwright? A fine Hotel exists at Bakewell. Comfort and excellence of food will act like arnica to the shinbone injured by fielding practice, restoring to their normal bonhomie minds distressed by commerce and bodies weakened by catarrh.

'Bud' Spenser: facial functionalism

It was during the previous year of 1921 that word first came to the factory of an American buyer who had appeared on the Best & Lloyd stand at the British Industries Fair, Castle Bromwich. Later, he introduced himself as Mr. Spenser—'Bud' Spenser to his friends. Dark haired, his heavy eyebrows seemed accentuated by the horn-rimmed glasses, at that time especially associated with the New World.

My wife is French but has spent many years in the U.S.A. and England. As a result of observations in these three countries she has formed an interesting theory regarding the design of faces. The shape of the lower part of the face, especially the mouth, is largely, she holds, the result of the language, the manner in which it is spoken producing a further modification.

To a Latin, the English faces appear slightly 'buttoned-up' and impassive, due, she maintains, to their indolent articulation. With the Americans, however, the bass voice, cultivated by the male, gives somehow a fullness to the jowl, which is accentuated by the need for wholesale cheering and cheerleading, to say nothing of overcoming the din of cocktail parties, jukeboxes and radio. All their drinks have names which require lip-work, such as 'John Collins', 'Bourbon', 'Mint Julep', 'Whiskey Sour', 'Gin Rickey' and so forth. No Englishman would make the effort. He would rather go without his drink. In short—and here she has, by a different route, come to the same conclusion as Edward Johnston and Mr. Fletcher—the Americans think of their mouths as implements with which to make a noise.

Design for the U.S.A.

Soon after our first meeting, Bud Spenser began to talk of designs for lighting—he called them 'fixtures', not 'fittings'—and standard lamps in his own country, comparing them with what he had seen at Castle Bromwich. Although he approved, in general, of the company's designs, it would be necessary, he insisted, to make some alterations in order to conform to certain American conventions. The arms of wall-brackets should be shortened; a different kind of lamp-holder (or 'socket', as he called it) was standard and this affected the design of the upper part of table- and floor-lamps. There was, furthermore, a demand for a much richer-looking article than in Great Britain. The necessary modifications were accordingly carried out to his instructions.

The collection of casting-patterns has already been described.[21] Visitors generally find it surprising. Spenser was not only surprised but delighted and at once began moving eagerly from one drawer to another, picking up a spindle here, a neck there, fitting them together and building up new and interesting shapes. Some of these suggestions were most unexpected.

Colour on lighting appliances had been popular enough in its time. Following M. Argand's invention in 1784 of a new burner for oil lamps, there had been many reading lamps of *tôle*, or sheet-tin, which were painted by hand in a charming way. But apart from an imitation of darkened verdigris, called 'green antique', the company had supplied nothing in colour for many years. It had been the unmistakeable appearance of metal the public seemed to prefer. At Spenser's suggestion, the natural colour of the metal was combined with enamels in green, blue or red, often in articles of a general shape suggested by the eighteenth-century oil-burning reading lamp. He revived, furthermore, the old practice of combining with the metal spindles, vases and cups of coloured glass.

---

[21] ['and compared to some 'Tomb of the Kings'.' Deleted by R.D.B.]

Through him we rediscovered the many excellent books in the company's library and even enlarged our collection. Leonardo da Vinci in his famous treatise on painting recommended the painter to look at certain walls stained with damp, or at stones of uneven colour, in which he would be able to see divine landscapes or battles or an infinity of other things. It was in the same spirit that we turned over the fine photographs of furniture and metalware, often finding, in the angle of a chest, a piece of carving or unit of pattern, something which if enlarged and possibly turned upside down or sideways would make a lively-looking article and a good seller.

Pictorial presentation

Lastly, Spenser added yet another of the many methods of representing the articles we were offering for sale. These had been either 'rendered' in simple pen-and-ink drawings, or in flat washes on white paper 'tickled up' with brown ink, or in wash drawings on tinted paper shaded with pencil, after which the highlights would be picked out in body colour, this last often being overdone.

Spenser showed how, if a drawing on tracing paper were coloured at the back with crayon, the same colour appeared at the front as a delicate tint. All articles destined for the States were presented in this way. This simple convention of the time led to the scale sketch on tracing paper, from which positive prints were made by the Ozalid process and afterwards coloured by hand. The method is commonly used today.

The members of the firm liked all this activity and were warmed by the high spirits of some of the new designs and of their creator. It was impossible to remain indifferent to these tales of a land where 'good-class' period fixtures and standard lamps were adequately appreciated.

Bud Spenser's visits had far-reaching results. The journeys made on behalf of the firm first by one person, then by another, and the opening and subsequent closing of a showroom in New

York are outside the scope of this essay on industrial design; but through this contact with the New World, we were faced—luckily right in the early stages of our pilgrimage—with a viewpoint contrasting with that presented by the D.I.A. and the growing school of thought which preferred simple, functional designs.

'Fitness for Purpose' had little to do with many of these ebullient American models. The fact that many Americans then, if not now, preferred an eighteenth-century idiom to the manner of Morris, Lethaby or Gropius should, I have always thought, be accepted by the manufacturers as part of their raw material: it is neither good nor bad. It is nevertheless surprising how many industrial designers seem to forget that it takes all sorts to make a world.

CHAPTER 6
FROM LALIQUE TO GROPIUS

The 1925 Paris Exhibition

From the manager of Best & Lloyd's Paris showroom came a strong recommendation to visit the *Exposition Internationale des Arts Décoratifs Modernes* of 1925. Accordingly, the Spring of that year found our head designer Will Morris and me in the French capital, equipped with sketchbooks for discreetly recording our impressions while wandering round the pavilions which filled the *Esplanade des Invalides* and flanked the Seine. The exhibition was intended to display contemporary work of all nations, but especially to show that the French were capable of producing furniture and fittings in styles other than the classical ones.

There were many books about the exhibits. One, *Le Luminaire*,[1] was much consulted by the drawing-office staff at home during the following years. In an introduction to this work, M. Guillaume Janneau wrote:

> Of all decorative art, the realm of 'luminaires'[2] or light fittings was most prolific in happy finds [*trouvailles*] and one exploited to most advantage … . After many years of electric candles the luminaire had at last been given an independent existence.

What we now call 'architectural lighting' was then becoming popular. The luminous cornice was being incorporated into the

---

[1] Guillaume Janneau, *Le Luminaire et les Moyens d'éclairages nouveaux* (Paris: Editions d'Art Charles Moreau, 1925).

[2] This term for light fittings has now been taken up in the U.S.A.

construction of the room, along with other indirect lighting effects such as luminous borders, soffits, panels built into the wall and so forth. 'Certain strict purists,' M. Janneau suggested, 'were contesting the legitimacy of a lighting effect which conceals the means, but this was carrying scruples too far. The modern spirit is more supple: it appreciates, furthermore, the new charm of scientific magic; and just as it is alive to the abstract beauty of the radio, it senses the enchantment of illumination effected without material means.'

Gone, it would seem, were the flutes and mouldings of the classical styles. Contemporary decoration substituted for them 'imbrications' or scale-like surfaces, falling leaves, 'Marguerites-seen-in-plan' and various geometrical forms. But all this was of secondary importance, thought M. Janneau; what really mattered was form and there, lighting appliances had definitely entered a new phase:

> The modern spirit, a little austere in its tastes, disdains knick-knacks. Desk lamps and wall brackets take the form of reflectors which direct light in a sheet onto the surfaces to be illuminated ... . They are at once works of art and logically constructed implements, the clean outline of which is marred by no superfluous decorations.

Looking once more over these illustrations, one cannot help wondering whether M. Janneau was not perhaps describing what he would have liked, rather than what was actually there. If the modern spirit was then a little austere (*un peu janseniste dans ses gouts*) and disdained knick-knacks (*le colifichet*), how can we account for the glass balls of M. Dilly's '*applique murale*',[3] the flutes and volutes of Paul Kiss[4] or the spirals of Edgar Brandt?[5]

It would indeed be interesting to make an anthology of

---

3 Wall light.

4 Paul Kiss (1885–1962), French artist specialising in Art-Deco ornamental ironwork.

5 Edgar Brandt (1880–1960), French decorative artist-blacksmith of the Art-Deco period.

introductions to exhibition catalogues during the period covered by this essay. One would undoubtedly find a certain sameness about the principles propounded, whereas the articles themselves would show a variety that makes futile the perennial attempts to codify the principles of good design.

There was a British Pavilion which showed the work of two young architects, Murray Easton and Howard Robertson, names that will reappear in this story. According to Mr. H.C. Bradshaw, writing in an official report, the pavilion

> was original and in keeping with the spirit of the Exhibition ... a definite contribution to the object of the Exhibition, and equalled in architectural interest many of the foreign and French pavilions.[6]

The British exhibits, on the other hand, 'gave but an incomplete idea of the real strength of British art production':[7]

> Many competent observers who visited them, while impressed by the excellence of their craftsmanship and finish, were also struck by their comparative dullness and aloofness, and the absence of the spirit of adventure. The question arises to what extent and in what respects are these characteristics the marks of high or low vitality? How far do they relect the qualities of sanity, restraint and continuity of tradition which are signs of health and power? ... Or how far do they imply ... rigidity and ossification?[8]

By contrast the French display was highly impressive. It also occupied at least two-thirds of the entire space and would not have been attained without the expenditure of a good deal of public money. Did that mean its exhibits were 'superior'? Mr. Bradshaw felt the test of this had been occluded:

---

[6] *Report of the Present Position and Tendencies of the Industrial Arts as indicated at the International Exhibition of Modern Decorative and Industrial Arts, Paris, 1925, with an Introductory Survey* (UK: Department of Overseas Trade, 1927), 45.

[7] *Report of the Present Position*, 12.

[8] *Report of the Present Position*, 37.

When we seek to compare the results produced by this artificial encouragement with those produced under ordinary economic conditions ... it is very necessary to remember we are not comparing like with like. It is only when 'exhibition pieces' come to be tested by exposure to ordinary market conditions, without artificial shelter from the full blast of economic forces, that it can be definitely known which of these developments represent new and permanent factors in the art history of the world ...[9]

My company exhibited a five-light pendant for electric candles; it consisted of a shaft of blue glass, with candle pans and other parts of the same material but mounted in brass. Designed by Will Morris, it has, throughout the last twenty-five years, successfully withstood the full blast of economic forces.

'Firelite' glass

Having been introduced to the 'modernistic' in the *Salon d'Automne* of 1912, I was not overwhelmed by the effect of the Exhibition of 1925. After returning home, however, and working on what we had seen, the full possibilities began to be realised. It was the new use of glass that struck us most forcibly: panels, moulded or etched, arranged vertically, in tiers, in horizontal layers or in triangular pieces, suggesting rays of light spreading upwards.

We soon found we were not alone in liking the moulded glass, especially that of M. René Lalique. It appealed to those who wanted more light and less metal. One young architect, I remember, with a reputation for sound contemporary building design, showed me a photograph of a highly romantic moulded glass pendant and said, in all seriousness, 'This is so beautiful, my eyes fill with tears ...'

But moulded glass meant expensive dies, and we had no confidence that the demand, in this country, would justify the

---

9 *Report of the Present Position*, 14.

outlay. We therefore turned our attention to texture and, after searching around, selected an 'orange peel' surface, called 'Obscured Rimpled'. Colourless glass, we decided, would produce an unbecoming light but tinted glass was not readily obtainable. We therefore had to use cellulose spray.

A warm orange shading off to a primrose yellow was eventually selected. Applied to the back of the glass, it seemed to glow when the lamp was alight. Secondary effects were also to be seen. As for a trade name, we naturally turned to Bobbie Simon. 'How about "Firelite Glass"?' came the answer, 'but let sound D.I.A. principles prevail, my dear Sir, or as soon as the name is uttered, some cotter-pin will give way and there will be the sickening crash.' His suggestions were accepted. Later this type of treatment became very common and various shades of tomato-red, applied coarsely to the front of each panel, appeared under other fancy names.

'Firelite Glass' was commercially successful with the buying public. Some of the designs of this vintage, as we shall see, also appealed to distinguished architects. One model even found its way into the Club Room of the Architectural Association in Bedford Square. It consisted of three superimposed discs; but any 'continental' spirit had been exorcised by profiling the edges, softening the angles and modelling the metalwork. In general we deliberately tried to smooth the outlines of our 'happy finds' where they seemed too stark and constructional, while simplifying others in which the imbrications had gone too far, thus adapting them to English preferences.

Selling policy and design

These experiments in design were bound up with an important change in the selling policy of my company, which in its turn further modified the appearance and construction of the product.

In the trade under review, the manufacturer, keeping rather in the background, may dispose of his wares through dealers who buy for resale; or he may make direct representations to individual architects, trying to convince them that his products should be incorporated in their buildings. The two methods may be combined but for many years it had been the policy of my firm to follow the first course, selling standard models to the trade from samples and catalogues. These were mostly designed at the factory.

Since 1918 few lighting schemes had been specially drawn up for architects; still less was much influence felt from that quarter. But these new products of the company were clamouring for a setting and it seemed to me that such might be provided in some of the 'modern' public buildings going up at the time. My colleagues at the factory, however, were not at all convinced that this policy was sound. 'We should be dropping the substance for a shadow,' was the phrase I then heard repeatedly. That I must have discussed this problem with Bobbie Simon is borne in upon me as I record the following incident.

I was returning with Bobbie by road from Bedales in 1926 in my new Essex car, which fixes the year as 1926. As we passed through Alton I became aware that one of his mental film presentations was in progress. It was more than usually allusive. Dramatic scenes at his old school—Charterhouse—appeared briefly, to be sandwiched between parallel incidents at the co-educational school we had just been visiting.

Design and the D.I.A. were continually cropping up in his screenplay, the design of the headmaster's grey flannel trousers being presented, as it were, in a close up. These somehow suggested themselves, to his imagination, as a symbol of power, which led to a curious theory of succession to the headship reminiscent of Fraser's *Golden Bough* at its gloomiest. But however striking the visual imagery, a certain kaleidoscopic quality made detailed attention difficult.

Somewhere near Basingstoke I must have lost the thread but as we were coming onto Newbury Downs I found it again. For just as a secret-service agent, listening idly to the buzz of conversation in a café or restaurant, will suddenly realise, from a chance remark at the next table, that important events are on the move, so my attention was arrested by a change of key in the Simon soundtrack which told me that, flashing across the screen of his private film-show, was something affecting seriously the future of my own business. This, I began to understand, was nothing less than the complete plan for a major campaign. A vigorous sales assault was about to be opened.

The objective was to conquer the whole architectural profession, and we were to start on the citadel—London. Furthermore, I had been detailed for the first wave. Additional representatives, specially engaged, were to follow. Letters of introduction were to be provided (though by whom was not very clear), 'sales lunches' arranged and a new West End showroom opened at the first opportunity; and of course, for all this, we should need some attractive sales literature: show cards, stereos for advertisements and a new catalogue specially designed for architects.

Lastly there was to be a clean breakaway in the matter of design. Mr. Fletcher, blended with the 1925 Exhibition, would, it seemed, do the trick! Later, when we had a number of fine jobs to our credit, there would be a slender handbook with illustrations of the interiors we had illuminated and, on the opposite page, at each opening, a photograph of the actual article installed. It was an excellent programme which, item by item, was eventually carried out in full. 'Mr. Great-heart' … .

Unfortunately, the edge of my sales attack was blunted by a nervous affliction, probably partly a result of the war, which affected my voice and sometimes made communications with prospective customers difficult, if not embarrassing. Before keeping an appointment, I would often walk up and down outside in an agony of agitation. Once, on reaching the door of a well-known architect and being asked what my business was, I could only blurt out the words, 'sales propaganda'.

I have every sympathy for the professional man, short staffed and interrupted by calls from manufacturers' representatives; but I also have a fellow-feeling for those whose job it is to explain and demonstrate manufactured products—in short, who have to sell. Theirs is generally an honourable job.

My first actual introduction came from an old friend, then director of the Stratford-upon-Avon Festival Theatre Company. W. Bridges-Adams[10] was not only interested in design for the theatre but made some excellent projects for domestic equipment. Together we would discuss any models and sketches and he would offer useful suggestions for improving them. When I had explained my plans to him, he put me in touch with an acquaintance of his, practising as an architect in London.

Percy Morley Horder

It was perhaps fortunate that I should thus, at the start of this phase, have met with such an unusual and temperamental personality as Mr. P. Morley Horder.[11] Sometimes I would be so taken aback that I could scarcely speak. He would drift in through one door, like some character in a theatrical presentation, making a sound usually written thus: 'Ugh?' He would perhaps glance at what I had brought to show him and then exit vaguely through another door, making the same non-committal noises.

His hair, blond but greying slightly, was parted down the middle and rather long. He wore pince-nez on a black ribbon-guard and the deep ascetic lines round his mouth suggested some clerical or academic character. At times there would be

---

[10] [William Bridges-Adams (1889–1965) was born in Harrow and educated at Bedales School with the author. After Worcester College, Oxford, he became a theatre director and designer and was closely associated with the Shakespeare Memorial Theatre, Stratford-upon-Avon, from 1919 until 1934.]

[11] [P. Morley Horder (1870–1944), English country-house architect working in the Arts and Crafts style, mainly in the Cotswolds and West of England. He also specialised in Congregational churches, among them those in Queens Avenue, Muswell Hill (1900), Bushey, Hertfordshire (1904), Ealing Green (1911), Brondesbury Park (1911) and Penge (1912), as well as designing the Cheshunt Congregational College in Cambridge (1915).]

tempestuous scenes. One could hear them working up in the next room. When the storm burst I was too inexperienced to say or do the right thing and I am sometimes astonished, looking back on these early encounters, at his consideration and restraint, in the face of the most clumsy and provocative behaviour on my part.

Morley Horder, whether or not he knew it, was opening up an entirely new world for my delectation. He wanted to find some contemporary form of lighting as much as I wanted to design and make it. The occasion would be his 1925 competition entry, with his partner Verner Rees, for a building to house the London School of Hygiene, on a site on the corner of Gower Street and Keppel Street that had been bought in 1913 to build a Shakespeare Memorial Theatre.

Bridges-Adams's introduction had, in fact, come at an opportune time. Well under the influence of the Paris Exhibition, I set to work on a complete scheme. It was a kind of thesis on lighting, with tables setting out floor-space, volumes, foot-candles, wattage and so forth. There were also drawings of the different recommended types of articles, all done on tracing paper, quarter scale, and tinted up with crayon in the manner recommended by Bud Spenser. The whole compilation was bound and lettered in good style. It undoubtedly made an impression.

(I mention this project because hitherto it had been uncommon for the company to treat a lighting scheme as all of a piece. Rather had it been the practice to offer isolated examples unrelated closely to the space which had to be lit.)

Morley Horder himself was engaged on the new University College at Nottingham. It had reached a stage when definite decisions about lighting had to be made. But he was not to be hurried. In as much as he believed in the experimental method, he was fully in agreement with Sturge Moore. 'Taste and see' was undoubtedly his doctrine and this meant that although the results of his work were generally satisfying to the eye, they tended to be costly. If the effect of some feature proved to be disappointing, down it would come, to be rebuilt in some other form. The same empirical methods certainly applied to the lighting.

Some of the suggestions offered for the London School of Hygiene were utilised but no formal scheme was ever put before him, and very few drawings. One had first to entice him into giving even the roughest indication of the sort of thing he wanted. The stump of a soft pencil would be laid on a blank surface and perhaps a few challenging lines roughed in, of a sort that he could not resist correcting. The next stage would be a journey by road to the building, the back of the car being loaded up with full-size models and templates.

Then came a most critical part of the proceedings. There was no guarantee that Morley Horder would be there at all on the day arranged but if one was lucky, he might pass by just as the cardboard model was held against the ceiling by an assistant or myself, standing at the top of a trestle. 'Ugh?' he would say; 'Ugh? Why not make it then?' As for the written word, the most that ever came from his office was a narrow strip of paper, about two-and-a-half inches wide by eight inches long, covered with small, fine and completely illegible handwriting.

It would be unfair and ungrateful to leave the impression that Morley Horder was generally 'difficult'. He was excellent company. I enjoyed some pleasant times with him in London and at the Court House, East Meon, near Bedales, which he later restored magnificently. I cannot think of him without pleasure, partly because of this first successful engagement of the Simon campaign but also because he introduced me to a way of designing products, namely 'the three-dimensional experimental method'.

Or maybe this method, which had occurred to me after the Sturge Moore talks, was to him perfectly customary—as it was for many architects working for clients who could afford it. That some designers could carry out all this three-dimensional experimentation in their heads and put down on paper what later needed no alteration was something upon which I had not then pondered very deeply, but I soon found that Horder's partner Verner Rees [with whom he won the competition for the London School of Hygiene][12] had this capacity.

Luminous boxes

Verner Rees, a much younger man, was quiet but easy to talk to and discussions about the lighting must have taken place in the early stages of the building, before even the foundations were started. The chief material involved was glass rather than metal and this represented a break with the past.

Most of the rooms were to be lit by what were, in effect, luminous boxes, with a minimum of metalwork, either hanging from the ceiling or attached to the walls; but the right design for some of the points was not easy to find. The Library, for instance, puzzled us both. It called, we thought, for three massive box-like pendants. We played about with several ideas but failed to find a solution until in January 1926 I went down with influenza. While lying in bed I had an idea for the Library pendants which I thought was an improvement. The arrangement of glass triangular lustres was to produce a brilliant effect. Its great merit, thought Verner Rees, was definiteness and simplicity and he even went so far as to suggest that the prism and mirrors were 'glorious'. With some minor modifications it was carried out.

In 1926 basic shapes, now fully exploited, were being worked out and offered for the first time. The box, carefully proportioned, was a new idea and it was a box, or suspended tank of light, which appealed to Murray Easton, of Easton and Robertson, for the new Royal Horticultural Hall[13] in Vincent Square, in London. There were twenty of them. Each measured about six foot by two foot and comprised three Holophane reflectors surrounded by skirting to avoid glare. The side panels were decorated with a

---

[12] [Deleted by R.D.B.]

[13] [Now known as Lawrence Hall, the newer of two halls built by the Royal Horticultural Society around Vincent Square, built between 1925 and 1928 and awarded a gold medal by the Royal Institute of British Architects.]

geometrical pattern sprayed onto the glass. When the light was switched on, the bottom panels cracked with the heat; but this difficulty was overcome by replacing them with narrow strips of glass. The whole design was the result of experiment. Of three preliminary projects, one was actually made up in full size and tried in position but was discarded because the low level of the light sources caused glare.

Architects, manufacturers and design

Whatever may be the process of creation in the fine arts, industrial design is much bound up with discussion, and this should take place in the early stages of a project. Nowhere is this more true than in the designing of light fittings. Far too often, these important articles of equipment are left till the last moment. The original estimate for the building may have been exceeded, designs are rushed through and a whole scheme improvised. The delivery time is inadequate and in consequence the work suffers. Everybody gets anxious and excited, and all for the want of the provision given in the cases described above.

But these discussions are really only one aspect of the whole complex question of human relations between individuals and groups, in competition and cooperation, on which so much of industrial design really depends. It is important, therefore, to consider some of the forms these relations may take. The happy form of cooperation described above may have been peculiar to the times. The manufacturer seems to have played an important part in the early stages of creation, whereas he is now often confronted with a complete scheme, scope for design being chiefly in respect of detail and interpretation. [What is worse, according to a Board of Trade report, copying and plagiarism are sometimes encouraged

by a policy becoming more and more practised by architects. The architect will prepare a schedule of scale sketches, many of them taken from the catalogues of different firms, and invite competitive tenders based on these sketches. A manufacturer may thus find himself asked to give a quotation for supplying some of his own products and some copy or near copy of a competitor's product. This procedure (which might have excellent and beneficial results if the designs were really originated in the architect's office by some gifted and technically skilful designer) ... cannot but help but encourage copying with distortion, or even piracy of a designer's property.[14]][15]

Nor was this trend, I soon discovered, peculiar to the trade under consideration. Division of labour and specialisation were increasingly to be found in the printing trade as well. The independent 'typographical specialist' and advertising agent filled, it seemed, an analogous role by supplying the consumer with designs and layout work.

'Free competition' between printing firms was, in this way, said to be promoted, since none is then protected by the quasi-monopoly of its own design staff. 'We are faced with conflicting aims. On the one hand, it is clear that from a social viewpoint the more a first-class design may be broadcast the better ... and this is specially the case where there exists a large number of small manufacturers not able to afford highly paid designers.'[16] But on the other hand, it has always seemed to me that this splitting up of the design and manufacturing functions must take away from the 'factory-group' much of the interest and responsibility connected with the job.

It is a complex question to which there is no simple answer but the practice of broadcasting sketches taken from catalogues of different firms is difficult to justify. 'The designer ... tends to lose by such an arrangement, for the employer or patron is unable to pay him as highly as would otherwise be the case, and his status suffers.'[17]

---

[14] Best, 'Design and the Designer', 55.
[15] [Deleted by R.D.B.]
[16] Best, 'Design and the Designer', 55–56.
[17] Best, 'Design and the Designer', 56.

The Paramount theatres

In 1931, for the first time, I was confronted with a large collection of quarter-scale prints and asked to give an interpretation and price. The Paramount Company was then building, at Newcastle-upon-Tyne, the first of a series of buidings that would double as theatres and cinemas. The architects of the building itself were Messrs. Frank Verity and S. Beverley but the light fittings, and indeed all the interior decoration, came under the supervision of Mr. Charles Fox, of New York.

And here I hasten to add that, to the best of my knowledge, these outline sketches were taken from no manufacturer's catalogue. They nevertheless showed, very clearly, the influence of M. Edgar Brandt and the 1925 Exhibition. The imbrications, falling leaves, 'marguerites-seen-in-plan', were all there; in fact, the Janneau publication seems to have been as freely consulted in Mr. Fox's office as it had been in our own.

With his customary speed and ability, Frank Cashmore got to work on the lighting scheme, which was an ambitious one. In the auditorium was to hang a central fixture, shaped like an inverted umbrella of glass, twelve feet long by eight feet in diameter. In it were to be 240 lamps. Round the walls were to be a number of large luminous capitals to the pilasters. Each took thirty-six lamps and was 10ft-6ins long. Over the grand staircase were to be three pendants measuring 9ft by 4ft diameter, each a mass of obscured and stippled-etched glass panels and moulded glass pockets. For the rest, a quantity of smaller brackets and whatnot, ingenious in shape and detail, offered a challenge to the ability of the company. All these articles were to be of cast bronze electroplated with *real* gold.

But the most difficult problem lay not so much in the metal-work as in the glass. The scheme called for hundreds of leaves or fronds. Not only was each to curve gently throughout its length but the edges were undulating and the veins picked out by a special process.

An essential but at the time unusual part of the contract was the assembly and erection on site of the pendants and brackets and the fitting of the many hundred glass panels. The employees of the company had had little experience of such a task, made immeasurably more difficult, as we shall see, by the chaotic conditions of the last week before any new theatre is opened. Sensing the atmosphere from afar, I decided to be present, if only as a spectator.

The large umbrella-like pendant in the auditorium was of somewhat delicate construction. I was therefore horrified, on alighting from the train at Newcastle, to find a photograph in the local evening paper showing this article swinging around with a human figure sitting inside it.

But this was only a mild taste of what was to come. It was difficult to imagine how the work could possibly be completed on time, and the last few days of the adventure were, for me, passed in a state of extreme nervous tension. It would clearly be a close thing for our own men, but one could not help being distracted by the obvious difficulties besetting the people in other trades. There were the men with spray pistols, trailing lengths of rubber tube; the electricians prowling about with instruments for locating electrical defects (some, unfortunately, due to our own products); the ventilating and air-conditioning technicians; the fitters of theatre seats, kept back, as it seemed, almost to the last moment; and then the furnishing people, waiting to roll down the carpets and place on the walls oil paintings lit by specially designed picture lights. Weaving in and out of all this was a drilling—a marching and counter-marching —of attractive usherettes and, as accompaniment, a male-voice choir rehearsing, not without some pretty severe criticism from the choir master, the 'Pilgrims' Chorus' from *Tannhäuser*, supported at times by the mighty Wurlitzer organ. To this mixture were added excerpts from the film *Monte Carlo*, starring Jack Buchanan and Jeanette MacDonald. Breakages of glass were extremely difficult to avoid.

The members of our team were quite unused to working on scaffolding but it soon became clear that they would have to do so, for although the large auditorium fitting could be lowered to the floor by means of a winch and the glass panels fitted there, not so the luminous pilaster capitals. These were fixed to the walls, some fifty feet from the stalls. But the climax was reached when it came to fixing the large pendant over the Grand Staircase, for to complete this operation the whole weighty object had to rest on the shoulders of two men standing fifteen feet above the floor on narrow planks.

Throughout this exciting episode, I was encouraged by the round and ever cheerful face of Mr. Charles Fox. He liked our work. He was himself a practical man and in order to give a lead, he would climb up onto the scaffolding and even help to paint, on walls and ceiling, the fruit, flowers, fauns and female figures peculiar to this scheme of interior decoration. And on the last day, when my nerves could no longer stand the sight of that expensive pendant hanging precariously over the Grand Staircase on the two men's shoulders, he led me off firmly to a nearby restaurant, where we drank sparkling Burgundy.

All the less attractive features of this style of interior decoration are to be found displayed under 'Modernistic' in Osbert Lancaster's delightful series of caricatures, *Homes Sweet Homes*.[18] It was, he says, 'a nightmare amalgam of a variety of elements derived from several sources ... the fruit of a fearful union between the flashier side of *Ballets Russes* and a hopelessly vulgarized version of Cubism'. His prejudice is indicated by the fat oriental-looking woman seated on the sofa.

To the industrialist and designer, there was more to it than that. Those ascending rays in his drawing of the wall-bracket and mirror somehow express ebullience. It was indeed a creative period for many and the Paramount episodes represented a sort of Indian Summer, before the heavy hand of functionalism, combined with an unprecedented commercial depression, had sobered up the trade.

---

[18] Osbert Lancaster, *Homes Sweet Homes* (London: John Murray, 1939), 72.

Suggestion and autosuggestion

The ascending and spreading rays in the lighting brackets that Mr. Lancaster had illustrated had for some years suggested to me a problem connected with the design of electric fires: how to combine heat with the appearance of heat. Thus in January 1927, during an attack of jaundice, I occupied myself with making cardboard models of electric fires, about a quarter full size and painted in water colours. The idea was to reinforce the actual heat radiation with the visual effect of fire.

During the post-Versailles period, the French pharmacist Emile Coué had created much popular interest in autosuggestion (then known also as Couéism). In his book *Self-Mastery Through Conscious Autosuggestion*, Coué talked about 'an attitude of mind directed toward progressive improvement' and became a sensation during his lecture tours of England after 1921, notably curing bouts of insomnia suffered by Lord Curzon.[19]

I alternated my model-making with the reading of Charles Baudouin's classic work *Suggestion and Autosuggestion*,[20] which appeared at the same time as Coué's and which was described, somewhat surprisingly, by Havelock Ellis as 'the most exciting book since *The Origin of Species*'.

A well-known firm, as I informed Verner Rees in a letter at that time, was making 'a fire which imitates, in a very realistic fashion, an ordinary coal fire, even to the flicker of the flames and heat'. But I was doubtful then about the 'artistic integrity' of

---

19 [Emile Coué, *Self-Mastery Through Conscious Autosuggestion* (London: George Allen and Unwin, 1920). Coué (1857–1926) was a provincial pharmacist in Nancy, France, who gave psychological counselling sessions that encouraged self-improvement through willpower and positive thinking. After founding the Lorraine Society of Applied Psychology, Coué published a book about his method which became a bestseller in its UK (1920) and US (1922) editions. R.D.B. was attracted to autosuggestion in the hope of its curing various 'nervous' afflictions, including stammering.]

20 Charles Baudouin, *Suggestion and Autosuggestion* (London: George Allen & Unwin, 1920).

this device—though why, after the many design-camels we had swallowed, I should have strained at this gnat seems now difficult to understand. I was willing to allow, however, that from one point of view, the design was good because it filled a psychological need:

> If you can make people imagine warmth, through suggestion, Baudouin tells us, they really become actually warm; and I believe, therefore, that the imitation coal fire performs a useful service. My idea is to design something which, in some way, gives the psychological reaction of heat and light, without being a blatant imitation of a real fire. At first I thought something in the nature of a 'futurist' or 'stilisirte' (stylised) fire might do the trick. Model A would consist of a metal back with a *repoussé* design which would be oxidised and relieved, and then, in front, a sheet of glass on which the flame pattern could be etched and sand blasted; a red light between the glass and the metal might, I hope, give some sort of fiery effect. Model B is rather more simplified. ... We still have a *repoussé* back, but a glass dome would take the place of the sheet glass in A.
>
> I showed the models to Bridges Adams who did not think much of them and I am inclined to agree with him. He fully appreciated what was desired, as he had recently been on a P&O liner where a flickering fire was installed in the drawing-room. He thought the solution to the problem was to be found in the luminous window of an anthracite stove. Working on that idea, I have done a little sketch of a heat box. The elements are in the front and the box consists of a metal frame with a nice grid to form the walls: an eighth of an inch or so from the frame (to avoid breakage) would be glass panes and a red light inside.

Verner Rees replied:

> I have had your little models in front of me for some time. I think I agree with your friend that they are not very appropriate.
>
> To me the electric fire is more akin to the radiator than the coal fire—something on the lines of your B crossed with the amusing little box would seem the nearest, I would imagine ... . I do not like the glass flames but, as you say, there may be a lot of people who

would. I think you showed me a photo of a fire in your room, which struck me as looking extremely suitable … .

One day, pondering these problems, I remembered a curious toy with which I had played as a boy. It consisted of two glass bulbs connected by a thin tube and filled with coloured spirits. If one of the bulbs was clasped in the hand, all the liquid was forced into the other, where a violent bubbling was seen to take place. The toy had been in the family many years when it was first shown to me, and I have always understood that the device was used by quack doctors. The bubbling was attributed to fever in the victim's blood. He could then easily be induced to buy a bottle of medicine.

I went straight to the cupboard wherein lay this toy and held it in such a way that the bubbling spirit came between an electric lamp and a piece of paper, on which I beheld a pattern of leaping flames.

With youthful optimism, I patented the device. Thereafter, helped by friends, I initiated a series of experiments in order to make it as effective with water as with inflammable spirits. After about a year, a satisfactory solution was found and as, in the meantime, the design of the elements and screens had been settled, we were ready to put the article on the market.

There remained the printing of catalogues and leaflets and the provision of a suitable trade name. As usual we turned to Bobbie Simon. He suggested 'The Rippleray'. The name was not only applied to this fire but was given to a cocktail—composed chiefly of apple-jack—which was dispensed copiously at the opening of our new showrooms in Great Marlborough Street.

Whether this cocktail ever found a permanent place in the repertory of cocktail mixers I do not know. If it achieved popularity it fared better than the electric fire for, truth to tell, the Rippleray, on which so much time had been spent, received only moderate support from the buying public. Some examples, nevertheless, brought the company a certain *succès d'estime*; one, made originally for the showrooms of Messrs. Jacquard in Bond

Street, may be shown in reproduction without any special feelings of embarrassment to the present writer.

The public was, as usual, *right*. Even now, a great many people, including some respected in their professions as designers, prefer electric fires to represent glowing coals. In the year 1950, I was interested to find a fire of this type, designed by one of our most successful architects of civic buildings, installed in his beautiful London office. Whatever the merits of the Rippleray as abstract moving design, it was too *voulu*, too roundabout and theoretical.

Steel tubes and electric fires

Not in the least discouraged by this episode, I nevertheless decided to go further afield for the design of my next electric fire and accordingly, in 1931, turned to Murray Easton for advice. It would be difficult to imagine anything less like the Rippleray than the product he showed me, in sketch form, some weeks later.

Tubular steel chairs [first designed and made under the direction of Marcel Breuer at the Bauhaus in 1925][21] were becoming popular. There was a suggestion of the tubular steel chair about Murray Easton's design. I liked it immediately and when it came to 'exposure to ordinary market conditions, without artificial shelter from the full blast of economic forces', it withstood the test; in other words, it was a commercial success. It also attracted Dr. Gropius, the founder of the Bauhaus at Dessau.

In 1935, as we shall see, I began to meet this master of design. During his time in England, before accepting a position with the Architectural Department of Harvard University, he saw a photograph of this electric fire and ordered one for his own use. He then suggested carrying out a little experiment in design such as would have earned the approval of Sturge Moore, writing to say that he had been much preoccupied with the shape of the article and had taken the liberty of working out a simplified

---

[21] [Deleted by R.D.B.]

version of it in the hope that it would constitute an improvement. A prototype of his version was then constructed and put before him while he was staying in Birmingham. He made some minor alterations and approved it. The two examples may be compared.

The 'Bestlite'

> If Best & Lloyd had never done anything but produce the Bestlite lamp, we should still have a good deal to be grateful for. Practically every architect seems to have one in his office. It has probably been the thin end of quite a large wedge, for it must have been many people's first introduction to rational design in light fittings ... It is still one of the best standard models.

Thus wrote a contributor to the *Architect's Journal* ten years after the Bestlight had first appeared.

Bent tubes finished in chrome or nickel, combined with a frankly mechanical appearance, must have been behind the design of a certain desk lamp which I first saw in Zürich in 1929. Its affinity to my father's adjustable gas pendant, the 'Surprise', was at once obvious to me, as it was later to Nikolaus Pevsner.[22] The lines of the shade and the square outline of the base might, I thought, be made more suited to British taste; we therefore set to work to go one better. The clip-joint was to be retained but a new universal ball-joint introduced above the lamp-holder. Efforts to find another version of the metal shade—rather too 'continental' in its original form—led to what was probably one of the happiest shapes the company has ever produced. The base became slightly radiused and a shallow dome instead of a cheese-shaped finial seemed to complete the process of naturalisation.

Directly the Bestlite came onto the market, expressions of approval began to appear in the press. It seemed to please the growing number of architects and others who were seeking

---

[22] Nikolaus Pevsner, 'The Humane Industrialist', *Architectural Review* (January 1941), 26.

inexpensive things that *worked*. Pictures of it were soon to be seen in magazines, films, advertisements for other products and in humorous drawings, as a type of the contemporary and efficient in interior fittings.

The New Puritans

The Bestlite was indeed the thin end of quite a large wedge. Of all that has been written about 'Rational Design', Osbert Lancaster gives surely the best summary in *Homes Sweet Homes*. There is little exaggeration in his accompanying drawing of the 'functional' interior:

> The voice of the new Puritans, nourished on the doctrines of Gropius, Le Corbusier and Mumford, first attained a really authoritative ring in the late Twenties, but even in the succeeding ten years, while it was listened to with ever-increasing respect, the number of persons who felt compelled to act upon such advice as it so generously gave remained disappointingly small. This apparent failure of the reforms ... is, one fancies, one of psychology. The open plan, the mass-produced steel and plywood furniture ... are all in theory perfectly logical, but in the home, logic has always been at a discount. The vast majority, even including many readers of the *New Statesman*, crave their knick-knacks, though not in Victorian abundance, and are perfectly willing to pay the price with broom and duster.[23]

But though the response to the new Puritans may have been, generally speaking, small, the company was much affected by their doctrine. It was during the first shock of the 1930 trade depression that its force began to be felt and there is little doubt that the movement was connected with poverty and the need for economy.

This was particularly the case in Germany and it manifested itself in a growing demand, especially amongst the younger

---

[23] Lancaster, *Homes Sweet Homes*, 76.

architects, for what, some years previously, would have been looked upon as bathroom or kitchen fixtures. Many of them were based on German models, sometimes adapted for production in metal from originals in ceramics or plastics.

Foremost amongst them was the opal glass sphere. This was 'the first known example of a lighting fitting so satisfactory that it has become a standard article for the whole trade and yet so simple that it has been impossible to copy it with distortion'.[24]

During the early stages of the chrome and opal period, Bobbie Simon was building himself a house in Jubilee Place, Chelsea, and introduced me to his architect, Christian Barman. The appearance of this building did not loudly proclaim the doctrines of Gropius or Le Corbusier. It embodied, however, some unusual features, such as a small fives court on the ground floor where one might have expected a kitchen or dining room, and was distinctly 'Modern'.

As a result of this project, I turned to Christian Barman for advice as to how best to trim the company's sails to catch the wind then blowing from Central Europe. His proposals were presented in the form of silhouettes or outline drawings, leaving us to fill in the details and develop the constructions, a procedure which I have often found, in working with consultant designers, gives satisfactory results.

Amongst his designs were three glass diffusers shaped so as to give different patterns of light distribution, two recessed ceiling lights, two bell-shaped shades made from glass in a preliminary stage of manufacture and referred to above and two ceiling lights with flattened glasses so as to throw the light along one axis. These were to be used in corridors.

Students of this period cannot fail to notice the contrast between the simplicity of the articles and the somewhat lavish way they were often presented to the public. It was the custom to show the most inexpensive sphere of opal glass in a superb large-scale photograph with telling highlights and an accompanying

---

[24] Best, 'Design and the Designer', 55.

line drawing setting out the principal dimensions. These line drawings are still used but often in a vestigial form; that is to say, no longer showing the dimensions, they appear as a pleasant decorative device, possibly against a coloured background, relieving the monotony of the half-tone photographic reproductions. The company's version of this fashion showed the article in a white line on a blue background, suggesting an engineering blueprint.

The return to Germany

It was not surprising that through the spirit of these design tendencies, my attention should have been redirected towards Germany. With memories of my father's achievements I made some continental journeys, looking up old customers in Bremen, Hamburg and Berlin. Throughout these visits I was keenly alive to the progressive trend of German design. I was, furthermore, continually being reminded of my youthful experiences at the Düsseldorf School. Nikolaus Pevsner, in a generous notice of my book *Brass Chandelier*, compares my father's experiences with my own:

> Thus the appreciation of Germany, initiated (by R.H. Best) as far back as 1862, still inspired the attitude of a new generation three quarters of a century later. Yet within this appreciation interesting changes of emphasis had taken place. To R.D. Best the son, Germany of 1910 and 1930 meant the Modern Movement. To his father it had first meant Schubert. Then, between 1875 and 1900, roughly speaking, he had admired Germany as the country of industrial enterprise and initiative until, after 1900, his attention had been focused on German social progress ... . The Modern Movement, though already strong in Germany in 1910, when he first met Kerschensteiner, the leader of the continuation school and monotechnic ideas, he does not seem to have noticed. The need for abandoning the period styles had not been seen by him. This was left to his son. Thus the necessity for the introduction of new forms, when gas chandeliers were replaced by electric chandeliers, was

> bound to escape him too. He accepted the alabaster bowls which in
> 1910 … were brought from Italy by his Sales Director. That is as far
> as he went.[25]

No doubt there is much truth in Nikolaus Pevsner's contention but I sometimes wonder whether, perhaps, he fully grasped the factors determining industrial design during my father's time. R.H. Best was actually well aware of the Modern Movement in Germany, admired much of it, but, when it came to factory production, was discouraged from experimentation by his own sales director and by the exigencies of the market. To the English buyers, designs which would have been approved by Wilhelm Kreis were too 'continental', as we have already seen, while German customers wanted the 'schöne einfachen englischen Formen'—by which they meant, in fact, English period pieces. It is indeed difficult to appraise the performance of a designer or industrialist without reference to some market.

As for my own poor part, Nikolaus Pevsner is quite right in suggesting that, for me, Germany of 1910 and 1930 meant the Modern Movement. But alas for my hopes of renewing the moderate inspiration of my youth, I soon found that the source had been poisoned. Seeking Gropius during one of my continental journeys I arrived in Berlin some months after the burning of the Reichstag. Evening traffic was frequently interrupted by torchlight processions. Gloom had spread over the office of the Deutscher Werkbund and the Bauhaus, which by then had moved from Dessau and was under the direction of Mies van der Rohe. Gropius had left for England.

Dinner with Gropius

Jack and Mollie Pritchard were militantly on the side of the New Puritans and their flat in the well-known Lawn Road Building, designed for them by Wells Coates, contains certain elements to

---

[25] Pevsner, 'Humane Industrialist'. In *Architectural Review*, 89, January 1941.

be found in Osbert Lancaster's caricature of the 'functional' interior. These elements are combined, however, with *objets d'art et de vertu* of great charm. The furniture too and general arrangements have always pleased me, but never more than on the evening of Thursday 17 January, 1935, when I found myself sipping aperitifs with four other guests, Dr. and Mrs. Walter Gropius and Moholy-Nagy and his wife. It was a setting admirably suited to the occasion.

Admiration for the teaching and practical achievements of Walter Gropius, enhanced that night by his striking appearance, coloured my thoughts as, during dinner, the subject of his work began to be developed. With this regard was mingled speculation regarding some of his theoretical principles. He spoke of the danger that 'modern' architecture would become fashionable and that formalistic imitation and snobbery would distort its fundamental truth and simplicity.

Surely, it occurred to me, snobbery—in the sense of exaggerated respect for the judgment of those we felt to be our superiors—was so common and so difficult to estimate that we must accept it as one of the elements in liking, at least in the sphere of industrial design. Without it, many of the articles created in a spirit of truth and simplicity—I was not too clear what this actually meant—would never get on the market at all.

As consumers we should certainly try, by self analysis, to make ourselves aware of snobbish elements in our own selections and to resist them. As producers, our chief concern should be to treat the preference of the snob in a spirit of market research, neither over- nor under-estimating its effect on demand.

Although to be found in many members of the D.I.A., squeamishness about 'style' and fashion is something I have never been able fully to understand. I was therefore puzzled when Gropius said that a Bauhaus Style would have been a confession of failure and a return to that very stagnation and devitalising inertia they had tried to overcome. My bewilderment would have been even greater had I read prior to this conversation an article by Colin Rowe in which he seeks to show an affinity between the Modern Movement—as exemplified by, amongst other designs, the Bauhaus at Dessau—and the 'Mannerists' of the later sixteenth century.[26]

'Style', according to the *Concise Oxford Dictionary*, is a manner of expression or of doing things, as opposed to the matter or thing done. Manufacturers generally connect the idea of style with *repetition*—certain shapes, patterns or 'cuts' applying to a number of different lines. But the elimination of the style element, even if desirable, would be far from simple. Is a light diffuser in the form, let us say, of an opal sphere conforming to a style or not? If there have been, previously on the market, glass diffusers of different shapes, and perhaps hanging on chains instead of rods, it is difficult to say what is matter and what is manner of presentation—what is 'style' and what is 'not-style'. One suspects that 'not-style' is another name for a plain shape which cannot easily be modified or applied to other articles.

'In all great epochs of history,' Gropius had written, 'the existence of standards—that is, conscious adoption of type-forms—has been the criterion of a polite and well-ordered society; for it is a commonplace that repetition of the same thing for the same purpose exercises a settling and civilizing influence on men's minds.'[27]

I cannot see how, in practice, the consideration of these issues helps the industrial designer at all. Whether the changes in group-preferences are 'style', 'fashion' or 'standard type-forms', he would be well advised to accept them as a most important condition of his job.

How sum up the main contribution of Walter Gropius to manufacturing and the theory of industrial design? At the risk of being misunderstood, I would say that he gave a new significance to the idea of *cheapness*: the maximum effect with the slenderest

---

[26] Colin Rowe, 'Mannerism and Modern Architecture', *Architectural Review* (May 1950), 297.

[27] Walter Gropius, *The New Architecture and the Bauhaus* (London: Faber & Faber, 1934), 27.

means—*mit geringsten Mitteln grösste Wirkung*.[28] This principle, as we have already seen, had, in a general way, always been accepted by the company; but the proposition, as presented by his creative genius, took on a different form. The cheapness was, as it were to be displayed, almost as if it were an essential feature —a 'style', if you like—so that a standard lamp made out of wire, paper or even string was to be looked upon as having particular merit by virtue of the economy of the means employed.

Seated on my left, on the other side of Frau Gropius, was Ladislaus[29] Moholy-Nagy. A Hungarian, he had moved to Berlin in 1920. Gropius had recognised him as a promising experimental artist and put him in charge of the beginners' class at the Bauhaus, where he had given especial attention to photography and abstracts made by placing different objects on sensitive paper. During the late 1920s, he had also attracted considerable attention by his designs for film and stage.[30] His work commanded my admiration and does so still, but I found the same difficulty, as with Gropius, in accepting some of his theoretical programme.

I have a vivid recollection of his genial countenance and expansive grin. I remember too his trick of emphasising his thoughts by making small movements with his thumb, as if in clay. But it was light, not clay, which attracted him as a medium.

His proposals, furthermore, were of particular application to my own trade, for he wanted to project luminous patterns onto walls and ceilings from specially designed projectors. He also outlined plans for systems of light generators, enabling an operator to flood the air with brilliant visions of multi-coloured light. There were to be vast halls with flat or curving walls of unusual material or perhaps filled with artificially produced fog.

---

[28] Walter Gropius, *Bauhausbauten Dessau* (Munich: Albert Langen Verlag, 1930), 8.

[29] [More usually, now, László.]

[30] L. Moholy-Nagy, 'Supplement to *Telehor*'. *The International Review New Vision*, Year 1, Issue 1-2 (Brno: Fr. Kalivoda, 1936).

By manipulating a series of switches, the whole structure was to be transformed into a resplendent symphony of light. Much affected, I could not help thinking of the Rippleray as a half-hearted attempt to realise these radiant dreams.

With perfect candour, he informed us that no patron had ever been found to back his monumental schemes. The ruling caste of society, it seemed, had instinctively resisted them, just as it sought to retain antiquated forms of economic organisation. For the same reason, every creative achievement, every work of art prognosticating a new social or economic order had been categorically condemned.

So here then was yet another 'general character' of 'good' design—the sort that prognosticates a new social order and is resisted by the ruling caste. Aware that a ruling caste had, in fact, made it impossible for these two gifted designers to work under its tyrannical rule, I could not help looking round for examples, within my own experience, of resistance by any ruling caste to the sort of simple inexpensive things associated with Bauhaus design. Had the Birmingham Education Committee resisted the installation of opal spheres in schools? On the contrary, it had led the way. Were the moneyed classes resisting or encouraging 'modern' furniture and interior decoration? Abysmally ignorant of Marxist theory, I felt it would be unprofitable to pursue the matter further.

It was at this point that the party broke up quietly and moved on to take part in some lecture or meeting of the D.I.A. In my diary, I find the record of that day ends with the words: 'One of the best evenings I have ever spent.'

Mottled thinking

Throughout the 1930s the main stream of thought, not always crystal clear, eddied around the subject of industrial design, broadening and swirling about as book after book appeared, as lectures and meetings multiplied and as one exhibition after another was organised. To it was added my own intermittent and cloudy trickle and in 1934, along with some other manufacturers as well as designers and teachers, I was invited by Mr. Geoffrey Holme of The Studio to express my views on 'Design for Industry' by answering a series of questions. The replies were afterwards published, along with a preamble and some illustrations, under the title 'Industrial Design and the Future'.[31]

Oddly enough the definition of 'good design' was left till Question 4, where we were asked, 'Have you found good design at variance with popular taste?'

The editor, commenting on the replies, said they showed a certain vagueness; some industrialists tended to think of good design as a slight improvement on popular contemporary taste and fashion, others as expressive of fitness for purpose. Some replies asserted that the public had no fixed or definite taste.

There was, thought Mr. Holme, a case for finding out what the public really wanted. We are all members of the public, he reminded the reader, but it is always the 'other fellow' who is meant when we say that the public has no taste and does not know a good article from a bad one or positively prefers a bad one. One thing, he said, was clear: 'that you cannot persuade the vast majority to replace as many of their possessions as do not conform to contemporary standard; for the simple reason that they cannot afford to. It is a question, not of taste, but of cash.'

As for my own reply, having just read J.H. Badley's The Will to Fuller Life, I led off with a garbled version of his illuminating analysis of 'craftsmanship'. There were, it seemed, two main elements: one line of development being aesthetic—'for delight', he called it—including 'all such things as gave scope for fancy in decoration, pattern that could be made in weaving or impressed on clay or added by colour; the other, centred on the idea of making things to satisfy our needs, and the bestowing of care to make them as perfectly suited to their purpose as possible.'[32] To this I added: 'These two elements, which are equally important

---

[31] Geoffrey Holme, Industrial Design and the Future (London: The Studio, 1934).
[32] J.H. Badley, The Will to Fuller Life (London: Unwin Ltd, 1933), 154–157.

in design generally, are combined in different proportions in different things. The beauty of the car, for instance, lies chiefly in its "fitness for purpose" whereas that of the textile or fresco must be largely judged by the aesthetic pleasure it gives.' As for the second part of the question, I replied: 'It is difficult to say whether good design is at variance with public taste, since this has never had a chance of really expressing itself. Until more things of good design are offered, we cannot really say.'

In replying thus, I was obviously at sea, trying to explain the fact that the 'other fellow's' preferences were not always the same as mine by suggesting lack of opportunity for *real* public taste to express itself.

The question of what industry wanted from the designer did nothing to clear the air. 'As industry has to make a profit,' I suggested innocently, 'a foundation of saleable designs may be required, even though not "good". My reply is therefore a) saleable designs, b) saleable and good designs, c) good designs.' 'Saleable and "good" designs' would have been a better answer.

Machine and craft production

One other question in the questionnaire put out by *The Studio* may be mentioned: 'How far do you consider the capacity of the machine to go, and what, if any, is the place of handicrafts in industry?' 'Design for machine production,' I replied, 'must, of course, be treated differently from design for hand production. Machine-made articles are better if simplified, though even here one cannot dogmatise (medals and coins frequently succeed artistically in elaborate patterns). Good design requires that the fundamental things should be considered first, and good design in social life requires that the essential instruments of living should be had by as many people as possible. Generally speaking, therefore, machine-made articles should be simple and cheap. Hand-produced things will develop naturally when the machine is doing its job satisfactorily for the community, which will then be able to afford them.'

Some years later this idea was developed, in his usual stimulating and scholarly way, by Herbert Read, in a lecture to the D.I.A.[33] 'We must,' he said, 'establish a *double-decker* civilisation,' comparing such an organisation with that of ancient Egypt. 'In the valley of the Nile,' he continued, 'there existed for many centuries side by side two types of art of entirely distinct character. One consisting of public buildings and sculptured monuments was religious; the other, consisting mainly of paintings, small carvings and decorative vessels of various kinds, was domestic. The religious art was geometric, rational, objective, abstract; the other was naturalistic, lyrical, even sentimental. These two arts did not represent the highbrow and lowbrow extremes of expression within a social unity; they were completely divorced styles, uninfluenced by each other, almost unaware of each other.'

Similar stylistic division had, he thought, already become apparent in our own time, though few people were yet conscious of it, aware of its significance or willing to draw conclusions from it. And yet it is this 'double-decker' structure which should be developed. On the upper deck the factories will spill out their products 'in an unending stream of glossy jube-jubes whereas, though there seems to be some confusion, on the lower deck we shall certainly find there the naturalistic, the lyrical and sentimental modes of expression ... . We cannot ... oppose the machine ... but do not let us make the mistake of assuming that a civilisation can be based on rationality and functionalism alone.'

For this viewpoint the Council of Industrial Design showed little enthusiasm, dismissing it as a 'strange proposal' ... 'pedagogical suggestions not conspicuous for their originality.'[34] And yet there is probably no doctrine more worth the attention of designer and industrialist at the present time.

---

[33] Herbert Read, *The Future of Industrial Design, Being one of Four Lectures on Design Delivered at Meetings of the D.I.A.* (London: Hutchinson, 1943).

[34] *Design Digest: News from the Council of Industrial Design* (November 1946).

Theory and practice

This summary of trade experiences may illustrate for the reader what I said in my first chapter about a gap between the earthy nature of industrial design itself and the theories, conceptions and explanations offered by critics to explain what they like of it and how they think the designer should work.

The critics' pronouncements nevertheless deserve the attention of those engaged in manufacturing and selling, and should be treated in a spirit of market research; but the market in question will often prove to be a small one. The intelligent professional, who believes in 'trade-design integrity' as opposed to 'artistic integrity', will continue to accept with humility the preferences—sometimes lyrical and sentimental—of the main body and *seek to interweave them with his own*. Whatever may be the practice of the 'serious' painter or composer, his condition is isolated compared with that of the industrial designer—although, to be sure, the former may not be working for himself quite so much as he thinks or claims.

With few exceptions, industrialists tend to be inarticulate, and when they do enter this field show a certain reluctance to be frank about the influences which have moulded them. Much will be made of the pots of pure design, but little is said about the highly decorated dinner services sent across the Atlantic; and yet in both classes are examples of 'good' industrial design.

It is astonishing how the ideology of the fine-arts man has been forced to fit the conditions in this other sphere until much that is mythical has become widely accepted. Unfortunately, design criticism easily leads to the formation of cliques and coteries; these only too often tend to become centralised and preoccupied with questions of prestige and influence. It is to this aspect of design that we must now turn our attention.

Cenacles and coteries

Along with our main theme of design, the counter-subject which, broadly speaking, concerns the activities of artistic groups and their leaders is manufacturing and selling.

The propaganda of these groups has little in common with the previously described teaching of Sturge Moore, the poet, and Fletcher, the art master, neither of whom was seeking influence or power. But amongst some groups of critics, committees and government bodies, processes may now and then be seen at work that are analogous to the struggles of political parties. That the motives are often unconscious, or only partly realised, does not make them less real. At their worst, the common purpose of all such groups is to hinder the individual from making a 'free' choice.

Artistic pressure groups have for long been a subject of unfavourable comment by many a writer and artist. Sturge Moore, for instance, held that

> Cenacles[1] and coteries seek importance, not contemplative delight, and their would-be leaders are merely busy forming cabinets of authority.[2]

---

[1] ['Cenacles', from the Latin *cena* (meal) and *cenaculum* (room, specifically a dining room, upper room or attic), pronounced 'sennacle', is a plural noun that refers not just to a room but, by extension, to a group of people who meet in it. Hence, a discussion group, seminar or clique.]

[2] Sturge Moore, *Armour for Aphrodite*, 132.

The relationship between the struggle for power and confused thinking has been much studied during recent years. It is no accident that the propagandists of authoritarian governments use circular arguments and double-think in order to accomplish the Rape of the Masses. By presenting the non-rational or mythical as objective and scientific truth, the public mind may be divided and ruled.

Unfortunately, much that enriches life, such as some art and all music, is quite non-rational and non-objective. The problem is to know when we are on the fertile but spongy soil of the non-rational and when on the solid rock of objective truth.

In our difficulty we may, with advantage, turn to the logician and semanticist, if only to learn how many human experiences now lie outside the sphere of logic and words, or for that matter, of the scientific and predictable; though to be sure, this is no reason why scientific methods of investigation should not be applied to these experiences.

Crawshay-Williams and 'The Comforts of Unreason'

Reference to words and meanings has now become the small change of public discussion. Though grateful to the popular philosopher, who many times repeated that the answer to a given question depended on what we meant by a certain term, we are periodically reminded that over-preoccupation with semantics can become extremely tiresome, especially in conversation.

It is often, to quote Eric Gill, 'what the psycho-boys call a "defence mechanism".' All statements about art are in the form of analogies and metaphors and when you are using a metaphor, you are, by definition, not using a word in its correct meaning. One is appealing to what William James called the 'fringe meanings' of a word. They are spread into other contexts besides those in which they are normally used.

For this reason, in discussing the shape, colour or pattern of a product, it is generally the fringe meanings that count.

Accuracy of terminology may therefore stop the free flow of expression.[3]

Amongst the many who have discussed the tyranny of words, two authorities suggest themselves. Both have, in their time, caused irritation to leaders in the design world by pointing out needless vagueness and ambiguity in what purported to be clear, if not objective, dissertation. C.K. Ogden comes to mind, not only because he was a friend of and co-author with my father[4] but also because, with I.A. Richards, he was one of the first to study the influence of language upon thought. In their classic work *The Meaning of Meaning*, these authors have a good deal to say about the different main types of definition given to the idea of 'beauty'.[5]

This material is used by Rupert Crawshay-Williams in his excellent study of the motives behind irrational thought, called *The Comforts of Unreason*. The average man, he reminds us, is unconsciously against rational thinking; there is, however, no reason to be ashamed of this tendency, provided we are aware of its dangers.

'Reality thinking' is for the specific purpose of dealing successfully with the objective world. It has experimental observation as its criterion and leads to 'practical' certainty in prediction. So much is obvious; but not all apparently straightforward statements are what they appear to be. Although assumed by many eminent people to be reality thinking, a proposition such as 'two plus two makes four' tells us things

---

[3] [Deleted: 'Some reagents in the semantics laboratory are nevertheless useful in precipitating the dross in design criticism.']

[4] R.H. Best and C.K. Ogden, *The Problem of the Continuation School and its Successful Solution in Germany: A Consecutive Policy* (London: P.S. King and Son, 1914). This consecutive policy for day continuation schools, based on the Munich trade schools, makes some excellent proposals for the teaching of industrial art and was in advance of its time.

[5] C.K. Ogden and I.A. Richards, *The Meaning of Meaning: A Study of the Influence of Language upon Thought and of the Science of Symbolism* (London: Kegan Paul, Trench, Trubner & Co., 1923), 142.

about how we use language but not about the phenomena of the objective world. It is, in fact, a tautology. Its truth depends on the fact that the words 'two plus two make four' have been so defined as to make it true, and one can always so define words in a statement as to make them true. Consider, for instance, the following statement:

That's not really a candle because it's electric.

All that the critic has done is to define 'candle' so as to suit his own argument. He has said nothing about the object in question. Such generalisations as the repudiation of 'ill-considered bedizenment of meaningless and unrelated ornament'[6] are tautological for the same reason.

If 'ill-considered', the ornament in question must, by definition, be worthy of repudiation. And yet much design criticism seems to be of this plausible but intellectually dishonest character. Equally misleading but common are dogmatic statements like 'Epstein's *Genesis* is a monstrosity.' It tells us nothing about the design but only describes the feelings of the individual concerned, unless of course the word 'monstrosity' is explicitly or implicitly described.

A rigid moral code has again and again led to persecution. It is not always realised, however, that aesthetic standards can lead in the same direction. That dogma and confused thinking are closely related Crawshay-Williams makes clear in the following passage:

The belief, or unthinking assumption, that such words [as 'democracy' or 'beauty'] have a one-and-only correct meaning is, I think, a comfortable concept. ... The answer in fact seems to be not that there is such a thing as 'beauty' but that there are numbers of different concepts, or emotions, which have all been given the same label, sometimes because there is an actual similarity between them

6 Walter Crane, 'Of the Revival of Design and Handicraft', quoted in Gorell, *Art and Industry*, (London: HMSO, 1932), ii.

and sometimes, on the basis of a fancied similarity, because there just aren't enough labels to go round."[7]

From practical experience of discussions about design in industry I believe that Crawshay-Williams is right. Definitions of beauty or good design are a waste of time, whereas informal conversation about what people like—cost, colour, shape, texture and so forth—is useful to the commercial man. Examples of specific objects should, therefore, be on view while argumentation about 'that added loveliness' is in progress. In public discussions (except, of course, on 'sound-radio'), there is no excuse for barring illustrations.

X and Y

I have already introduced certain ill-defined notions, such as 'authoritarian governments', in connection with the 'cenacles and coteries' of the design world. But Crawshay-Williams suggests that it is advisable sometimes to substitute for an emotive word a 'colourless letter of the alphabet, with the object (a) of getting rid of preconceived associations and (b) of making sure that one is really arguing about the phenomenon in question and not about the meaning of words'.

I therefore propose to use the letter X when discussing certain unpleasant manifestations such as power-seeking, sycophancy, devices for exacting conformity, aggression disguised as criticism, the search for scapegoats and the path of the careerist. (If I were to say that X, at its worst, stands for the Police State, with its regimentation of artist, designer and composer, the reader may wonder whether we are not perhaps losing our sense of proportion; and in one respect he would be justified. The Police State is X in an extreme form.)

---

[7] Rupert Crawshay-Williams, *The Comforts of Unreason: A Study of the Motives behind Irrational Thought* (London: Kegan Paul, Trench, Trubner & Co., 1947), 50, 51.

I suspect that all these milder forms of behaviour are evidence of the same principle, and it is our task to examine how it should become involved in so apparently neutral a subject as that of industrial design. Just as it should be part of a liberal education to learn to distinguish between dogma and scientific truth, so children should be taught to recognise symptoms of X in its early stages, and how to meet it; for X germs seem fairly prevalent and people of all ages should know how to prevent them spreading.

Contrariwise, the letter Y will be used to stand for such factors as decentralisation, sharing power and responsibility, and two-way traffic in ideas, as well as facilities for answering the critics.

The interpenetration of X and Y into the world of art, design and literature is a field that the social psychologist has hardly explored. But as soon as we begin to speculate about these aspects of imposition and more benign leadership, we are inevitably faced with the question, 'Who are the experts?' I accept that there are design and art experts, just as I believe that some design and art is 'better' than the rest. But how to arrange examples in order of merit is a problem I have never been able to solve.

Of all those who have written about the expert, from George Bernard Shaw to Mary Parker Follett, none seems to be of much use to the industrialist trying to find his way amongst the many who cry out that *they* are the real leaders.

Shaw differentiates between 'the quality' and 'the mob' [but goes on to make clear that they] 'do not indicate two classes of entirely different persons' [but that] they [can be] the same persons'. In literature and drama, for instance, he declares that he belongs to 'the quality'. In mathematics, athletics and mechanics he admits that he is one of the mob and not only accepts and obeys authority but claims a neighbourly right to be told what to do by those who know better than he.[8]

A sound enough view; he fails, however, to meet our difficulty. For whereas, in a hundred years' time, if marathon races are still

---

[8] George Bernard Shaw, *Everybody's Political What's What?* (London: Constable & Co. Ltd, 1944), 30, 31.

run, we shall know exactly how the performance of a twenty-first-century runner compares with that of Jack Holden in 1950, no one on Earth knows how the 'quality' of that epoch will place Shaw's output in comparison with today's literary opinion.

Though she is not concerned with the question of how to recognise them in the art world, Mary Follett's teaching about the leader and expert is Y—of at any rate commercial purity. That we should lay less stress than formerly on the leader influencing the group and more on the leader being influenced by the group seems excellent advice. Centralised art groups need to be continually reminded, however, of this reciprocal relationship and of the necessity for the 'circular response'.

Mary Follett says the currents must go both ways. 'The channels should be kept open for this continuous flow to go on all the time. When it gets dammed up, effective leadership stops.'[9] But even if we agree to accept this conception of 'power-with' rather than 'power-over'—a jointly developed power; a co-active, not a coercive, power—we shall still have to admit that in the Fine Arts and in the Arts-Not-Fine we know very little about the power itself and still less about who should share it with whom.

The power of the art expert or critic seems, nevertheless, to depend upon certain positive qualities. First, he must be able to detect fine differences of measurement, texture and colour, an ability that can often be verified by specific tests. If, for example, he is known to have mixed up a Ming with a Sung, accepted a van Meegeren for a Vermeer or bought a Boulton[10] for a Ballin,[11] one

---

9 Mary Parker Follett, "The Leader and Expert" in *Dynamic Administration: The Collected Papers of Mary Parker Follett*, Vol. 3 (*Early Sociology of Management and Organizations*), ed. Henry C. Metcalf and L. Urwick (Bath: Management Publications Trust Ltd, 1941), 247, 248.

10 [Matthew Boulton F.R.S. (1728–1809) was the business partner of the Scottish engineer James Watt. Like R.D.B., he was born in Birmingham to a manufacturer of metal products, and R.D.B. seems to have identified with him.]

11 [Hugo Ballin (1879–1956), American painter of classical and religious subjects.]

may with justification doubt the sensitivity of his eye. Another (less reliable) touchstone, especially relevant to directors of galleries and museums, is their ability to gauge market prices and anticipate trends. For however much the fine-arts man may protest that artistic value exists in its own right, the 'expert' who continually buys things that depreciate in value may forfeit his leadership, much as if he had acquired actual fakes.

Lastly, in order to become a leader, it seems probable that a critic must be able to write or speak about his subject in an interesting or entertaining way, and one is tempted to believe that this is an indispensable qualification for the job.

But even if we agree that there are certain objective criteria of the 'expert', it seems perplexing that, because he has established his knowledge of Chinese Porcelain, Dutch Painting or Eighteenth-Century Metalwork, his preferences should be taken seriously when it comes to 'electric fires for the medium-income bracket' or carpets for the Australian market. Unfortunately, in addition to the art expert, almost everybody claims to have expert knowledge regarding the things bought for the home: 'I know what I like!'

It is difficult to see what the positive qualities of the 'experts' have to do with 'beauty' or 'good design'. And yet it is the painters and sculptors who receive such experts' approbation who also become the 'leaders' in their sphere of criticism. Eric Gill expressed his disgust at the situation in the following words:

> My high-art friends seemed to float on the top of things, both unanchored and unfounded ... with no reason of being but the vapourings of art critics—art critics whose position depends upon 'art prices' obtainable by the machinations of the art dealers ... . What is a sculptured figure for? What's the good of it? To give pleasure of course, says the high-art world—i.e. the high-class and very refined pleasure of those minds which have been well informed by the best art critics. Obviously the first thing to do is to get round the best art critics. You won't get far until you've done that.[12]

---

[12] Eric Gill, *Autobiography* (London: Jonathan Cape, 1940), 177, 178.

And now, having subjected the 'leaders' to critical examination, I am reminded of those who seem destined to command respect and admiration by virtue of something one can only call 'stature'. Their creations are massive, and organised in a manner requiring great intellectual powers. In sheer volume their output is impressive, while at their work they are honest and single purposed, ignoring all issues which do not help them to realise their noble conceptions. In the fine arts of today no such giant has crossed my path; but in the field of industrial design, Frank Pick seemed to answer to my idea of a 'leader'.

The Design and Industries Association

Until the beginning of the twentieth century the politics of industrial design differed greatly from the struggles between rival cliques that had hitherto irritated the creative artist. The designing and production of commercial articles was a complex process and, unlike the creation of a picture, involved a whole train of human beings. In spite of advertising, accepted by the public with caution as normal commercial special pleading, pressure groups claiming transcendental authority for their personal preferences had not developed. Criticism was mostly exerted by the selection of customers in the open market. There were therefore a great many critics who, without any means of grouping themselves and publishing their views, nevertheless had a lot to say.[13]

Around 1910, however, the critic–approval–artist relationship entered upon a new phase. Groups of critics coalesced spontaneously, much as in the fine arts, and to give point to their pronouncements they were forced to claim that the working of the market was scarcely relevant to the appraisal of good design.

The German Werkbund was formed in 1907. Societies with similar aims sprang up in other countries; and in England during

---

[13] [Deleted: 'Since then the scale of some industries has increased but the designers still remain spread over a wide field.']

the First World War, a group of businessmen, encouraged by the Board of Trade, exhibited a number of articles which they maintained were of 'good design', previously imported from Europe and now unobtainable. Here was an example of useful group buying, in the sense that their main object was to encourage potential suppliers to produce what had once sold well. Having performed this service the group, in which Mr. B.J. Fletcher played an important part, formed itself into the Design and Industries Association (D.I.A.), a propagandist body 'working towards the stimulation of appreciation of fine design in all goods which everyone has to live with'.

Though there is plenty of evidence that the doctrine of the D.I.A. affected other bigger bodies, no one will ever know just what influence this association had upon the production of commercial goods. The D.I.A. claimed that the public was interested in its teaching about 'good' design and instanced the 100,000 people who went to see the Dorland Hall exhibition in 1933,[14] and others that followed. This seems to be, however, a variation of the contention—repudiated by the association—that a design must be good because so many examples of it have sold.

An engaging quality of the D.I.A. in its early years was its childlike innocence. The crusading spirit and dogma were so ingenuous and on such a small scale as to be fairly harmless— small particles of X, if you like, but of a sort to make us smile. The society claimed expertise and at the same time repudiated it. It appointed selectors and yet hotly denied that it had set itself up as an arbiter of design. It maintained that in some mysterious way selection was *not* a criticism but an *investigation*. How can one resist the appeal of the prospectus offering the services of the Association in organising exhibitions in shops and department stores:

The D.I.A. sends to the stores a *selector* who ... *without being expert in*

---

[14] ['Exhibition of British Industrial Art in Relation to the Home' at Dorland Hall, Regent Street, London, 1933 and 1934, described in Chapter 9.]

any sphere of merchandise ... will select ... those goods which he considers to be the best. [R.D.B.'s italics.][15]

But the most valuable feature of the Association was that it provided facilities for discussion amongst professionals. This was a comparatively new activity. In my father's time businessmen did not meet to compare notes on design, which was accepted as something important enough, but a strictly commercial matter, to be kept as a secret from competitors.

Preferences and needs: the planned economy

It is a long way from the mildly revolutionary activities of the D.I.A. to the struggle between conflicting interests associated with the planned economy. There is, however, a connecting factor between them, suggested by the doctrine, still much discussed, of 'preferences' versus 'needs' in design.

A moment's thought will show that behind this conception lies the assumption that one group knows better than the others what they should have. The first group says, in fact, 'You may *prefer* this, but what you really *need* is that.' And of course this is often demonstrably true. Governmental expenditure on school buildings is based on the assumption that education cannot be left to the uncontrolled operations of the market. That an adult who can neither read nor write will be badly handicapped can be predicted with practical certainty. Large-scale designs for districts (town planning) must be carried out for the same reason and on the same principle, since the penalty in terms of human health and of overcrowding can be measured.

It is conceivable that the production, in large quantities, of certain utility articles was best undertaken in the same spirit. But here we must be careful or the designs will be riddled with X. For just as, in the case of reality-thinking and non-rational

---

[15] *Exhibition Held in Department Stores* (Design and Industries Association, circa 1936).

thinking, it is important to know on which plane we stand so, when it comes to industrial design, we must constantly be on our guard lest the leader present as a 'need' his own unimportant personal preferences. The doctrine of needs versus preferences applied to the patterns of carpets appeals to those who have a high opinion of their own taste but is as dangerous to Y as vague and misty sentiment masquerading as objective truth.

How precarious is the maintenance of Y, directly we begin to organise 'good' design for others, will be seen later when we examine the work of Frank Pick.

We are not in this context concerned specifically with nationalisation or indeed the programme of any political party. We cannot however ignore the school of economists which has attempted to show the connection between collectivist planning and various forms of oppression. Conversely, it is held that open competition and the working of the market are related to democratic freedom, in the sense that every time one makes a purchase it is as if a personal vote for this or that form of production had been registered.

Even if we find it difficult to agree with many of the arguments of the 'Road to Serfdom' school we should take heed of the warning that there is a connection between the market and X and Y factors. [F.A. Hayek's *The Road to Serfdom* (1944) discussed the danger of applying wartime principles of economic and social planning to peacetime problems. Hayek later argued that Nazism reflected not on the character of the German people but on the popular socialism that Germany had embraced in the 1920s and 30s and that was now starting to be emulated in the post-war free world. He warned that intellectuals—'second-hand dealers in ideas'—were attracted to what he considered socialism's confusion in wishing to redesign society rationally but also according to utopian ideals, and without recognising the undemocratic, even totalitarian, imposition of intellectual tastes.][16]

---

[16] [Editor's note.]

If we accept ordinary market research and commercial selling, it is difficult, at first, to see why we should jib at the sort of conformity demanded by pressure groups which claim to know the sort of shapes and colours that the public 'needs'.

The supplier often has to take up an accommodating attitude towards his customer who, as we are commonly told, is 'always right'. Why should he object to catering for the tastes and preferences of cabinets of authority? The answer is that a) the customers are generally multifarious, whereas the design committees tend to be centralised, and b) that the customer, whether buying for a business or as a private consumer, generally has to accept personally the consequences—financial or in terms of private satisfaction—of his own choice. This sort of personal responsibility does not apply to the typical exhibition selection committee.

The buyer, furthermore, is appointed by his employer and the private customer, as it were, by his pay packet or bank balance. The exhibition committee, however, is self appointed and is in effect responsible to no one except itself. This condition arises, as we shall see, from the peculiar way that artistic or design groups form themselves; so that although, nominally, they may be appointed by some governing body or minister of the crown, in fact, tastes and preferences being intimate and personal, people who like the same sort of things 'get together' and appoint themselves.

Centralisation and size

The designing and production of commercial articles, we must repeat, has been, for the most part, carried out by a large number of competing individuals. But against this happy form of decentralisation in design, certain factors are working:

1. Firstly there is the growth of large-scale industrial enterprise resulting from technical developments or the desire to avoid competition.

2. Then, closely connected with it, is the development of nationalised industry.

3. Lastly we have the intervention of the state supporting, out of public moneys, councils, corporations and groups of design propagandists and critics.

All these bodies can impose a certain style on the consumer and all can place themselves in the X or Y sectors according to the way they work. Reducing the size of administrative units is not incompatible either with planning, large-scale industry or academies and design coteries. The difference between X and Y is often largely a question of size. When the design group gets too big it tends to become corrupt, dogmatic and rather aggressive —attitudes as fatal to 'good' design as to our export trade.

That the lie of the land is appreciated by those who believe in a measure of nationalisation is clear from the proposals of a group of Fabians for reforming the B.B.C.:

The existence of more than one Corporation would help the solution of most of the problems that have been so hard to solve under monopoly, from staff relations to vigour in the programmes and free expression of ideas. In particular, it would allow a much greater variety and sense of adventure in the programmes. Moreover, under the present centralised system, there is a regrettable tendency for all young artists to gravitate to London, whereas devolution and competition would assist in the creation of a pool of local artists—thus helping to develop and enrich the cultural life of other parts of the country.[17]

Cutting across the grouping of left and right, there is a second division: those who believe that the complexity of modern civilisation makes decentralisation imperative versus those who tend more and more to get sucked into the metropolitan pressure groups of the art and design world.

---

[17] *The Future of Broadcasting: Report of a Research Group set up by the Fabian Society* (London: Fabian Publications, 1950), 7.

X tends to corrupt

All this, as we have said, is speculative, difficult to prove and as non-rational as many design preferences. But whether the politics of design groups and their effect on the individual will always remain on the plane of intuition is uncertain. The science, if it can be so called, of 'Human Relations' or 'Group Dynamics' is young and will no doubt throw up as much of the bogus as psychoanalysis has done.

But if, as is claimed, one may consider 'a "group atmosphere" as something which is as real and measurable as a physical field of gravity', and if it has been demonstrated that 'it is quite possible to measure, and not only to "judge", leadership performance',[18] then the sooner these investigators get busy on the councils, academies and boards of Beckmessers[19] the better.

Lord Acton's famous saying 'Power tends to corrupt, and absolute power corrupts absolutely'[20] should, I suppose, be classed at present as non-rational, though who knows but that some future study may not prove an objective relationship between administrative power and the corruption of duodenal ulcers, high blood pressure and so forth. From personal observation I suspect that those who try to mix up design activity with too much prestige get irritable, bossy and generally unhappy. Their work, inevitably, suffers.

---

[18] Kurt Lewin, 'Frontiers in Group Dynamics', *Human Relations,* Vol. 1, No. 1 (1947), 7.

[19] [Beckmesser, a clerk and Meistersinger, is a character in Richard Wagner's *Die Meistersinger von Nürnberg* and epitomises the narrow and pedantic critic. R.D.B. was an enthusiast for German opera.]

[20] [Comment in Lord Acton, 'Letter to Archbishop Mandell Creighton' (5 April, 1887).]

CHAPTER 8
CENACLES IN THE MAKING

One day in the early part of 1931, calling by chance on Bobbie Simon, I found him examining the material for a catalogue of wooden bedsteads and proposing to himself all the while possible codenames for each article. 'The Ardent?' he suggested, as he showed me a generous-looking double-bed in a rather aggressive Jacobean idiom. 'What this firm needs, my dear Sir, is some advice from the D.I.A. and, by the way, are you aware that, at last, the banner of sound design is to be floated in the Industrial Midlands?' Whereupon he began to tell me of a D.I.A. exhibition about to be opened at Barrow's Stores[1]—as well known to citizens of Birmingham as Fortnum and Mason is to Londoners.

On the last day of the exhibition, there was a public luncheon to form a new branch of the Association. From the report of the proceedings in the *Birmingham Post*, I find that

> Councillor O. Morland (Chairman of the School of Art Committee), who presided, said that one by one some of the old English crafts had vanished until we were left with little traditional art in England; [whereas] Sweden, which had not the advantage of cheap labour and long hours ... had been able, through the encouragement of the national crafts, to demonstrate the importance to industry of good design. Noel Carrington, a vice chairman of the Association, deplored the neglect of design in industry and said that ... it was proposed to hold a large-scale exhibition in London on the lines of the Paris Exhibition of 1925.

---

[1] [Barrow Stores was an expensive department store located in Bull Street, Birmingham, originally started by Richard Cadbury of the Cadbury dynasty.]

My own contribution, reported with disconcerting fulness, contains much that to me now is completely unintelligible. It is clear, however, that I intended to work out the Sturge Moore method of 'Taste and See', even in this design circle, with its rather rigid doctrine. 'Good design in commercial work,' I said, 'and indeed in any form of artistic work, is essentially a practical matter—a matter of experiment and demonstration.'

The press report continued:

> The alternatives of manufacturing cheap articles by mass production or of the expenditure of thought over beautifully designed products were discussed by Professor P. Sargant Florence of the Birmingham University. If we were not going in for either of these, we were heading for bankruptcy. It was very difficult for us to compete with America in mass production, but there was no reason why England should not produce designed work, or why she should not place herself in the vanguard of design.
>
> A committee was then appointed to proceed with the organisation of the branch.

No records or minutes were kept of the transactions of this committee, for everything was extremely informal. When talk was relevant to the activities of the branch, it was of a Quaker-like simplicity, comparable to the designs we advocated. Some of the founder members were in fact Friends[2] and something of that Society's attitude seems to have entered into our earlier deliberations. But I have never been able to understand why, if one can dispense with the intervention of priests between the human being and the Divinity, there should be any need for institutions to come between the consumer and his enjoyment of the designs he chooses.

---

[2] [That is, Quakers. The Quakers, officially known as the Society of Friends, were strongly represented in Birmingham, along with other dissenting religious groups, and included the Cadbury family.]

The programme

At this first luncheon meeting were laid down some of the main planks in the party platform. We were to follow the shining example of Sweden. The Stockholm Town Hall stood to the D.I.A. as the Kremlin to the Communist Party; and by way of inducement to emulate the Swedes, there was much talk by our leaders of the benefit to the export trade of that country arising from their enlightened policy.

I was already vaguely aware, however, of a certain inconsistency in the programme. 'Better' design might lead to more business abroad; and yet if a manufacturer innocently offered for discussion a design, good of its sort and saleable in some foreign market but which did not conform to the Association's preferences, it would be severely criticised.

Artistic and design groups are invariably formed to gain strength of purpose in some way or other, if only by 'taking in each other's washing', and promoting internal discussion. But in most cases they are also out to bring others round to a certain point of view, to persuade them that the group-style is the right style and, in short, to sell what the members are producing. This is often called 'exacting a high and uniform standard'.

The D.I.A. sought to spread its influence by means of

a. printed matter
b. lectures illustrated with slides or films
c. exhibitions, including 'exhibition houses'—i.e. houses furnished and equipped by the Association, and
d. discussion by small groups round and about actual examples.

Of these activities the last, in my opinion, has proved the most useful, stimulating and least tainted with X. There was also an annual dinner, followed by a meaty speech, and a discussion (for which members were often briefed) in order to get some point across to an influential guest who had been especially invited to receive our message and to give it practical effect.

We would generally have a short-run objective, as, for instance, the promotion of more practical instruction for the School of Art Students, more machinery, lectures on costing and so forth. In this manner we hoped to hasten the age of 'Design Laboratories': the name hypnotised us. In all this, the young society was not only received with tolerance but on the whole encouraged by those concerned with municipal affairs.[3]

The Gorell Report

The first lecture was given by Bobbie Simon at his own house and, as if to subject himself to some third-degree ordeal, he directed a powerful light into his own eyes, after first throwing the room into complete darkness. He then began to tell us of certain governmental proposals which, had we but known it, might well have been worked out by some Giant Despair of the design world—for the committee, under the chairmanship of Lord Gorell, was the first to support the theory that a centralised group, if free from competition, might set a lofty and constant design standard throughout the land.

The committee, appointed by the Board of Trade to investigate 'The Production and Exhibition of Articles of Good Design and Everyday Use', had accepted the propositions that:

> First, a reversion to handicraft cannot, for economic reasons, solve the problem of beautifying the articles of common use within the purchasing power of ... consumers (of moderate means); secondly, that the fundamental differences between the technique of industrial manufacture and of handicraft make the problem of adapting design to industry a wholly different one from the production of unique specimens of artistic workmanship.[4]

---

3 [Originally 'the governing class in municipal affairs'. Wording changed by R.D.B.]

4 *Art and Industry. Report of the Committee appointed by the Board of Trade under the Chairmanship of Lord Gorell on the Production & Exhibition of Articles of Good Design and Everyday Use.* (London: H.M.S.O., 1932), para. 17.

So far so good. It was the consciousness of these problems, as Bobbie explained, that had given rise to the D.I.A. in 1915. The main recommendation of the Gorell Committee was that there should be in London a standing exhibition (i.e. always open but constantly changing), if possible housed in a special building.

> The object of Exhibitions should be improvement of the taste of designers, manufacturers, distributors and the general public by the display to the best advantage of beautiful modern manufactured goods, due regard being paid to the purchasing power of the householder of moderate means.

There were also to be exhibitions in the provinces but the really important aim was to be centralisation of control and unity of policy.[5]

The Gorell Report therefore laid the foundation for concentration of design criticism. The central group was not to be advisory but entrusted with executive powers. Local committees were to be allowed 'the maximum degree of administrative responsibility, including arrangements regarding publicity and other specific local details' but the ultimate control was to be in the hands of the central body, 'in order to ensure a high and a *uniform* standard of quality throughout the country'.[6] The exhibition activities of existing associations were to cease, in order that 'a newer, stronger and more efficient body' might function *without competition* (author's italics).[7]

These arrangements were, in some mysterious way, to 'facilitate discussion with manufacturing interests' ... and produce a degree of cooperation that had not hitherto been forthcoming. There was no suggestion, however, that the discussion with business folk was to be about the goods themselves, their prototypes, their specific designs, their markets and their manufacturing problems.

---

5 Gorell, *Art and Industry*, para. 66.

6 Gorell, *Art and Industry*, para. 72.

7 Gorell, *Art and Industry*, para. 63.

Mary Follett's 'circular response' was not in evidence. Selection was to be unilateral, by persons of taste and cultural standards, with 'an up-to-date ... and an international outlook' on art. The members of this central body, in which a few people with experience of manufacture, wholesale and retail trade were graciously to be included, were to be 'appointed' by the Board of Trade. The committee-men expected that manufacturers would send their wares to be judged and would look upon the acceptance by the selectors as in itself a 'crown of merit'.

No opposition to this focusing of prestige was anticipated, nor did it occur to the Gorell Group that the industrialists might look upon the persons of 'taste and culture' as [no more than] gifted amateurs. The goodwill of businessmen was nevertheless deemed to be especially important and there was to be the closest possible liaison with them both individually and in association.

The attitude of the committee to the market and its relation to design was cloudy. The report stated that:

> Conflicting evidence has been laid before us on the question whether propaganda or sales should be the commercial objective. ... In our view ... the two can and must go hand in hand; propaganda is of little value unless there are ready means of translating its precept into practice; immediate sales are too narrow and circumscribed ... therefore the object should not be sales, though they may follow, but the improvement of taste etc. etc.[8]

Here the Gorell Committee-men failed to recognise that, if the objects exhibited were to be considered as industrial design at all, it was not enough to suggest that sales *might* follow. Sales may not have been a primary objective; they were and are nevertheless an indispensable condition. Geoffrey Holme had this sort of vagueness in mind when he spoke, in the passage already quoted, of the tendency to think of good design as a slight improvement on contemporary taste or fashion.

---

[8] Gorell, *Art and Industry*, para. 55.

The report ends with a most readable appendix by Roger Fry, concerned, amongst other things, with exploding the 'Fitness for Purpose' dogma. It would, he maintained, prevent any real development of artistic design, since aesthetic satisfaction is quite distinct from the pleasure of recognising functional adaptation. 'Good architecture must always remain distinct from good engineering and this principle holds equally in the design of the objects of daily use.'

Gropius in Birmingham

Another notable lecture was given by Walter Gropius, and before he came to Birmingham there was much pleasurable anticipation amongst the members. So great was our enthusiasm that his name was even introduced into D.I.A. charades as 'Grow Pious'.

As for myself, I was vaguely aware that excitement was mingled with apprehension and I was moved to explore the foundations of this attitude. Gropius, as we have seen, had warned us against the dangers that 'modern' architecture would become fashionable and that snobbery would distort its fundamental truth and simplicity. But snobbery, I thought, may well, unfortunately, begin at home. Unable to assess the snobbery of others I set out to find out how much there was of it in my own attitude towards the sort of designs my hero would approve.

The ideas thus related pointed only too clearly to the questionable motives for my so-called 'preferences' in modern design. Not very far below the surface was fear of disapproval— fear that the electric candles in my house might be looked upon as 'imitations', that the charming antiques might be regarded as 'selling the pass' or that the pleasant chintzes would not be accepted as truthful and sincere.

'Hadn't we better stow away the Rippleray in the cellar?' I burbled on in my diary. 'Shall I change it for something else? ... He'll be frightfully shocked, etc.' And yet I had not only myself designed the electric fire in question but had sat in front of it every day for several years without experiencing any displeasure. These notions, I immediately realised on reading them, were childish and ridiculous, especially bearing in mind the tolerant and kindly attitude of my guest. Here, nevertheless, was a permanent record of what lay behind some of my design 'preferences'. Was this blatant form of sycophancy unusual? I have since been given reason to believe that it was not.

My impressions of the actual visit, our talks together and of Gropius's appearance at the D.I.A. Annual Dinner in 1935 were recorded in my diary fairly 'straight'. It was 'an experience I shall always remember,' I wrote. I expressed a wish to see the timetable of the Bauhaus, as I thought it might be applicable to the teaching at the Birmingham School of Art. 'It would not tell you much,' Gropius replied. 'It was the *atmosphere* ... .'

I then asked him what he thought would be the most useful activity for the D.I.A. in Birmingham. 'Exhibitions,' he answered, without hesitation. 'Entrust them to one man at a time. Let him choose his collaborators. Let them be extreme and revolutionary. At the Bauhaus the students always revolted once a year, although two of them invariably sat at directors' meetings.'

He liked the idea of 'cooperative design groups', which we were then putting forward, for non-competing smaller firms which, so we proposed, might share a good designer between them and perhaps help each other by criticising or by discussing each other's products. (I still believe that this form of grouping would be worth trying in some trades as an alternative to the ambitious 'Design Centre' scheme for single industries.)

After the meal, we went up to another room and listened to his lecture, illustrated by lantern slides. He stressed the virtue of design which was in tune with the spirit of the times—the consequential product of the intellectual and technical condition of the age. On the other hand, he criticised designs which were the whim of a few architects, hungry for innovation. It must be difficult, I reflected, to exorcise this hunger for innovation and at the same time carry out the extreme and revolutionary exhibitions he had been advocating for the D.I.A.

I felt myself nevertheless in sympathy with his desire to free the movement from false slogans. All slogans are false, I thought, in the sense that it is unpredictable whether a design constructed according to some slogan will be 'good' or 'bad'. He said he had tried to solve the ticklish problem of combining imagination with technical proficiency and, as we were very much aware, of the need for more opportunity for practical experience for the students of the Birmingham College of Arts and Crafts; there was enthusiastic approbation when he explained that the workshops at the Bauhaus were really laboratories in which designs for present-day goods were worked out as models for mass production.

There seemed less reason to agree, however, with his suggestion that the future field of handicrafts should be in research work for industrial production; or with, as he put it, 'the Bauhaus School of thought which believes that handicrafts and industry must be understood as opposites perpetually approaching each other'. Attractive though this dialectic theory might be, it seemed to me far more likely that the two different kinds of design would continue to exist in different layers, each in its own right, as Herbert Read had argued.

'The object of the Bauhaus,' he concluded, 'was to exert a revitalising influence on design, since it did not base its teaching on any particular idea of form but sought the essence of life itself behind life's ever-changing forms.'

A novel experiment

'An artist,' Sturge Moore had written, 'wishes that, when discussing aesthetics, philosophers would argue with examples rather than phrases,'[9] and I was soon convinced of the hopeless inadequacy of words in the deliberations of the D.I.A.

---

[9] Sturge Moore, Armour for Aphrodite, 83.

Manufacturers were furthermore only too easily embarassed when asked to discuss the fine principles propounded by distinguished visitors. But once an actual article was put before them, their reticence vanished. Talk became real.

Something more was needed, however, than mere disquisition though, to be sure, 'disquisition on a work helps powerfully to focus attention on it and so may reveal its beauty to others; yet the degree in which analysis becomes complementary to the admired structure remains necessarily unanswerable.'[10] I felt we were in want of some special kind of discussion about actual articles. If it were simply discussion for its own sake it would be sterile. The discussion must lead to positive results, such as changes in the design of the article or information useful to the members.

Mr. Fletcher, as we have seen, had already shown me how some of the company's products might be improved by altering the position of an arm, the proportions of a casting, the fining down of some piece of detail. To this process he had given the name 'Quizzing'. It was a game that many could play and I found that often the most unexpected people had the ability to improve a design if allowed a free hand to experiment.

One or two meetings were held before the members found a procedure most fit for the purpose of 'improving', in some way, our designs. The first took place during a small exhibition at the University in the early part of 1932. The following is a summary of the prospectus:

A NOVEL EXPERIMENT
A growing number of people including Architects, Designers and potential buyers have expressed the opinion that British design is lagging behind that of other countries. Whether this is so or not, it seems highly probable that many of the objects for domestic use produced in Birmingham are capable of improvement.

The object of this exhibition is to test, in a practical way,

---

[10] Sturge Moore, *Armour for Aphrodite*, 49.

whether by constructive suggestions and cooperation any improvement can be made to specific articles without increasing their cost or decreasing their saleability.

The exhibition was to be open to members and their friends but not to the public, although the press was to be invited. There was to be no charge for admission and no selection panel. Articles might be sent in, either as examples of what, in the manufacturer's estimation, was his best work or because he considered them to be capable of improvement. The committee made only one stipulation: that the samples were to be subjected to constructive criticism by those who thought they could improve them. There was, of course, to be no obligation to put into practice any suggestions which might be made. Members were asked to give their criticisms in writing and a small panel was appointed to discuss the exhibits, in a critical vein, at the special meeting referred to above. The price of each article had to be stated but the name of the manufacturing firm need not appear unless desired.

In shaping this procedure we were influenced by the words of Dürer: 'If any man thinks my work can be improved, let him show me what he means with his hands.'[11]

The final paragraph of the prospectus read:

THEORY AND PRACTICE IN DESIGN
The idea we are trying to stress and which is behind this exhibition is that improvement in design can only arise as a result of practical experiment, trial and error. Vague generalisations and theories are useless where the actual worker is concerned. On the other hand, there is little work being produced which cannot be improved, and in Birmingham there may be great scope in this direction.

The experiment was interesting and may have been useful to some but, so I felt, was not wholly what was wanted. The seats were arranged in rows and the design of the key meeting was too

---

[11] Quoted in Sturge Moore, *Armour for Aphrodite*, 96.

'one-way'—from the platform to the floor. There was not nearly enough discussion and the number of people assembled was too large. There were, furthermore, scarcely any suggestions of a practical or graphical kind. Dürer invited the critics to show what they meant with their hands but although, in a manner of speaking, use was made of hands, it was not for holding the pencil but as a gesticulatory aid to the spoken word—the index finger touching the thumb, the little finger pointing to the ceiling and the arm, first extended, then withdrawn, as if the activity of applying paint to canvas were being combined with that of range-finding.

Beispiel gegen Beispiel

In spite of Sturge Moore's warning against trying to compare an apparently satisfactory example of one kind with an obviously faulty specimen of another, the next experiment took the form of inviting members to bring to a drawing-room meeting contrasting examples of everyday domestic articles. These were laid out on trestle tables covered with fine linen and looking for all the world like some display of wedding presents—'like the wedding breakfast of Design and Industry,' Bobbie Simon suggested.

The meeting was interesting and enjoyable. The members sat around informally in groups and after each exhibitor had introduced the knives, forks, plates, glasses, coal-scuttles, electric fires or table standards he had brought along, the fun started.

Although this was the first meeting I had attended at which there was lively discussion about actual articles, the idea of contrasting examples had been tried in an exhibition organised by the Deutscher Werkbund in Munich during the year 1908. According to the Secretary of the Werkbund it was called '*Beispiel gegen Beispiel*'—Contrasting Examples.

A simple interior, for instance, filled with modern furniture was shown alongside a fussy crowded room—alleged, according to the catalogue, to belong to a certain retired businessman, Herr Privat Rentier Nudelmeier. Unfortunately the lesson was missed by many of the visitors, who in fact approved Herr Nudelmeier's appartment but found the other cold and inhuman.

The Quiz

Thereafter it was found that the most successful meetings were about manufacturers' actual products. Often the prototype of a new design would be put before the members in an early stage of production or as a mock-up. The designer or responsible businessman would go to the centre of the group and give a short explanation of the sample, how it was made, what it had to do, what it cost and what were the peculiarities, if any, of the market.

The ensuing discussion was usually stimulating in a general way and often of practical value to the professionals concerned. The opinions of the private members as consumers were worthy of attention as a form of market research, while the comments and suggestions of other manufacturers were frequently technically well informed. Pencil and paper would be produced and detailed proposals for modifying the construction or treatment would be talked over.

Held in private houses, these meetings were small—more than two dozen people were seldom present—and this was an important factor in promoting useful discussion. They were looked upon as social occasions in the sense that members were there to enjoy themselves, to meet friends and to talk about things other than design, should they feel so inclined.

Visitors from outside the Midlands were often invited and amongst them was Noel Carrington. A publisher and author of several books on design and an untiring worker for the Association, he was looked upon as a high-priest of D.I.A.-ism. He happened to be present at a meeting called to discuss, amongst other things, some examples of furniture submitted by a member of the Rudolf Steiner Colony at Clent,[12] and designed according to the principles recommended by that prophet. These pieces, presumably suggesting organic growth, were somewhat reminiscent of the Art Nouveau Period and did not conform to D.I.A. doctrine. 'This is rank heresy,' said Noel Carrington.

In these discussions the wags gave full measure. I was as little as anyone else able to resist the temptation of making humorous comments, and could not therefore complain when my company's products came in for criticism mingled with persiflage. They were generally made a special target and, as I went before the group, I could see the professionals rubbing their hands in gleeful anticipation.

One evening, amongst the company, was a gifted visitor from abroad. A former member of the Bauhaus staff, he had actually designed one of the articles I now offered to be 'quizzed'. His name, to British ears, sounded somewhat arresting and when I stated, in my introductory remarks, that this article had been designed by Slutzky,[13] my meaning was grossly misunderstood. Bob Best must have his bit of fun, they thought, and there was a shout of laughter. The distinguished designer then rose from his seat and at once tripped over a length of electric wire. Somewhat disconcerted, I tried to explain the principle of the design. It was a table standard. The lamp bulb, placed in a vertical reflector, directed the light upwards against a wide inverted dish which reflected it down again onto the working plane. My explanation failed to quieten the hilarity. I continued to flounder. Then when the tumult began to die down, it was restarted by a suggestion from Bobbie Simon that the lamp might be fit for its purpose at a spiritualistic séance.

---

[12] The Sunfield Children's Home, started in 1930 by Friedrich Geuter and Michael Wilson and based on Steiner's principles. Clent is a village in the Bromsgrove area of Worcestershire, just south-west of Birmingham.

[13] [Naum Slutzky (1894–1965), goldsmith and designer in metal. Taught at the Bauhaus 1919–1924, Central School of Arts and Crafts in London and in Birmingham, where he became associated with Best & Lloyd.]

During the last twenty years, I have been a member of several cenacles and coteries. I have come into contact with many more. From these experiences I have reached the conclusion that if design can be improved at all by measures other than the play of supply and demand, discussion is the best tool for the job, and the happy form of it we called 'The Quiz' is the most helpful activity these bodies can undertake. Almost entirely free from X, it may be regarded as a manifestation of 'the circular response' that Mary Follett called for. The current goes both ways. The channels are kept open. The leadership is continually changing. The leaders are not only influencing but are being influenced by the group.

The weekend festival

Although this pilgrimage has reached no delectable mountains that I have so far been able to discover, it has passed through many pleasant valleys. Amongst them must be counted the weekends in the country arranged by the Association. Nobody could have called these events 'conferences', and a stranger would have wondered what they were all about; but they provided Bobbie Simon with a rich field whereupon to cultivate the sort of *fleurs de farce* which delighted him. Few escaped his attention and few were able to withhold it. I have a clear recollection of his sitting in the middle of a half-circle of women members and talking about fitness for purpose, mingled with pleasantness in use, to an accompaniment of light soprano laughter.

The weekend at John Fothergill's hotel, The Three Swans, Market Harborough, was exceptionally felicitous and more than usually without any sort of link with the programme of the Association. Fothergill's account of our visit reads as follows:

When Bobbie Simon came with 18 members of the Design and Industry [sic] Association for their weekend festival, their beautiful bill-head printing stamped on their clear foreheads, I told them that their presence would do me no end of harm and worse, for even as the one or two highbrows who had trickled in since we came had driven away at sight some of our commercial travellers, so these arty hearties would in turn drive away the highbrows and leave me with no one. Bobbie Simon talks, talks, but it is worth it. I asked him why he didn't throw his leg across a horse whilst here and go a-hunting. 'Well, I didn't bring my _____'s 13/6 pair of grey flannel trousers,' he said, but in fact he had and wore them the next day, the very worst bits of bad fitting I've ever seen on legs.[14]

[14] John Fothergill, *Confessions of an Innkeeper* (London: Chatto & Windus, 1938), 244.

CHAPTER 9
DORLAND HALL

When Noel Carrington, at the inaugural luncheon of the Birmingham D.I.A., said that it was proposed to hold a large-scale exhibition in London, he was referring to the 'Exhibition of British Industrial Art in Relation to the Home' which was to take place at Dorland Hall during the following year, 1933.

The government had shown a sympathetic attitude towards the project but gave it no financial support. Much of the initiative came from the D.I.A. A general committee of about three dozen people, called by the inner circle 'the Snob Committee', was formed and in its turn appointed an executive committee of fourteen. This was found to be too large and was whittled down to six or seven. Thirteen individuals offered, or were persuaded, to act as guarantors, but they were not called upon to honour this obligation, since the exhibition was financially successful, as, indeed, it deserved to be.

This excellent private enterprise was organised for exactly the same reasons as apply to all exhibitions by advanced artistic groups, namely to give the bright boys a chance and help them to sell their products. According to the catalogue, however, its justification was that 'the latent creative power of the country was not finding expression as it used to do,' the sponsors claiming that the exhibition was the product of a widespread national movement.

Lord Gorell denied that it was an isolated endeavour on the part of some enthusiasts. It did not stand alone, he maintained, but was 'the forerunner of a concerted national movement ... a national system of exhibitions controlled by a permanent body'. Fortunately it was nothing of the sort.

Selection and selectors

After 'contact-men', appointed for each trade, had persuaded manufacturers to submit samples, these were offered up to one of seven selection committees, most of which consisted of four individuals. Noel Carrington, who was on the executive committee, thought that two would have been enough and that every additional member made it harder for them to agree. Nobody seems to have asked, however, whether it was necessary for them to agree at all or why there should have been this desire to form a united front to maintain a 'high and uniform standard of design'.

No selective exhibition of industrial art has, to my knowledge, been held without the creation of unnecessary difficulties through trying to establish agreement when, in the nature of things, this is impossible.

A formidable problem arises through the very under-standable desire to keep the selection free from trade interests. In theory it would be invidious for one businessman or designer to pass judgment on a competitor's products. In practice, as we shall see, this difficulty need never arise, if we were to give up the search for uniformity.

At Dorland Hall it was claimed that the exhibition, for the first time in England, contained only articles which a catholic and expert jury regarded as including aesthetic excellence among their other attributes. But one cannot help wondering how that jury, though it might have been catholic, could possibly have had sufficient expert knowledge of the 'markets' for which a designer has to work or the sort of things the public won't have at any price. The industrialist hesitates to offer up his pet products to publicity agents, young architects, journalists, publishers and museum directors and longs for some 'old sweat' with common experience of the earthy conditions in which he works, some first-class retail buyer, or if export trade must be considered, some importer from abroad, with whom to discuss his design problems. As he looks over the selection panel, he wonders how many of the team of selectors will have stood the pace in twenty years time? Who will have cut any ice? Who will be known and accepted then?

In the exhibition under review, the term 'selector' was, in some cases, slightly misleading, for certain of the team were not so much 'neutral' people, free from trade interests, as live young interior decorators and architects having a most enjoyable time designing and arranging the rooms and flats in which exhibits were to be displayed. As we have suggested it was partly on behalf of these gifted individuals that the exhibition was organised. These were the manifestations of the 'latent creative power of the country' which was not finding expression and I believe they deserved the opportunity thus given to them but there was, in their selections, no need for unanimity because they were all working on different projects and expressing a purely personal point of view.

The architect with whom my company had most to do was Serge Chermayeff. He approached the problem of selection in an accommodating and cooperative spirit and for his 'Weekend House' made an admirable adaptation of the Bestlite Standard as a wall-bracket. But according to a member of the committee, the selectors turned down an immense amount of stuff and tried to put across the idea that it would be a privilege to be accepted.

Whether or not they succeeded in promoting this form of artistic sycophancy is doubtful and unimportant. What should concern us is that here, in the sphere of industrial design, we find an attempt to set up the same sort of critic–artist relationship as disgusted Eric Gill. Thus do creative individuals and their camp followers seek to increase their prestige by appointing themselves as 'cabinets of authority'.

Preface and product

We have already drawn attention to the discrepancies, sometimes noticeable in exhibition catalogues, between the theoretical principles advocated by the writer of the introduction on the one hand and the exhibits themselves on the other. An alert but experienced visitor to Dorland Hall might have noted, perhaps without much surprise, some of these anomalies. The Gorell Committee had reported that a reversion to handicrafts could not solve the problem of beautifying articles of common use within the purchasing power of consumers of moderate means and the catalogue stated that the artist-craftsman had been excluded, except where his work was suitable for industrial production. But if this was the plan, why exhibit the elegant articles by Spencer, Harold Stabler, Cooper and others—the fruit bowl costing £48, the candlesticks at £40 per pair, the powder-bowl in silver, gold, ivory and enamel at £20?

An alert visitor might well agree with the general principle that 'a twentieth-century synthesis must provide for the economic no less than the cultural needs of the public'. Even though, as a theoretical ideal, it might have been accepted for his own epoch by any benevolent designer, industrialist or politician during the previous hundred years, liberal-minded people should recollect with pleasure that in 1933 a new factor was about to appear: design for rationing, for we were then on the brink of the era of Utility furniture and production for the common man.

It is difficult to see, however, what all this had to do with most of the designs exhibited. They pleased me personally, but the style and prices of the articles showed clearly that they could only appeal to certain middle-class people with money.

The sponsors themselves did not care for ornament and rationalised their preferences by arguing that 'we have no money to pay for unnecessary ornament'—tautology again—or that 'since ornament repeated by machinery is meaningless, the place of ornament should be taken by using the great variety of materials now available'. Our alert visitor, on reading these words, might well have paused to examine the coin with which he paid his entrance fee or the finely printed ornamental borders in the book section.

New materials and new forms

And what were the materials which were to take the place of ornament in the modern home? According to the catalogue, they were: 'laminated wood, chromium steel, glass and textile fabrics' and the articles produced from them, as displayed in the entrance hall, represented 'the basis of the industrial synthesis: mankind's needs supplied, through industrial technique, from the capacities of materials'. The alert visitor might have enquired as to which were actually new and what precisely was the synthesis.

Now, a manufacturer must, as part of his daily job, search for new materials, and an intelligent consumer will naturally welcome those which combine both cheapness with serviceability and (to him) a pleasing appearance. If this is a 'synthesis', it is difficult to see how, as manifested at Dorland Hall, it differed from the ordinary play of supply and demand which had been gathering impetus during the nineteenth century.

And this is in no way to belittle the influence of the materials and processes then appearing. Some were in fact fairly new and are still saleable. Tubular steel furniture has come to stay, certainly in the form of nesting chairs, though one may doubt whether the chromium-plated chair, as pictured in Osbert Lancaster's 'Functional' interior, will become a permanent feature of domestic equipment. Plywood construction was then being developed and has had important effects on design. Plastics, probably one of the most significant new things in my time and trade, had not then come into their own, although there was an exhibit by the British Xylonite Company. It is not clear, however, why the sponsors should have included glass and textile fabrics amongst the constituent parts of the twentieth-century synthesis.

In looking over the catalogue, the materials composing most of the exhibits do not seem to have been particularly new. What was indeed new was a style or idiom, just as in the case of the Art Nouveau. The chromium-plated tubes, applied to furniture, reappeared in the light fittings, for no reason except that it was the fashion at that time. Indeed, unlike some other design leaders, the chairman of the executive committee did not hesitate to declare that 'the economic value to a nation of possessing a characteristic and flourishing style need not be pointed out'.

While passing through the entrance vestibule our alert visitor might have noticed signs of the same mental confusion as caused Roger Fry to comment that 'design in industry is menaced … by the … idea that when an object fulfils its function perfectly, it is, ipso facto, beautiful and a work of art,'[1] for displayed there was a collection of tools and implements of a sort which we have since learned to associate with so much propaganda for producers of 'modern' shapes and styling.

While questioning some of the verbiage and theory, this visitor would undoubtedly have enjoyed examining the actual products. The courageous attempts to carry out forms of unit construction advocated by Walter Gropius and others would certainly have held his attention.

Unit construction

There was, at that time, nothing new in principle about design which allows the user to arrange units, such as book-case sections, in any way required. Each unit is intended to be complete in itself, unlike the 'Meccano' plan where a series of purely structural standardised components can be assembled to form a variety of objects.

An intermediate method, then exhibited, took the form of different basic units such as trestle, drawer, box-shelf and link. It seemed, at the time, reasonable to suppose that they would 'fulfil every furnishing need and solve every possible contingency as individual pieces or combinations'. The public appears to have thought differently. Perhaps there was something too 'continental' about the scale. A Birmingham dealer tells me that he thought

---

[1] Gorell, *Art and Industry*, 44.

the pieces too big from back to front—the drawers looked like tunnels. As a selling point, he considers that unit adjustability has the same drawback as the adjustable chair. It is set once and then never touched again.

The theory may be sound but the customer is far more likely to be influenced by some detail—what is known to the trade as 'nonsense-value'. At any rate the quantity of this kind of article actually sold must be small compared with the total furniture sales, which amount to about £80 million per annum.

In my own trade, for at least a hundred years, the unit principle has taken the form of combining, in different ways, castings, or perhaps bent tubular arms, glass bowls, stampings and capstan-lathe products. I know of at least one firm which has used this method with great success and almost every manufacturer in the trade introduces some component parts into more than one article. Certain stampings, called 'parish goods', may indeed be supplied by one firm to a number of others for assembling into complete articles. But in the writer's experience the results tend to be disappointing, and the device can be easily overdone when the prospective purchaser feels that he is being fobbed off with an adaptation, a 'codged-up job', not properly made through and through.

In an exhibition such as the one under discussion it is debatable whether there should be a place for the frankly experimental. The fact that a model may subsequently prove to be a failure certainly shows that it is poor industrial design or perhaps not even industrial design at all. On the other hand it may be argued that it is still worth showing as an idea, a personal viewpoint, an expression—a form of fine art, if you like.

Just before the Exhibition closed there took place a delightful consummatory party for members of the committee, the D.I.A. and friends. Standing in a circle, sipping sherry, some members were joined by Eric Gill. I listened attentively.

'In the entrance,' so the catalogue informed us, 'the symbolical figures of a man and a woman, by Mr. Eric Gill and Mr. Frank Dobson respectively, are seen in relation to examples of industrial plant,' and in the available space the actual processes of manufacture had been indicated decoratively. I have often wondered since how Eric Gill came to find himself in that *galère* at all; for few people condemned mechanised production , more than he; whereas the D.I.A. not only accepted but welcomed modern techniques and set itself to make the best of them.

George Orwell suggested that, in repeatedly criticising factory life and its products, Gill was, in fact, 'nagging away at a half truth'. But in spite of his trouncing of us industrialists, I find myself more and more drawn towards his teaching on account of his insistence that, somehow or other, factory work must once again be made worthy of responsible human beings.

Industrial design and religion

Eric Gill, as we have seen, deplored the art critics and dealers and disdained the sycophancy they engendered. After much heart searching, he took the view that art (or, for that matter, industrial design) was very much mixed up with religion and he seems to have reached this conclusion in the following way.

First he found that his artist friends, Jacob Epstein, Augustus

John, Ambrose McEvoy and others, disagreed as to what was good and bad art; what they worked for was aesthetic emotion as understood by the art critics. Art was in a watertight compartment and the artist was the lapdog of the wealthy.

Gill was unable to tolerate these values; nor could he even accept the material ideals of better housing and social services. 'You can abolish cruelty and injustice,' he said, 'but still have the Civic Centre at Cardiff.'[1] The evil, he believed, arose somewhere in the sphere of religion. He was therefore forced, as he put it, to 'invent' a religion as a 'reason' and standard for all his creative activity and afterwards found that this religion corresponded to that of the Roman Catholic Church. So although he suggested that the Catholics of his day were almost completely corrupted by the world we live in, he applied for membership and was accepted.

A cursed breed

In spite of his Christian faith, Eric Gill turned on businessmen in a way that recalls Hitler and his Race Theory. He cursed 'the monstrous filthiness of the man of business' who 'laid his evil hands on every corner of the earth' and 'pandered to the lowest denominator of taste'. It was foul—worse than lechery and drunkenness. It was idolatory—destructive and desolating. The desire for money was the root of all evil. The businessman applied only one test: 'does it pay?' Science and industry might be good things in themselves but they both led to the degradation of man and the isolation of the fine arts. The pages of his autobiography[2] are scattered with variations on this theme.

Sales: sole aim or limiting condition?

Like Catterson-Smith's condemnation of machine production, referred to above, Eric Gill's strictures were, I believe, based on a

---

[1] [Cardiff City Hall, Lanchester, Stewart and Rickards 1900–1904.]
[2] Gill, *Autobiography*.

misunderstanding of the actual motives and conditions governing the conduct of the sales—the works- and design-managers who are primarily responsible for what is put on the market. When he said that saleability was the businessman's criterion, like so many others even today, he was confusing a 'limiting condition' with a 'sole objective'.

It cannot be too often repeated that, if unsaleable, an article is by definition *not* an example of industrial design.

On the other hand, even if it *can* be sold, the design may nevertheless be inferior, if not downright bad, and is often therefore consciously avoided by many, though by no means all, manufacturers. The man of business is *not only* concerned to buy cheap and sell dear. But at any rate the need to *sell* the designs which industry produces may be looked upon as a kind of insurance against the egotism of any particular group, since those engaged in designing have perforce to please others as well as themselves. To accept this condition does not class them as 'pimps and thieves'.

As a young man Gill had been disgusted with the 'go-getting' antics of the architectural profession—the individual's ambition to obtain all the jobs there were; also with the sorry fact that the 'grand conception of architecture as humanised engineering' appeared to depend upon the 'degeneration of workmen'. He therefore gave up this occupation of architecture, went to a craft school to learn lettering and thereafter was never out of a job.

But surely such a job can only mean that one accepts the 'customer–supplier' relationship as a condition of work. The sale of his products was certainly not Gill's main interest but it was undoubtedly part of the job, just as it is in the case of the businessman. Gill commented critically when his artist friends pretended to despise the 'silly old customer who wanted a picture and would pay' and yet he denounced the manufacturer for taking his customer seriously.

Art, he maintained, was neither a hot-house flower nor primarily self-expression—not a manifestation of the precious personality of the artist. It was simply a job of work, like building a house, as it had always been before industry rejected the idea of production as something sacred and holy.

But the industrialist cannot help speculating as to the actual conditions of production when art was simply 'doing a job'. Was the job not almost invariably performed to the order of some customer? Some rich patron, secular or clerical? Was the job not, therefore, a two-way or even a many-way process, the artist having to consider the preferences of other people beside himself?

Responsibility unshared

Perhaps I have oversimplified the issues. Gill was careful to explain that his actions and beliefs were not always to be understood in logical terms. He did not doubt the efficacy of reason but put no trust in the reliability of his own reasoning powers. He was intellectually humble.

May not the real explanation for his disgust with the whole business world have been that mechanised industry, he clearly saw, deprived human beings, from the time they clocked in until the whistle blew in the evening, of the responsibility for ordering and designing their own affairs? This reduced the workman to a sub-human condition of intellectual irresponsibility; the machine-factor destroyed all power of discrimination, and if these conditions continued, industrialism would, he prophesied, go down in blood and tears. In all this I find myself very much on his side.

He was probably mistaken, however, in supposing that the necessary responsibility for and participation in the work-act, with exercise of hand-skills, could only be brought about by reverting to some older form of craft economy. Questions of industrial administration are outside the scope of this essay; it must nevertheless be stated that there seem to be many ways, as yet largely untried, whereby the responsibility and skills might be shared out and the headlong downward course arrested.

One may even be developing through the stratification of

industry which, according to Herbert Read, is already taking place, whereas another is suggested by James Gillespie in his *Free Expression in Industry*.[3]

From this healthy distrust for the humiliation of the conveyor belt and with the detached and socially irresponsible attitude of his artist friends arose his theory that even music should be *Gebrauchsmusik*,[4] designed for a special occasion,[5] and that all artwork should fill some real need or serve some useful purpose. If he could have seen any evidence that it might be possible to give back to the men on the workshop floor manual skills and the function of making administrative decisions, he might have changed his views.

What is sauce for the factory goose may also be sauce for the ministerial gander. If it is desirable that the managing director should share with the other members of his firm the fun and excitement of his job, then should we not condemn the Gorell-men and all who have subsequently supported them for recommending that the primary control of industrial art exhibitions should be given to a central body with executive powers?

Provincial groups should therefore be encouraged to organise and plan their own affairs, and government grants for such purposes should not become the perquisite of a coterie based on London.

---

[3] James J. Gillespie, *Free Expression in Industry* (London: The Pilot Press, 1948).

[4] Utility music; music of need.

[5] Eric Gill, *Work and Property, etc* (London: J.M. Dent and Sons Ltd, 1937), 31.

CHAPTER 11
THE MIDLAND INDUSTRIAL ART EXHIBITION

Like the artisans from whom, as Eric Gill complained, all responsibility had been taken, many exhibitors at Dorland Hall, especially provincial ones (such as my own firm), found themselves very much on the outer rim of things. The following year, however, I acquired first-hand experience of being at the centre of an artistic sect while engaged in the frontal attack on design standards generally associated with selective exhibitions.

At the Union Club, Birmingham, I used to meet S.C. Kaines-Smith, Keeper of the City Museum and Art Gallery, and together we would discuss, amongst other things, contemporary industrial design. K.S. was not enthusiastic about domestic furnishing and equipment deliberately styled to suggest the machine age, but nevertheless accepted tolerantly my suggestion that we should organise, locally, an exhibition similar in scope to the one at Dorland Hall.

In the Autumn of 1933, therefore, at his suggestion, the Design and Industries Association wrote officially proposing such a project but made it clear that the local branch was neither big enough nor rich enough to undertake the organisation single handed. A group consisting partly of members of the Art Gallery Committee and partly of the D.I.A. was formed and, in February 1934, appointed K.S. and me as organising secretaries.

I have often since pondered this starting point for an experiment in group criticism and propaganda. The coalescence was spontaneous and indeed it is difficult to see how it could be otherwise. The good D.I.A. apostles were probably fired by the example of the London venture but, I think, many of us also liked, for its own sake, the activity of spreading a gospel. We enjoyed stating a point of view and testing its truth by public and private discussion. We wanted to convince others. As for myself, it so happened that events, so to say, switched on the current of conviction the reverse way, as we shall see.

Throughout the enterprise, the attitude of the Art Gallery Committee was like that of a benevolent ministry supporting some group of enthusiasts thought to be worthy but not fully informed. The formation of such coteries deserves the closest attention from a qualified and impartial investigator.

Office work

Comparable problems of administration must be faced by the committees of all industrial art exhibitions. There is the preparation of a schedule of trades; the collection of names; the drafting and distribution of a prospectus; arranging meetings; answering queries and following up enquiries; deciding the class of goods to be admitted; and so forth. Any examination of the activities of design coteries should cover the question of finance: by whom? In this case the sources were:

- a grant of £100 made by the Dorland Hall (London) Exhibition trustees;
- a like amount from the Birmingham City Council;
- smaller sums from the Birmingham Chamber of Commerce and other bodies; and
- a charge of two guineas to exhibitors.

Of interest to the student of the 1951 Festival of Britain, with its travelling show which in some cases affronted local patriotism, is the following extract from the 1934 prospectus:

A part of the British Industrial Art Exhibition held at Dorland Hall last year was formed into a travelling exhibition which has been shown at certain provincial cities. The suggestion that it might be brought to Birmingham was rejected by the Art Gallery Committee on account of the Art Gallery Jubilee Year programme, which is devoted entirely to Midlands artwork. Furthermore it is certainly the case that sufficient material can be found amongst the Midland industries to justify an exhibition of goods in which design is of major importance. The Birmingham Art Gallery is the appropriate place for such an exhibition.

The D.I.A. equipped a stand for the sale of literature, and to demonstrate the two factors in design suggested by J.H. Badley in *The Will to Fuller Life* (mentioned above) there was a large-scale diagram in three horizontal bands. At the top were functional appliances in different stages of development, starting with the stone axe and working up to the machine tool and aeroplane. At the bottom were ranged examples of design including those connected with the play instinct, such as articles of personal adornment—beads and body decoration leading on to modern jewellery, patterned wallpaper, textiles and so forth—which satisfied no need except to please the eye; while in the middle band there were articles in which the two factors were intermingled: furniture, pottery, glassware, early lamps, light fittings and electric fires.

Selection

The marshalling of the exhibits, organised by the D.I.A., followed much the same lines as at Dorland Hall. A body of 'contact-men' was supposed to ferret out the most likely firms and 'Advisory Selectors' followed them up to recommend which products were most likely to be accepted. This involved much hard work from our volunteers but progress was disappointing. Few days went by without a phonecall from my co-secretary asking for news of the contact-men, who for intervals remained strangely silent.

The committee decided to invite three 'experts' to make the final choice and on 23 May, Noel Carrington, B.J. Fletcher and Sir Eric Maclagan (of the Victoria and Albert Museum) were confronted with the results of all this activity.

I thought I noted a certain lack of warmth in the atmosphere. Picking their way carefully amongst the exhibits parked on the floor, they began to sort them out and at the end of the day had divided them into two lots. Although I later observed with gratification that divers products of the writer's company had been selected, I was dismayed to see that, in spite of the work of the advisory selectors, the pound enclosing the rejected models was a large one and contained many articles of, in my view, sound design, bearing in mind the limiting factors peculiar to commercial production.

It was precisely at this point that I began to reflect in earnest on the question:

> Who has the necessary 'expert' knowledge and experience to make selections for this kind of exhibition?

The preferences of the three distinguished jurors was of interest, in the same way as, let us say, Byron's *chaise-longue* at the Garrick Club, but I could not see what all this had to do with 'design for sale', as I knew it.

Shortly afterwards I had to go abroad for a fortnight. While away, I heard from K.S. that he had been using a good deal of latitude in adding to the exhibits and hoped the judges would not disapprove. I was glad that he had taken this course, for I could see no useful purpose in irritating capable manufacturers and designers by rejecting designs of merit, simply because they did not happen to suit the predilections of the selectors.

Furthermore, his wise rearrangement provided a key for future *selective* exhibitions, in which the preferences of *different* individuals might be shown separately and alongside each other for comparison.

And, for that matter, I thought, why should not the manufacturer himself have some choice? Such an exhibition would at least answer to reality, industrial design being the result of different points of view.

A broadcast discussion

Amongst other publicity measures, there was to be a radio discussion, with Kaines-Smith acting as chairman and the other members being Mr. Donald Milner, then principal of the Gloucester School of Art, Mrs. C.V. Miller of Edgbaston, to speak for the ordinary housewife, and me, to put the manufacturer's point of view.

At the rehearsal, the slight nervous affliction which affected my voice and had proved a handicap in my earlier sales adventures reasserted itself so that K.S. advised me to renounce my part in the discussion and rely on a 'ghost'. I decided, nevertheless, to go through with it.

On the night of the broadcast a pleasant diversion was provided by my friend Cyril Batho, of Birmingham University, who was entertaining two colleagues, Harold Fox and Julian Huxley. Made aware of the somewhat tense state in which I found myself, the others created just the right atmosphere to distract me. They consoled me by saying that however disastrous my microphonic contribution might be, these three would not be amongst the listeners, since there happened to be no wireless instrument in the house.

After dinner, resigned and in elevated mood, I went round to the studio. We sat around a table and K.S. opened the discussion by suggesting that while the manufacturer tried to blame the public, the housewife complained that good design was unobtainable. 'A plague on both your houses,' he said. Mrs. Miller confirmed that ordinary modern furnishings and fittings seemed to her so ugly that she had started buying antiques; Mr. Milner, intervening, argued that the designer was not given a chance by the manufacturer. The chairman then turned to me.

Disliking the prevailing search for scapegoats, I led off, somewhat hesitantly, with the suggestion that the public got the design it deserved. Many men did not think a great deal about furnishing their homes and left it to their wives; and designers and manufacturers were not, I continued, a separate class from the public but, in private life, consumers just like anyone else. As for the theory that trade buyers and retailers were preventing new and saleable designs from being put before the public, the whole notion was, I suggested, absurd. In every town of any size was to be found at least one shop specialising in up-to-date design. If a public hunger truly existed for the new, these shops would be flooded out with orders while the more conservative ones would be going badly downhill. As this was not the case we must look elsewhere for an explanation, if any is required.

I added that never before in history had there been so much technical change in so short a time. Human nature could not adjust. It was like taking a person with a taste for light wines and suddenly putting him on to raw spirit. His palate would be ruined.

And then I worked round to the exhibition and somewhat lamely brought this set piece to a close by recommending that on the board of every company manufacturing designed goods there should be someone with experience of designing, and arguing for more opportunities for workshop experience at art schools.

I then returned to Cyril Batho, who immediately gave an excellent imitation of the whole broadcast, especially my own hesitant opening; for as soon as I had left, the party had hurried round to a friend's house and had been chuckling over the shortcomings of this presentation. At one point the radio receiver had been offered a whisky and soda to steady its nerves ... .

Next day the exhibition was opened by W.G. Ormsby-Gore M.P., then First Commissioner of Works. Bobbie Simon came down especially for the opening, and we met as I was about to join the platform party. 'Ah, my dear Bob,' he said, 'You have arrived, I see.'

Another foreword

Having commented on introductions to catalogues of other exhibitions, I must not ignore the foreword to this one, written, I find, by Kaines-Smith and me. Certain passages, no doubt those in which I had a hand, revealed the same cloudiness of view as is found in other catalogues. There were, however, some telling points, bringing the reader right down to earth. I have no doubt these were the work of my partner who, throughout these preparations, showed a cautious and sensible attitude towards the more extreme theorists.

In the first paragraph is the following quotation from a book written in 1766 by John Gwynn, the designer of the bridges at Shrewsbury, Atcham and Worcester:

> How much more valuable a manufactury would Birmingham be (as well as many others) to this nation if it was in the hands of people of taste! At present, quantity not quality seems principally to be considered, and everything is loaded with much confused and superfluous work, which is falsely called ornament, when less labour, guided by judgment, would be much better, and every article be rendered more valuable by its elegant simplicity in shape and form, and the expense of that unnecessary labour might be added to the quality of the materials. The making things cheap and good is of infinite advantage to commerce, as cheap and bad are certainly to the contrary.

The object of the exhibition, we said, was to show that whether by virtue of machinery or despite it, design in industry could be good and inexpensive. We quoted the recommendation of the Gorell Report that the great artistic genius of the nation should be used to the full to beautify our products 'for the sake of national self-respect, as well as profit', though we claimed that the order should be reversed and that the phrase should read 'for the sake of profit as well as national respect'.

'The public, however,' we went on, 'is intensely conservative.' The guidance of experts, who often differ amongst themselves, may even be a source of bewilderment,

> and, moreover, the capacity of machinery to produce designs is increasing more rapidly in scope than the public can possibly realise, so that at any moment they may be confronted with some new development in design which bears no relation to anything

within their experience, and may find themselves swept by the enthusiasm of writers and shop windows into following a fashion which they neither understand nor like, only to regret bitterly when the fashion fails.

Now, the only way to enable the public to judge a new movement in design ... is to show them the products themselves, as chosen by the expert. After all, in the long run, the buying public are the judges. It is they who set the fashion and, as likely as not, terminate it, sometimes more quickly than the manufacturer and the expert expect, and it is ultimately to the public that manufacturer and designer must look to learn how far each may stray from tradition and to what extent new adventures must be based on old principles.

A successful exhibition?

Three years later Kaines-Smith addressed the Council for Art and Industry on 'Museums and Displays of Contemporary Products'. The Midland Exhibition, he thought, had been a complete failure. It had been impossible to get the cooperation of the manufacturers. They hesitated to submit themselves to the judgment of the selection committee and to allow their competitors to see their designs. The public, furthermore, was not interested in the somewhat heterogeneous collection of objects thus brought together.

But the larger trouble was that the rules of the Gallery forbade actual selling and, according to K.S., prospective exhibitors were thus unwilling to pay the small charge. He was disappointed that the jewellery trade had been almost entirely unrepresented and that silversmiths' work was also meagrely shown ... .

There was no doubt much to be said for this summing up. For myself, I felt that the most unsatisfactory feature of the plan was the attempt to foster the illusion that the opinions of the selectors had great importance or objective backing—the weakness of so many selective exhibitions. In demonstrating the absurdity of approaching the project in this way, the Midland Industrial Art Exhibition was, for me personally, an eye-opener.

CHAPTER 12
NIKOLAUS PEVSNER

Some weeks before the opening of the exhibition, I had been introduced, by Philip Sargant Florence,[1] to a young art historian. Driven by oppression from his own country, Nikolaus Pevsner had been made research assistant in the Department of Commerce of Birmingham University, the subject for his investigation being 'Industrial Art in England'. He became a frequent and welcome visitor to my house.[2]

I found his great knowledge of things artistic impressive and stimulating, whilst my earlier experiences at the Düsseldorf School and my admiration of German design gave us a sort of common ground. He was, even then, giving excellent lectures on the subject he was examining and his rapid mastery of the English language and customs was, indeed, astonishing. It seemed, as it were, to polish itself almost as one talked to him. Since those days, I have read much that he has written and never without interest and enjoyment.

To carry out his research it was necessary for him to visit and interview manufacturers and managers of retail shops and I was able to help him with introductions and advice as to the sort of

---

[1] [Professor of Commerce at Birmingham University. Known for his statistical research into fatigue in industry. Said to have been the first person to spend a night in Wells Coates's Isokon building, otherwise known as Lawn Road Flats (1932–43). Associated with C.K. Ogden and Basic English.]

[2] Before coming to Birmingham, Nikolaus Pevsner (Hon. A.R.C.A. and Hon. F.S.I.A.) had been Lecturer in History of Art and Architecture at Göttingen University. He subsequently became Lecturer in Art at Birkbeck College, Art Editor of Penguin Books, Member of the Editorial Board of the *Architectural Review* and Slade Professor of Fine Art, Cambridge University.

approach most likely to bring out the information required. Our letters did not always produce the desired results. One director replied that this questionnaire was 'in the nature of an inquisition with which (he) was not in sympathy', while another wrote: 'Our commercial arrangements are designed to advantage our factory in competition with a host of competitors, and I should not be prepared to have them brought into a general discussion.' But even when the manager's office had been penetrated there might be difficulties. 'To discuss the aesthetic value of English products,' Nikolaus Pevsner tells us, 'involves criticism of present methods and suggestions as to practicable improvements.' Sometimes these suggestions failed to secure the attention they deserved.[3]

Scapegoats

When he began this research, Pevsner seems to have assumed that there was a wide gulf between what the public wanted and what they were actually allowed to buy. 'The shopkeeper,' he reported, '... unconsciously pushes what he likes and conceals in dark corners what seems to him unattractive. He may also kill articles by bad and overcrowded display, let alone the fact that he may have his special and objectionable reasons against good modern design in cheap merchandise.' Referring to the carpet trade, he suggested that the shopkeeper tends to place, at the top of the pile, the designs he wants to sell, while sounder designs disappear at the bottom.[4]

The small manufacturers were too indolent or too much concerned with securing orders and keeping afloat to recognise their social duties, while it was often the case that they were misinformed as to what the public really wanted. They depended largely on suggestions from their own sales departments, i.e.

---

3 Nikolaus Pevsner, *An Enquiry into Industrial Art in England* (Cambridge: Cambridge University Press, 1937), 3, 7.

4 Pevsner, *An Enquiry*, 207, 65.

from information received from travellers who would come home and state what had been a 'flop' or what was selling 'like hot cakes'. 'Moreover, the class from which most travellers, buyers and smaller shopkeepers come is supposed to be one of the most reactionary classes in the country.'[5]

For these reasons, Pevsner urged that it would 'never be sufficient to consult the manufacturer and the shopkeeper only; the public itself should be consulted. Much too little has been done so far to induce consumers to express their opinions of the goods which they are offered.'[6]

The evidence on which this theory rested seemed to me inadequate and I felt that the hunt for scapegoats was unpleasantly reminiscent of some race theories then achieving notoriety. But the plea for more direct market research had my whole-hearted support. It was a move in the right direction; in fact, according to Stuart Chase, there are now 'a number of experts who believe that after the culture concept in anthropology, public-opinion research is the outstanding accomplishment in social science. The polls have helped to vindicate political democracy.'[7] At the time, however, my interest was confined to getting a few tips for our own design department.

A questionnaire

To short-circuit the influence of unworthy manufacturers and distributors, Pevsner felt that a useful opportunity offered itself in the Midland Industrial Art Exhibition. He therefore compiled a questionnaire which visitors were asked to fill in and himself attended at a desk to clear up any difficulties which might arise. The text included questions as to sex, age and profession and then enquired as to which objects in each department of the exhibition

---

5 Pevsner, *An Enquiry*, 207, 209.

6 Pevsner, *An Enquiry*, 5.

7 Stuart Chase, *The Proper Study of Mankind* (London: Phoenix House, 1950), 186.

(electrical goods, hardware, furniture, glass, pottery, jewellery, textiles and other goods) were liked most and which least.

'Only 92 answers were given, 30 female and 59 male [and three not disclosing], which is not a high percentage considering the total number of visitors,'[8] Pevsner noted. The answers were provided mostly by young people with an interest in educational and artistic matters but, as Pevsner reminded us later, from a questionnaire on industrial products in the States it had been found that the answers from twenty-five students were up to 70 per cent identical with those from 390 people of mixed social status.[9] Frequent reference is made to this questionnaire in his stimulating and provocative report on *Industrial Art in England*, which was published in 1937.

Taste and the Expert

In that introduction, Pevsner attempts to answer the question how, from his personal judgment, he could state what is good and bad design. This is, as we have already seen, a question uppermost in the minds of many business people when asked to submit designs for selection by people outside the commercial world. Nikolaus Pevsner allowed that he was not infallible in his judgments on taste, but they might be taken 'as the conscientiously considered judgments of one who has tried to follow the ways of the Modern Movement in architecture, industrial art and the so-called fine arts on the Continent, and above all in Germany'. 'Slightly less subjective,' he continues,

> is another argument which, in fact, may settle the matter, so far as we need it settled. Anyone who has ever been present at the meetings of the jury for a big art exhibition of really live importance will have noticed that, if out of 5,000 objects sent in only 1,000 can

---

[8] Pevsner, *An Enquiry*, 5.

[9] Pevsner, *An Enquiry*, 5, 6. Quotes Dan Starch, *Principles of Advertising* (Chicago, IL., 1923), 299.

be shown, there will be 500 which, from the first examination, are accepted by all experts, at least so far as they belong to the war and post-war generations. There will be 3,000 at least, say 3,500, which hardly one of the jurors finds himself able to take seriously. The remaining 1,000 will be border cases, the cases where arguments arise and convictions clash. In a discussion on 3,000 objects of industrial art (e.g. the British Industries Fair) the procedure would certainly be the same. There would be, from the first, unanimity as to two thirds at least being out of the question, unanimity as to one tenth being definitely good or acceptable—provided again the jury consisted of experts, that is men who are keenly interested in living art and industrial design, have seriously attempted for some time to evolve a power of discrimination and are prepared to judge disinterestedly, objectively and conscientiously.[10]

Since this argument has been used by other critics of unquestionable integrity who, like Nikolaus Pevsner, are quite unaware that it is peculiarly fitted to uphold the prestige of certain artistic groups at the expense of others, it may be worthwhile pausing to examine whether it does, in fact, 'settle the matter so far as we need it settled'.

Firstly, if it is true that a proportion of articles submitted are accepted by all the experts, how explain the selections for the Exhibition of Industrial Art at Burlington House the following year? The latter, Pevsner held, was doomed from the beginning because, although the Executive Committee did not want to do so, 'it did in fact set up standards, of which ... it was impossible to approve'.[11] Secondly, how can we even start to examine this proposition unless we know how the jury is itself chosen, and by whom, or whether it simply chooses itself? Thirdly, would it not be possible to collect some useful facts as to the *actual* proportions unanimously rejected and accepted by certain specific selection committees, a job perhaps for the D.I.A. or some Department of Social Study of Human Relations? And lastly, why should this

---

[10] Pevsner, An Enquiry, 9, 10.
[11] Pevsner, An Enquiry, 168.

intangible something we call 'beauty', which at the last resort exists simply to give pleasure and satisfaction, be subject to the judgment of a unified central panel at all?

Strength through juries

Pevsner thought that the principle of rigid standards and selection should be extended. Even the ingenuous D.I.A. required 'strengthening' and 'renewing'.

> One means of improving its position would be the introduction of an entrance jury which would see to it that only men of real artistic conscience would be members. That would mean a quantitative loss for the moment, but one ought not to underestimate the amount of ambition and competition which might, by this device, be roused. It should become a desirable honour to belong to the D.I.A. and be allowed to use its initials, as was the case with the German *Werkbund* before the war.[12]

All this would lead quite naturally to the wished-for Dictatorship of Exhibitions. For it seemed, he thought,

> fundamentally wrong to entrust this work to vast committees, in an attempt to avoid personal standards. On the contrary, a muddled impression is bound to result unless the risk is taken of appointing one conscientious and distinguished expert belonging to the post-war generation (or, if that seems too dictatorial, a *directoire* of three), for the whole of the selection. ... The task of the organiser of an exhibition ... would be to act on his own standards ...'[13]

There should be set up, therefore, and ruthlessly maintained, 'a rigid standard of quality and of style'.[14]

Here, at the risk of wearisome repetition, we must point out the difference between, on the one hand, allowing several

---

[12] Pevsner, An Enquiry, 227.

[13] Pevsner, An Enquiry, 225.

[14] Pevsner, An Enquiry, 171.

designers each to furnish and decorate certain ensembles with the sole object of giving pleasure and presenting a purely personal point of view and, on the other, the setting up of an illusion that 'rigid standards' exist and that certain individuals have a monopoly in the capacity to recognise them.

The Zeitgeist

A glimpse of what these rigid standards might mean is afforded by Pevsner's doctrine of design in accordance with the Zeitgeist, which differed fundamentally from that of Eric Gill, in that Pevsner accepted mechanised production and all it implied. The reasoning went something like this: the Modern Movement had found a more genuine and complete expression in unadorned shapes and surfaces than in any kind of decoration and a new beauty of our century was suggested by 'the pure and clean-cut shape of a liner, an aeroplane, a racing car. Any decoration applied to them would be ludicrous. Hence most modern architects have almost renounced ornament, and consequently keep aloof from purely decorative work.' When they were asked to design a monumental entrance gate or bronze doors for a bank for which the customer wanted more decorative treatment —i.e. 'some elaborate design, not a piece of work whose effect lies in the pureness of proportion and the beauty of the material alone'—the architect either took refuge in some modified classical style or left it to one of the Guilds to design something that would satisfy the customer.[15]

To all of which one is entitled to ask, by way of reply, 'Why not?' Is not this argument a case of what Eric Newton calls 'assuming the truth of the very thing he wishes to prove— thereby arguing in a circle'?—an error into which, as Newton reminds us, Ruskin sometimes allowed himself to be drawn.[16]

---

[15] Pevsner, An Enquiry, 19.

[16] Eric Newton, The Meaning of Beauty (London: Longmans Green and Co, 1950), 40.

Although certain basic English qualities, of which on the whole he approved, might delay its adoption, Nikolaus Pevsner maintained that in the long run the 'modern style' he himself liked would be generally accepted because it was simple and rational. He held, quite rightly I believe, that this style would be characterised by 'mass qualities' and clearly adumbrated the design for rationing we find in 'utility goods'.

He may, however, have gone too far in assuming that it would be as devoid of ornament as the fast-travelling machine, when the human being may, for all we know, insist on furnishing his home in a way that does not remind him of these objects. On grounds of cost, too, 'mass qualities' may not always be in accordance with his particular conception of the 'modern style' since, as he points out, plain surfaces show up any blemish and are, therefore, sometimes actually more expensive to produce than decorated ones.

But in many ways we saw eye to eye. In practice he was not dogmatic but felt that 'modern purposes favour modern design, traditional purposes traditional design, and that the desire for a display of art favours bad design'.[17] Even though buying reproductions, he thought, means 'fleeing from contemporary life, and buying period pieces means destroying the market for good modern pieces ...',[18] he admitted freely that reproductions of eighteenth-century silverware were more pleasing to him than anything modern offered by many jewellers. They were so immaculate and simple that he did not see how anyone could improve on them.

Commercial aspects

'To plead for better design in manufactured wares,' Pevsner wrote, 'will remain a futile task, unless the commercial aspects of the problem, unpleasant as they may sometimes be, are

---

[17] Pevsner, An Enquiry, 94.
[18] Pevsner, An Enquiry, 229.

carefully taken into account.'[19] The keyword is 'unpleasant'; for however hard he may try, it is extremely difficult for a fine-arts man to accept the part played by the market in industrial design. Nikolaus Pevsner would agree, in theory, that the designing of an article depended upon teamwork but thought that designers should not allow 'their freedom of invention [to be] considerably restricted by suggestions from the sales departments and travellers, as to what competitors have successfully produced and merchants repeatedly demanded'.[20] There was no reason why the sales manager should not indicate to the designer which of the year's new models had been successful, but when he 'tries to indicate what ought to be done in the future, the result is, as a rule, aesthetically disastrous'.[21]

In my own experience, however, the real difficulty arises not so much from suggestions from the commercial sales staff—a wise designer will accept them readily—as when a director, manager or some outside consultant has strong convictions as to what is 'pure design' which differ from those of the head designer or the company's best customers.

Pevsner was completely in favour of the manufacturer himself, the managing director or the works manager acting as a creative designer, providing they were sufficiently interested, well educated and 'not devoid of inborn sensibility'. It rested with the manufacturer to improve the design value of his wares. It was his responsibility. 'He must realise the seriousness of the problem, must train his appreciation and deepen his consciousness of beauty in his house, in his office, in the articles of his personal wear and use.'[22]

The manufacturer and the retailer who say that they are proud of not having any taste, that they are ready to supply anything which is asked for, and that educating the public is no business of theirs,

19 Pevsner, An Enquiry, 4.
20 Pevsner, An Enquiry, 16, 17.
21 Pevsner, An Enquiry, 194.
22 Pevsner, An Enquiry, 196.

must be called public enemies plainly and bluntly. They must change their outlook, or sooner or later public enterprise will interfere and make life rather unpleasant for them.[23]

Moral responsibility

At that time, we both of us failed to realise that there are always to be found groups of people who are only too ready to interpret their own personal preferences as moral rectitude and are often the first to group themselves as candidates for backing by public enterprise. Once installed, the temptation to 'make life rather unpleasant' for those outside their own circle of producers is difficult to resist. Their excuse is that they are 'upholding moral responsibility'.

Even though there may be, as Sturge Moore suggested, a sort of parallel between 'artistic integrity' in the fine arts and conscience, it is, in fact, not the same thing as morals and truthfulness and very little to do with industrial design, which is, of necessity, riddled with compromise (sometimes called 'teamwork').

What this doctrine of moral responsibility might mean in practice is suggested by Nikolaus Pevsner's attitude towards imitation:

> In a cardboard travelling-case made to imitate alligator skin, in a Bakelite hairbrush made to imitate enamel—there is something dishonest. A pressed-glass bowl trying to look like crystal, a machine-made coal scuttle trying to look hand-beaten, machine-made mouldings on furniture, a tricky device to make an electric fire look like a flickering coke fire, a metal bedstead masquerading as wood—all that is immoral. So are sham materials and sham technique. And all that is showy, pompous, blatant design.[24]

He admitted that the principle could not be pushed to its

---

[23] Pevsner, *An Enquiry*, 231.
[24] Newton, *Meaning of Beauty*, 11.

extreme but it is precisely as a *principle*, divorced from actual examples, that the above pronouncement seems meaningless, if not mistaken.

I was reminded of Sturge Moore's words, already quoted, that 'Aesthetic mimicry does not aim at deception but glories in an avowed distance that makes its nearness miraculous.'[25] No one is taken in by the electric coal fire; people just like it that way. But how easy for a group interested in some other product and backed by 'public enterprise' to suppress this type of commodity in the name of 'moral responsibility'. That some designs are 'better' than others seems clear enough to me personally, but not because they conform to any moral principle. Yet the exclusive modern-minded designer, quoted by Pevsner, who talks about 'that wretched woman's-dressing-table mentality' shows enough intolerance to want to make life rather unpleasant for those who disagree with him.

But in moral condemnation, Pevsner's bark was worse than his bite. At the back of all this *vertu farouche* was much kindliness and common sense. He showed that he had, indeed, the right end of the stick when he wrote that,

> [i]t would be absurd to suggest to the producer that he ought to ruin himself for the community, but what one is justified in asking is that he should consider carefully and conscientiously how he can best obtain a balance between his business and his public duties.[26]

Perhaps, as a manufacturer, I should describe this balance somewhat differently. If the producer has no preferences in design, his job must be so loveless and unpleasant that he should either acquire some or find another occupation. If, on the other hand, he has strong tastes he should seek to interweave them with those of his customers, including, if necessary, the manifestations of 'that wretched woman's-dressing-table

---

25 Sturge Moore, *Armour for Aphrodite*, 46.
26 Pevsner, *An Enquiry*, 191.

mentality'. He should do it patiently, with a certain humility, and he will eventually enjoy it.

The 'superior' fine arts

Like Eric Gill, Nikolaus Pevsner harks back to an age when the painter was also a craftsman, an age when he was not 'brought up with the idea of the great message of free and independent art'. But 'since about 1800,' he tells us, 'the artist has begun to consider himself as a superior being to whom the ordinary person ought to look up. His task is to express his own infinitely important experiences and thoughts.' Manufacturers told him that they found 'it difficult to deal with painters or sculptors, or to have them about the factory, because they were unbusinesslike and touchy'. He thought that

> We still suffer badly from this morbid conception. The medieval painter was a craftsman. As such he would not have thought of objecting to the carrying out of orders. Holbein designed cups and ephemeral decorations, and he painted the sign for a schoolmaster as well as he painted his portraits. We may have gained much by this liberation of the artist which started during the Renaissance, but in the end this irresistible development has proved fatal. Without it we should not have had Rembrandt, but neither should we have had the unbearable oversupply of artists whom nobody wants and whose private feelings are totally uninteresting in a century such as this. And we should also not suffer from the equally disastrous lack of good designers ... . If the painter is not so great as to express with the utmost intensity and vitality the essence of his time, let him starve, unless he is willing to find his way back to serving the community.[27]

This is well expressed. Two comments suggest themselves, however. Firstly the great painter today is just as likely as not to starve even if he does express, 'with the utmost intensity and

---

[27] Pevsner, *An Enquiry*, 198.

vitality, the essence of his time'; and secondly he will certainly be unable to find his way back to serving the community unless he accepts, when called upon to do so, 'the wretched woman's-dressing-table mentality' and seeks to mingle his own creative notions therewith.

CHAPTER 13

FRANK PICK AND THE COUNCIL FOR ART AND INDUSTRY

Few people in the sphere of industrial design have commanded more respect than Frank Pick, Vice Chairman of the London Passenger Transport Board. To us members of the D.I.A. his influence on behalf of clean-looking and practical aids to transport seemed to be unprecedented, while his posters showed that, in pictorial art, he was reaching forward towards the experimental and exciting.

Whatever truth there may be in the story of the highly-placed person who, after an interview with Pick, was heard to mutter, 'Don't let that impeccable bus-driver darken my door again,' he made an impression of uncompromising integrity. His appearance was unforgettable. The poise and shape of his body, the regular features and clear blue eyes all suggested honesty, serious endeavour and strength.

Perhaps at times he felt the need to rationalise his own aesthetic preferences—for young artists, so I was told, often had to explain why they placed such an object here or such a colour there. But his own estimation of his achievements was modest. At one point in our correspondence I suggested sending round to members of the D.I.A. and others a questionnaire enquiring whether their interest in design was the result of family influence or whether some process akin to conversion had taken place. What, for instance, had set Pick in motion? He replied:

As to your last question, the answer is a simple one. Just before the outbreak of the last war I was turned on to deal with the advertising work of the old Underground Group of Companies and after many fumbling experiments arrived at some notion as to what poster advertising ought to be. Everyone seemed quite pleased with what I did and I really got a reputation which sprang out of nothing. When the D.I.A. was formed I was asked to join the original group and agreed. I then met Peach,[1] Stabler,[2] Heal, Troup,[3] Brewer,[4] Lethaby[5] and other exponents of design. All I know about the subject I picked up from them. This must have been about the year 1914/15. Since then I have kept a keen interest and concern in the job.

In a way, his job shielded him from experiencing just how far compromise is involved in the production and sale of 'designed' articles; for although he was responsible for the selection of much material in which appearance values counted, his role was generally comparable to that of an end-consumer. He was seldom in the position of a manufacturer or buyer for a shop, having to consider carefully the tastes of other people.

This, as we shall see, led to a form of behaviour common enough in others but at variance with his fundamentally humble disposition; for one of the most astonishing features of our subject is the tenacity with which people cling to the illusion that their preferences are the only ones that matter. Just as an individual suffering from some compulsive neurotic trend will shield himself from unpleasant truths, so will the design purist refuse to acknowledge that other peoples' preferences may be as valid as his own.

People who knew Pick as a young man speak of his simple and engaging manner, but when, in the early thirties, we first met, shades of the administrative prison-house were beginning to close in upon him. And yet he impressed all with whom he

---

[1] [Harry Peach (1874–1936), businessman and author. Set up Dryad Furniture. Co-founder of the Design and Industries Association.]

[2] [Harold Stabler (1872–1945), sculptor, metalworker, ceramic designer. Partner in the firm of Carter, Stabler and Adams. Leading member of the D.I.A.]

[3] [Francis W. Troup (1859–1941), architect.]

[4] [Cecil Claude Brewer (1871–1918), architect.]

[5] [William Richard Lethaby (1857–1931), architect and historian. Founder of the Central School of Arts and Crafts, 1896.]

came into contact as an enlightened man—a *good* man. His father and mother were religious and sectarian. Perhaps it was a certain Puritan strain which led him to pronounce moral judgments on aesthetic matters. The Puritan reacts differently from the man of the world to administrative heights.

Reforming the Royal College of Art

In 1933 the D.I.A., looking around for the most suitable point at which to apply pressure, decided to set about the Royal College of Art and in August submitted a memorandum to the Board of Education. A deputation, subsequently invited to discuss the proposals contained therein, was first rehearsed by Frank Pick in his office and then taken round to Whitehall.

Anticipating by three years the Hambleden Report, we declared that the tuition at the Royal College—originally founded as a school of industrial design—was 'characterised by a bias towards the fine arts and a divorce from industry, which is equally a divorce from the needs of the time'. There was no provision, we argued, for adequate instruction of industrial design—which has its own problems of technique and aesthetics —by any national institution of university status.[6]

The pernicious theme of centralisation, introduced by the Gorell Committee, was restated; it was nevertheless recognised that there would necessarily be a textile branch of the college in Manchester, metal-working branches in Birmingham and Sheffield and a pottery branch in Stoke-on-Trent. 'But these branches must not be allowed to develop into wholly autonomous institutions. They should remain subject to the control of the Royal College of Art, to the extent that may be requisite to ensure a common standard of attainment and efficiency, etc.'

Frank Pick said that if we were to keep pace with foreign

---

[6] [Following the D.I.A.'s Memorandum, William Rothenstein, then director of the Royal College of Art, was interviewed by the Board of Education and offered his resignation.]

competitors, it was imperative to effect an improvement in British industrial design which, according to the D.I.A., was in a very unhealthy condition.

The other members of the deputation told the same story and my own evidence, delivered somewhat haltingly, worked on the need for properly equipped workshops in all colleges. 'In this country,' I said, 'draughtsmen were encouraged to look on the production of a design on paper as an end in itself, not as a means to an end.'

Later, at Pick's request, I prepared a scheme for a designers' workshop class in 'metal products from the mould (i.e. stampings, castings, etc.), setting out the plant and machinery, the workshop exercises and the examples of practical factors which would be brought out in the workshop course'.

Frank Pick's Council

The Council for Art and Industry was appointed by the Board of Trade in January 1934 under the chairmanship of Frank Pick. It had 'to deal with questions affecting the relations between Art and Industry' and 'to enquire generally into the subject of Design in Industry, with particular reference to the recruitment, training and position of designers'.

The Council did not try to push any particular style or claim sufficient expertise to 'maintain high and uniform standards'. It was not an artistic sect but above all a committee of enquiry, collecting facts and opinions from a wide number of sources, examining witnesses and sending out questionnaires. Some of its investigations, however, were frustrated through vagueness as to words and meanings. There was a strange lack of specific examples, so that questioner and questioned must often have been at cross purposes.

Consider, for instance, the following example from the Questionnaire to the Buyers' Association: 'Are British manufacturers in your lines designing their products generally *as well as*—*better than*—or *worse than* their foreign competitors?' Is it not almost certain that different standards would be used by different participants?

But the Council did at least keep in touch with all sorts of people—manufacturers, designers, teachers—up and down the country and acted as a clearing house for information. In 1937 it published a report of its investigations under the title *Design and the Designer in Industry*, from which certain extracts are given below. It contained much sound material although the recommendations took the form of ultimate ends and broad objectives rather than the means whereby they were to be attained.

The designer and market requirements

The Council assumed that managers were often 'unversed in the considerations of taste which should enter into a choice between designs'.[7] Its outlook was nevertheless commercially realistic, in the sense that designers were urged not to lose sight of the 'economic factor—the necessity for producing an article at a price and of a kind which will command a ready sale in the market for which it is intended'.[8] It was argued that 'fashion is a dominant factor in design, and the field of fashion is extending from short-lived articles, such as dress, to articles of a longer duration of life ... . The result is that fertility of design is now more necessary than before.'[9] Training of students, therefore, 'should be very definitely related to realities and should have a direct bearing on the student's work in the factory'.[10]

Witnesses brought out only too clearly the difficulty which arises through confusing ideals appropriate to the fine arts with those indispensable for industrial design. 'An artist will seldom

---

7 Council for Art and Industry, *Design and the Designer*, 11.

8 Council for Art and Industry, *Design and the Designer*, 8.

9 Council for Art and Industry, *Design and the Designer*, 10.

10 Council for Art and Industry, *Design and the Designer in Industry* (London: Board of Trade, H.M.S.O., 1944), 34.

become a successful designer. He will have his own individual conception of what is good or bad in art, and that will make it very difficult to subdue his mind to the requirements of those who are employing him.[11]

Inbreeding

Conditions fostered a 'process of inbreeding'. In the schools of art, a substantial number of students were 'pursuing their training with a view to taking up teaching in secondary and art schools'.[12] As for industry, many copyists, adaptors and setters-out were needed and the limited number of new lines which a particular firm could profitably place on the market often did not justify the continuous employment of a highly-trained designer producing a steady stream of fresh designs.

Employers finding that art-school work had little bearing on commercial conditions 'relied on the chance that sufficient creative talent would emerge from a personnel that had received no more than an elementary school education'.[13] For the rest, if the head designer was a man of limited outlook, he might well thwart his subordinates and destroy their initiative.

The Council failed, however, to mention another important factor which works against experiment and in favour of the status quo. A gifted head designer will invariably impress his personal style on the products of his company, which will return the favour by offering him security of tenure. There was much talk at this time of raising the status of the designer, but no one seems to have noted that such security might also hinder the inflow of new blood which, so it was argued, was much needed. That the freelance designer did not provide an altogether satisfactory solution of the problem will be seen later.

---

[11] Council for Art and Industry, *Design and the Designer*, 15.
[12] Council for Art and Industry, *Design and the Designer*, 35.
[13] Council for Art and Industry, *Design and the Designer*, 16.

Centralisation

'The regrettable tendency for all young artists to gravitate to London' mentioned in Chapter 7 also aroused comment in the Report:

> It might reasonably be supposed that an industrial student brought up, for example, in the textile industry, who wins a scholarship to take him to the Royal College of Art, would be likely to return to his place of origin and play a useful part as a designer for the industry and as a part-time teacher in the local art school or college. In practice, however, this has seldom happened, and it is hoped that openings will now be found in industry which will induce such young people to return to the industry and render it valuable service.[14]

Attention was thus focussed on supposed shortcomings in industry—much of it, by inference, provincial industry—but the idea that a new outlook was needed at the Centre never seems to have occurred to the drafters of the report. The Council favoured taking from foreign capitals their exclusive markets in designs. It was not realised, however, that a similar distribution of skills and influences, as between the Metropolis and provincial centres might also release latent creative ability within the home country.

An investigation

In 1937, by the same process of accretion as we have already noted, my name came to be included amongst the Council personnel. I was almost immediately asked to investigate conditions in the Light Metal Trades of the Midlands and to use the Main Report as a guide.

Pick told me that design in the small quasi-domestic factory had not till then been touched. So, helped and guided by Philip

---

[14] Council for Art and Industry, *Design and the Designer*, 42.

Sargant Florence of Birmingham University, some members of the D.I.A. and others formed a committee of enquiry centred on Birmingham.

The multifarious range of articles made it difficult to know where to start. Hearth and door furniture, light fittings and electric fires, spun hollow-ware and shop fittings were only some of the many commodities to be considered; and as for materials, brass, rustless steel, aluminium, glass, wood, plastics and in fact almost any substance was being used for many of the articles. The term 'Light Metals', however, was adopted for want of a better.

Birmingham is a city of small employers who could hardly be expected to attend meetings in order to give evidence. A full-time investigator, Richard Padley, B.Com., was therefore appointed to carry out fieldwork while the committee received such material as was available and prepared its own report. Padley's contribution was unusual if not unique in its frankness and the nature of the facts that it brought to light.

Padley made it clear that whoever proposed to mix himself with designing for the Light Metal Trades would have to be pretty adaptable, for few firms were content with a single product, and 'the logic which determines a businessman in the choice of a subsidiary product was often hard to find.' One manufacturer combined hearth furniture, beauty boxes and picnic outfits, while another added table lamps and shop-window display stands to the first product; yet a third made picnic outfits, watering cans and 'Brighter Kitchen Ware'.

Methodical designing

There were two main classes of business to be examined, namely, those which employed a full-time designer and those which did not.

Amongst the first category were firms making architectural metalwork, shop fittings, name plates, light fittings, slot machines etc. The nature of these trades made proper working drawings indispensable. The design process was initiated by a potential user, often through the intermediary of an architect whose influence, according to Padley, was on the whole beneficial.

The position, however, 'was not ideal,' he said, 'since a designer may be compelled to pander to individual foibles, one designer of shopfronts confessing that he kept careful check on architects' whims and "if a man likes a bit of Spanish then I give him a bit of Spanish."'[15]

Here we may pause and ask ourselves whether an important part of the designer's job does not consist of just this 'pandering', the term being generally only used by someone who does not happen to like a design in question. Otherwise the same process is called 'conforming to a high standard, which should be rigidly maintained'.

How, by promoting copying with distortion, the influence of the architect was not always helpful is described later in this chapter.

Haphazard designing

As for the second category—the firms employing no full-time designer—their designs, as Padley put it, were 'allowed to develop after the fashion of Topsy'.[16] In theory the method was sound enough. 'The process of creation begins with accumulations; so a bird builds a nest or feeds its young,' said Sturge Moore. It was usual, in industry, for many birds to take a hand in building the nest.

The stages of development were generally as follows: First a rough sketch was made, generally by a director after receiving a tip from one of the travellers. It would then be given to the head toolmaker or a foreman who would make a model. This would then be criticised and possibly modified. Who criticised it

---

[15] R.D. Best, 'Design and the Designer', 30.
[16] R.D. Best, 'Design and the Designer', 31.

depended upon circumstances; perhaps it would be taken home by a director who would ask his wife to use the article and comment or it might be left on the manager's desk for a few days in the hope that visitors would provide some useful suggestions for its improvement.

New designs were not, as a rule, produced regularly, or according to a definite schedule, but 'from time to time', 'when anyone had a brainwave' or 'whenever trade got a bit slack'. Certain firms, however, made a point of preparing new lines for the British Industries Fair. In some trades many designs were anything up to 50 years old, the most successful being often copied from foreign countries or the result of customers' ideas.

The freelance

Sometimes a firm in the 'Haphazard Design' category would employ a designer-modeller but the consequences were generally unsatisfactory. Not enough new designs were required annually to absorb his output. The obvious course of engaging a part-time consultant or freelance designer had also been tried but with disappointing results. An aluminium manufacturer, for instance, hearing an eminent designer of international reputation speak over the wireless, forthwith employed him, but refused to modify his design when asked to do so: the tools were very expensive and the price too high. The manufacturer summed up his experience in the words: 'Good design doesn't pay and it's a damned shame.'[17]

There were, however, exceptional cases. One very large manufactury had continued to work with outside designers even though, at first, these individuals 'didn't know how the metal could be put together', and their designs, 'while looking well on paper, proved less attractive when seen in the round'. The firm persevered because new ideas from within seemed nearing exhaustion and while, at the time of these investigations, they

---

[17] R.D. Best, 'Design and the Designer', 18.

had not yet had 'a bestseller designed in this way, they had had several quite satisfactory lines.'[18]

Those who wish to 'improve' British design should concentrate on the problem of the part-time designer. On its solution, as distant now as in 1937, depends more than anything else the ennoblement of design amongst the smaller firms. But it must be approached in a realistic mood. Personal preferences regarding style must be put in their proper place.

Pretty drawings

While Richard Padley was out in the field, the Light Metals Committee was probing into local methods of teaching. The crusade for 'workshop-laboratories' initiated by the D.I.A. entered into a more positive phase. In a memorable paragraph, the Committee expressed its distrust of mere pencil and paint brush:

> A saying sometimes used by architects is that such and such a design 'drips drawing board', meaning that the designer has shown more interest in pictorial effects than the happy solution of practical and structural problems. This is the great danger of all art instruction related to industry. Attention of the students is distracted from the all-important idea of the solution of practical and structural problems, because they cannot, through lack of technical knowledge, be even aware at what points these problems exist. An experienced technician would ring round in red pencil passages of their excellent drawings and point out that at this point they were seeking to solve some problem which had occupied the attention of designers in the trade for years. The knuckle or universal joint, the hinge, devices for securing glass etc. would then be discussed and particulars of cost and processes given.[19]

Nothing could be more frustrating to the student than the

---

[18] R.D. Best, 'Design and the Designer', 8.
[19] R.D. Best, 'Design and the Designer', 46.

production of design after design on paper without seeing any of them actually made. It was like marriage minus consummation. And yet this was the unhappy lot of most students at that time. Furthermore, without contact with the workshop, they were deprived of the powerful stimulus to the imagination of seeing the processes in operation and were thus never taught to design for the machine or process, or to find what machine would suit the design.

Obviously, to provide this practical experience, the workshops of the school itself needed development and this in the intervening years has slowly taken place. The workshops were then good enough for models and mock-ups, but what was also needed was a group of public-spirited manufacturers willing to allow students to have the run of their factories; the young designers might then either see their designs made up or actually help to produce them with their own hands. Such a group would also popularise the school and keep it abreast of the times.

Unfortunately the diversity of trades 'made it difficult to procure cohesion amongst employers in their relation with it'. During 1944, however, after full discussions with manufacturers and trade unions, an Advisory Committee, under the Local Authority, was formed for the Light Metal Trades. Since then a number of firms have opened their factories to students for about a month each year.

One day, in conversation, Frank Pick was speculating as to how much effect his Council was actually making—whether institutions like the Birmingham College of Art, for instance, would alter in any way as a result of his reports. Had he lived, he would have had the satisfaction of knowing that in one corner, at any rate, his work had born fruit.

Team work and conflict

Pick's Council had agreed that 'the creation of ideas is not the exclusive possession of any one person. It is the combined endeavour of a group or team of people each experienced in a particular branch, working together, who influence the producer. The manufacturer, the designer, the engraver, the colourist, the stylist and the research chemist all play their part.'[20] It remained for the Light Metals Committee to emphasise that

> the specialists in the team often have conflicting interests and there may be tension between them. The drawing office tends to consider appearance values, whereas the works staff may be concerned with ease of production, while the sales staff are demanding appearance and cheapness—value for money—and the cost office is continually brought into play to indicate how changes in design affect cost. Good industrial design depends on the solution of these conflicts.[21]

But being associated with 'skimping', 'cheeseparing', 'designing at so much an ounce' etc., instruction in costing tended to be resisted by some art-school teachers, one of whom, in his evidence, declared that 'an imaginative designer has not the patience nor the inclination as a general rule to think in terms of rows of figures,'[22] whereas, in fact, exactly the opposite is the case. A good industrial designer cannot start to use his imagination without questions of time, weights and values beginning to cross his mind.

In short, the best teaching of industrial design will reproduce, for the benefit of the student, the field of force we described in the first chapter of this essay.

How were they used?

The Council for Art and Industry immersed itself deeply in the study of museums and exhibitions, some of which appear to have been used by designers scarcely at all. Possibly there was insufficient participation by industrial people in the selection

---

[20] R.D. Best, 'Design and the Designer', 40.
[21] R.D. Best, 'Design and the Designer', 47.
[22] R.D. Best, 'Design and the Designer', 42,

and administrative policy of these institutions. Two witnesses, speaking on behalf of the Federation of British Industries (F.B.I.), suggested that it was important to get the enthusiasm of the various industries in a museum. Say to them 'This is your show; make a success of it.'[23] On the other hand, even when designers used what they saw, it seemed to me that scant attention was given by the Council to what exactly happened in the workshop and the drawing office as a result.

From New York came the news that three years after the Exhibition of Machine Art—held in the Museum of Modern Art (M.O.M.A.) in 1934—few objects worthy of inclusion in the permanent collection had appeared. In many instances manufacturers had merely altered and sometimes debased existing designs. This did not surprise me. Possibly their customers did not want 'Machine Art' of the kind which was displayed.

The Paris Exhibition of 1925 produced some major changes. Just how they affected my own company, I have attempted to describe in an earlier chapter. The complaint of a witness that exhibitions and museums 'were often used for copying rather than inspiration' would not mean much to the experienced professional. If frank, he would say that a large proportion of new lines were a form of copying. Talk to him of inspiration and he would probably have told you to 'come off it!'. As Sturge Moore said, 'All Art is derivative.'

During the between-war years, the number of designers sufficiently fresh and original to influence fashion was small; the Paris Exhibition of 1937 seemed to manifest a sort of levelling-up process, be it copying or inspiration, so that there was a certain similarity between the interior decoration of countries as far apart as Czechoslovakia and Japan. There was, furthermore, a queue of manufacturers furtively sketching the fittings in the Lighting Section. Bearing these considerations in mind, I suggested to the Council that more attention be given to the

---

[23] Evidence given to the Council for Art and Industry, 9 March, 1937.

derivative processes behind most commercial design. What could be done, I asked, to make the best of them, such as they were?

The anatomy of copying

The whole question was later taken up by the Light Metals Committee, which eventually reported that distortion was actually fostered by the existing obstacles to direct copying. Design registration gave little protection against the predatory manufacturer who was nevertheless reluctant to make accurate reproduction of a coveted design because

    (a) he wished to produce 'something different', to screen himself from competition;

    (b) he felt that one day the roles might be reversed and such designs as he himself originated might be purloined by the firm he had offended; and

    (c) the buyer to whom he offered an obvious copy was inclined to be critical and to rally him on his lack of creative ability.

'These and other unofficial sanctions,' the Report suggested, 'have far more effect than is generally realised in preserving the original designers' property. Thus it comes about that the copying, which is all too prevalent, is generally accompanied by some greater or lesser alteration from the original model. The original may be fresh and happy in its appeal but the alterations are often made by unskilled adaptors of undeveloped taste when the results are likely to be of the nature of a "Rake's Progress".'[24]

The influence of the architect on design was, as we have seen, generally beneficial. But in one respect this Rake's Progress was actually encouraged by those who would circulate a schedule of scale sketches taken from the catalogues of different firms and invite competitive tenders therefrom. A manufacturer might thus find himself asked to make a near copy of a rival product. What an opportunity missed! The procedure might have had

[24] R.D. Best, 'Design and the Designer', 51.

excellent results if the designs had really been made in the architect's office by some gifted and technically skilful designer.

In 1945 the matter was taken up by the F.B.I.'s Industrial Art Committee, but manufacturers did not want their names disclosed and had lost examples during the war years; the architectural bodies were reluctant to admit that anything was wrong and the question still remains open.

Parish goods

Copying, however, was not always of this undesirable kind. There were many cases where, by tacit agreement, an article might be 'copied straight', i.e. without any attempt to distort or alter the original design until it had been taken up by a whole trade. The opal glass sphere for lighting—satisfactory in use and too simple to modify without spoiling the effect—has already been noted as a case in point. According to Richard Padley, in aluminium hollow-ware many an article, and in door and window furniture about half the trade, was of 'parish designs'.

It occurred to members of the committee that if certain steps were taken, these conditions might be turned to good account. Obviously there were conflicting aims to be faced. Socially, the more a first-class design (such as, for instance, the opal sphere) was copied in its original form, the better, especially where there was a large number of small factories unable to afford highly-paid designers. To foster 'parish goods'—standardised and of good design—seemed a worthy aim; but on the other hand, unless suitably safeguarded, the designer tended to lose by such an arrangement. Was there any way to get the best of both worlds?

Free prototypes

The Light Metals Committee suggested that the Architectural Association, Royal Institute of British Architects and other organisations might well organise special competitions, the terms of which should be:

1. Prizes on such a scale as would attract the most gifted designers;
2. Winning designs to be available for exact copying by a trade and for use by architects in their broadcast schemes, a small charge to be made for blueprints and models; and
3. Unsuccessful designs not to be exhibited but to remain the property of the designer in order to avoid the risk of copying without payment.

Such a procedure, it was felt, 'would discourage hole-and-corner copying ... and would provide the manufacturer with some solid substance to reproduce honestly and openly'.[25]

Although the Utility scheme[26] had not then been tried, there was nothing new in principle about these proposals. As Francis Meynell pointed out in a letter to the *Times* some years later, pattern books for furniture had been widely circulated among cabinet makers in the eighteenth and nineteenth centuries. Chippendale and Sheraton produced such books. 'But there are even more august precedents,' he continued. 'Sixteenth-century artificers in every craft had their eyes and their mind's eyes filled not with original patterns but with lessons they learnt in the arabesque pattern-books which then abounded. I know of thirteen such books published in Italy, France and Germany between 1525 and 1535.'

The Royal Society of Arts, in its earliest years, had awarded premiums for objects in connection with 'arts, manufactures and commerce' and in 1760 decided to buy all the prize-winning models. In 1937 it was reported to Pick's Council that the R.S.A. was considering reviving competitions in industrial design.

Some of the specifications of the British Standards Institute covered objects such as wood-mouldings, shop signs, etc., the design of which was determined partly by considerations of appearance. There were, furthermore, other designs, such as the

---

[25] R.D. Best, 'Design and the Designer', 56.
[26] The Utility Furniture Scheme was introduced during the Second World War to encourage designs that accommodated shortages and rationing of raw material. The scheme lasted until 1952.

Coronation mug, which had been put at the disposal of a whole trade for manufacture.

Three years after the completion of the Light Metals Report the Birmingham D.I.A. decided to push the whole question into the open and in October 1943 organised a conference in London to discuss 'National Designs'. But the Utility Furniture Scheme and the wartime growth of state control had created some prejudice in the minds of the members of trade and professional associations attending. Antagonism was aroused by the very word 'standardisation'.

From the discussion it seemed as if the D.I.A. had lost some of the revolutionary zeal of its earlier days. The conference nevertheless agreed that it would be a good thing to make available certain standard designs 'of the highest order which could be copied without distortion' and that after further enquiries another meeting should take place.

No such meeting was ever held. An investigation by the F.B.I. Industrial Art Committee indicated considerable difference of opinion. It was true that the Leather Industry had held a competition and made the prize design available to the trade; the general feeling, however, was that individual designing should not be restricted in any way. Where industries were to be covered by Working Parties, perhaps something could be done to get 'National Designs' introduced, in which case some degree of inspection and perhaps the use of a national mark would be required. The name seemed to create prejudice and it was suggested that 'Free Prototypes' might be a better term.

All this information was passed on to the D.I.A. in order that another conference might be considered but the Association showed no enthusiasm for this particular form of 'design for use' and the matter was quietly dropped.

Plain or fancy?

Underlying the opposition to 'Free Prototypes' so bound up, apparently, with the fear of state interference were three factors which never came to the surface in these discussions. Firstly, it seems probable that many small manufacturers associated these standard designs, wrongly perhaps, with plain, antiseptic shapes, whereas their factories were more suited to the production of decorative products.

Secondly, as Richard Padley pointed out, 'In attempting to escape from the pressure of his competitors each manufacturer attempts to build up his own little monopoly. The frequent introduction of new patterns is one of the principal means whereby he does this.'[27]

Lastly, to quote Norman MacKenzie, writing of furniture, 'the public and the retailers alike demand variety and where designs are changed frequently, the small firm … can compete with the large one; it may actually enjoy certain advantages.'[28] These conditions apply equally to the metal trades.

The Light Metals Committee allowed that humour and even sentiment had their place in design, if not overdone. The members felt however that these qualities frequently found expression inappropriately. They were pained by 'the large output of articles in the shape of animals, such as comic dogs, cats, etc'[29] but thought it probable that wrought work and intricate detail in certain articles would be demanded for many years. They were not in a position to say that the 'plain' was invariably to be valued above the 'fancy' but were positive that it was much harder to design good 'fancy' than 'plain'—though what reason they had for reaching this conclusion was not made clear.

The National Register of Designers

Pick and his followers believed that to raise design standards, the status of the designer should be improved. The Light Metals

---

[27] R.D. Best, 'Design and the Designer', 6.
[28] Norman MacKenzie ,'Furniture and its Makers', *New Statesman and Nation*, 15 July, 1950.
[29] R.D. Best, 'Design and the Designer', 51.

Committee acknowledged that it should be 'equal to those in parallel executive positions, [such as the] works or sales manager', but could see no reason why it should be superior.[30]

A National Register of Designers was founded in 1936, its objectives being: firstly, to establish a status for the industrial designer identified by the initials N.R.D., awarded on a selective basis; secondly, to keep a record of designers, their qualifications and examples of their work; and thirdly, to introduce designers to industry. There was to be no limit to the membership and, unlike the D.I.A., the members were not being banded together to push any particular artistic theory. In February 1937 a Treasury grant towards the expense of office work was obtained.

To the student of group relations the Governing Body presented interesting features. It was nominated by

(a) Pick's Council,
(b) Art societies to represent Design, and
(c) Trade associations.[31]

Such an arrangement was admirably suited to the early stages of an association but to bring it to life, some form of regional grouping and representation was, sooner or later, absolutely essential. This indispensable condition was never fulfilled.

The government grant was severely cut at the outbreak of war in 1939 and was subsequently withdrawn. In February 1946 the members, many of whom had been paying a subscription for some years, received a circular starting with the stereotyped passive verb 'IT HAS BEEN DECIDED TO ...' In spite of this ambiguity as to just who had taken the decision, the Register was to be closed down. Conditions, it seemed, had changed. A new Council, the Council of Industrial Design (CoID), had been formed and a time had come for the liquidation of the National

---

[30] R.D. Best, 'Design and the Designer', 55.

[31] 'The National Register of Industrial Art Designers': Particulars of Registration and Bye-Laws.

Register, whose members soon found that its functions had been taken over by the Society of Industrial Artists.

The Royal Designers for Industry

In 1937 the Royal Society of Arts came forward with proposals for conferring on certain persons who had 'attained high eminence and efficiency in creative design for Industry' the title, 'Designer for Industry of the Royal Society of Arts.' Then, by a curious transposition, the word 'Royal' was brought to the front and the appellation became 'Royal Designer for Industry' (R.D.I.).

Following the example of the Royal Academy, the so-called Faculty of Royal Designers was to be limited to 40. The first list of awards was drawn up by a committee of the Royal Society of Arts but later, as almost invariably happens in academies and artistic coteries, it became the practice for nominations to originate with existing holders of the distinction.

From the first, the Royal Designers were, so to speak, imposed from above on their competitors. There was never any consultation with professional or trade associations as to whether so-and-so was acceptable or whether it was agreed that he was so far above his colleagues as to merit any advertising value suggested by the word 'Royal', with its implications of royal warrants and what not. When discussed by Pick's Council it was suggested that the initials might be misunderstood but eventually it was agreed that no objection need be taken to the use of the letters 'R.D.I.' and the proposals were approved.

Frank Pick argued that as the Council was constituted to promote industrial art, it ought to try to secure that the recognition of industrial artists should be as handsome as possible and comparable with that for Fine Art; but the logic of his reasoning now seems somewhat shaky. The phrase 'recognition of industrial artists' was ambiguous, if not misleading. There was no question of general recognition of a profession, but of one or two in each trade. If the distinction was to be of any value, then the others would be that much worse off in competition. And as for the suggestion that this recognition should be comparable with that for Fine Art, one wonders why no one pointed a warning finger at the Royal Academy.

Many fine designers and artists have become members of this R.D.I. faculty but what effect it had on those who did not should have been a matter for independent investigation. As I write this, I expect that the situation may in due course become fossilised, as in the case of the Royal Academy.

Discussion methods

At this point the reader may be tempted to ask how it came about that no one, especially the present writer, protested when these proposals were put before the Council. At the time I saw nothing much amiss. During the last war, however, many people, myself included, began to revise their notions regarding 'dynamic' administration, joint consultation, group relations and so forth, and began to perceive the close parallel between the reluctance of the authoritarian boss to share responsibility with his employees and the tendency, in ostensibly 'democratic' associations, to keep the real decisions in the hands of a well-entrenched minority—often the chairman and secretary.

It is doubtful whether such a conception ever occurred to my colleagues on the Council. If any felt inclined to question the Royal Society of Arts' proposals they were probably restrained by reluctance to criticise people they liked and respected. This, at any rate, is a powerful reason why many important issues are covered up. Frank Pick was a 'man of goodwill' in the sense that he wished to help his fellow human beings to achieve greater happiness and deeper satisfaction. As chairman of the Council for Art and Industry he took decisions and conducted affairs according to the most enlightened standards of that time. Had he lived he might have changed his outlook; but in 1937 there seemed nothing contrary to his integrity in obviously manipulating a committee.

Once, somewhat ingenuously, he told me how he would

place same interesting working model upon the table around which the members of some board or committee were to sit. They could not resist the temptation to fiddle with it and while their attention was thus diverted he would get through the agenda in the way he wanted. To those who think that the best committee is a committee of one, such methods will seem commendable, but others who realise that purposeful discussion by small groups is our only safeguard against the *Führerprinzip* will recoil in horror from the implications of such behaviour.

Stresses and strains

Sometimes there would be scenes. A certain member of the Council persisted in criticising until one morning there was a flare-up. The Chairman considered that he had overstepped the mark and threatened to resign. The rebel apologised but I never saw him at any further meetings. 'How very rough and tactless Pick was with ____,' I noted in my diary.

There were other incidents. I was involved in one and accordingly I wrote to him as follows:

> I would like you some time to enlighten me as to the functions of the councillors in relation to their chairman. It does seem strange that a major point of policy, such as ____ and ____ should not, at any rate, be put to the vote. It is a fact that there was a division of opinion on each of these points. The minutes do not describe the transactions of the Council fully [and] the fact that there was some opposition to the final decision regarding ____ does not appear at all.

Frank Pick replied:

> I am afraid you find me a difficult chairman. I am sorry. I cannot remember an instance where the Council has taken a specific vote. After all, is it necessary to record the fact that we are not wholly at one in putting forward our reports? Does it serve any useful purpose? ... As soon as I am clear the way the great balance of opinion lies I let the matter drop as not one for discussion usefully much further.

What you say with regard to minutes is more serious because the minutes should be a record of what takes place at the Council meeting. I will endeavour to get the minutes a little more accurate … . I am sorry to be a bother to you.

By contemporary standards Pick was undoubtedly a good—some thought an ideal—chairman. In refusing to create a situation in which one side is forced to vote the other down, he was only acting according to common sense and the most enlightened principles of administration. But there is another use for the show of hands. The so-called 'straw vote' does, at any rate, indicate what is the actual balance of opinion and yet commits the group to no specific action. Unfortunately, otherwise good chairmen all too frequently depend on their intuition to interpret 'the feeling of a meeting'.

Frank Pick's crusade for purity

The Council, as we have seen, existed for investigation and did not seek to set up standards or promote any particular style. These terms of reference, however, did not prevent Pick from trying to rally the members in a crusade to suppress an artistic idiom of which he disapproved.

It happened this way. In 1938, seriously objecting to some of the students' work at the Royal College exhibition that year, he circulated the Council 'with a view to representation that the aim and character of the teaching in the Royal College of Art in relation to commercial and industrial design should be changed before the present perverse tendencies spread and deterioration sets in in the provincial art schools'. He even wrote to the then President of the Board of Education on the theme of freedom and licence, suggesting that some of the work indicated

a mind ill-principled and diseased, without a clean and healthy content … . The splendours that there are, seem to be irridescent splendours that flow from a decay in manners and morals.

This invitation to join in a crusade for purity was firmly declined. Sir Eric Maclagan, Director of the Victoria and Albert Museum and a member of the Council, could not regard the attack as in any way justified. He had been astonished by the freshness of the work. It was 'arresting and original' and showed 'just those qualities for which there is the greatest demand in the artistic side of industry today' ... 'The illustrations,' he continued, 'were admittedly in the manner which is now popular; but it is no use hoping that students will get commissions from publishers if they work in the style which was admired when we were undergraduates and which I still find more congenial.'

To Pick's charges of indiscipline, slovenliness and moral decadence the Royal College Council replied by quoting from other 'experts', 'with whose names none of the decadent tendencies referred to could possibly be associated'. These disagreed completely with Pick and pronounced the general standard to be of great excellence.

Unfortunately there are still leaders of design groups who pretend that there is unanimity amongst the experts as to what is 'good' and what 'bad' design. But why Frank Pick, who had been so docile, if not aesthetically humble, should have allowed himself to give this exhibition of ill-judged dogma, Lord Acton only knows.[32]

Leave-taking

I met Pick for the last time in March 1939 at the annual dinner of the Birmingham D.I.A. He spoke about the craftsman and the machine. When a design originated in the mind of the former it became perfected and traditional. It borrowed life from its maker and civilisation entered. But when the machine takes over, copies and multiplies it, humanity goes out and 'mechanisticism' comes in. The design becomes dull, blunted or

---

[32] [R.D.B. is referring again to Lord Acton's comment about the tendency of power to corrupt. See page 133.]

warped to suit the machine or it is hardened, sharpened, straightened, because these are qualities the machine can give. We design for machines less frequently than we copy for them.

There was, Pick said, a divorce between mind and skill. Mind comes out of the art school; skill from the technical school. Mind was the designer, skill the works manager, and they were not brought up to understand each other. He wondered how many Birmingham manufacturers would have the courage to decorate the facades of their factories with the queer bevy of creatures—typical of modern business—that had replaced the nine muses: Cheapness, Big Sales, Success, Fashion, Sham, Quick Returns, Output, Turnover and Profit.

'The cure for all this cannot be taught,' he said.

> We could teach processes and methods. Show attainments and achievements. Try out materials. Experiment in construction. Play with colour and vary forms. And out of all these, *designs* would come —if we offered the opportunity, ordered the environment, changed the conditions—and hoped …

We continued to exchange letters until shortly before his death in 1941. The Report of the Light Metals Committee was completed in the spring of 1940. Pick was pleased and 'had been educated by the perusal of it'. He thought that the answers to our problem of design in the small firm were either a combination of jobs in the hands of one man or the provision of some pool of designers for the whole of the small manufacturers. He did not think the Birmingham College of Art could provide what was wanted. 'They need some more-easily secured and probably cheaper assistance, so that they will be able to improve design.'

In June, he wrote, 'I am now living in exile, having retired from London Transport. I am without any influence or authority of any sort … . I seem suddenly to have gone out of life.' Shortly after, however, he was on the move again with dock inspection. In October he wrote from the Ministry of Information that art and industry had receded into the background.

Design for utility and economic planning seem to appeal to

the same sort of mind and it is not surprising that many D.I.A. members flirted with mildly socialistic notions. I turned to Pick regarding the 1941 Committee.[33] He replied that politically he was a nonentity and had therefore no advice to offer. I nevertheless asked for his views on some questions I had put forward in an article in the *New Statesman and Nation* called 'A Manufacturer Wants to Know' and later expanded as a pamphlet. What did he think of the London Passenger Transport Board as a prototype of nationalised industry to be adopted in other fields? He replied:

> Herbert Morrison wrote a book on the L.P.T.B. which was cleverly done to show that the credit mainly belonged to the Labour Party. It is however fair and accurate ... . My experience of controls is that they are clumsy and expensive. The war technique will not do for peace and the task of devising an efficient economic control has still to be tackled. The Soviet seems the nearest venture so far! But the Soviet has gone wrong and deserted its first fine principles. Your pamphlet is excellent but bring it right home and answer all your problems ... . You have made me think, but you only can give the answers. [September 1941]

This was the last letter I received from him. He was 'up to his neck in an address on re-energising religion' but could not quite frame his views as he wanted and 'doubted whether it was worth printing'. It seemed to him an ephemeral effort. 'I may make a serious job of it later but it is a bit outside my experience,' he wrote.

To many of us members of the D.I.A. he was a father-confessor—a little austere perhaps—and a friend. We all looked up to him as a leader. 'If we had to have a dictator in England,' said Harold Stabler, 'I should like it to be Frank Pick.' Since his death others have tried to wear his mantle but the results have not been entirely satisfactory.

---

[33] [The 1941 Committee was a group of left-leaning public figures chaired by J.B. Priestley who pressed for efficient production to help the war effort.]

CHAPTER 14
DECENTRALISATION AND DIVERGENCE

From the many documents connected with the last stage of this pilgrimage emerge some seven main themes which have already appeared in these pages and are now restated with intensity and insistence. There is, above all,

1. The need to decentralise and lessen the influence of London in design criticism;
2. The need to share out government grants and encourage provincial bodies to organise their own exhibitions;
3. Scarcely less important, the right and duty of these bodies to appoint their own representatives to any central design council;
4. That exhibitions of industrial design should display articles in different styles, this seeming only common sense, bearing in mind the many fashion changes described in this essay;
5. The need to remind many boards of selectors that good industrial design should be saleable, which is not to say that what sells best is necessarily 'good' design;
6. The importance of discussion, in groups of a manageable size, around and about actual examples, as an accompaniment to selection and criticism, this having been made evident again and again; as well as the need for a continual interchange of ideas between provincial and London groups;
7. The need—perhaps a recurring need—for an expert and unbiased investigation into the whole question of state-subsidised design criticism.[1]

---

[1] [Originally drafted as: 'and, lastly, the resistance, in certain quarters, to an expert and unbiased investigation into the whole question of state-subsidised design criticism has always seemed, in itself, sufficient evidence of the need for it.']

The lesson of industrial relations

In 1941 my eyes were opened to what I have called 'Y' by Mary Follett's classic work *Dynamic Administration*, with its philosophy of consultation between responsible people in the early stages of a project and coordination as a reciprocal and continuous process. I soon learnt that her teaching should be applied not only to industry but to national groups, especially those with a head office in London and provincial branches, their vitality depending largely on a continual movement of constructive ideas not only between centre and rim but around the latter. Such movement, however, can only be maintained if there is widespread awareness of the sort of things which hinder communications between groups and individuals.

As a member, first of the 1941 Committee and later of the political party Common Wealth, I encountered many 'progressive' ideas; but the circulation of them seemed at first rather too much within the London orbit, where individuals tended to exert a disproportionate influence on the formation of policy; but not for long, for the Midlanders soon evolved some simple devices which enabled any member, even though living in a remote part of the country, to make a contribution in thought.

The most important tool in the democratic workshop was the detailed agenda—usually in the form of a series of challenging questions—issued in good time before a conference. Initiated in one of the provincial regions, the 'Discussion Plan' would often be sent round to all of them—'Peripheral Communication' we called it—thus changing the whole structure which in many organisations is like an old-fashioned prison chapel, where the convicts, seated in pens, could see the preacher but were unable to see each other and were forbidden to answer back.

We found, furthermore, that it was at first necessary for the provincials to be a little aggressive in their claims to equal political status and intellectual comradeship. The walls of Jericho do not crumble at the first trumpet blast.

In Common Wealth I worked with Wilfred Brown, the liberal-minded managing director of the Glacier Metal Company and later joint author of *Managers, Men and Morale*.[2] One should not try to manage others, he taught, since

> People are sick of having things done for them, however benevolently. They want not to have things done *for* them but *with* them. If management is done *with* them they often make surprising sacrifices for the common objective. If it were done *without* them they become irresponsible in the literal sense.[3] [Italics added.]

As to the soundness of these principles, my conviction was enormously strengthened when, in 1949, I began to put into practice 'Free Expression in Industry'[4] as propounded by, and with the help of, James Gillespie.

These new tendencies in administration were welcomed by many who helped to shape the policy of the 1945 Labour Government—but only as concerning employers and employed. That the same laws were applicable to any central trunk, be it governmental, professional or artistic, and its surrounding branches was not fully understood.

Crusaders

Under certain conditions, sincerity and enthusiasm degenerate into the 'crusading spirit'. Like Peter the Hermit, who may well have been prevented by the Turks from completing his pilgrimage, many modern crusaders are frustrated people. To save themselves the trouble of thinking, they crave discipline. The code of moral law, formerly enforced through the confessional by means of penances, has now become the 'party line', the call for a strong jury of selection, an 'assize in taste',

---

[2] Wilfred B. D. Brown and Winifred Raphael, *Managers, Men and Morale*, (London: Macdonald & Evans, 1948).

[3] Report of B.A.C.I.E. Conference in the *Birmingham Post*, 23 May, 1949.

[4] James J. Gillespie, *Free Expression in Industry: A Social-Psychological Study of Work and Leisure* (London: The Pilot Press, 1948).

with sanctions in the form of expulsion from the artistic group or refusal of export permits. The first crusaders showed deplorable prejudices against certain peoples. Their modern counterparts, today's crusaders, vaunt the superior taste of metropolitan designers as against that of the Ruritanians and provincials, and seek to create scapegoats—the employer, the wicked buyer, the suburban-dweller or the victim of the 'wretched dressing-table mentality'.

Dogma is part of the crusader's equipment and generally arises through confusing fact with personal opinion. A dogmatic attitude, especially if backed by the state, tends to hinder the development of industrial design. It must certainly impair export trade, which depends largely upon a sensitive feeling for other people's preferences. In industrial design the only permissible dogma is that there shall be no dogma.

The sincerity of a viewpoint may be assessed by the frankness with which alternative ones are stated and the thoroughness with which they are analysed. Crusaders seldom show this kind of sincerity.

In 1942 the Central Institute of Art and Design recommended, in an otherwise admirable pamphlet, 'a crusade' as part of a national art policy and 'carried through with all the powerful instruments of modern publicity ... the attack must not only come direct and open but also indirect and covert—we shall need much more than explicit praise and explicit criticism ... .' And yet 'if art is to be an integral part of our national life ... it cannot be imposed from above but must arise from the people.'[5] These two conceptions are not always compatible.

Enemies of design

By 1945 some of the Old Guard were beginning to have misgivings. Anthony Bertram, who besides broadcasting and

---

5 The Central Institute of Art and Design, *Memorandum: A National Art Policy* (London: National Gallery, London, circa. 1942), 9, 10.

writing on design had interested himself in the Birmingham D.I.A. quiz, published a pamphlet called 'Enemies of Design'. Such enemies, he said, were sometimes open and sometimes secret. The secret enemies lurked among the doctors and experts, by which he meant town-planners, architects, designers, organisers of exhibitions, critics and so forth. 'They are all to some degree affected by functionalist doctrine ... . The first (secret enemy) is automorphism ... , that common tendency which makes the man in the train assert what England wants when he is merely expressing what he and his like want. It is particularly dangerous when it is found in a minority that have some power to impose their wants.' The second is an excess of logic. 'Since man is not logical [and] is, one begins to think, barely rational, why build and design for him as if he were? Why always take into account what he should need when, in fact, that is not what he needs at all ... .'[6]

'I am more and more concerned,' he wrote to me in 1947, 'over the growth of official centralising control of the arts ... Design will only become really good again when we have ceased to think about it and get on with making things; but we cannot afford to adopt a *laisser-aller* principle at present because we know the chaos of horrors waiting round the corner to flood the market. The world is very sick; we must go on doctoring, but never forget that doctoring does not create health; it only prevents disease getting worse—sometimes.'

The Council of Industrial Design and Design Centres

Based on the Meynell-Hoskin Report and sponsored by the Federation of British Industries' Industrial Art Committee, the Council of Industrial Design (referred to hereafter as the 'CoID') was formed in December 1944. A more compact body than Frank Pick's Council, it was not so much concerned with fact-finding

---

[6] Anthony Bertram , *The Enemies of Design* (London: Design and Industries Association, 1946), 3, 6, 7.

or enquiry as encouraging a certain style of design—the 'contemporary idiom'—and with exhibitions. Amongst its other tasks was the promotion of Design Centres in those industries where design was of importance. The functions allotted to these centres were

(a) to study the problem of design in relation to the products of the particular industry;
(b) to collect and make available information relating to changes in public taste and trade practice in home and overseas markets;
(c) to hold exhibitions both at home and abroad;
(d) to conduct and encourage research and experiment in the design of the products of the industry; and
(e) to cooperate with the education authorities and other bodies for the training of designers and in the provision of special equipment, prizes and grants, and to arrange factory visits and training in factories for art students. They were to be financed by industry with the aid of a government grant.

Realising that something should be done to counteract the potentially excessive influence of the newly-formed CoID, in 1945 I arranged a meeting between Mr. S.C. Leslie, its first director, and what I thought might become the nucleus of a Design Centre for the Midlands. This was the then recently constituted Light Metals Advisory Committee, described above, which was already performing function (e), above, namely, cooperation with the local education authority.

The diversified products and materials peculiar to the region suggested that the different functions of the proposed Design Centre should, in this case, be split up and considered as separate projects and that detailed means should be evolved for performing them by using, where possible, existing institutions, the local D.I.A. being given a place in the plan. I doubted whether manufacturers would put up much money for anything as vague as 'Research', especially when told—as was made clear to me—that no actual designs would be forthcoming from these Centres.

My proposals were not encouraged. It was thought that there might be difficulty in using the Light Metals Industry as a starting point, as some of the producing industries were highly organised and 'it might become a question how far we should divide the field along the lines of its material resources', and so on.

Six years later, the anticipated broadening out of participation through these state-subsidised artistic groups had scarcely been achieved. Only two industrial design centres (Rayon and Jewellery) had been established by the CoID, both being located in London. May it not also be said that decentralisation of such groups can hardly exist unless, from time to time, there is some disagreement between them? If such has appeared, the outside world has yet to hear of it.

The 'Britain Can Make It' Exhibition

That the 'Britain Can Make It' Exhibition (B.C.M.I.) was forced upon the CoID is no secret. The reluctant members, after only a year, were given a whip by the President of the Board of Trade to undertake this enormous task and it is not surprising that mistakes were made.

Probably the most serious of them was that behind the whole project was the conception of an aggressive action. The manufacturers were to be taught a lesson and given a shock and 'a salutary reminder of the need to think again and think harder'.[7] Regarding methods of selection for exhibitions, there are, to use the Civil Service formula, bound to be differences of opinion; but Kenneth Luckhurst, in The Story of Exhibitions, shows convincingly that 'the worst of all possible kinds of body to entrust with authority in cultural affairs is an exclusive professional body supported by the State ...'.[8] Experience in

---

[7] S.C. Leslie, 'Some Lessons of "Britain Can Make It Exhibition"', Board of Trade Journal, February, 1947.

[8] Kenneth W. Luckhurst, The Story of Exhibitions (London and New York: The Studio Publications, 1951), 49.

France suggests that the right of election of juries might be given to exhibitors.[9] He also mentions the experiment of the Institute of British Photographers: 'Recognising the fallibility of all juries ... this society appoints no less than three for its exhibitions— one composed of artists, one composed of photographers and one representing "general interests". The verdict of all three is shown with the exhibits.'[10] But this comparative method was, as we shall see, incompatible with the principle, about to be laid down by the CoID, of 'unified standards'.

During the nineteenth century, exhibitions in Europe were undoubtedly popular. The medals and mentions seem to have been highly esteemed and valued by the industrialists, all the more so because the public had an opportunity of seeing what had not received awards and checking the judgment of the selectors. Whether selection by the CoID or its nominees was similarly esteemed is a matter for unbiased independent investigation.

Selection for the B.C.M.I., opened in September 1946, was supposed to be carried out by 'expert committees appointed by the Council', with technical assessors who were, however, without any jurisdiction in matters of taste. The *expertise* of the selectors was sometimes open to question. There were also suggestions that they tended to be cliquey and that certain firms were prepared 'to play up to them'.

The exhibition was supposed to be limited to 'new post-war designs'. My company submitted seven articles, all in a style 'favoured by the new puritans of the late twenties' and of these five were accepted.

What might have been an exciting and enjoyable event for all producers of designed goods was unfortunately bedevilled by political and aesthetic prejudices. The employers, who at the last resort were responsible for industrial design, became, of course, the scapegoats and in the general muddle the intelligentsia did

---

9 Luckhurst, *Story of Exhibitions*, 49.
10 Luckhurst, *Story of Exhibitions*, 50.

not always play a helpful part. Raymond Mortimer, for instance, who can write so discerningly about the 'rules (once applied by art critics to rationalise their intuitions but now exploded, every one of them[11]) could not resist the temptation to bait the manufacturers. His generalisations—quite meaningless without examples—were presumably intended to irritate. Although the effect of cut glass is appreciated by many who can use their eyes, he held that commercial glassware appeared to have 'suffered the Chinese torture of the thousand cuts. For what market these monstrosities were intended I could never discover.'

He had severe things to say about the manufacturers of other wares, too, including the potters. Their supposed complaints at finding their products rejected from the exhibition were noted with gratification. 'Fury is widespread amongst the manufacturers,' he gloated, 'and I understand that in the Five Towns protest is already shrill.'[12]

But protest was not nearly shrill enough to bring about much-needed changes in the outlook of the CoID. Manufacturers often grumbled but generally did nothing. Typical of their attitude was that of the eminent carpet manufacturer who said to me: 'What are you worrying about? We look upon the Council of Industrial Design as a noxious insect buzzing around. If you leave it alone, it will buzz off.'

Constructive counter-criticism

Fortunately, there was one group which was unwilling to accept the assumptions on which the CoID rested. By 3 December, 1946, the Birmingham D.I.A. had swung into action and called a public meeting at the City Art Gallery. In order that those attending should have ample opportunity to consider what was

---

[11] Raymond Mortimer, 'Artist, Critic, Public', *New Statesman and Nation*, 19 March, 1949.

[12] Raymond Mortimer, 'Britain Can Make It', *New Statesman and Nation*, 28 September, 1946.

at issue, the following 'Heads for Discussion' had been previously circulated:

What lessons are to be learned from the 'Britain Can Make it ' Exhibition?

(a) Is the aim to educate the Manufacturer?

(b) Could the selection be decentralised?

(c) Is there any danger of a Metropolitan bias?

(d) How remove any suspicion that design standards are being dictated by cliques?

(e) Should not photographs of rejected exhibits be submitted?

(f) How to integrate the Art Gallery into the Industrial Design activities of the City?

(g) How much space will be required and could be allocated to travelling exhibitions?

(h) Is the CoID organising travelling exhibitions?

(i) How are the permanent exhibits to be arranged?

The meeting was well attended.

The following resolution was unanimously approved: 'That this public meeting of the Birmingham Region D.I.A. wishes to record its admiration and approval of the "Britain Can Make It" exhibition, but would welcome an examination by the Council of Industrial Design of any proposals for decentralising selection and location of future exhibitions.'

Philip Sargant Florence, leading the discussion, said that when he was a boy his mother (a distinguished artist) had forbidden him to visit two places: the Chamber of Horrors at Madame Tussaud's and the Royal Academy. 'There were,' he continued, 'two extremes of thought typified by the centralised selection of the Royal Academy (which should be avoided at all costs) and by the individual selection of the B.I.F. This last free-for-all scheme was dangerous. We should avoid the slightest risk of selection being influenced by trade politics. Both extremes had risks and,' he thought, 'we should work out some compromise method.'

Sargant Florence advocated local exhibitions selected partly by assessors appointed by the Council who would choose the things they thought very good and throw out those they thought very bad—say, half of the articles submitted. This would leave half for the industrialists and, if necessary, a further selection might be made therefrom by allowing so many to each firm. If you wanted to educate the manufacturer, the important thing was to stimulate discussion.

This meeting was fully reported in a memorandum later submitted to the CoID and other committees. It included the following specific proposals:

> We strongly recommend that the principle should be worked out by a practical test on a small scale. Let us take, say, textiles or pottery, and if there were space for 100 exhibits and 500 were submitted, proceed as follows: let the CoID panel select 25 and reject 25 pieces and let them be shown in separate groups under some such label as 'Preferred' and 'Not Preferred'. This would leave 450 exhibits of which there would be space for only 50. These might be chosen by drawing lots or by the method known as 'Buggins' turn next'—i.e., so many exhibits from each prospective exhibitor, picked out with or without the advice of the CoID selection panel. Such a selection would answer more closely to the blend of leadership and anarchy essential to design development. The exhibition should be made a forum for the fullest possible discussion with the selectors of their preferences and dislikes, the public being also asked to express their opinions by voting, as at the B.C.M.I. Exhibition.

Psychological types

In conclusion, the memorandum suggested that:

> Design, good or bad, depends partly on the quality of thought about design itself, and it is interesting to find that discussion of these proposals has brought out certain well-defined types corresponding, we feel, to a general attitude to life.
>
> Firstly, for instance, there is the *Sportsman* who treats design selection as if it were a knock-out tournament. ('If your things have been thrown out, you've just had it, old man.')

Then there is the *Administrator* who likes to think that design can be tidily arranged, so to speak, as on a ladder, all above any rung on the ladder being 'better' than all below.

Closely allied is *the Legal* or *Judicial mind*, comparing the selective exhibition to an assize; welcoming any cries of protest from the unsuccessful as in themselves evidence of shortcomings; claiming that it is better for industry to be shocked by the Council's Selection Committees than by foreign competition later; *but at the same time denying that saleability abroad is relevant to the selection of designs.*

Fourthly, there is the *Individual* who assumes that criticism of the selection can only arise from disappointed and prejudiced would-be exhibitors. (Note: as far as we know, none of the Committee responsible for this memorandum has any personal or business reason to complain of the Selection panel's judgment. This criticism is based on important first principles concerning design itself).

Fifthly, there is the *Assumptionist*. Because in certain countries there is a high standard of design and also a degree of state intervention, he assumes that (a) the one is a result of the other, and (b) that state influence is always beneficial in art, however it is imposed and whoever is behind it.

Sixthly, there are those *Addicts of Automorphism* which, according to the *Shorter Oxford Dictionary* quoted by Mr. Anthony Bertram, means 'the ascription of one's own characteristics to another'.[13] We agree with him when he says that it is particularly dangerous when it is found in a minority that has some power to impose its wants.

Seventhly, there is the *Metropolitan*. London, he assures us, is the great retail market of the country and the centre of fashion and taste; 'provincialism' must not be encouraged and in some of the provincial cities, being aesthetically starved, decentralised selection must also not be encouraged.

Lastly, there are those who cannot believe that these criticisms can go hand in hand with a sincere and wholehearted approval and admiration of the work which has been done and is being done by the CoID.

This memorandum did little to accelerate the circulation of ideas. If the London groups ever read it, no counter-observations were

---

[13] Bertram, *Enemies of Design*.

forthcoming and still less any action. A flash of Y, however, was to be found in an article by Mr. S.C. Leslie two months after the meeting just described. Expressing his personal viewpoint regarding changes which might be made on a future occasion, he said that

> it might be better to organise Regional Committees in the provinces to ensure that local attitudes and points of view are not overlooked. This too is well worth careful thought; it is one of the Council's conscious aims to check and reverse the process by which the capital absorbs more and more of the creative ability and expert authority of the country as a whole.[14]

If this was, in truth, one of the Council's conscious aims, an unbiased investigation should be made as to what actually was done to achieve it.

Unified standards

Although some of the goods in the 'Enterprise Scotland' Exhibition were selected by trades, this was not, I was informed, as a result of the above proposals; and indeed one of the most astonishing results was the degree of opposition they aroused, not only from officials of the CoID but from the now rather pathetic National Council of the D.I.A. which, on the one hand, was in danger of being overwhelmed by the more powerful body but on the other hoped to get material support from it.

The situation was somewhat complex, for just as one political party may work within another, so some who were members both of the CoID *and* the D.I.A. used their influence to discourage criticism of the former. Others were held back by friendship and respect for personalities involved.

By piecing together publications, correspondence and my recollection of conversations, it is not difficult to understand

---

[14] Leslie, 'Britain Can Make It'.

why these Birmingham proposals were received at first coldly and then with growing hostility. By implication they struck at the whole notion of agreement on matters of taste; whereas, again to quote Mr. S.C. Leslie, 'the principle on which it (the Council) takes its stand is that the very idea of a national effort to improve the level of design implies that there is such a thing as a standard ... .' The goods presented were 'not the personal judgments of some individuals or cliques but industry's own best goods as selected by a fair sample of expert opinion.'[15]

Out of this circular reasoning arose the phrase 'depersonalising the selection', which was supposed to cover the personal selection of the 'experts' by the Council members and officers, and then those experts' personal preferences. To depersonalise selection is about as sensible as depersonalising love-making or the 'thrill of pleasure' which, according to the catalogue, the public was to expect by looking carefully at the choice of the 'experts'.

It was further argued that because of this 'depersonalising' process, any comparison with methods of selection in the fine arts would be wide of the mark; therefore it would be wrong to decentralise selection because, given the fact that objective standards existed, justice required uniformity. It would not do for an electric kettle from Birmingham to be accepted while another of 'equal merits' from London be excluded.

Raising a protest against the right of any high priest of design to come between us and our discussion of the things themselves —whether accepted or rejected—I explained that by trying to 'depersonalise' selection, the Council had actually erected a protective buffer between itself and the exhibitors.

By the end of 1947 the resistance to the whole concept of comparative exhibitions had strengthened and led to a crescendo of disapproval: it would be 'stirring up a hornets' nest' and 'sticking a knife into the back of the CoID'. To anyone asking why the B.C.M.I. should be 'good' and the other 'bad', given that any selective exhibition is a form of art criticism, there came the

---

[15] Leslie, 'Britain Can Make It'.

answer, 'Whether a design is good, bad or merely negative is something on which half-a-dozen selection committees, whose members have studied the subject over a period of time, will generally agree.[16]

To foster the illusion of uniformity, the Council published a pamphlet, 'Design Quiz', showing various household articles, in sets of three. The 'experts', who were to choose between them, were an artist, an architect and a 'housewife'—but no industrialist or designer with commercial experience. No indication was given of the setting in which these household goods were to be used but the experts 'all chose the same design from each set of objects in this book'.

There were some things the experts do agree about, the argument ran. 'Honesty is one. Always they reject a design which imitates something else: electric fires which imitate coal fires, wood which imitates marble, inexpensive things which try to look rich by wearing a lot of fancy decoration, just as we all dislike showy people.'[17]

Party discipline

As we have seen, the idea of the 'united front' appeals to crusaders or to those who do not like having to make up their own minds; in design matters, according to J.M. Richards of the *Architectural Review*, it also appeals to those who feel they 'are on difficult ground in condemning outright the rebel turned doctrinaire, because in doing so—in questioning the fixed value he puts on a transitory achievement—we may seem to betray, by sowing dissension in the camp, the cause we have all fought in common'.[18]

---

[16] Gordon Russell, 'Industrial Design as an Essential Element in Production', *Board of Trade Journal*, 8 November, 1947.

[17] *Design Quiz*, Council of Industrial Design (London: Council of Industrial Design, 1946).

[18] J. M. Richards, 'The Next Step?', *Architectural Review*, March 1950, 167.

It was with something of a shock, however, that in 1947, for the first time, I heard an official of the Council state solemnly that 'there was to be a united front for good design'.

From London came word that a 'comparative exhibition' might prejudice relations between the D.I.A. and the newly-formed Council of Industrial Design. It might perhaps be interpreted as a sign of hostility, even if the intention was otherwise. Was it worthwhile severing our connection with the Council? Was not the future of our ideals more important? Dissension might weaken our policy. Was it wise to divide our forces? Under existing circumstances a false step might prejudice the expansion of the D.I.A., and the Midlanders should therefore be discouraged from going ahead with this contentious project. In such matters it was inadvisable for branches to take active steps ...

Against all this came a contrary suggestion that the most important thing was to avoid even the appearance of unity, progress only being possible through disunity; for one had but to examine the varied styles required by different markets to realise the absurdity of trying to preserve a united front in such matters as design.

For myself, I argued that when the state mixed itself with design criticism, three things were liable to happen: the state's wielding of too much influence, the discouraging of counter-criticism, and the loss of intellectual integrity by those who allowed themselves to become too closely involved.

Permission was, nevertheless, granted to the Midlanders to hold an exhibition, providing that it was on a small scale and not open to the public. Up to the time of writing, however, it has never been held. The provincials wished to avoid discord, and the suggestion of disapproval spreading from London discouraged them. Post-war fatigue and apathy did the rest; but for some years a group of enthusiasts made repeated efforts to carry out the 'contentious project' and a good opportunity seemed to offer itself in Design Week Birmingham (1948).

Design Weeks

In May 1948 the CoID opened Design Week Manchester, the first of a series in provincial centres. The focal point was an exhibition called 'Design Fair'. Arranged to bring out certain principles and conceptions underlying all design, the show stands suggested stalls and roundabouts. They were gay and, to my eye, pleasing.

But Y involves consultation *before* a decision on major policy is reached. Strictly speaking, the project was *imposed* upon Manchester and the other provincial cities by a central group. The fees and *réclame* went to designers, artists and contractors of its choosing. Organised, designed and carried out by local people, aided by a grant, the exhibition might not have been as large or impressive but would surely have stimulated the cultural life of the provincial cities by increasing local participation.

Anticipating the start of this touring exhibition, I had written to the CoID, suggesting that an experimental Comparative Exhibition should be held during Design Week Birmingham. It would be quite small. 'The important thing,' I wrote, 'is to try out the principle of comparison, decentralisation and joint consultation ... . There is always a great need to remove barriers to free circulation of ideas and discussion; there is no sphere in which this applies more than in questions of aesthetic taste and design standards.'

But the National D.I.A. had already planned, with the help of the CoID, to take advantage of these Design Weeks in provincial cities. New branches were to be formed or old ones developed, and to make this programme effective, enthusiasm and material resources were necessary.

Thus it came about that any criticism of the taste or methods of the Council on this occasion was especially unwelcome. If Design Week Birmingham were to be seized upon as 'a golden opportunity to shoot at the CoID, it would not make cooperation easy' and 'no cooperation' meant no regional development of the D.I.A.

Decentralised discussion

A feature of the Design Weeks was that running concurrently with the public events was a series of discussions between representatives of the CoID and others on 'the best way of improving design practice and raising standards'; but when it came to Birmingham, the members of the Council were willing to talk over any differences of opinion *before* Design Week. Certain main topics, drafted by the Midland group, were accepted by both sides as a basis for discussion and were circulated prior to the meeting, together with some comments by the Council. In the following paragraph, however, they have been split up and rearranged according to subject, alongside certain points arising from the discussion and other relevant material.

To promote further predigestion of the issues, an illustrated advertisement was included with the agenda. A lamp standard of steel tube, accepted for the B.C.M.I. Exhibition, was shown side by side with another (which would certainly have been rejected) in a style not unpopular in the U.S.A. Accompanying the illustration were copies of letters about these articles from (a) the Director of the New York Museum of Modern Art and (b) an experienced and gifted distributor of British-designed goods, also of that city. Each expressed contrasting points of view.

This illustration of actual examples gave point to the following 'Head for Discussion and Enquiry': 'Are we agreed that, in order to avoid an appearance of unity in Design matters which does not and cannot exist, the Council should, if required, provide publicity for divergent points of view?' To which the Council replied: 'Yes, provided that the divergent view is aimed at improving standards (which is the duty of the Council).'

A further comment was also circulated to the effect that this reply seemed a little inconsistent since 'there can hardly be a "divergent view" unless there is some difference of opinion as to what is "improving standards".'

The discussion, memorable and to me enjoyable, was held on 4 October, 1943, at the Queen's Hotel, Birmingham. Five representatives of the Council attended, and amongst the others were industrialists, a designer-architect and the principal of the City College of Art, making twenty including a woman-chairman, experienced in design matters and of engaging personality.

I led off with a reference to the contrasting designs and the comments from New York. Our object, I suggested, should be to bridge the gap between these two points of view, the Museum Director having shown a certain lofty attitude not entirely absent from the Council's propaganda, which was fatal to sound commercial design. There should be no *hauteur* towards either customers or to those whose job it was to carry round the bag and sell the things.

Asked by a Council officer whether I maintained that there were no standards in design, I replied that there were four factors, namely:

(a) what works,
(b) what pleases my customers
(c) what pleases me personally, and
(d) (which was wholly bad) what I think I ought to like because other people, who claim to be experts, like it.

It was important that professionals should develop sensitive tentacles to feel out what a customer wanted. I recommended caution about telling others what they should like. The officer protested that

everyone in the room, except Mr. Best, has an idea in his mind about standards and about improving them. But he reduces it every time to the personal standard of the individual—what he likes. No publicity could be provided for persons who said there were no such things as standards. Those who worked with them should be with them and not against them. The Council had been set up to do one particular job, and if there were no standards of design it could not do it, because there would be no standards to judge by. There would be no point whatever in having an organisation like the CoID to prove what doesn't exist.

Another aspect of the matter was later put to me by a member of the CoID who wrote:

> You may deny absolute standards in theory and have very good reasons for doing so; but those who deny them in practice ... belong to the army of the damned. It is through them that much of our lovely country has been ruined during the last hundred years ...

And here, perhaps, one might quote from Karen Horney, the well-known psychologist:

> By adhering to certain standards the individual also acquires a certain firmness which hides his essential weaknesses, a firmness analogous to that which a corset provides for an individual whose backbone is injured.[19]

Selection of exhibits

Three of the 'Heads for Discussion' amplified the proposals worked out at the meeting in 1946. They were:

(a) that liaison officers and selectors should include people of commercial and industrial experience
(b) that some of the exhibits should be selected by trade associations; and
(c) that there should be full opportunity for discussion between the selectors and the prospective exhibitors.

Much of the controversy ranged round these three questions. The Council claimed that qualified tradesmen and people of experience were already being employed, but that the question of status, depending as it did on the individual, must be reserved; it could not bind itself to confine its selection to part only of the exhibits, and no exhibition could be mounted if unlimited discussion with a great number of groups took place beforehand.

---

[19] Karen Horney, *New Ways in Psycho-Analysis* (London: Kegan Paul, Trench, Trubner & Co., 1939), 219.

Amongst the points made by the industrialists were:

1. Manufacturers should be allowed to put into any exhibition what they themselves thought was their best work, without 'vetting by any kind of expert'. The managing director of one famous firm told of certain articles, at first rejected, which had later been especially altered to suit the taste of the selectors for an exhibition. They had then been accepted, but in the modified form had ceased to sell.

2. Alternatively, it was suggested, a group of manufacturers, at a certain point in the proceedings, should collect together their products and decide amongst themselves what should be shown.

3. A list of juries should be sent to the trades for acceptance, and if this were given, then 'for Heaven's sake let them stand by any decisions the jury might make—let the argument take place *before* and not *after* selection'.

4. Manufacturers could not be expected to act as 'instructors of taste' overseas; the Council should, therefore, accept financial responsibility for its own ideas and actually have made and paid for exhibits of their own design. They should lead rather than criticise.

5. It be accepted that manufacturers were reluctant to sit in judgment on their competitors' products.

6. The selection of the Council might be compared with that of the Third Programme, the criticism of the general mass of the public being supposed to be worthless; but if the aim was to increase the sale of British goods, it would fail just as surely as the Third Programme failed to bring in revenue to the B.B.C.

How were they appointed?

That selection committees, councils and artistic sects tend to be self-appointing and self-perpetuating is an opinion that has been expressed more than once in these pages. The appointment of Council members by the President of the Board of Trade was obviously a *façon de parler* (like the term 'Crown appointments'). Which geographical areas or pressure groups actually made nominations and who chose from them was, it was felt, yet another question for impartial investigation. The CoID had been formed without any link with the industrial Midlands, a matter of some practical importance to many within the region, and amongst the 'Heads for Discussion' the following was therefore included:

> That the Constitution of the Council should be revised and some form of regional representation tried out. At present, Scotland is represented as a region, but the Scots do not choose their own representatives. We suggest that not only should there be representation of territories but that the people most concerned in those territories should participate in the selection of their representatives on the Council.

The following written reply was circulated prior to the discussion:

> The revision of the constitution of the Council of Industrial Design would be a matter of policy on which our Council and the Board of Trade would have to be consulted, but,
> (a) Scotland does choose its own representatives
> (b) the first consideration is what a Council member can personally contribute to the Council's work. The second consideration is his or her representation of an industrial interest or region.

That there were well-trained, sensitive and creative designers and commercial people, some of whom did find their way onto the CoID, is clear enough. It is also obvious that there was no place there for those who were content to do hackwork and thought of nothing but the short-run profitability of their efforts.[20] In artistic matters it is difficult to check or verify 'personal contribution' but there is something positive about the conscious choice, by interested bodies within a territory, of someone to speak for them in London and to them of what is going forward there. That he has been accepted and not

---

[20] [Deleted by R.D.B, following 'of their efforts': 'The conception of "Personal Contribution", though understandable, is unfortunately only too well adapted to the self-perpetuation of design coteries.']

imposed upon those he is to help makes the promotion of 'two-way traffic' easier. It does not require a superman to do valuable educative work if this method is followed.

Industrial design is a team job. Its fruits must be enjoyable to a great many people. Of the hundreds of industrialists, designers, architects, publicists and teachers with equal qualifications, it is important that members of the Council should not be drawn predominantly from any particular group. But the fact that, in 1952, very few of them actually claimed for out-of-pocket expenses incurred in attending Council meetings seemed to point to the contrary.

Nothing in the discussion threw further light on the difficult question of nomination and selection. I said: 'What has to be avoided, at all costs, is a spontaneous generation of groups, implying that their claims to distinction in the arts have been confirmed by an outside authority, unless we know (a) the names of the individuals who conferred these honours, and b) by what reasoning process they find themselves in a position to do so. We have seen quite enough of the results of the Royal Academy to wish to avoid any similar situation being created in Industrial Art ... . If there were a Council of Music, it would interest musicians very much to know who appointed that Council.'

Continuing, I suggested that regional representation and 'two-way traffic' could be achieved without altering the constitution, if there were an unwritten law that nominations from associations and societies within a region should be accepted. Failing this, one member of the CoID should be earmarked as liaison officer for a certain territory; this would presume, of course, that such an officer would be well-acquainted with his area.

Long-term benefits

The theme of saleability as an indispensable factor in industrial design has occurred frequently in this essay. Because it threatened the conception of 'design standards' on which authority rested, a certain squeamishness about it had always shown itself amongst the prophets of good taste. The CoID was, of course, reluctant to face up to the full implications of such a doctrine. Amongst the 'Heads for Discussion' by this 1948 meeting, the following was, therefore, included:

> Are we agreed:
> (a) That the main task of the Council is 'to play a vital part ... in stimulating the *sale*, at home and *overseas* (the italics are ours) of a wide range of goods of which we can be justly proud,' long-run influence of the Council on design standards being almost impossible to check and verify.
> (b) That unless it can be shown that the Council is making a contribution in this respect commensurate with its cost, its activities should either be discontinued or drastically reduced.

The quotation in (a) was from the last sentence of a letter from Hugh Dalton to Sir Thomas Barlow setting out the main function of the Council. The following comments by this body were circulated prior to the meeting:

> Regarding a), the italicising of 'overseas sales' is historically incorrect. The main task of the Council is the improving of standards, which was to confer long-term benefit upon British trade. The direct promotion of immediate overseas sales is the job of the Export Promotion Department of the Board of Trade.
> And on b), parallel with the Council's main educational task, certain services to industry are in being or in preparation, such as small technical exhibitions of new materials and products, the record of designers ... and a rota of correspondents chosen for their ability to answer manufacturers' questions on design matters.

Whether or not the underlining of 'overseas sales' was historically correct, the heavy expense of the Council (a quarter-million pounds in 1951) was often justified on the score that design played an important part in maintaining commercial solvency. 'If we were to be able to sell our goods in the markets of the world, and it was essential for our very livelihood that we should,' said Sir Stafford Cripps in 1948, 'we must be far more alive to the place of design in industrial production than we ever had been in the past.'[21] It was a time for a quick expansion of export trade by offering new designs in a *saleable style*—a subject on which the excellent Export Promotion Department of the B.O.T. generally referred enquirers to the Council.

But for the Council to mix itself too much with saleability was to tolerate the heresy of personal taste and to weaken the doctrine of absolute standards. Impossible to verify, the conception of long-term benefit was therefore an expedient way out. Obviously designers and industrialists had to look ahead, and the penalties for not doing so were serious. But this form of provision, easily confirmed, was quite different from the vague policy of the CoID, which depended on what Aldous Huxley calls a 'time philosophy'; because the ultimate good lies in future time, people feel justified in making use of any temporal means for achieving it.[22]

Eric Newton, in *The Meaning of Beauty*, puts forward some sensible notions regarding the actual year-to-year swinging of taste, fashion being different from it only in degree and not in kind. 'Having decided that a particular quality is desirable it exaggerates and isolates that quality and rejects all others. If simplicity is in vogue, fashionable good taste will always prefer no ornament to simple ornament; if squareness is modish, even a teaspoon must be square; if suavity of line becomes desirable, then sloping shoulders come in and the ideal is a champagne bottle.'[23]

While agreeing that there is such a thing as 'bad' design, Newton doubts whether organisations like the CoID and the D.I.A. had a clear notion of what their purpose was or of how to put it into effect. 'Presumably chosen from the "moderately rich

---

[21] Address by Sir Stafford Cripps at the convocation day ceremony at the Royal College of Art, as reported in the *Sunday Times*, 16 July, 1948.

[22] Aldous Huxley, *The Perennial Philosophy* (London: Chatto & Windus, 1946) 221.

[23] Newton, *Meaning of Beauty*, 143.

intellectual" stratum,' he suggests that 'their job, as they envisage it, ... is to see to it that fashion spreads with the utmost speed. If it has been decided that aspidistras are "bad", then it becomes their duty to preach against aspidistras until an obedient public has banished the last offending specimen ... . The illusion that the gift of "good taste" was withheld from the previous generation, but granted to a few enlightened members of the generation to which we belong, is a useful one. It would certainly damp the enthusiasm of the prophets of good taste if they realised they were, in fact, the victims of an illusion; ... Both enthusiasm and scorn are indispensable motive forces.'[24]

It is doubtful, however, whether enthusiasm which is based on an illusion is compatible with the 'awareness' of the sensitive eye and the mature individual, or whether it can remain alive after Eric Newton's glorious debunking of lantern slides showing contrasting pairs of teapots, chairs and refrigerators, piously bequeathed by ardent and sensitive men to educational institutions, which no longer point the moral they so aptly pointed twenty years ago.[25]

A new style?

How far the CoID, while ostensibly insisting on certain 'standards', was actually, perhaps unwittingly and even unsuccessfully, pushing a particular style, constitutes yet another question for expert and unbiased investigation. After spending such large sums as in 1951, it would have been strange if some influence on fashion were not detectable. Asked to give evidence, I could only point to examples from my own trade and compare certain design-types encouraged in the Council's publications with actual models being offered for sale.

The magazine *Design* (in June 1948) showed a light-pendant consisting of three scoop-like reflectors attached to a central rod

---

[24] Newton, *Meaning of Beauty*, 146.
[25] Newton, *Meaning of Beauty*, 143.

which formed part of an interior in an Amsterdam department store; and from other publications it looked as if preference was to be given to a type of lighting fixture which consisted largely of sheet-metal cups, often cut off at an angle at the rim, or bowls or dishes pierced with slots or stars so as to allow some light to pass—a feature, of foreign origin, which I personally found pleasing. There is no doubt that a quantity of this type of design found its way onto the market.

As for exhibitions, evidence would have to be sifted as to how far certain companies supplying the required style were given preferential treatment by the promoters. The National Brassfoundry Association found that in one class of article, for example, over 50 per cent of the exhibits came from one firm.

I have also seen another process at work, whereby influential people—not necessarily interested in 'modern' design, at any rate, for their own homes—who were associated with the Council became persuaded that a certain fashion should be pushed and accordingly gave instructions, in their own businesses, that such a policy should be carried out. If it were established that the Council had, in fact, influenced fashions, then it would be very important to find out whether this change had affected a substantial volume of merchandise either for home consumption or export. If the output of goods in the 'Council-style' had been short-lived, one would have to conclude that, in whatever sphere the CoID might be working, it was *not* industrial design, in the sense of design to sell.

I would add that in the particular foreign markets dealt with by my own small company, there had been no encouragement to offer goods in the idiom favoured by the CoID. The reason is simple. We operated by the principle: *What is expected from Great Britain is something which looks British.*

And if the *raison d'être* of the CoID was, from the start, to hasten the spread of a new fashion, how much easier would their task have been had they frankly invited the cooperation of manufacturers towards this end? It was to arouse discussion of this general proposition at the 1948 meeting in Birmingham that the two illustrations, 'Plain and Fancy', were circulated. The Director of the New York Museum of Modern Art[26] said that British good taste was 'notably absent from the "Adam" travesty which debases the reputation of two great British designers, at the same time that it debases the taste of transatlantic friendly customers'. One of those transatlantic friendly customers ventured to disagree with him. 'To say the least, (these) comments are most amusing, and definitely misleading,' he wrote; 'they are confusing to manufacturers, not only in England but throughout Europe. He expresses his personal viewpoint and —as the saying goes—is feathering his own aesthetic nest.' Be this as it may, we must give serious attention to the criticism of such a distinguished devotee of modern design.

Like the crusaders of the CoID, the museum's Director seemed to oversimplify his case. The 'Adam' travesty was designed in 1926. There may be nothing particularly high-spirited about it; but let anyone alter the proportions or treatment in such a way as to give it 'a contemporary feeling' and it immediately ceased to appeal to a wide public. Why this is so has been lucidly explained by J.M. Richards in his book The Castles on the Ground:

> The voice of the school teacher (i.e., the apostle of 'good taste') is powerless against the instinct of self-preservation. Nothing is to be gained, the instinct of the suburban resident tells him, by condemning the make-believe of spec-builder's Tudor when the thing that is most valued about it is its cosiness and familiarity, which make it a secure anchorage in a changeable world.[27]

Furthermore,

---

[26] [Editor's note: MoMA had no director in 1948. Alfred Barr, MoMA's first director, was dismissed in 1943 but kept on as advisory drector before becoming Director of Collections. Best may have been referring to Philip Johnson, curator of MoMA's Department of Architecture and Design from its foundation in 1932 to 1934 and again from 1946 to 1954.]

[27] J.M. Richards, The Castles on the Ground (London: Architectural Press, 1946), 56.

it will do no good to impose an advanced or academic idiom on people who are already evolving at their own slow pace a vernacular style based on very different standards but suited to their own peculiar needs and aspirations, contemptible though this style may appear to the sophisticated.[28]

For a minority art is a closed art, closed to the warming influence of popular enthusiasm and understanding. It also tends to be dogmatic and to lack the common touch that should enable it to reflect those human vagaries which are the foundation of architectural richness.[29]

This analysis of suburban architecture by the joint editor of the *Architectural Review* applies equally well to much industrial design. It is significant that even a great creator like Picasso, according to Gertrude Stein, is so completely ahead of his generation that 'to calm himself in his daily living he wishes to live with the things in the daily life of the past'.[30]

Rational functional or irrational organic?

Gordon Russell may well remind us of our rôle as akin to '... that of original thinkers or daring innovators,' the creators of the Spitfire, radar and Mulberry.[31] But only confusion is caused by assuming that these technical inventions have necessarily anything to do with the living room. 'Daring innovation,' as often as not, is simply a style. The 'Modern' lamp standard made of bent tube conforms to a style. The application of bent tube to furniture was already eighty years old when, in 1925, Marcel Breuer revived it, emphasising the curved corners reminiscent of bicycle handlebars. In style neither good nor bad, the table lamp appealed to those who liked tubular furniture and repelled those who detested it. In my own experience it is useless to talk to

---

[28] Richards, *Castles on the Ground*, 76.
[29] Richards, *Castles on the Ground*, 82.
[30] Gertrude Stein, *Picasso* (London: Batsford, 1938).
[31] Russell, 'Industrial Design'.

customers about the 'maximum exploitation of mechanisation' or of 'making use of contemporary techniques in the course of logical evolution', unless they happen to be predisposed towards that sort of thing.

To quote J.M. Richards again, 'machines are tools to be utilised exactly as far and as frequently as it is to our advantage to do so, but no further.' A moment may come, he continues, when we wish to call a halt and say that further mechanisation cannot bring the ultimate quality we want. What is wanted is a move in the direction of conscious humanisation. The functional solution is only a means to an end. Our task, as Dr. Giedion observes, is to 'dare to leap from the rational-functional to the irrational-organic' and to 'discover an emotional equivalent that may rescue us from drowning in the flow of technical processes that is being poured over us'.[32]

A contradiction must have been obvious to the many designers and industrialists in 1951 visiting both the South Bank Exhibition and Battersea Park in the Festival of Britain. If the first was in a contemporary idiom, the second, with its suggestions of seventeenth-century architectural fantasy, most certainly was not. Offered for inclusion in the South Bank *Design Review*, the Battersea lighting pendants would surely have been rejected, if only because electric candles had been incorporated.

These conflicting viewpoints struggled to find expression in the discussion at the Queen's Hotel in October 1948. What Gordon Russell had called 'third-hand imitations of second-rate originals'[33] were, as an industrialist expressed it, the living tradition of the eighteenth century, a way of life and a type of home.

But the businessmen felt that all was not well. The basis of any export trade must be a lively home market. Conditions made

---

[32] J. M. Richards, 'The Next Step', 180, 181. The case is worked out in Sigfried Giedion, *Mechanisation takes Command* (Oxford: Oxford University Press, 1948).

[33] Russell, 'Industrial Design'.

this impossible to realise, so we were thrown back on our achievements of the past. The good design is the one you can go on living with, liking it more and more. Selectors unfortunately were not forced to live with what they chose.

From the other side of the table came the thought that the fancy bent-tube article need not also be traditional. It was the play of light and shade, a relation of big forms to small forms, that appealed—a colourful quality, if you like. In certain historical periods, design had this charm and distinction and it still had a tremendous attraction for discerning people; but it needed transmuting, through the designer, into something which was more contemporary in spirit. What we wanted was a modern design with charm—a range of articles which echoed the functional, the frivolous and the classical, but which was not a superficial effect of a past period. We had got ourselves into two watertight compartments: those who think of themselves as traditionalists and those who look upon themselves as contemporary designers. There might even be a place for 'vulgarity', as long as it was wholehearted and clever.

To all of which the experienced designer or industrialist could only reply, paraphrasing Dürer once again, let those who make proposals of this sort show what they mean with their own hands—and with their shoe leather, as they go round selling the results of their labours. Let the Council have prototypes designed and offered to the trade for production and sale, as suggested by the industrialists. Then let the results of these operations be reviewed impartially, after sufficient time has elapsed, to give the designs a fair trial. In not doing this the CoID was irresponsible, since it incurred no financial liability for the results of its aesthetic preferences.

In normal times there is much to be said for seeking inspiration amongst foreign designs. My father's exploits and, indeed, my own less impressive efforts are only characteristic of what occurs in any progressive firm. But wise national planning means that first things should come first. The times were exceptional. Export trade was desperately needed. Paradoxically enough, by favouring an idiom already popular abroad, instead of one acceptable to overseas customers as coming from this country, an insular policy was, in fact, being encouraged. Was it consonant with the plea for daring innovation to push these foreign styles? The designers and manufacturers of Great Britain were and are waiting for a saleable new fashion as distinctively British as the modernistic creations of 1925 were French. Could it truthfully be said that the CoID had shown wise leadership in this respect?

After reviewing the changes in fashion described in this essay, I am tempted to point to Osbert Lancaster's 'Vogue Regency' as a hint—not to be taken too seriously—of a possible line of development. To his admirable caricature of this idiom he adds:

> Luckily the furniture of the Regency period possesses in an exceptional degree the quality of adaptability: it 'goes' as well with a strapping pink nude by Picasso as with the less generously proportioned nymphs of David or Etty. And a Recamier sofa is in no way embarrassed by the close proximity of a rug by Marion Dorn.[34]

An independent investigation

A subsidiary item scheduled for discussion at the Queen's Hotel meeting was a suggestion that the activities of the CoID (particularly its relationship with industry) should be the subject of investigation by an independent body. But neither on that occasion nor since has the proposal been accepted. And yet there must surely be a need for some impartial fact-finding body, like Frank Pick's Council, uncommitted to any particular style and innocent of the crusading spirit. Otherwise, free from effective criticism, self-contained and self-perpetuating, the CoID must, sooner or later, tend to deteriorate. But who should undertake such an enquiry and who should appoint the investigator?

---

[34] Lancaster, *Homes Sweet Homes*, 74.

I have always hoped that social psychologists might be asked to produce a pilot survey to find out how far fashion, style and design are affected by the search for influence and prestige; what have been the commercial and financial results of the Council's activities; what attitudes have been engendered amongst the manufacturers, teachers and others; how the 'leaders' have been appointed and what has been the quality of leadership; whether there have been serious obstructions to communications; whether the traffic in ideas has been one-way, and so forth.

Industrial design should be treated not as an isolated subject, but as the result of a whole complex of social forces. According to one school of thought, 'bad' design is an indication that individuals and communities are concealing facts about themselves which they partly know but are unwilling to admit, and the objects they prefer are a symptom of neurosis, anxiety and repression. But against this, it has been argued that illness is always illness while conceptions of bad taste alter. Did George IV and Ludwig of Bavaria, men not conspicuous for psychological health, have bad taste? Professor Charles Madge, of Birmingham University, the well-known sociologist and part-founder of Mass-Observation, observes that there is a sense in which all things are equally 'beautiful' but that there is something wrong—or odd—about the things which are liked by large numbers of people today. He believes

the malady to be by no means confined to speculative builders or humble art-school students who design wallpapers. The members of the Council of Industrial Design, for example, are (to judge from their own printed propaganda) sadly in need of therapy. Well intentioned as they are, and beneficial as their efforts may prove in the long run, they are struggling not only with mass taste but their own psychological maladjustment.[35]

---

[35] Charles Madge, 'Reflections from Aston Park', *Architectural Review*, September 1948, 107.

The Midland Design and Industries Group

To return to the evening of 4 October, 1948, after some hours of discussion the participants came together in amity to eat and drink, rather like rival teams after a match. Later at my house we continued the debate on unified standards, disagreeing radically amongst ourselves about the merits of a picture in my small collection of contemporary paintings.

The air, to some extent, had been cleared, but the National Executive of the D.I.A. was still reluctant to encourage a regional exhibition or to raise the controversial issue of rival styles. At this point, it did not wish to be identified in any way with the Birmingham proposals. It was necessary, therefore, to consider the formation of an alternative organisation, especially in view of the forthcoming South Bank Exhibition.

Kenneth Luckhurst believes that through increasing control and centralisation, exhibitions now offer an opportunity for more perfect planning and harmonious design, but are 'less advantageous to the individual exhibitor and lose a natural element of liveliness'. The Festival of Britain Exhibition, he maintains, 'unlike all its predecessors, (was) planned in every detail from above, even to the selection of its industrial exhibits'.[36]

The Midlanders were fully alive to these conditions and the dangers of commercial design cliques arising therefrom. And so another programme was prepared, three of the six points repeating themes already stated, namely:

(a) Discussion
(b) Giving consideration to what those in industry consider to be their best in relation to their own markets, and
(c) Regional Representation.

The other points asked whether it was agreed

---

[36] Luckhurst, *Story of Exhibitions*, 216.

(d) that, whatever may be the plans for the 1951 Exhibition, the occasion should be used for a city or regional industrial design exhibition?

(e) that, by definition, Industrial Design should be saleable (Industry exists to make goods for sale). Though all that sells may not be good industrial design, no industrial design can be considered good unless it sells, at a price to cover the cost of production, either now or at some time in the future?

(f) that we would welcome the evolution of a contemporary style, peculiar to this country, in which the requirements of modern production methods would be tempered by the graciousness and human appeal apparent in the best periods of English traditional design; we also recognise that an exhibition displaying this evolutionary trend might stimulate our export trade and increase the pleasure of living on this island?

Preceded by an attempt to arouse the interest of trade associations by speeches at Rotary lunches and other functions, the first meeting of the Midland Design and Industry Group was held in May 1949. It was attended by members of eight trade associations; the Birmingham College of Art and the architectural profession were also represented. A resolution was passed that a group be formed 'to act as a forum for discussion of design matters, and a focus of opinion in dealings with governmental and other bodies, and that the Council of Industrial Design at an early date be invited to appoint a liaison officer to attend meetings'.

At a second meeting the following month, the Six-Point Programme was agreed as a general statement of policy. Attention was then given to the method of selection laid down by the CoID for the South Bank Exhibition which, as is now well known, set out to display the British contribution to civilisation, past, present and future. The collecting of exhibits was an immense undertaking, and there was no reason, to be sure, why the CoID should not help in this task and thereby find its place on the Festival bandwagon.

But in so doing the travel vouchers somehow became

confused. The designers of the exhibition were, of course, at liberty to select their articles to suit their theme, much as an artist chooses his colours; but this was surely a different matter from selecting 'good' designs and rejecting 'bad' ones. And yet, to the surprise of everyone who troubled to give attention to the principles involved, this was exactly what the Council now took upon itself to do.

The result was called 'The Stock List'. Circular No. F.O.B. 1a. declared that, 'Although the precise methods of selection ... have not been decided ... the principle can be clearly stated: the highest standard of contemporary design, etc.' The industrialists were vaguely aware that the methods of selection had *not* been clearly stated and that once again they were being asked to give *de facto* recognition to a selection panel whose members were unknown.

The prestige of the Council and the selectors was to be increased by encouraging firms to advertise that such and such a product had been accepted.[37] Why should there not be, furthermore, a 'hallmarking process', they opined, comparable to the endorsements of reviewers on book jackets? No one had complained of the dictatorship of taste on the part of book critics ... .[38]

I wondered how far this was actually true. What had writers got to say? If there were no protests, was it not perhaps because critics advanced their own opinions and were unsubsidised by public money? In design criticism, by contrast, as suggested by the National Brassfoundry Association, dissident groups were 'unorganised and inarticulate through a) being spread out over the country, b) lacking secretarial help, and c) lacking cash'. By contrast an artistic group, centred on London and backed by

---

[37] *Design Newsletter*, No. 26, March 1951. 'It is satisfactory to note in the trade and technical press that firms advertising their goods are beginning to draw attention to the fact that such and such a product 'has been accepted by the CoID for inclusion in the 1951 Stock List', etc.'

[38] P.R., "Hallmark for Good Design?" *Design*, No. 20, August 1950.

public funds and a propaganda magazine, was in too strong a position and might very well become exclusive. Such were the topics discussed by the Midland Design and Industry Group.

In 1950 the National Brassfoundry Association had advised its members to send in their photographs of products for the Stock List. These, it was proposed, should also form the material for a small exhibition, arranged locally, to which the CoID selectors should be invited. The occasion was to be looked upon as a social function. There should be informal and free discussion about the exhibits and the selectors were to be treated as customers, their preferences being the requirements of one particular market.

Selection, therefore, did not necessarily indicate that an article was either 'good' or 'bad'. For this reason member firms were advised not to claim, through advertisements or in any other way, that selection was a sign of any particular distinction.

An official quiz

Meetings between the CoID and the National Brassfoundry Association culminated in a small private view of articles which had been, or were to be, offered for inclusion in the Stock List. Held in Birmingham in March 1950, the experimental discussion between people of dissimilar outlook once again justified itself. Twelve people were present, an ideal number for a meeting of this sort, although a 'strangers' gallery' might also have been worth trying. The proceedings began with aperitifs and lunch.

'After the table was cleared,' to quote the official report of this memorable and enjoyable afternoon,

> the 'opening batsman' placed his products on the table and the fun started.
>
> The first exhibits were by a well-known firm making 'Period Reproduction Brassware'. The catalogues were looked over and then three actual articles were produced:
>
> 1. a spirit measure in the form of a copper jug measuring about

twelve inches high

2. a shallow dish; and
3. a chestnut roaster, popular in the U.S.A. for roasting popcorn.

Mr. Hartland Thomas selected all three. The chestnut-roaster struck him 'as something which is as valid now as it ever was'.

There was a discussion on what was 'traditional' design. Mr. Hartland Thomas said the word meant 'handing on and adding your bit'; traditional design was ancient design, but made better. We should set our face against conscious literal reproduction of old designs. The fact that an article sold in the U.S.A 'had nothing to do with the case. It doesn't happen to be what the Exhibition is about.'

Why was the Council allergic to ... knobs for hearth furniture [in the shape of galleons]? 'Galleons,' answered Mr. Hartland Thomas, 'were not such a good wicket, especially when submitted for the Festival'. But he would look at a finial for a poker with a very different eye, if it were in the form of an aircraft carrier. He hoped that, amongst the souvenirs, there would not be too many galleons, crinolines and comic Scotch dogs. Manufacturers should take modern things if possible.

Lighting fittings were next discussed. A manufacturer suggested that it was not the most efficient design which was wanted for domestic use. Mr. Hartland Thomas entirely agreed. 'A narrow definition can be a bad one. You've got to consider emotional efficiency. The lighting engineers ought to be countered; some of them were suffering from "foot and candle disease"; for this reason they've changed the term to "foot-lamberts". There's a lot more to it than lighting efficiency.' He thought the designers of lamp-bulbs had come too much under the spell of the flame.

Other points were:

1. Indirect lighting makes you yawn.
2. Too harsh a contrast between the luminous portion and the metalwork is unpleasant.
3. Are electric candles bad? And if so, what about vestigial candles? In this connection a manufacturer drew attention to the distinguished 'artistic' people who seemed to like electric candles and the Modern Danish candles reproduced on page 251 of the *Architectural Review* (November 1948). Mr. Hartland

Thomas thought it was too easy a solution for what has hitherto been an unsolved problem. He had no objection, however, to 'vestigial candles', i.e., extended covers to the lamp-holders.

4. Push-bar holders and how they should be housed on a table standard.

5. Glass chandeliers: have we got the right answer yet? They are essentially for a weak light source.

6. Perspex as the modern version of the lustre fitting.

All these points were discussed, as the photographs of the manufacturer's exhibits came before the group. Mr. Hartland Thomas selected a number for the Stock List. 'We are not at all satisfied about the present situation in lighting fittings,' he said, 'and we certainly do not think that the clinical fitting is the answer.'

Two door springs and checks, both made by the same firm, were then explained and discussed. One of the articles was a restyled version of the original design. In making this second version, the firm had been influenced by the fact that there were already many thousand of the first form in use and therefore spares had to be interchangeable. The restyled design had already been accepted for the Stock List.

Another firm later produced an article which had been rejected by the Council on the grounds that it was not 'Modern'. A most interesting discussion then followed, during which definite suggestions were made to modify the appearance of this model. Mr. Hartland Thomas asked the manufacturer to take this matter up again with him personally. Some display equipment was then placed before the group and was a hundred-percent success. 'The fact that you can hardly see the display stand when the articles are in position is a great advantage,' said Mr. Hartland Thomas.

A manufacturer then submitted a design for a fluorescent fitting which had been turned down. Mr. Hartland Thomas, while approving the general lines, suggested that the reason for rejection might be that the tubes had not been screened. 'The fluorescent tube is, even now, an unsolved problem, because you still have to screen the thing. In this case the designer has appreciated that the lamp is a long bar and shaped the metalwork accordingly, but he hasn't begun to tackle the awkward surface brightness of the tube.' He then went on to describe a series of baffle plates which had been evolved at the

Building Research Station at Watford. They were registered (or patented) but were available to the trade.

Another firm then produced a number of photographs of lighting fittings, from which Mr. Hartland Thomas made a selection. He suggested that, on an adjustable table lamp, an alteration might be made to the shade—at present a metal spinning. This caused too harsh a contrast with the illuminated surface. A translucent version might be substituted as an alternative.

Mr. Cooke offered interesting suggestions for two products which, he thought, were needed. One was a special lamp standard for use when the television was being watched; it should possibly incorporate an adjustable dimming device. In the other, a bent perspex tube was to be used for hotel twin-beds, so that one party could read without disturbing the other.

The proceedings ended with a discussion as to whether, in time, something like a 'Standard of Good Design' would be created in this country.

Throughout the discussion, the two representatives of the Council of Industrial Design showed a commendable absence of doctrinaire feeling towards commercial designs, but made their selection within the standards and conditions appertaining to the industry concerned. At the same time, they made it quite clear that certain designs were preferred to others, and why. From time to time specific proposals for improving designs were sketched out on paper, and throughout the afternoon there was a lively give-and-take in discussion, often of a humorous nature.

Even though the possible number of such discussions is obviously limited by the time available to the officers of the Council of Industrial Design, it seems important that the industrialists and the selectors should meet, periodically, in the presence of the articles themselves. Without the face-to-face contact, selection is of doubtful value and often only causes resentment.

Similar discussion amongst the industrialists themselves may also be valuable, but the presence of someone from a central organisation, who claims to be an expert, by setting up a mild and friendly clash of viewpoints, is most beneficial to both sides.

The Official Report, quoted above, was signed by R.A.

Wolstenholme of Messrs Pearson Page Jewsbury Co. Ltd., H.C. Shead of Messrs W. Newman and Sons Ltd, and the present writer.

Important only as a prototype—as an experiment on a small scale to be developed later—the discussion just described between critics, nominated by a governmental body, and provincial industrialists, might well form part of a regional programme. The official visitors entered into the spirit of the thing and acquitted themselves well. I believe they themselves learnt much. They also gave freely of their ideas and experience to the industrialists.

As for the Midland Design and Industry Group, we may hope that it will become a permanent and official body and that by the time this essay is published it will have nominated and have had accepted the first member of the Council to be appointed in this way. It will then be simply a question of time before other industrial territories follow its example.

And here, with the Delectable Mountains just in sight—but only just, like small mounds on the horizon—we shall break off this pilgrimage, and in order to plan the way ahead, use that convenient literary device of describing future events as if they were already history—a free fantasy or development section, perhaps. Thus we might imagine a survey, much condensed for foreign readers, of events leading up to the Twenty-First Annual Comparative Exhibition, then just opened at Kidderminster, decentralisation within the region having been practised from the time of the big breakaway from London. This survey might form part of a section devoted to Midland news in a governmental publication called *Design*. Other industrial districts would each have a part of the magazine allotted to them for articles and reports of meetings and exhibitions.

After explaining how it came about that in 1951 the only state-subsidised group of design critics was centred on London, the writer might continue:

> Already it was becoming clear to many thoughtful people that sensitivity of public taste was not helped by the presentation of a one-sided and confused artistic theory, or by pushing a certain fashion as if it were the only form of 'good' design; clear, too, that good health in design criticism could only be maintained by removing the artificial restrictions to free circulation of ideas, chief of which was the quasi-monopoly then existing in London.
>
> The first positive move was made by the National Brassfoundry Association, which in 1951 submitted a memorandum to the Board of Trade criticising the taste of its nominees and the organisation of the CoID, and suggesting that its members should not be 'relieved

of the salutary obligation to keep provincial groups informed and to take back facts and opinions to the central body'.[1]

These representations were at first without results. Later, however, Mr. W.K., nominated by a number of Midland trade associations, the local architectural association and the D.I.A., was officially accepted as a CoID member by the President of the Board of Trade. A new principle was thereby established; for hitherto Council members had been appointed primarily on the score of 'their personal contribution' and not as representing any particular territory. By keeping in touch with like-minded people in other parts of the country, the Midlanders caused this practice to spread until it became unofficially recognised by the Board of Trade that about one half the members of the CoID were to be, as it were, elected, the remainder finding themselves members by the same process as hitherto.

The coming together of trade and professional associations in order to secure representation in London seemed to make easy and natural the essential cooperation in further projects, first of which was the formal organisation and constitution of the Midland Design Council, whose members were all nominated by the associations referred to above.

The second positive move was an investigation into the whole art examination system of that period as it had been set out in the Ministry leaflet, 'Rules Governing the Award of the Ministry's Diplomas and Certificates in Art'. For some years far-sighted people had been asking themselves in whose interests these examinations were held. The students'? Or were they not perhaps unconsciously fostered by hard-working and not particularly well-paid teachers to underpin the whole hierarchy? Had the Ministry actually made up its mind whether to train students for the teaching profession or for industry? Were there not indeed two quite different styles of industrial design: art school design, shielded from the market, and industrial design proper?

The report of this Midlands investigation had a profound effect on the teaching not only of industrial design but of art generally. The Ministry brought into clearer focus its own concepts. It came to be recognised that it was quite unfair to treat the industrial

---

[1] P.R., 'Hallmark for Good Design?'

designers like the fine-art students of that epoch, or to encourage them to 'express themselves' without reference to some 'customer'. Market research became an important feature of the curriculum. The whims and fancies of the examiners were to be studied carefully, not because there was anything good or bad about them but because, for the time being, they were the customers, and the customer is always right.

Partly right. If, for example, an examiner was known to draw upon biological specimens for inspiration, the effect upon the entries for the three-dimensional section was most marked. The result of these and other reforms was to reverse the process which, in 1905, had caused R.H. Best to complain, referring to the drawing from nature then practised, 'I ask Catterson-Smith for Louis-Quinze and he hands me a rabbit.'[2]

Equally remarkable were the changes brought about in examinations for the fine arts, for it must be remembered that the doctrine of artistic integrity was then professed by nearly all 'serious' teachers of art, and it has only recently been recognised that the artist-client relationship should only differ in degree from that of the commercial designer towards his customer. Both involve a two-way process. On the grounds not only of artistic but intellectual integrity, the students were protected from all tests which could not be measured in an objective manner. Any tendency to conform to the preferences of a teacher or examiner generally led to the student's being ploughed.[3]

Complementary to this examination of examinations and no less important in its results was the university survey published under the title 'Design Criticism and Group Dynamics'. It covered such matters as fashion changes and how far they could be accelerated by artistic groups; hallmarking; group attitudes towards selection and criticism; and geographical distribution of art professorships. Other matters, of great practical importance, were presented in the phraseology of the social psychologist, which the reading public has now come to realise describes fairly simple and valuable concepts.

The Table of Contents included: 'Socio-Aesthetic Equilibria',

---

[2] Best, *Brass Chandelier*, p. 223.
[3] [That is, being failed his or her examination.]

'Subjective and Objective Elements in the Critical Field', 'Scapegoating and the Interdependence of Levels of Conduct', 'Socio-Aesthetic Feedback', 'Metropolitan Fantasy and Prejudice', 'Autistic Hostility and Commercio-Aesthetic Reality', and so forth. This investigation showed that, although the South Bank Exhibition and Battersea Amusement Park of 1951 had had some influence on fashion in the home market, its effect on foreign trade had been negligible.

Soon after the publication of these two reports, an important National Design Conference took place, not in London but in a picturesque Warwickshire setting. Small group discussions and circulation of memoranda beforehand resulted in ample predigestion of the issues. It is now acknowledged that this was the first occasion on which those who had been invited to attend were also allowed to take a hand in the shaping of the agendas, and many awkward questions, hitherto covered up, were at last brought into the open. The conference allowed the fresh air of free criticism, based on facts, to dispel the mists of prejudice. Industrial designers, teachers and business folk went away refreshed and prepared to start again.

In 1952 the CoID had decided to continue the collection of photographs started for the Festival and known then as the Stock List or Design Review. Little enthusiasm had been shown for this undertaking as long as it meant ceding the right of selection to unknown London critics. The Warwickshire Design Conference resulted in a new approach. That the doctrine of 'depersonalised selection' was the result of confused thinking had been clearly demonstrated in the university survey referred to above. As a regional study in personal preferences, this sequel to the Design Review was widely supported. The method of selection was in accordance with the plan proposed by Professor Sargant Florence at a public meeting of the D.I.A. in 1945, i.e., partly by assessors appointed by the London and Midland Design Councils and partly by industrialists. Further selections were made by the local Society of Industrial Designers, by certain teachers from the colleges and schools of art within the region, by the D.I.A. and by the local architectural association. Until all had declared their preferences, no group of selectors knew what the others had chosen.

It was then found that cases of disagreement were far more numerous than those of agreement. The subsequent discussions around these selections were lengthy and spirited. The public display of the Midland Design Review was followed by a series of small exhibitions organised to show the personal preferences of different well-known individuals, each being asked to undertake, with the help of the Midland Design Council, the furnishing and decoration of an interior.

Of two citizens occupying prominent positions in the artistic life of Birmingham, one produced a charming scheme in a period idiom while the other chose a restrained form of modernism showing more affinity with the style of Ernest Gimson than with that of Walter Gropius. Other personages to take part in this interesting experiment were a Lord Mayor, the President of the Birmingham and Five Counties Architectural Association, a well-known actress and film-star, and a distinguished artist. Since there was no suggestion that these manifestations of personal taste were 'good' design in an absolute sense, however helpful they might be as an indication of fashion-trends manufacturers, designers and decorators showed a lively interest and supported the project by freely lending their wares. This principle was later extended to 'exhibition houses', hitherto generally furnished by metropolitan interior decorators and imposed upon the provincial cities.

Because these exhibits revealed such divergent tastes, the Midland Design Council, helped by Mass-Observation[4], organised a

---

[4] Mass-Observation was an organisation set up in the U.K. in 1936 to observe aspects of everyday life and measure public attitudes through questionnaires, in much the same way that the B.B.C. measured audience response to its radio programmes. It was started by anthropologist Tom Harrisson, the poet Charles Madge and the filmmaker Humphrey Jennings, all of whom had been at Cambridge University together. It was supported by the literary critic William Empson, the photographers Humphrey Spender and Michael Wickham, the collagist Julian Trevelyan, novelists Inez Pearn and G.B. Edwards, the celebrated spiritualist medium Rosemary Brown, the journalist Anne Symonds, and the Euston Road School painters William Coldstream and Graham Bell. It was prompted partly by a lack of trust in the reliability of newspapers reporting. After the war and the departure of its founders, it turned increasingly from sociological research to more commercially driven market research and in 1949 was turned into a limited company, Mass Observation (UK) Ltd. See also page 242.

survey of the preferences—as manifested in their homes—of the designers, industrialists, publicists and others who at different times had served on the CoID. The report was well illustrated and at once became a bestseller and proved the absurdity of dogma in design matters. It also showed that even those who had taken part in a crusade for 'honesty' in design and the 'contemporary idiom' were not squeamish about electric candles and flickering electric fires for their own homes.

The Quiz Meetings originated by the D.I.A. in the early 1930's took place each year. Although primarily for specialists—industrial designers, sales staff and manufacturers—there was invariably a sprinkling of lay people, often members of the D.I.A., who made valuable contributions to the discussion and represented the viewpoint of the enlightened consumer.

Striking—and saleable—designs followed the exhibitions which were brought to the region by the powerful trade groups producing primary materials. A number of free prototypes, the result of competitions, also began to appear. Many of these suggestions were taken up by practising designers and turned to good account.

From its inception it became the policy of the Midland Design Council to give a social character to all exhibitions, lectures and meetings held under its aegis. Coffee and refreshments tended to be served. Many of the smaller exhibitions were so arranged as to allow, by moving stages and other devices, something of the human interest and appeal of the mannequin parades staged by the Birmingham School of Dress Design, and indeed the fashion and dress trades year by year played an important part in these activities. Londoners, especially members of the Council of Industrial Design, were frequently invited, and, as the pronounced metropolitan bias became eliminated, were treated in a thoroughly comradely fashion.

Succeeding directors of the Birmingham Museum and Art Gallery, themselves members of the Midland Design Council, were able to help local activities in a number of different ways. The parts of the building damaged during the last war were at last restored. Since then much of the additional space was allotted to visiting exhibitions of industrial art. Through cooperation between the Midland Design Council and the Friends of the Gallery Association, the permanent collection of this type of exhibit was also greatly extended and enriched.

As, one by one, regional design councils formed themselves in other parts of the country, the group of officials within the Board of Trade responsible for these matters were persuaded to divert 80 per cent of the grant from the CoID to the provincial bodies. With its share, the Midland Design Council was able to maintain a part-time secretary and pay for hire of rooms for meetings and exhibitions. A substantial sum was also spent on a portable exhibition setting, consisting of screens and revolving stages. In time it came to be realised that all the functions of a design centre, as set out in a Circular appearing in 1944, were thus actually being carried out for a number of industries.

Of first importance was the cooperation with the local education authority. Practical training in factories and refresher courses as well as competitions and so forth were being fostered by advisory committees which, through individual members, were linked with the Midland Design Council. Other functions laid down by the 1944 CoID Circular had, for the first time, been given practical form and were being performed as efficiently as the limited income would permit. The collecting of information relating to public taste, the research into industrial factors and requirements, as well as the holding of exhibitions, was prominent amongst the original proposals for design centres. How these activities were actually carried out in the Midlands has been reported above.

As for 'research', the Midland Design Council came to the conclusion that this word, originally applied to exact and systematic experiments the results of which were subject to rigorous objective tests, was quite inappropriate to the operations of a design centre. In view of the multifarious nature of the Midlands products, it was felt that so-called 'research' or design development was best carried out by individual firms. It nevertheless came to be realised by the Board of Trade that this regional design council was, in fact, a 'design centre' and therefore eligible for an annual block grant, fixed in amount for a number of years, on condition that the industries concerned would maintain contributions at a specified sum.

It was now possible to occupy a permanent office with a small exhibition room attached. But from the first the governing body refused to accept nebulous projects put forward under high-sounding titles, and restricted itself to the activities already named. Its most important function never appeared officially amongst its terms of reference; this was to maintain some sort of balance of power in 'commercio-aesthetic' matters.

Perhaps the most important result of this readjustment showed itself in relation to the prevalent fashion, style or idiom, hitherto influenced perhaps unduly by the particular artistic group which happened to have control of the public purse-strings. While ostensibly encouraging originality, these conditions had in fact made it increasingly difficult for provincial designers to inaugurate a new style or fashion in 'modern' interior decoration. Decentralisation reversed this process in some cases and in others mitigated its evil effects. There was a release of creative energy, which coincided with a slight lowering in the temperature of the cold war.

One of the first manifestations of the new spirit was the idiom, now famous and called, amongst other names, 'Five Counties Festive'. It grew naturally out of the mild reaction from geometric forms. Recent developments in tools and materials for the production of furniture and fittings lent themselves as much to curves and broken surfaces as to smooth planes and straight lines. This new style was also well suited to the tendency, noted by Dr. Herbert Read in 1943[5] towards the increasing stratification of industry—he called it then a 'double-decker civilisation'—so that small semi-craft undertakings and large firms were able to cooperate, often on the same article.

As for textiles, wallpapers and interior decoration, the public had become a little tired of the small dots, stars and crystalline structures, admirable though these patterns had been in their time, and took readily to the plant patterns which became characteristic of this now famous 'Festive' style. It was completely contemporary, because natural forms are always contemporary. It was also adaptable and went well with the heterogeneous collection of furniture to be found in many homes.

In helping to promote and popularise these stylistic tendencies, the Midland Design Council played an important and enlightened role. Consultation and coordination were effected even in the early stages. All the trades concerned together with representatives of the buying public were encouraged to come together and nurse it

5 Read, *Future of Industrial Design*.

through its infancy, while contact with other Design Councils was continuously maintained.

One can now say that Twentieth-Century Great Britain will probably go down in history as the home of civilised and humane planning: planning, that is to say, which was combined with the widest possible participation and sharing of responsibility. Symbolic of this spirit was the furnishing and decorating idiom which originated in the Five Counties.[6]

---

[6] [R.D.B. deleted the final sentence from the last version of his manuscript.]

CHAPTER 16
LAST WORDS

Here I offer modest advice based on the arguments I have advanced in the preceding pages.

To the man in the street

Furnishing the home should not be undertaken in too exalted a mood. Violent likes and dislikes may lead to trouble. More than one point of view must generally be represented, since wives as well as husbands take a share in selection and parents bequeath furniture to children. Many homes are therefore the result of diverse influences.

Examine carefully and with docility the things which the 'experts' offer, comparing them with what you see in the shops.

Pay no attention to art jargon. Reject all ready-made rules and standards and, insofar as consideration for others will allow, quietly make your own choice and reserve intensity of feeling for painting, music, poetry or sculpture, which are more capable of supplying your spiritual needs.

To teachers and examiners

Keep in mind the aesthetic spectrum from the ultraviolet of artistic integrity to the infrared of producing only what sells. Teachers and examiners should make clear to young people on what part of the spectrum they are supposed to be working. If in the ultraviolet zone, the teacher should be cautious about interfering. A student with anything in him will get it out of his system somehow. If in the middle bands, the teacher should never be squeamish about introducing market research into the curriculum, making it clear that, although the student may laugh up his sleeve at examiners, he can hardly ever afford to work for his public with his tongue in his cheek.

Teachers and examiners should also consider the diagram shown at the 1934 Birmingham Exhibition[1] with three horizontal bands, functional appliances at the top and articles that only please the eye at the bottom. Examiners have no place on the lower band, except perhaps to test designing for a special market. But the solution to design problems in the functional group may be capable of objective assessment.

Students should carry through their projects. Whether they make the prototypes with their own hands or not is not so important as *getting them made* and seeing the different stages of production in the workshops.

Teachers associate costing with skimping, cheeseparing or designing 'at so much an ounce' whereas, in truth, a good industrial designer cannot use his imagination without questions of time, weight and values beginning to cross his mind.

Art has great educational and even therapeutic value.[2] In this respect the schoolteacher has much in common with the art-school teacher confronted with a middle-aged student taking up a craft on doctor's orders. I suspect that much of this activity takes place in the ultraviolet zone. The teaching of art is itself an art. How far it can be tested by examinations is outside my sphere, but in assessing art school attainments it seems to me to be a mistake to confuse the educational or therapeutic with industrial design.

To industrial design students

Pay more attention to what your teachers do than to what they say. Acquire all the technical knowledge you can. If your art

---

[1] See page 163.
[2] See Read, *Education Through Art*.

school is unable to supply what you want, get round to a technical school or into a factory. Should you find that your instructor is pushing some particular style—it may be 'Modern Design for Mass Production' or perhaps 'Craftwork of Quality'—remember that both sorts are wanted in industry.

God forbid that you should become involved in the examination system! But if you are unfortunate in this respect, throw aside some 'artistic integrity', find out the sort of style your examiners like and then pander to them. Unlike the professional designer, you need not be unhappy about catering for tastes that you find repellent. When you have passed your examinations and established yourself, join the company of protestants and reformers.

To design councillors and officers

This is a confession of faith in freedom of liking and removing obstructions to the circulation of ideas. To restore circulation it is necessary to carry out the proposals in the last chapter—for decentralisation, for sharing government grants and exhibition policy, and examining afresh the way leaders are appointed.

Argue with examples of design rather than phrases. Treat aesthetic theory with caution and throw away dogmas and slogans. If design can be improved other than by the play of supply and demand, discussion is the best tool for the job. 'The Quiz' is the most helpful form of it.

Don't be taken in by talk about the *Zeitgeist* or the age of aeroplane shapes and plain surfaces.

There may be as much need for the Battersea-Park manner as the South-Bank manner. You will find them side by side in the better shops in Europe. Keep in mind Herbert Read's 'double-decker civilisation, in which there must be room for the naturalistic, the lyrical and the sentimental modes of expression'.

Try out more 'Free Prototypes' and 'Parish Goods' designed in a manner that you approve of—but only after consultation with the regional groups which are to produce them. The market will provide indispensable information.

Let us have more facts and illustrated analyses of design trends in different parts of the world, more data regarding what our customers abroad *want from us* (as opposed to what they want from their own nationals) and more comparative statistics about the sales of designs pushed by the CoID. But let all this be unbiased and not part of a crusade for some particular idiom.

The public is entitled to an independent investigation into the relationship between the CoID and the business world. The cost of the Council is often justified on the score of increasing exports, but part of this overhead is carried by industry. Do not be surprised if tangible results are expected.

Never despise saleability. Some exporters may seem to be 'muddling about, trying to adapt the Adam Style to something which people in Rio or New York will buy'. If you think you can help them, show them what you mean with your hands. You will probably learn a lot in the process. Never adopt a superior attitude towards the Ruritanians or suburban-dwellers.

To my fellow industrialists and designers

Sweet are the uses of adversity but only if we are willing to do more than grumble. Set up your courts, therefore, in the forests of Stoke-on-Trent, Sheffield, Birmingham and Kidderminster. Appoint your own councillors, run your own exhibitions and select your own exhibits.

I assume that there is someone trained and interested in design matters at the top of your company, that you have a Design Day on which the managing director gives attention to design problems, and that, before a new model is put on the market, the prototype is examined critically by your staff, by friendly and respected customers, and by private consumers as well, male and female.

We should interweave our preferences with the styles favoured by our customers. Whatever is to be done should be done *deliberately* and *con amore*. If we find that prevalent tastes make it impossible for us to design or produce without extreme revulsion, then let us look for another job.

We may as well admit that many of our designs are 'pretty awful'. Inevitably industry produces much that may embarrass us. But do we shrug our shoulders and say, 'Oh well, it's a good seller'—in which case we really do belong to the army of the damned—or do we believe that improvement is possible?

As for the prophets of good taste, especially those centred on London, treat them as friends and colleagues but don't mince words. If you don't like what they like, challenge their taste. To help them in their difficult task, treat them occasionally to the soul-liberating retort, 'Sez You!'

BAROQUE
MEMORIES

PAUL CARTER

BAROQUE
MEMORIES

CARCANET

First published in 1994 by
Carcanet Press Limited
208–212 Corn Exchange Buildings
Manchester M4 3BQ

A CIP catalogue record for this book
is available from the British Library
ISBN 1 85754 070 0

The publisher acknowledges financial assistance
from the Arts Council of England.

Set in Bembo by Koinonia Ltd, Manchester
Printed and bound in England by SRP Ltd, Exeter

Contents

Maravíllate, memoria!
Recuerdas lo que no ha sido.

Fernando Pessoa

Christopher discovers a Father

Entering the city this morning my eye was caught by what I can best describe as a dazzle of darkness. In the distance where the white-walled street ahead of me curved out of sight a doorway of shadow kept opening in the glare, and as quickly closing again.

I blinked as I had blinked when the light first struck me. I wanted to check the darkness was not in my eye. But when I looked again, the tiny eclipse was still happening.

Like the shadow vanes of a turning windmill sliding down a blank wall; like a flickering screen, like a crocodile of black-habited nuns threading a sunlit cloister, like the stutter of a film unspooling...

But I must not go on. It is a fault of mine to go on. Similes are like gunshots, Grazioni used to say: one focuses the eye but a battery of them puts up a smokescreen.

Besides as I drew closer it began imperceptibly to change, to fluctuate, to slow down, to grow ragged at the edges – a scarecrow, dangling from a stick by one gripless talon, fluttering dismally, a black sheet being shaken out or the felling of a dark-foliaged tree, the shuddering, the imminent collapse.

I am only trying to make you see it. Perhaps there is too much detail but you must understand that we travellers pass our lives among people who do not share our point of view. We become used to repeating ourselves, describing the simplest event in a hundred ways.

But to come to the point: I saw at length a black sleeve and a white cuff frantically waving, beckoning me urgently to approach.

When I first set foot in this country I was struck by the variety of birdsong.

But I get ahead of myself.

What I should say is that I was surprised to find only one sound I could identify.

Behind the beaches, along the tea-coloured creeks and among the alabaster groves nightingales sang constantly.

All the afternoon and early evening they filled the air.

For the rest, I seemed surrounded by voices.

Calling to one another across the spaces in whistles and clicks.

Answering one another in guttural croaks or far-carrying whispers.

I had alighted in a country where men had not learnt to speak in sentences!

And where were the inhabitants of this place?

I heard their naive calls but, except for the passage of feet, I could find no evidence of occupation.

The shadows began to lengthen. Many strange thoughts passed through my mind.

Perhaps they are invisible because they cannot speak.

Perhaps millenia of talk have eroded their tongues to the smoothness of water.

Perhaps they have gone back to mimicking nature. Their sounds indicate nothing except their distribution in space.

Perhaps I had discovered the home of poetry where there was no difference between the leap of feet and the intervals of sound –

Where birds and men understood one another.

I called out my name but nothing came back.

I imitated their clicks and grunts but, like echoes, my noises created a pool of silence.

The silence was infinitely worse than the sound.

I became angry. What game were they playing?

I fired my gun.

I gave up seeking a cave where I might rest.

In case anyone was looking for me.

I lay down in the cleft between two sand dunes.

I fired my gun.

To frighten them away.

And again.

In the silence I fell asleep.

Drawing nearer I observed what looked like an old man leaning over a stable-door.

He had stopped waving (had he been waving?).

As far as I could make out, he was craning his neck to see me, looking fixedly in my direction.

I was not so naive as to take his gesticulations at face value. In some countries our sign for 'Come here' signifies 'Farewell'. I was careful to give the impression that my mind was elsewhere.

Besides I resented his assumed familiarity. I disliked the idea that my arrival had been anticipated. What right had he to assume he was the focus of my visit?

My instinct was to turn aside, to pretend I had not seen him. But what would this prove – except that I had seen him? Besides, I reflected, perhaps it was not bad manners but the custom of the place.

L— was renowned for buildings whose animated facades, in the words of one guidebook 'almost turn to meet the passer-by'. Why shouldn't walls look back? Why shouldn't voyeurs poke their heads out of every aperture?

Why, in a city made for seeing, shouldn't my eyes dance like puppets on a string to the architect's master hand?

I looked away to take a photograph. But then again, checking the aperture I had the distinct impression he was winking at me … like a smuggler's lantern drawing me on to the reef … like a bubble of foam in a flowing gutter …

I determined to look straight through him and set my course at an acute angle so that if by chance he were to stretch out to grasp my sleeve, I would remain just beyond his reach.

Now that I had seen him, it was important to give the impression I had not seen him; that I was about to notice him for the first time. If nothing else, it would give him a chance to greet me differently.

Accordingly, I kept my eyes turned upwards where the quaintly carved balconies (for which L— is famous) crowd like puzzled eyebrows until, drawing abreast of him, I glanced as casually as I could in his direction.

To my surprise he had disappeared. In his place was a scarlet parrot tugging at a silver bell which, as it tinkled, twinkled in the sun.

'Christopher! Christopher!'

I awoke next morning to find a woman kneeling beside me, lightly stroking my brow.

'Christopher?' I said, imitating her rising inflection.

'Your mother, she will be so pleased to see you. Your father … but how could you know?'

'No?'

The voices that last night filled the air had become scarcely distinguishable from insects, frogs and the gentle hush of waves on the sand.

'Why did you leave us? My daughter …'

The noise was intolerable. I shook my head.

I thought I could detect thunder and dogs distantly baying.

'You are imagining it,' she said.

Was I also imagining she spoke?

Perhaps it was birdsong.

And if she did speak, was it in my tongue or simply in a tongue that sounded like mine?

Did she mean what I took her to mean? Or was the resemblance purely coincidental?

And if it was mere coincidence, our dialogue nothing more than a musical duet emerging haphazardly out of the noise, how could I reply?

Anything I said would mean something else in her tongue.

The more nearly I imitated her, the less likely I was to convey my meaning.

'You have made a mistake,' I said, contemplating her beaked nose.

But she went on stroking my brow.

'Do not panic, it will all come back in time.'

What kind of metamorphosis was this where I had become recognisable to strangers and unrecognisable to myself?

'Christopher,' she said with the same rising inflection.

There was no question about it: she had clearly mistaken me for someone else.

※

To disguise my confusion I pretended to stumble: looking where I was going would give me a reason to glance away.

I righted myself, pretending to check my camera for damage. But out of the corner of my eye I had the distinct impression that the parrot, rocking back and forth on its perch, mimicked my motions.

I drew myself up to my full height: he drew himself up to his full height! Without daring to look back, I hurried on.

That night when I went back over what had happened I reflected: if I was ever to reach the Piazza and my rendezvous with Nostalgia, I had no choice but to return to what I now dubbed 'The Street of the Mimic'. I could not allow a little misunderstanding to constrain the freedom of my wandering.

If yesterday's experience were repeated in every street I ventured down, I would shortly find myself unable to go out for fear of stirring up awkward memories.

Exploring L— would not enlarge my freedom but serve to imprison me: instead of feeling ever more at home I would redouble my strangeness.

Returning next morning to the Street of the Mimic I found the cage had been removed. No trace of my former passage remained: I began to tread with a distinctly lighter step.

Then, just as I was passing, the old man casually opened the upper-half of his door, gesturing with an eyebrow to the paving stones at my feet.

Inwardly I stamped my foot. I was not going to be tied down by a crack in the pavement. I had no intention of making it the premature epitaph of my journey.

I had only pretended to stumble. He knew that. Why did he pretend otherwise? His air of sincere concern irritated me. It was a pretence and he knew it …

I had no choice now but to greet him.

I fixed his eye and nodded. If I did not look where he looked, he would see that I had no recollection of what he alluded to. He would discern that I found his knowing glance comically absurd. Feeling embarrassed, he would naturally alter his expression, pretending that nothing had been meant by it.

I half-smiled, signalling my lack of comprehension; I looked away taking a photograph, giving him time to rearrange his features, to pretend that nothing had passed between us.

To my embarrassment, when I looked back, his face had disappeared.

Out of politeness I assumed my new identity. But what did it amount to? A past I could not remember, a language that mocked and silenced me.

Hearing the words come out of my mouth I felt like a runner who sees his shadow gliding ahead of him.

I could neither outpace my phantom self nor detach myself from it.

Besides someone was bound to trip me up.

I lived in constant fear of missing a chance allusion.

I lay awake at night wondering if I had given myself away.

My mother, my father – and her, what had my relationship been with her?

I became neurotically sensitive to signs. I could not distinguish the intended from the unintended: a casual glance, a crossing of legs, an unusually flattened vowel – I interpreted them all as the Janus-faced arbiters of my destiny.

For safety's sake, to conceal my nothingness, I studied to imitate the manners of those around me, but it was becoming unbearable.

So anxious had I become not to miss a trick, I developed a nervous tic.

Every time a bird called out overhead, a door slammed or a telephone rang, I twitched involuntarily. Was it for me, I could not help asking.

But it was more dangerous to undeceive than to deceive.

'Nostalgia,' I said one day to my fair discoverer, I cannot go on like this, pretending to be someone I am not.

'I thought you had nursed me back to health but you have imprisoned me in a solitude more profound than any I knew at sea or shipwrecked on the shore.

'I am not who you think I am.

'I am another Christopher.' (I could not bear to deny my new name altogether, and besides my former name I had forgotten).

She slapped me.

'Not a word more. The conceit of idleness makes you prey to these fantasies.'

I buried my nose in her cleavage trying to forget.

＊

His disappearance did not produce the desired effect, making it easier to grasp the street. My photographs seemed to lack scale and any significant point of view.

The old man might have been a blind spot in the retina of the city but it was through him that I was most likely to penetrate to the form of L— , to discover and possess the mystery of its inner eye, the Piazza – without which nothing that has been built here could have been imagined.

He was a gateway to L— , a necessary point of departure from my own way of seeing. Seeing him see me, I could imagine myself as another person – a photographer commissioned to record the city from the inside, to render visible what travellers never saw.

Without him I might remain forever outside, shipwrecked on a foreign shore. If he recognised me as a stranger, this merely proved the accuracy of his judgement? Who after all carries a camera at home?

Seeing I wore an instrument for seeing, he could not fail to see through me.

The next day I advanced towards The Street of the Mimic with a new eagerness. I keenly anticipated our meeting. I looked forward to placing our relationship on a new footing.

I found him there as before, his spectacles catching the sun. I greeted him unequivocally, saying 'Good Morning', and saluting him frankly with an outstretched hand and a smile.

The anxiety passed.

Day by day it became easier to be Christopher.

Friends were constantly reminding me of childhood incidents or adolescent pranks, and as my memory was naturally good, I found no difficulty in retaining these new sensations.

What they put behind them as superstitious relics I began to welcome as prefigurements of Paradise, whose nose-crowned cone is said to resemble Nostalgia's breast.

The spicy details they dismissed as travellers' tales held for me the fragrance of all the Indies.

I swam in an ocean of first impressions. I became a theorist of tides; I made a principle of the heart's fluctuations. I became adept at reading the signs, mimicking gestures, interpreting directions ...

Before long I found myself able to correct errors of fact. As a student of Christopher, I was becoming without equal. I began to keep his diary. I tried to imagine the city he lived in, asking myself whether he felt, as I did, like an explorer walking backwards over mirrored ground. I contemplated writing his biography.

Many things though remained unclear: neither then nor later did I make any progress in resolving how he spoke. All I could say with confidence was that as my own speech altered insensibly I came to feel I spoke as Christopher would have spoken if he had gone away and after a time come back.

It was disconcerting that they seemed to take my flattened vowels for granted, never asking me where I found them, as if they had not noticed my other life slipping slowly over the horizon, but by and by I also began to put it behind me.

My new confidence did not have the desired effect. Instead of responding with an equal openness, the old man seemed taken aback, at a loss how to reply.

Taking a leaf out of his parrot's book, he shifted uneasily from foot to foot, as if he did not feel at home.

I began to entertain the suspicion that he was not the owner of the house he appeared to occupy but merely its janitor. This would explain why he was always there and why he kept a parrot to raise the alarm.

It would explain why he greeted every passer-by with the same affability – and why the passers-by neglected to answer his friendly salutations: they knew he was standing in for someone else and only pretended to be at home.

When he fixed his beady eye upon them, instead of a man in full possession of his faculties they saw a man-sized parrot ... a parrot which kept a little man in a cage ... a little man who repeated every sound his father-parrot said and rocked far into the demented night remembering happier times at sea ...

He was the guardian of a palace to which he himself was forbidden entry; a face in the wall that could lay no claim to an interior. His smile was all surface ...

He was exactly like me, lodging in L— at someone else's pleasure – and the unpleasant thought occurred to me that in greeting him as an equal I seriously lost face, undermining my chances of getting in: would not the true inhabitants of L— perceive at once my lack of judgement?

I made myself vulnerable to being hoodwinked. I risked becoming the people's parrot, incapable of distinguishing sense from nonsense, right from wrong. Asking the way I might one day reach the Piazza but at what cost?

Condemned to repeat every sound I had ever heard, I would resemble the stylus in the record groove which, minutely approaching the centre, stops short of it, and lifting off jerkily swings back to the outer Void, there to begin all over again.

Suppose, I thought to myself, that the Contessa or whoever owned the palace, disturbed by our conversation, were to draw aside the curtain of an upstairs-window, and see me in the street: she would conclude I was a vulgar tourist – the more earnestly I entreated the janitor to let me in, the more irrevocably I would find myself exiled from her presence.

'The speech of these people is flat, monotonous.

'Little more on first hearing than a collection of nasal explosions, laconic hesitations and children's cries.

'Imperatives, propositions, exclamations and promises are all pronounced as questions.

'Subordinate clauses are unknown and for the most part communication is confined to simple canonic phrases which serve as a sort of shorthand, circumventing any need to speak more precisely and at greater length.

'Here is a people,' I wrote, 'that stands at the Antipodes to Baroque excess.

'No fear of the Void assails them.

'If they communicate at all it is not through words but through the gaps between words.

'These are truly a people of the surface, devoid of metaphysical anxiety.

'They do not even listen for the echo but finish changing a tyre, slam the cab door shut and grating the gears pull away in a plume of dust, pilgrims of the horizon.'

Looking into his pebble-lense spectacles, I reflected I had not seen into his eyes. The welcoming wink I had discerned had been a chance effect of light glancing off a bubble in the glass or sliding along the rim's steel hoop.

His greeting had been as mechanical, as impersonal, as the parrot-eye of the camera shutter: I began to see why I had been taken in. I was a photographer. I was used to seeing the world through a lense.

The little blindness of the camera closing its eye to take a view was my way of getting in – and wherever I saw a little eclipse of light I imagined photographers like me beckoning me to approach.

I had been taken in by my own mechanical way of seeing; I had mistaken my own blindness for a sign of recognition.

We – he and I – were alike janitors of the dark, pretending to illuminate its depths while staying imprisoned in the blindness of our own seeing.

I began to understand why so few photographs of L— had been taken, and why they so singularly failed to convey the city's effect.

At the same time I was not such a fool as to forget that, like it or not, the old man had been a witness to my arrival. No photograph of my entrance into L— existed except as an image in the old man's eye.

And even if it was the image of a man whom staring had rendered blind, it would be blindness to deny its importance.

I had no choice, I concluded, but to find another way of meeting him; another way in.

'It seems to me that my first impressions were superficial.

'I begin to notice that, despite the absence of eloquence in this place, the language is not without expressiveness.

'In compensation for the extreme contraction of verbal forms, the narrowed vocalic spectrum, the attenuated musicality, there is an extraordinary variation in the idiolect.

'One speaker may agree with another in using only the present tense, in reducing polysyllables to monosyllables, differentiated vowel sounds to single slurred diphthongs.

'But within these reductive verbal enclosures enormous variations exist.

'Take the ejaculation F—, a word sound universally employed to punctuate dialogue, indicating surprise, disdain, the whole gamut of emotions (and a remarkable instance of the genius of the tongue).

'I have heard F— pronounced fock, foock, fack, faick and even fake!

'Although in a primitive state of development, the language is capable of truly Baroque elaboration.

'Nor is this elaboration without rules.

'Not without some risk to myself I have ascertained that certain intermediate vowels are unacceptable.

'The short "i" (fick) for instance is not recognised as a form of F—, being taken instead for labialised "thick" …'

To place our relationship on a stable footing, it was essential to surprise him, to catch him off-balance.

While he remained a door-keeper, I must remain an outsider: so long as he looked at me a mutual dazzle would obscure the surface – I would not see past his glasses, while he would judge me by the flash of my camera.

This morning, determined that he should not see me before I saw him, I approached stealthily. But when I got there I found the upper door ajar and no one in … and then, as I turned to go, he surprised me, popping up like the parrot-nosed Punch in the show, and gaily greeting me. And although I was pleased to see him, I could not conceal my annoyance.

The frankness with which he said 'Good Morning' recalled my own behaviour a few days before when I had tried to branch out, steering our myopic past towards a more clearsighted future.

Only now, in his repetition, the phrase seemed tinged with nostalgia – as if, I thought afterwards, he wanted to pay his respects to a path that had once beckoned us but which was now no longer available.

I felt tears coming into my eyes. I turned. I walked away. And as I walked on I became aware of an irritation spreading down my spine, as if I was being minutely tattooed.

Another would have said it was the southern sun beating down but, with that third eye peculiar to travellers and photographers, I knew better: the old man was looking after me. They were his tears, not mine, that formed between my shoulder-blades; his gaze that bored into my brain; the map of his loneliness I wore on my back.

His memory of journeys taken and not taken propelled me on, drew him to me, his son, destined me to leave him, my father, always behind.

Parrots of each other, our only freedom was to fall silent. Mirrors to each other, our only choice was to turn our backs and under the illusion we found ourselves to shatter what remained of the past, sailing into the Void.

As I embraced the vocation of philologist a new anxiety assailed me. Was Christopher interested in the way people spoke? Or was he as I half suspected attracted to noise?

I felt the need to know him better. It was not enough to speak as he might have spoken had he come back: I needed to listen as he listened to the sound of his voice, to hear as he heard the sounds around and picking up their counterpoint to catch the rhythm of his consciousness.

He was a man or a woman who habitually allowed what he was saying to trail away to nothing, who modelled his speech on the archipelagos of islands printed at the world's end. But for this open-endedness, this disposition to dissolve into the background with its hubbub of insects, lawnmowers and numbers being dialled, his voice would still be here and he among us.

Perhaps I was only permitted to live here because his former friends were deaf to everything except the sounds of their own voices – whose murmur I imitated. I, it occurred to me, was tolerated as a noise in the background pleasantly amplifying their own self-importance, flattering their laughter.

I felt a need to master the ocean of sound. It was in the sea of noise they ignored that I would find the inner voice that was missing from my life. In an ear attuned to the tremulous screaming of the city, say, I might discover an explanation of his elusiveness.

Nosing my way through that parrot of all parrots – the city at night – I might find myself on his wavelength: amid the strangled pipes, abused children and squealing wheels, I might pick up his dwarf-cackle, his tin-whistle arias, his farts and intestinal stutters.

I was beginning to hear him all about me – but when I asked those I knew to listen, they merely shook their heads. When I gestured to the roar of the traffic they responded by closing the windows.

And when one day Nostalgia caught me talking to her parrot, she sharply dropped a curtain over its angry poll.

Deep in the pavement's core I could hear his heartbeat regular as the thud of distant waves, but when I put my ear to the ground I merely drew attention to myself, a man all ear, dangerously unable to say what he was doing.

A further obstacle stood in my path. Was it not certain that on these illicit descents into the caverns of noise Christopher had disguised himself, disappearing from sight and sound in order to reemerge as another person?

It was likely that he had disguised his speech, lapsing into another language? And what of his clothes, his sex, the outline of his nose, the colour of his eyes? How many masks had he possessed? How many voices? And did he speak all of them like the parrot or none of them – like the parrot?

I wept with frustration.

Perhaps he, too, had come from another place and, washing up against this doorway on his first day here, had remained there ever since like a hermit crab avoiding the tidal tug of the streets. In my few days here I had probably seen more of the city than he had in a lifetime.

If I had invested him with a citizenly authority he completely lacked, it was possible that he had similarly misunderstood me.

Besides, what could he make out through his pebble glasses? The people in the street, the very shadows of the balconies slowly waxing and waning throughout the day, were fishes swimming behind glass.

I was suddenly moved by compassion for him, short-sighted, alone but for his ventriloquist's dummy. It was clear he only greeted me because he could not see me, because he mistook me for someone else, because he was terrified that his blindness might be found out, and his disability used as an excuse to dismiss him from his post ...

This was why he kept the parrot: it was his camera, without which he was lost.

Was I one person who kept coming back? This would explain his eagerness to recognise me. Or was I everybody in the city, no one in particular, and his greeting always a first greeting, merely a habit?

To ease any misgivings he might have, I saw I had no choice but to disguise myself. To dispel the terror he must be feeling I must take care to greet him differently every day lest he think I were singling him out.

I began to shift my ground playfully, one day addressing him in his own dialect, another day scarcely nodding, yet another speaking too softly to be heard.

How this changeableness struck him I cannot say but it considerably lifted my own spirits. Regularly altering my place, never approaching by the same path twice, I began to feel I was getting the measure of L— .

The character of my photography changed. I gave up trying to frame the view; I increasingly focused my lense on the spaces in-between; I contemplated specialising in empty doorways and in recording the noisy aftermath of events.

I would wait for a pigeon to cross my field of vision and, as it passed out of sight, shoot the torn space unfurling behind it.

Yes, finding a subject, I began to feel at home.

A new anxiety assailed me.

I had become resigned to the fact that there were aspects of Christopher's life that must remain a closed book to me.

Things are forgotten; even the most attentive make mistakes, confusing places and faces. Bridges are associated with countries that are flat. Meetings are located in buildings long knocked down. Diarists who stole an afternoon together in bed find long after they had cast-iron alibis.

Had we met in the street, the chances are we would not have recognised each other. He would have mistaken me for someone else: I would have thought I was in the wrong place. Either way we would have been like two streets which, converging on a piazza, are of one mind though they never meet.

Now, when former friends of his taxed me with some old indiscretion, I felt perfectly relaxed. I affected not to remember. It was obvious that only by forgetting him could I expect to find him.

And it was with some gratification that I noticed I carried off this truthfulness rather better than my old deceptions. No one suspected I was lying. They attributed my insouciance to bad memory – from which anyone might occasionally suffer.

But now something far worse began to disturb me. I became aware that Christopher resented the fact that he and I were growing apart.

I remember when I first realised this. It was as I began to write the first words of what I hoped would be my life's work. I felt (at that very moment) a physical resistance, an electric charge run up my arm and settle like a hump on my back.

It was Christopher, incubus on my incunabulus, trying to stop me going on. He knew that once I began to write his biography I would enjoy a separate existence. I might go for days without speaking – and then where would he be? As good as dead.

That same night I dreamt I was in a cemetery, only all the headstones were ant hills and, as I kicked each one over, parrot-nosed ants swarmed out and scattering round my feet looked up at me cursing, and those that remained silent as they ran carried in their jaws little effigies of Christopher.

The truth was that I had become tired of his migrant evasiveness. We have all come from somewhere else, migrants or not, and I was fed up with his dandyish posturing, his moodiness, his philandering, his unwillingness to do anything with his life.

Christopher was an invalid I had had to nurse and, hard as it was to admit, the truth was: I wanted him to die.

My chameleon behaviour had an unexpected consequence. Instead of pushing our friendship forward, it produced the opposite effect.

Instead of dissolving the distance between us, it pushed us further apart. The studied spontaneity of my different greetings turned him to stone. In a curious way we had retreated to the time immediately before my arrival.

Only now the future lay behind us not before, in the realm of the might have been; and the façades I looked forward to seeing now merely reminded me of a past not mine.

Now that I had become anybody except myself I was like any traveller arriving; and he, the good father that he was, could no longer look forward with simple pleasure to the homecoming of his prodigal son.

To guard against disappointment, to shield himself against repeated disillusionment as, one after another, likely-looking young men approached him down the street only to pass by on the road's far side, he had no choice but to cultivate an air of reserve, as if the balance of the present remained permanently weighted in favour of the future.

His face glazed over; he no longer recognised me, although he looked into my face; and if this pained him, be assured it was equally painful to me. I had come to rely on his fathering gaze to lend my wanderings their sense of purpose, of adventure.

Increasingly my photographs had been taken for him: to give him an idea of the city where he lived. By every means possible I had tried to stand where he stood.

But now he did not look at me. He did not look away. As if I were a parrot's eye, he gazed stonily through me, like a man condemned to die.

One night, pen in hand, I was contemplating the final coup de grace when the conic shadow of Nostalgia's nose fell across my page.

'Beware of doing Christopher in,' she began. 'So long as he is alive he cannot harm you. So long as his immortality depends on your refusal to give him up, he is your prisoner.

'You may libel him; you may despise him; you may pretend he does not exist. But while you keep his name he cannot live without you.

'Consider your position. It is years now since you first landed on our island. Perhaps you are Christopher; perhaps not – frankly the issue is no longer of much interest: for you have become more Christopher than Christopher ever was.

'You have been privy to all his secrets: the parts of his life he kept sharply apart have mingled in you. The thoughts of friends, the impressions of lovers, the private correspondence of bureaucrats, the photographs he took in L— – with unremitting zeal you have assembled them preparatory to publication.

'Out of them you have created a character whose powers of recall and self-understanding far outstrip the modest abilities the old Christopher possessed.

'You have created a Christopher that Christopher would envy, a Christopher that Christopher would kill for. Do you follow me?

'We love you, Christopher, more than your original.'

I looked into her eyes carefully.

I wanted, I admit it, I desperately wanted to see him again; I was ashamed of my stratagems, my lack of filial piety. So that when one day, passing his way, I found the double-door closed and a note to the effect that he had gone away, I was beside myself.

I had visions of his dying, neglected, unseeing; and blamed myself for torturing this good old man's patience.

I made enquiries; with much effort I located him in a nearby sanatorium; I undertook to care for his parrot until he was released; and I began to visit him, regularly taking him ... taking him not flowers but photographs.

I was determined to make him see again, to find a way of bringing the city back to life again. I dimly knew that if the stones of L— could be resurrected, the erosion of age might be stayed and the old man's blank eyes once more twinkle as they had on the first day of our meeting – our not meeting.

Each day I helped him to sit up in bed. I showed him a selection of shots which I had taken of the city – in the hope that he might recognise any of their images.

Quaint stalls with their conicular fields of oranges, retroussé belfries golden-tipped, the dripping noses of gargoyles, reproductions of the pre-Fascist Piazza, where archways loomed as large as nostrils; details of illustrated nostrums that had survived the Great Library Fire ...

Fiestas, masses, baptisms and burials: I showed him every conceivable familiar face without eliciting a spark of recognition.

Instead of reviving him my views had the opposite effect; it was as if they drew the life-force visibly out of him, as if tiny ropes passed through the openings of his eyes and drew out gradually the very stuff of memory, until nothing was left but an empty skull – an album of ghostly images.

From that time on I knew no peace.

I was like an autobiographer who, as he establishes the facts about the past, filling in the blanks, begins to perceive a pattern that he has not noticed before. Who begins to find that, in order to be himself, he must be someone else; and that the person he formerly inhabited is a savage in comparison with the savant he has now become.

Christopher had ceased to be a living creature and become instead a historical fiction. No longer a branching tree where birds might flock and where a hundred thoughts might branch like the streets of a city, he had become a strangling liana at my throat which, slowly enclosing me in a coffin of wood, prevented me from embarking on a road of my own.

The terrible truth was: the Christopher I had invented and so successfully mimicked was not the real Christopher at all. The real Christopher was the one who had slipped away and disappeared; and who now, one supposed, lived a parallel life on another island, where at noon the sky was darkened with skeins of screaming parrots making for the paw-paw trees ...

I realised I had been tricked. Had I not been willing to step into his shoes, to assume the burden of a past he was anxious to leave behind, he might never have escaped.

I was the mask he needed to conceal his flight.

It was my migrant nostalgia that gave him the strength to leave Nostalgia behind and migrate.

This irony racked me. I felt an impulse to smash his mirror, to burn his diaries, to lock up the house and leave.

But I could not bring myself to do it: I was seized by the thought that I might meet him somewhere.

If we met face to face, how could I explain what I had done? Without the appropriate documents how could I be certain he was who he claimed he was? Without a biography what proof would I have I was he and he not I?

I had despaired of his life, I had all but exhausted my photographic reserves, when one day I detected a glint of animation under his hooded lids.

One of my in-between images appeared to have captured his attention; I passed it before his eyes a second time. There was no mistake; he had clearly glimpsed in it something he recognised.

I enlarged the picture, I projected it on to the wall, dropping a white sheet over the door I had come in by; whereupon he himself seemed magnified in vitality; and hauling himself up, scanned the view intently.

A cross-roads was depicted, or rather one of those curvilinear meeting places where two of L— 's nobly curving streets briefly interwine before parting to go their separate ways.

Along the left hand edge could be made out the dark half-moon of a street sign, an extract of cornice; on the right hand side was part of a wall and the sharply raking shadow of a shutter; a peep of typical sky at the top, a mottled sea of cobbles near the bottom.

But it was the centre that appeared to engage all his interest: the focal point which, contrary to the best photographic practice, I had left blank, where undistracted by a pretty face, motor car grille or monument, it was possible, I flattered myself, to contemplate nothing at all.

Before I could restrain him, he pulled on a dressing-gown and slippers, and with a step that would have done credit to a man half his age, advanced towards the wall.

I was impressed: he felt like me the fascination of the image. He understood, as I did, the appeal of the Void. I noticed for the first time the prismatic refractions rainbowing the sheet and the faint flutter of shadow leaves projected sidelong on to it through the window. He was an artist of the eye like myself ...

Yes, I thought to myself, rejoicing in his resurrection, for the first time in our acquaintance I had presented him with a view that was unmemorable. No precious associations threatened to see through it to another place. No memories conspired to turn wall and image into cruel illusions.

On the white sanatorium wall the skin of the outer world and the skin of the inner world coincided. Yes.

The ward in which he lay all day, idly watching the flies in their spirals, and the world outside the ward, indifferently winding and unwinding a thousand destinies, miraculously wrapped round one another.

Yes. Remembering nothing, he found the world remembering him.

But then, instead of falling on his knees to worship, he extended his hand towards the screen and firmly grasped the little projection I had not noticed until then: the infant mountain, the Paradisal nipple, of the door-handle swelling underneath the sheet.

And before I could draw him back, he pulled aside the veil and sailed out, and teetering down the winding stair steered out of the hospital's harbour of shadow, into the surf of the everyday.

I ran after him with his parrot. But habited in light he had already disappeared.

✳

The possibility that Christopher had not simply disappeared and perished at sea but was alive and well somewhere else put a fresh complexion on my situation.

I envied him eating his guavas, freed from the burden of re-membering, and gave up my ambition to penetrate to the heart of the city – which at that time I envisaged like the amphitheatre of the ear.

Could he still speak or had he relaxed into island ways, dumb trading?

His independence appealed to me. His objective existence proved I wasn't mad? It was a guarantee against internment, inter-ment.

I could understand Columbus's relief when his Paradise turned out to be a handle on the sky, a place where parrots spoke a tongue he remembered and where the natives intuiting his love of these birds brought him them in golden cages, as if they were speaking books.

Removing his hand from Nostalgia's breast he might well have felt strong enough to go back.

Even in her arms I had never felt at home here, and now I understood his history I had a reason for going back, for going on.

I knew things about him of which he was unaware.

I could put him in contact with useful people.

I could put his mind at rest about his debts, about Sternatia, Egnazia, Euclidia and the rest of those island-women that had beckoned him siren-like.

I took a likeness of Nostalgia to show him; a profile as promising as a charted cape.

Perhaps – it seemed highly probable – the old navigator was already looking for me.

I comforted her, saying she would surely find another like me
...

If he was anything like me, his past life would be on his conscience. I began to imagine his gratitude, my condescension. He
would fall on my neck as on a loved one.

Yes, he was the lost one who must be found.

And when she did find my double, I told her, who knows but
he might be more like the person she thought I was ...

My blind hypotheses, my troubled dreams, my researches into
the surface of things, had not been wasted.

Like Columbus's scribblings in his copy of Marco Polo, they
were the speculative departures without which the true departure
would have been impossible.

And when Nostalgia cut off her hair, insisting I take it, I said I
would tie it to the stern where all day and night it would stream
out baroquely behind me.

In the meantime I began buying maps.

Doctor Duende forgets a Daughter

Doctor Duende started and opened his eyes.

Every morning it was the same. The white façade opposite caught the first rays of the morning and beamed them through the lace curtains of his bedroom. And every morning Doctor Duende started as if he were dreaming and for a split-second or so lay on his side unable to remember where he was.

He closed his eyes again but it was useless. The after-image of the white façade was cicatrized on his eyelids. Its Baroque complication of scrolls and pediments, of wreathes and scallop-shells seemed to have no other function than to hold up the light and bring it to fever pitch.

Doctor Duende had no one to blame but himself. When he first came to this country, he had taken up residence opposite the white façade because it reminded him of home.

Duende had never taken much notice of L— 's distinctive style, but he could appreciate that A— 's mass-produced urns, double-cusped pediments, emperor's head corbels and cloisonné wall panels bore little resemblance to it.

But this was the point. Contemplating the stuck-on rosettes across the road, half eclipsed by electricity poles or peeping through a trellis of wires, Duende was pleasantly reassured that this was not Paradise and he was not at home.

'It is not contrariness that draws me to noises. I do not understand what people have against noises.

'It is clear that they dislike them. If they did not find them disturbing, they would not attempt to drown them out with the roar of traffic.

'The climate of this country is especially congenial to the proliferation of noises. But let me explain.

'On days as warm as this the neighbourhood begins to deliquesce and shimmer. Angels dance on tin roofs; polished leaves sweat amber. Sheets of glistening water fit to beguile an explorer seethe on the crown of the road.

'Surfaces that used to package forms begin to vibrate, to unwrap themselves and levitate on quivering pinions. They do not wander away. Like souls they retain a sentimental attachment to their graves. But they rise far enough to put their former forms in doubt, suspending the difference between ground and air, visible and invisible.

'It is the same with noises. On warm days you have the impression they have taken leave of their senses and in the full face of summer radiate an aura of ambiguity.

'If we lived in a perfectly cold climate I dare say that every sound would be sensible. Words would be as palpable as stones sent skittering across the ice.

'But here they have no substance at all. They are vibrating walls shaking themselves apart, constantly collapsing in clouds of white mortar that, on closer inspection, reveal angels' wings dusting themselves off.

'But where was I?

'These micro-noises of which I was speaking make mockery of the imperial distinction between language and music.

'The soft pneumatic tread of motor cars becomes one vast and rumorous "hush", a mirage of maternal syllables, as if a giant were putting her child to sleep.

'As for radio's consonantal divisions, they crystallise and shatter, moting the intervenient air along with the sparrow's suburban chirrups, the cricket's rasping file, the cockatoo changing gears ...

'I hear what I want to hear. The language I have left behind. The language I am learning. All made one. Rising and falling.

'A language without names. A country without places. A ground drawn taut as a drum skin, and the feet that walk it lightly beating palms.'

※

While his wife was alive Duende had kept photographs of L— on display along with studio portraits of the family.

It had been her idea. She had wanted to make it plain that they had no desire to put the past behind them. They were proud of their heritage. They had nothing to be ashamed of. She had never really wanted to leave in the first place.

Duende acceded. He saw that any admission of indifference to the past would have been interpreted as infidelity to her. The little façades in their frames came to stand for all that stood behind them, the depth of their attachment.

When they had drifted to A— , which by the way they had

reached via many other ports of call, they had certainly not prepared the path for reminiscence by taking photographs.

They had had to collect their pictures of L— by cutting them out of architectural magazines.

The images were stored in a shoebox under the stairs. Every time a new detail was obtained – a section of balcony, the corner of a palace or even a well-known monument viewed from a different direction or in a different light – the shoebox was emptied on to the carpet and an effort was made to see where the newest photograph fitted in.

There was no end to the fragments that could go in to the reconstruction of a façade but it was always hoped that the new detail would prove the final piece in the jigsaw.

In reality it usually seemed to be the first piece of yet another new building.

Perhaps this explains why they went on adding to their collection until images of L— covered every available surface. Not having an image of their own, they could not assemble a recognisable L— except by imagining every conceivable viewpoint.

And who could say that even a collage of five or six photographs gave a complete picture of a palace, a fountain or a piazza?

No wonder that as he contemplated the growing collection Duende began to feel he was seeing L— for the first time.

'Not understanding the inner life of the country – not even being sure that it exists – I have to make the most of appearances.

'I understand enough about the electrical propagation of power not to suppose that the noises emanating from its finger tips – the sockets whence the vocal radios and deeply-inhaling vacuum cleaners draw inspiration – have their origins in the wires overhead.

'However I venture to say that the fate of noises here is correctly represented by the spindly forms of transport electricity favours.

'The arboreal reduction of the electricity poles, with their nailed-on yard arms and metrical rigging, represents the triumph of noise over noises.

'The peacetime roar of traffic makes conversation impossible. The slipstream of trucks and fast-moving cars is too strong for any human sound to escape. Consequently, to make oneself heard here it will be necessary to find another way of communicating.

'To overcome the noise it will be necessary to speak silently, to create a form of communication that is free of ambiguous signals, unique inflections, equivocal variations.

'This is what the lofty network of wires etched against the famous sky represents: graphic speech. No wonder that when the ibis fly over in V's they suggest a musical accompaniment or the invention of the alphabet.

'But these Baroque metaphors are a typical migrant's trick and betray nothing more than an impatience with the ambiguity of appearances.

'I have noticed that the electricity poles are not round but octagonal. Currently they carry wires in parallel north-south or east-west. But the carpenters of these bare trees clearly imagined a maypole of wires festooning the sky: eight directions of wires cobwebbing the city, darkening the sun at noon and, where they crossed, seeming to rub against one another, winding and unwinding reels of light.

'Resembling Leonardo's infinity of lines connecting all things to each other, isn't there something Baroque about this vision?'

🔖

Visitors to the house could not help noticing the burgeoning collection of photographs.

The Duendes' visual inventory of distinctive buildings, elegantly curved streets and breast-shaped domes was an obvious talking point.

At first Duende used to explain in the simplest terms that they were pictures of his and his wife's place of birth.

But he could see that this explanation left them puzzled. If L— really looked like this, their quizzical silences seemed to say, what on earth possessed him to leave it? Duende felt they suspected him of concealing some unimaginable crime or perhaps a temperamental instability – either of them fatal to his professional prospects.

He took to explaining that L— was by no means as it appeared in the photographs. In fact, he said, in its fragmentary juxtaposition of different styles it resembled to a surprising degree the visual character of an average suburb in A— .

This line of argument proved even less satisfactory. He found himself suspected of a double disloyalty – to the memory of his former country and to the reputation of his adopted land.

To close friends and acquaintances he confessed that he

tolerated the photographs in the interests of his wife's health.

The trauma of coming to a new country, he explained, had brought on a 'breakdown'. She had felt for many months unable to piece the pieces of her life together. She had babbled like an infant. She had gone for days without speaking.

Putting together the parts of L— , you understand, he said, is therapeutic. It is, he said, as if she were rebuilding herself. And then they began to smile and nod their heads comprehendingly.

'A tattoo of heels, the pavement has a different sound.

'It can also be thought of as the residue of the rain's drumsticks.

'Single notes pool in its depressions, expand its fissures, exposing wounds of aggregate.

'A minute sand migrates across its surface in high winds, making a scarcely audible "sshhh".

'In dry weather it grows pale as if it were withering away. Its natural pitch rises. "E-eeeeee-ah!"

'The pavement aspires to the condition of smoothness but eruptions of life from the underworld have aged it.

'It is criss-crossed with shadow trenches. The ice flows of private drives unceremoniously cut through it.

'Prosthetic tubes crowned with signs sprout from its bruised, still-cooling scar tissue.

'Exotic trees sprout like nightmares from white-lipped planters cut out of its skin.

'Its grooved and etched surface comes to resemble a miniature landscape which feet and children's bicycles navigate.

'It comes to resemble a record which the heel plays not the stylus. Only the grooves of the pavement criss-cross each other.

'As a result one does not hear the melody. One hears the interference pattern of scratches, scuffs, clicks and squeals where grooves meet one another and momentarily modify each other's signal.

'Different styles of walking reveal different pavements.

'Different speeds of walking compress the surface to different degrees.

'The running child makes the path mount up into a single standing wave.

'The two women who stop to talk are unaware of the surface threshing behind them like a serpent's tail and gradually calming down.

'The man walking at an even pace leaves behind him a profile of blocks and towers that resembles nothing so much as the skyline of the city.

'The dancer leaves behind no pavement at all.'

The solution to his conversational dilemma came one morning when a patient by the name of Egnazia, whom he had been treating for selective amnesia, remarked out of the blue that she recognised his photographs from her family album.

The album, she explained, had been lost but she had not the slightest doubt that these images came from it. Indeed she could remember having taken some of them herself.

She recognised the buildings; she could even put a name to some of the decapitated heads that loomed along the edges.

Over the course of the next few weeks a minute examination of them enabled her to recover an extraordinary range of repressed memories.

Duende was introduced to the members of her family; he heard about their holidays; about the war; about the difficulties they had experienced as migrants.

He learned that they had once owned a scarlet macaw which was a perfect mimic and that the bird had escaped when she was still a little girl and that she had firmly believed it had stolen her voice and had refused to speak for six months.

Photographic Recall, Duende's most distinctive contribution to psychiatry, arose directly from this experience – from the simple perception, as he later observed wryly, that in order to get at the origins of things the origins of things must be disguised.

'At night the traffic comes from a greater distance, like thunder after lightning.

'Cars slow down and fall asleep along the kerbs.

'When everyone is in bed the giraffe-necked street lights lower themselves and peer through the windscreens for signs of inner life.

'The wires hum. They hear galloping horses. They pretend they are tightly-held reins.

'Televisions betray their lovers, projecting their crouching forms on to curtains before being turned off.

'The roads tremble. For they never forget the war from which they came.

'The erotic rush of locomotives. Boom!

'The jangle of couplings. The jingle of the boomgate's flails.

'A toilet flushing.

'The fire engines in their fire-coloured shells dream of crowds, involuntarily alarming bells.

'Underground, souls half a world apart dream of each other, setting off a thousand telephones.'

All this time his view of the white façade was slowly changing.

The mere coincidence of its resemblance to buildings in another country had provided Duende with a way of orienting himself in strange surroundings; it had given him a reason for settling down.

He had the impression it shared his sense of irony. Its array of rooftop urns and curlicues cut out against the flawless blue sky might, at a glance, be mistaken for their Mediterranean originals.

But it was enough to widen the glance to see that there was no question of a genuine connection. Among its welter of volutes and scrolls, the white façade boasted wrought iron verandahs and fretwork grilles that suggested a recent visit to the Alhambra.

Nothing was pure or original. Nothing was represented, even though a dozen styles were mimicked. The white façade recalled famous buildings but there was no real connection, nothing behind it.

Its self-mockery had appealed to Duende. After all what is more absurd than the efforts of a migrant to appear at home? But before long its insouciance began to irritate him. He started to resent its lack of drama, he grew suspicious of its indifference to history.

The only event in its life, he used to say, holding the curtain aside and peering across the street, are the little saucer-shaped clouds that occasionally rise from its parapets and flock above it.

Blank emanations of its whiteness, they are the dreams the white facade harbours, formless, faceless, disappearing.

And he would look away, cover his face with his hands and, to all appearances, allow tears to course down his cheeks.

'The vagueness of clouds should not be mistaken for a lack of direction.

'They are the oldest inhabitants of this country.

'They do not die, they simply continue to change.

'They are the spirits that bring our houses back to life.

'Windows understand them, translating their passage into a film of moods.

'Their shadows lend weight to our choice of roof.

'Their aversion to drama is reflected in our furniture.

'Clouds inventory the life between events. For this reason some zealots describe them as anti-historical.

'The truth is: they never repeat themselves.

'Clouds give the lie to dreams. Pure outer life, they are never so much themselves as when they fall asleep drifting over the city.

'They can teach the migrant a thing or two. "Clouds," he exclaims on his first day here, naming the one thing he can recognise from the old country.

'But the one thing he can bring with him from the old country is already changing before his eyes into something new.

'And another thing: don't imagine the clouds are voiceless. It is reliably reported that the sound of clouds coagulating into water and forming rain far surpasses the thunder of Niagara in full spate.

'As for the production of snowflakes, even the din of the steelworks cannot be compared with it.

'If you think the clouds are quiet, you must have cotton-wool stuck in your ears.'

On other occasions the white façade moved him to eloquent compassion. He longed to restore it to its family, to animate it with the shadows of buildings that shared its forms.

If only, he would explain, it could be surrounded by balconies, opening and closing windows and the rise and fall of children's voices as they played ball in the cobbled lane below, it might recover its voice and begin to speak in confident tones.

But here its face was eaten away with loneliness and spoke, if at all, of the blank intervals that separated people and which spawned hybrid sounds too peculiar to be shared.

Duende noticed that his patients baulked at clusters of consonants. Inserting vowels, they made three syllables out of one.

So with the white façade, he exclaimed: elsewhere its fluted columns might have clustered in one composite mass. Here they were ironed out, pushed apart by a hollow grille of round-mouthed roses.

Duende had also observed a contrary impulse towards the simplification of vowels and the consequent reduction of vocabulary to a minimum. Sentences were left unfinished, phrases hung unanswered in the air.

Again, the white façade expressed it.

The triumphal wreathes for example that spanned the pediment underneath the attic were stuck on to the surface mechanically, without accent.

No fat cherubs shouldered them as they danced gaily in and out. They did not mingle with *bucrania* and *fasces*, discovering a hundred associations of Life and Death.

They resembled, Duende thought, a line of dactyls, signifying the loss of a verse in an ancient author. They indicated the sound of a meaning that could no longer be recovered.

They reconstructed what could not be heard, trying to connect what could not be connected, lending the silence a measure.

'Sometimes in the summer the tarmac despairs of its softness. It regards its amphibious in-betweenness, neither water nor stone, as a punishment its inventors imposed upon themselves.

'Those who conceived it were driven by a desire to cover ground more quickly. To this end they devised a means of surfacing the earth smoothly, a material as lissom as silk.

'But they were like novice ice-skaters navigating this frictionless lamina and kept falling over. Although they wanted to travel they did not wish to slide endlessly across a level plain.

'To slow themselves down, to disguise their vertigo, they modified the formula to make the surface sticky and impressionable.

'But the results were not as they had expected. Instead of giving them a better grip on the ground and allowing them to corner more quickly, to accelerate more rapidly, to steer more nimbly, the new surface adhered to their feet and on hot days was so viscous they found themselves slowed down and trapped.

'They were like limed parrots beating their wings more and more feebly.

'Perhaps they did not try to resist. Instead of seeking to spread their wings, perhaps they became addicted to tarmac's slowness. For people without a ground of their own, it provided a pretext for settling down.

'This is what the pavement thinks to itself in the summer.

'Lithic flagstones would be stepping stones, inspiring leaps of fancy, bouncing balls and the trickle of water.

'Fluent streams would support canoes, swimmers and trans-lucent depths.

'And it cannot conceal the depression it feels, which others call the migrant condition.'

※

Duende began to be grateful to the white façade. He even took to sleeping with the curtains open.

He saw that he had been wrong to write it off as an imitation of other places. True, it could not compare with the finest buildings of the Occident, but it had an identity of its own, a fractured, frag-mented personality that he could instantly recognise.

He saw that its lightness was more than an accident of light. It represented its attachment to the surface, its refusal to accommo-date nostalgia.

He began to warm to its lack of introspection, to its forward looking windows with their interrogative cusps and ear-muff mouldings. It was deaf to the past, it kept a clear weather eye out for the future.

He found its punning attitude towards reality entering into his own way of thinking.

He began to keep a notebook, dedicated to everyday appear-ances, which began 'It is not contrariness that draws me to noises. I do not understand what people have against noises.'

He developed a taste for paralalia. He found it increasingly easy to talk about nothing and to punctuate his discourse with silences that signified nothing.

And I mean nothing.

Some mornings he allowed the pale shadow of its brightness to populate his dreams. He watched the rod-like bacilli, the grooved paramecia, the atoll-like streptococci rise in the east and float spas-modically over the pink meniscus of his eyelids.

As they flocked, forming chains of islands, and, as easily, detached themselves, creating new arrangements, Duende had the distinct impression he was watching the birth of a Baroque façade.

Only it was a façade of the Void, without syntax, rhyme or reason, without origin or end.

※

'A writer of the old school would not be content to make lists. He would view everyday appearances with suspicion.

'Sometimes, pretending I live somewhere else, I have tried to put the fragments together, to make a picture out of them.

'A place where I could live like a writer.

'I have tried to construct a house that I could call my own. To develop a style of construction that would qualify me to say I was the architect of my own destiny.

'But the more I look and listen, the more they spread out – the wires, the clouds, the walking feet and the bird calls – and lose themselves elsewhere, and I have the impression that, but for my noticing them, they would have nothing in common at all.

'If I were to move a foot to the left or to the right, a completely different set of phenomena would pass through me and I would make different sounds.

'Personality is not a house, it is a pavement, a set of wires, a thin and tender pole.

'It resembles a vibrating surface suspended in the air.

'In the old country excitability of the limbs or countenance was regarded as a symptom of neurosis. The cure for the condition was poetry.

'Poetry was therapy for lightness of attachments. Metaphors were to migrants as cages to parrots: a way of making them talk and feel at home.

'The swallows assembling and flocking on the electricity wires could be compared to notes on a stave.

'It was a commonplace when writing of roadside puddles to describe the clouds floating over their face.

'These casual likenesses bear witness to the fragility of our grasp on reality. But caught in the poem's photographic plate and held there forever, they change their nature.

'They come to signify a hidden relationship or affinity which, before long, is felt to express the character of the place.

'But here the clouds go on, the puddle evaporates, the birds cannot be identified and have flown on without alighting.'

After his wife died, Duende changed completely. The examinations to which she had been subjected in the last months and weeks of her life had upset him.

The artillery of X-rays, ultra-sounds, intravenous drips and catheters with which the hospital had sought to penetrate to the heart of things had filled him with horror.

It was as if they were already digging under the green sward; already exhuming her skeleton. Seeing into her, they had rendered her invisible.

Duende became convinced that nothing of human value lay beneath the surface. His own practice concentrated more and more on the face, which he came to imagine as a cross-section of space revealing the fourth dimension of time.

The mistake, he now began to see, was to look past their eyes, to ignore the new capillaries bursting along the cheekbone, the recent shadow under the eye, the extension of a line on the brow.

A history of the skin was needed, a psychology of continuous substitution.

He developed an Art of Forgetting that enabled his patients to keep abreast of their ageing.

His diary took a new direction. Duende became sceptical about the value of recording appearances. He feared that his lists of birds and sounds, his car counts and voice recordings concealed a metaphysical nostalgia.

Duende no longer looked for patterns in his lists. He gave up expecting a meaning to emerge.

He began to imagine a literature of amnesia. He made sketches for a book called *Clangers* which, he said, would be free of metaphors.

Metaphors, he said, were rear-view mirrors. He wished to be free of backward-looking associations, to describe a world whose ground was as mobile as his mind.

The early motorists in this country carried sheets of iron with them – with which they fabricated roads across the desert. Repeatedly laying them down, picking them up, carrying them forward and laying them down again, they edged forward.

Making tracks, they covered their tracks: Duende said this was how he would like to write.

When colleagues commiserated with him on the death of his life-companion, he had increasing difficulty understanding them.

When she first came to this country it was, she said, as if she had died. But for his part, he said, it had been as if he had opened his eyes for the first time.

A moment he associated with the white façade.

Which his wife had dubbed 'The Nose'.

Such is the ambiguity of appearances here.
And he would smile wanly.

'Nothing adheres here. But this is not a criticism. Lightness of attachments should be cultivated. It is an excellent cure for displacement.

'A patient of mine by the name of Vincenzo has recently knocked down the old shed at the end of the backyard and begun to build little structures out of sticks – which, with the help of string and sackcloth, serve to shelter him from the sun.

'For years, he said, he had been in the habit of retiring to the shed to write. It was the ideal environment for writing a book, for enclosing the past, for closing the door on it …

'In reality it merely brought home to him his own isolation. When he forgot himself and began intoning aloud, he would be interrupted by heart-rending sounds. He would hear his daughter crying and deduce that she had been listening at the door. As he spoke in a language she did not know, how could she tell he was not mad?

'He played classical music he had loved in his youth in order to hide the sound of his own voice, but the gramophone was continually breaking down; and besides the records eventually wore out.

'When, on my recommendation, he knocked the shed down, he was surprised to find it had no foundations. It merely sat on a slab of concrete. He took this as a sign that his own writing was similarly ill-founded and gave it up.

'Now, each weekend he builds a new string and stick shelter, inside which he sits, sometimes with his family, sometimes alone, listening to the sound of the wind in the canvas.'

From this time, according to his family, Duende began to go down hill. He gave up his practice and took to spending days on the verandah apparently gazing into space.

His housekeeper complained that she had the eerie sensation that he was looking right through her. Even when she stood in front of him, it was as if she did not exist. 'It's as if we live in two different worlds,' she explained the day she left him, closing the door behind her for the last time.

Duende did not regret her departure, but she had misunderstood. His vacancy was not the result of yielding to a nostalgia for absent things. It was the rapture of one who felt himself to be in the presence of the Present.

He had woken up to the fact that he had been living in a dream. He did not mean to say that he had woken from life's dream but he was certain that he had correctly diagnosed its condition.

Where he had come from, they had taught him that dreams belonged to the realm of sleep. They dwelt in a country that could not be found on any map of the world, in an interior too deep to be excavated.

But they had been mistaken. There was no difference between our dreams and the daily appearance of things. When we rationalised appearances, penetrating beneath their surfaces in search of an underlying structure, we turned a blind eye to the dreaminess of reality.

When he looked as if he were dreaming, he said, he was most awake; and if he could not communicate with his daughter or the new social worker who now began to visit him, it was because they were under the illusion they were awake, when in reality they were fast asleep.

❧

'The brightest light here is a form of night or moonshine. It tends to disperse rather than define appearances.

'This can be proved by the application of associationist principles. When last night the houses and streets, the wires and car roofs were bathed in mother of pearl, it recalled to my neighbour the mountains of Thessaly. While on the other side it was Etna that came to mind or Ararat.

'When moonlight lies like snow on the suburb, it does not bandage up divisions. It does not gloss over misunderstandings or smother disagreements. It magnifies differences, burying us further in our separate pasts.

'This is not an argument against light but against the doctrine of associationism – from which we need to dissociate ourselves.

'The brightest light here is the shadow of death. It presages forgetfulness and resurrection. The uniformity of light's appearance is proof it is immune to nostalgia.

'The bereaved – I know from experience – not only mourn the loved one, but the seeming death of light. Light loses its familiarity, its colour, its Italian focus. It glazes over, grows mirage-like. The heart of darkness visibly pulsates within it.

'But, I hasten to explain, this detachment of light, its blank refusal to solace the bereaved eye, its bland occupation of other surfaces, signifies the migration of new life.

'This is why we never see more clearly than in the shadow of death.

'This is why the funereal moonlight makes us stir in our sleep and wake up.

'Why the Void is so valuable.'

⚜

Shortly after that Duende gave up speaking. Or to be exact he gave up speaking a language that anyone could understand.

His new dialect excited professional interest. A well-known specialist speculated that his mumbling rigmarole of proper names represented an unusual cathexis of what the great Russian psychologist of language, Lev Vygotsky, called 'inner speech' – in which the discourse of reverie involuntarily vibrated the vocal chords rendering audible what was normally not fit to be spoken.

Others from the University, surprised by the literary quality of his ramblings and by the exactness of his descriptions, wondered if he was quoting verbatim from James Joyce – a writer whom, they had to admit, they had never succeeded in finishing.

Others, however, reluctant to admit that anything original could occur in A——, argued that his speech in no way imitated the multilayered Baroqueries of the great modernist master. Duende's speech, they said, represented a drastic reduction of verbal possibilities. His whole discourse, they claimed, boiled down to the repetition of three words: 'do', 'end' and ''e'.

While Joyce embarked on naming the whole world, Duende, it seemed, could not even name himself properly.

And they remarked on how difficult he seemed to find it to settle on one pronunciation, one stress pattern, pitch or intonation.

Sometimes 'du' floated up the scale and disappeared into a flute-like whistle. At other times the consonant cluster 'nd', repeated over and over again, recalled nothing so much as an idling engine rattling on its mountings.

As for 'e', it frequently harboured a frightening, dry-throated death-rattle.

⚜

'I am not a narcissist but I cannot deny that I looked in my patients for indications of my own condition.

'There were many days when their symptoms, totally foreign to me, were little more than a buzz in my ears; many occasions when I saw their lips move without hearing a word they said; and when, if I spoke, I must have been deaf, for I remember nothing of what was uttered.

'I often wondered whether they experienced our conversations as I did. If the way they felt obliged to talk to me was as alien to them as it was to me, could not this be, I thought, a symptom of their illness, rather than a description of it.

'One day a man came to me, saying that he experienced the speech of others as a scream. When his daughter asked him a favour, he heard only a high-pitched whining. When a shop assistant asked if she could help, it sounded like the squeal of water being turned off. His father's laughter reached him as a dreadful underwater groan.

'He was sensitive to sounds others ignored. He described the white noise of snowflakes falling. As for the white noise of the radio left on between stations, that, surprisingly, he heard as speech, as perfectly modulated syllables, sweetly flowing, euphonious, light.

'I warmed to him. I was not the least offended when he informed me that my bedside tones cut into him like a chainsaw. I had often thought the same myself.

'Using a walkie-talkie and occasionally conversing by telephone, I devised a method of talking to him, which later enabled him to translate most screams into a semblance of common sense.

'But in retrospect I wonder whether the cure was the illness, the illness the cure. He heard what we refused to hear: the scream of a people unable to speak to one another, the calls of a people who, like parrots flying over, strove to keep in contact as it grew dark.

'Watching the people in the street vainly trying to communicate above the roar of their surroundings, I believe I can add a new species of scream to his inventory.

'Their wild gesticulations, their scraping and bowing, their gaping mouths and furrowed brows, their turning away and parting: what do these represent, if not the grammar of the silent scream?'

One day his daughter came to him. She said that she was tired of his harping on the 'end'. It would have been better, she said, if he had never left home in the first place.

Or, having left home, he might at least have had the fore-thought not to throw away his photographs of the place. They might have come in useful now; and besides – she would bring it up now, though she had said nothing at the time – how did his pyre of photograph albums reflect on the memory of her mother, his wife? Had she no claim on posterity?

She had a proposal: that he should depart these melancholy sur-roundings and move into a home where he could be assured of proper care. It was high time, she said, that he put the past behind him. It was useless to brood on the might have beens of history.

Duende smiled up at her. 'Your nose,' he said, in a tone intended to convey fondness, 'since you raise it, resembles your mother's nose.' But she took it the wrong way, attributing his sudden sentiment to an incipient softening of the brain. 'Come,' she said, and by all accounts attempted physically to lift him from his chair.

'It is not a white façade you see before you but an ambulance waiting to take you away,' she said – or so afterwards he says she said.

But Duende, the mobile, the cloud-watcher, the slurrer of sylla-bles, the nomad of nostrums, knew when to put his foot down. He refused to stand up. He did not look round him for the last time, his eyes watering. He sat resolutely down and, taking his white stick, swept the cut flowers she had thoughtfully brought from the table.

'You are a man,' she said, 'with two hearts,' and after that she stopped coming home.

Later, much later, Doctor Duende received a picture postcard from L— . 'Greetings from Home,' it said, signed 'Nostalgia' – a name, he said, that meant nothing to him.'

'It does not surprise me that our society's most intimate revelations are reserved for walls not bedrooms.

'Wherever houses are abandoned, car parks deserted or factories half-wrecked, more surfaces multiply than the petals of a rose.

'Inner surfaces, wallpapered with bouquets in military forma-tion, unfinished surfaces, oozing cement from their wounds, surfaces cicatrized with zigzag staircases recently removed: they all expose their tender, unlovely faces to the night.

'It is a moment not to be repeated. These scalped surfaces are on their way to dust. They will never become museums. No memories will attach to them. Like make-up, they will be completely removed.

'This gives the midnight writers courage and a sense of freedom. But invading these territories formerly forbidden to their vagrant eyes they also feel cheated.

'They had hoped to gain entry to the insider's world. Rich colours, sumptuous textures, gilt frames holding pictures of another country would have justified their sense of being left out, of being outsiders, exiles in their own land.

'But to their surprise and disappointment they find nothing to covet or despise. The interiors conceal no hidden depths: no shelter, no form of escape. The doors lead nowhere. The ceilings are open to the stars.

'To find no signs of their own absence, no reason for breaking in, only makes it harder to explain what they are there for, and to whom they speak.

'What dialectic can there be, where people simply drift from one empty place to another, like clouds across the face of the moon? They confront the nightmare of a world without readers.

'If the buildings have no eyes to read, who will bother to stop them writing? Who will prevent them from becoming attached to the surface and remaining there forever, forever elaborating their first remark?

'Perhaps they are grateful when the guard dog begins to bark: it gives them a motive for ending.

'Their violent slogans are a form of reparation. Spray-painting against rape, they mourn the disappearance of intact buildings. Urging us to save the forests, they wish they could bring the electricity poles back to life.

'Their 3-D capitals, which give the illusion of relief, the illusion of depth, express deep disillusionment.

'I have come to love the invisible tribe that paints the suburb each night with hearts, with phalluses and dripping swords, that transports its Baroque friezes of doom from one place to the next on the backs of railway carriages.

'They love the surface.

'They paint by starlight.

'They live on the run.'

Duende woke for the first time feeling perfectly happy.

The white façade beamed in benevolently through his windows. Its blank surfaces glowed with good will. The sky overhead was luminous, cloudless.

Leaning on an elbow he could see heads undulating along surfaces and sliding out of sight.

A woman and her shadow jogged by. He had the impression of a continuous surface, as if he were standing on a headland looking along a coastline bending in and out of sight. The head had not disappeared. It was merely traversing a hidden inlet, a fold in the cliffs.

And sure enough, there she was, coming out again, walking the other way, dressed like a man.

He could hear the underground of traffic trembling in the floorboards and the windowpanes; a turtle dove sounded deep in the chimney.

A telephone began to ring and kept on beginning to ring. He did not make the mistake of trying to get to it in time. The future lay before him like a curve forever trending towards a line without reaching it.

All the while the white façade went on glowing. There was nothing behind its luminous presence. It carried no message of comfort. It was not inclined to lean over and kiss his brow.

It was not a breast. It was not his white-haired grandfather. It was not a photograph.

It had nothing to do with him. It walked a mile with him out of sheer good will.

For the first (and last) time in his life Duende knew what it meant to feel at home.

M.E. Grazioni's Camera Profonda

As I began to retrace the photographic journeys of the master, I became aware of another mystery.

Grazioni had recorded meeting places, this much was clear. Rather than reproduce what after all anyone could see for themselves, he had used the Camera Profonda to discover hidden connections.

He had used his new invention as an instrument of analysis, to demonstrate certain historical connections in space.

This was a significant discovery to have made and went a long way towards explaining the complete eclipse of the man and his memory. Yet it left one question totally in the dark.

Retracing the master's journeys, I frequently found in-between spaces or meeting points which, at least to the untutored eye, might have served just as well as points of departure.

It was often difficult to see why he had chosen this arrangement of roofs and balconies as opposed to another in a neighbouring street.

Even a couple of paces further on, one would have thought, a more comprehensive arrangement of fragments was possible, a greater concentration of motifs.

I began to see that, within the master's vision of invisibility, a deeper invisibility lurked – one that even the camera could not record.

Last week my enquiries – which in reality had amounted to little more than wandering the sunlit streets – took a new turn.

I had assembled an archive of photographs that would have done honour to an exile. If, as some said, L— was, architecturally-speaking, a collection of fragments drawn from half-a-dozen different cultures, my collection of mouldings, balconies, arcades and oculi was authentically L— se, enhancing as it did the fragmentary character of the place.

And yet instead of helping me identify with the spirit of the place, my representative shots, my famous façades, seemed to locate me at an ever-growing distance from what most mattered to me.

In my pensione, examining my photographs I grew uncomfortably conscious of the room looking over my shoulder; as if to say: there is another place the camera can never see ...

I wanted to fathom the genius of a people so foreign to me that I felt I had stumbled like a second Christopher upon a New World. The old façades – wave-rippled, conch-studded, encrusted with twisted columns – represented a way of life that had long disappeared, a folk whose love of the surface suggested a propensity for travelling but who had no conception of the tourist.

If I did not feel at home here, it was because I lacked the art of seeing as they saw, thinking as they thought – even walking as they walked.

If I were to draw closer to them, I thought to myself, if I were to go beyond The Street of the Mimic towards the sounds of the Piazza, I must conceal my camera and give myself up to the pleasure of spaces.

I must breathe more deeply. I must distinguish the cool air exhaled by arches from the cobble-shimmer of the shadeless street.

I must close my eyes and feel the surface of stone rippling underneath my feet. I must find my way by fingering the walls, dating them by the friability of their crusted surfaces.

I must become the artist who, living at home, has no sense of walking into the past ...

Who has no truck with parrots and mirrors ...

For whom Nostalgia is a foreign visitor ...

It's been a week now since I started nosing my way like some coral-grazing denizen of the south among second-hand bookshops and dealers in curios.

Turning over pages of engravings, thumbing through hand-coloured maps, fingering tortoiseshell snuff boxes, trying on linen-lined wigs, corroded pince-nez ...

To find out what they were like.

I began to study the master's photographs for what they left out. I began to look for a deeper city within the city, a form of space that even the camera's wide lens could not capture.

It occurred to me that the deeper invisibility was simply an indication of the narrowness of the camera's outlook.

Modern instruments were incapable of recording the sites Grazioni had left unrecorded.

Perhaps Grazioni had also had to confront the limits of his camera's gaze, to acknowledge an edge to his Baroque imagination.

Certain spaces leaned out so far, wound about themselves so intricately or simply bent away into hidden courtyards, that the linear focus of the camera could not grasp them.

This thought pleased me, for it seemed to ground the master's philosophy objectively, scientifically.

It occurred to me that by mapping the courtyards, the archways and flowering walls that Grazioni had failed to record, those in-between relationships that he had taught us to see but which he had of necessity left unremarked, I could at once pay homage to his legacy and distance myself from it, finding a place where I might be.

It occurred to me that a notebook of my divagations might serve a double purpose. It would have an invaluable historical function, bringing to light a forgotten genius, an aesthete and savant whose meditations, better than any guide book, hold the key to the city.

It would also be an autobiography in the true sense of the term, saying not a word about the 'I' of the writer, focusing instead clear-sightedly on the mobile roundabout, the flux of impressions.

What better way, I thought, to infiltrate the labyrinth of the past. And falling asleep that night I imagined my coverlet was Grazioni's cape falling motherly over me and drawing me deep into its folds.

My mind's eye rapidly came to resemble a pond where thousands of microscopic creatures breed and swarm: wimpled Capucines, cavorting saltimbanques and simpering pulcinellas.

The noisy ritornello of cartwheels mingled with street-cries, blaring hautbois and snatches of opera buffa.

I was like a shop of shops where chequered masks hung side by side with mozzarellas in their waxed sacks, puppet paladins of tin and copper pans.

At night the city that my dreams produced surpassed anything that History had ever seen.

Two columns rose to the sound of a harpsichord, twining round each other as they climbed. There came spinning out of their spiralling crown nests of songsters, unravelling ribbons and slowly-revolving stairways of butterflies descending.

Statues walked, books spoke, marble planks chattered like teeth; in windows like eye-sockets silkworms sat stringing instruments.

Painters suspended from hooks were finishing off the sky.

Pattern books, turned over by the wind, stuttered into life, multiplying scarlet cardinals in files, gamboge criminals in chains and fluttering trains of pigeons.

Parrots shouted orders and were obeyed.

And everywhere the rat-a-tat-tat of hammer on chisel, the minute rain of stone-dust settling like volcanic ash.

One morning, coming out into the street, I mistook the swish of the watercart for the curtain rising, and advancing to acknowledge the applause of the stalls, was knocked to the ground.

'To understand the Baroque it is necessary to stay on the surface. To penetrate beneath the surface presupposes presuppositions, underlying motives which the surface expresses only imperfectly.

'To look behind, to reconstruct the historical forces represented in the surface, is to engage in a logical solipsism: for, dissecting the body of work, we destroy the spirit we intended to praise.

'The first step is to acknowledge the ambiguity of the surface.

'Baroque forms characteristically bear opposite interpretations. The rose is at once celestial and earthly, cultivated (surpassing nature) and natural (surpassing art).

'The Baroque buildings of this colonial town are not disguised expressions of the popular will. They are not Spanish imperial impositions. They exist in-between, suggesting a punning meeting-place where foreign and local influences converge and interpenetrate.

'But even this fails to capture their distinctive evasiveness.

'They are not the result of a pioneering intellectual synthesis. It is not a far-seeing Utopian who has manufactured these homely symbols of another place. They arise spontaneously out of the colonial temperament.

'In colonies appearances characteristically wear a double face: they have a local meaning, but they also have a foreign reference. What is rarely understood is that the colonist accommodates both meanings simultaneously.

'This is why colonials are metaphysical sceptics, why they have no curiosity to delve beneath the surface. For the surface is always something else, and stone is always resolving itself into air and light.

'This taste for ambiguity, this intuition of the relativity of appearances, appears to encourage passivity. On the contrary it is a subtle political strategy.

'Inducing irony, it permits colonists to look on their own place from somewhere else, to imagine things otherwise.

'And this second sight – so irritating to their political masters who can obtain the appearance of loyalty without its substance – becomes the means of wearing down authority, or eroding its forms until at length they crumble.

'For how can you deal with someone who does not mean what he says? Or: says exactly what he thinks?'

Coming to in the Ambulatorio there swam into focus a bald-headed Madonna; or so it seemed to me, who owed my life to her charity.

The ancient contadina bathed my brow, attended to my knee, adjusted my sling, righted the bandage that had slumped over one ear.

As I came to I could not help remarking a resemblance between the city of my imagination and my own condition: were we not alike ruins only time could repair?

It was a relief to find that I was only superficially injured. It was a greater relief to find my Baroque delirium had completely cured itself; and while it was disconcerting to find I could barely remember it, I consoled myself with the thought that even forgetting is a form of art.

I had thought I was swimming into deeper water, plumbing History's opaline depths. In reality the tide of time had been draining away leaving me high, dry and gasping.

I had not been the current but the sediment the current left behind. When I fancied my fingers were glistening fins, my feet slapping flukes, I had been the sediment turning to stone.

I had peopled L— with actors; I had turned it into a theatre. As if they did not belong here either and disguised their embarrassment by dressing up; as if behind the sets there were nothing.

Or rather a city that none of us had ever seen, where no one acted, where perhaps no one had ever been.

Seeing my agitation the good woman gave me to eat, extending on the tongue of a knife a clown's smile of watermelon, which I gratefully took.

'Grazioni,' I murmured, 'Grazioni', not speaking the local tongue as well as I would wish, and supposing this to mean 'one or more big thankyous'.

The wrinkled face broke into a smile and as I sank into that semi-conscious state where the hedges between languages turn into stiles, where words leap back and forth without let, I heard her say -

'Doctor Duende would have understood your condition ...'

And her hand, rough as the sunbaked hand of a stone Madonna, stroked my brow; and the hiss it made sounded like distant waves breaking.

'The stone of this city is scarcely harder than soap; well-adapted to carving, it rapidly turns to moted air.

'Which is to say: it demonstrates the historical dimension of the surface. In a material so prone to weathering, the surface, the precise granular topography, represents a point in time and space. Insensibly it is on its way from one state to another.

'The ephemerality of this stone places in sharp relief, if the metaphor may be allowed, the fetish of depth associated with Tuscan marble. Artists and aesthetes agree that the task of the Tuscan artist is to release the form in stone. The figure that is brought into relief by paring back the surface of stone embodies, expresses, the fundamental stability of stone.

'Without this faith the northern sculptor could hardly bring down hammer on chisel. Without his comforting illusion of the third dimension, his artist's violence would be revealed for what it is: the artificer of representations and mere appearance's destroyer.

'Our stone by contrast induces in the sculptor a certain scepticism about his powers, a measured irony towards his own fantasy. However Baroque his stone detailing, it will shortly be outdone by the natural effects of weathering.

'The work of wind and rain carves the stone into nodules and sockets that in their vague suggestion of battered angelic forms capture the paradox of limning the divine much better than any artist can.

'Eventually the sheep's-brain intricacy of the eroded surface, its bold resemblance to certain species of sea sponge, surpasses even the ingenuity of romanesque capitals.

'In this land if the sculptor has a fantasy it is that the surface will go backwards, growing more and more primitive until, finally, it crumbles away altogether, resolving itself into dust.'

Lying there, mote-filled light streaming through the window, contemplating her wizened face, its crow's-feet of concentration as she plied her needle, it occurred to me that the key to the city might be its invisibility.

The fact that I could not see the old academicians stepping out of their carriages, could not witness the perfumed tea parties and awkwardly crinolined excursions into the campagna might be what saved the city from disappearing into the third dimension of the past.

By not seeing them I saw as they saw; not figuring them as picturesque creations in an exotic setting, I preserved the unmarked order of their appearance and disappearance.

I lived in their faces, gazing outwards towards what was yet to come into view.

I preserved the future of the past.

At the very least by embracing my blindness I drew closer to a way of seeing that was different from my own. And without further hesitation, as light of head as I was nimble of foot, I sprang from the bed.

Flinging off my bandages – which I now compared to so many photographic images suffocating the very spaces they purported to preserve – I grasped the handle of the door and strode out.

The first consequence of my deeper insight was an intoxication with the city's spaces.

Doorways which had formerly saddened me because they were empty – and which I had inhabited with ancient faces in an attempt to provide them with human interest – thrilled me by their spacious vacancy.

The deserted piazzas which had struck me before as melancholy indications of civic decay now delighted me with their open-handedness.

Contemplating their invisible community of sightlines and subtly exchanged proportions, I felt (for the days were hot) that I commanded the very dreams of the builders and their patrons.

I flew as their eyes and hands flew from rooftop to rooftop.

I began to think that the surest way to maintain the city's vitality would be to desert it.

If the people who now lived there could be persuaded to abandon their houses and leave the city perfectly still, what experiments in living we might inaugurate.

We could contemplate without distraction the sunlight's dividers devising a thousand ephemeral tents of shadow, while the echo of a solitary sounding bell might endure a whole day.

Time would slow down and the spirit, no longer miserably enslaved by the puny human frame, would find the whole city its corporeal investment.

I went even further, wondering whether the essence of the city's contingency, the true invisibility it copied, might only be discovered by destroying the city itself.

There were plenty of archaeological sites in the region which preserved only the bare two-dimensional outline of their former palaces, temples and baths; and there was little doubt that the paradox of these shelterless cities, these carefully cobbled, buildingless spaces, was attractive.

For here we found the farthest bourne of the Baroque imagination: the past as pure surface.

Such sites were grooved with cart-tracks and pitted with hypogeums, but these were not like cellars cancerously undermining the city fabric.

They were merely undulations extending the surface area and inviting one to walk sideways across the site or even upside down.

How much further I would have wandered in these speculations had I not collapsed one day in the street, I cannot say.

'L— is an incrustation of the surface. The solitary upstanding nose of the cathedral bell-tower is only the tallest among many tall edifices. The streets are tall; the windows tall. Even the cool whitewashed entrances lead into courtyards which consist of cubic bales of light piled up to the eaves.

'Walking these streets one lives on three levels, perhaps more. Voices float down from upper storeys and mingle with the cries of swifts. Engine noises terrorise the winding streets and crowd upwards towards the wires, aerials and quaintly carved balconies.

'Progress in this town without gradients is always helical. One is always advancing towards a revelation, the further discovery of space within stone. Trending down this side street one comes unexpectedly on a corner, a parting of the ways; one travels these streets as a squirrel threading the continuously dividing branches of an oak tree.

'And always the gold, the treasure that comes to you, is the shimmering space that lies just along the surface of the buildings, the intimation of a room that obeys a multi-dimensional geometry, that, though regular, is infinite, inexhaustible, a charm against the termination of death.

'For this is the promise of the true labyrinth: not to lose you in the central darkness, but to wind you deeper and deeper into the only cocoon worthy of grown ups – the womb of space.

'And this is the meaning of those staircases found on the rooftops of the houses. Rising from the roof they lead up to – nothing, simply expiring against the blue sky.

'Atavistic altars, former sites of lookout, domination and sacrifice, they become now places to consummate a different kind of translation, platforms where houses renounce their quotidian structures and, lightly as birds taking off, step back into invisibility.

'Stare long enough into the whiteness before looking away and you can see Baroque angels pulling a negative staircase up into heaven.

'No! No! No!'

Coming to in the coolness of the Ambulatorio, I became aware of someone sitting quietly in the shadows.

'Allow me to introduce myself,' she said, 'The Contessa Von Economico ...'

As she stepped into a pool of sunlight, I saw that it was none other than the bald ministering angel of my former acquaintance, who now sported a wig, a hairy aureole of astonishing proportions and whose face, when she smiled, seemed to explode into a cloud of powder.

'Von Economico?' I repeated. And she, mistaking my mystification for a sign of recognition, went on: 'Seeing you are a photographer, and one what is more who is not impatient to find the centre, my husband would have wanted you to have these,' and she thrust into my hands a parcel wrapped in newspaper.

Opening the package I found myself in possession of a dozen or more glass plates on which there was vaguely discernible photoluminescent outlines.

Scratched on the reverse of these smoky panes were various dates belonging to the eighteenth century, notes on the weather and most puzzling of all the names of locations the plates were presumably intended to represent.

Puzzling because, although the names were familiar enough – and featured in my own visual inventory of L— – I could not recognise them from the exposures.

It was as if, unaware of the future's positivist preoccupations, a mechanism had been invented for seeing nothing, for investing the surface of air with depth.

Or better, for representing the Void.

'Grazioni,' I said. And she: 'At any other time in history these would perhaps have remained in the family. But nowadays the old genealogies mean nothing. A city like ours belongs to foreigners, visitors like you who have nothing in common except nostalgia.

'You run our tourist agencies and bars; you give private lessons; you double as professors and pimps, gigolos and maids. You attach yourself to archaeological digs; you mind our palaces over the long summer; you rifle our shelves for evidence of scandalous ancient life; you publish inventories of fading walls. Here ...'

And dissolving into tears, she handed me a calfskin parchment: 'To my honoured friend and fellow Academician, Constantino Von Economico, my only child which I created in my own image: the camera profonda.' Signed 'M.E. Grazioni.'

Is this how new stories begin, in a chance convergence of sounds? Two unrelated destinies, drawn into each other's orbit by a mere coincidence of names, twine round each other to form a new history, a new dynasty: could it be like this?

❈

No, there was no future in imagining him like this. Writing my diary I had been carried away: the very route intended to bring me to the master's point of view was proving a way of departing from him.

It was vital, I realised, to do as he had done, to leave no trace of my peregrinations behind; to yield myself wholly to History. But how to proceed? How to go forward without going back? How to go back going forward?

Up until now I have avoided mentioning a difficulty I have encountered. Once I understood that Grazioni's great picture collection depended on me for its fulfilment, I felt a deep gratitude to the master. I understood his will, I embraced what a friend of mine came to recognise as my 'historical fate'.

Yet I was assailed by an increasingly pressing sense of guilt. Was I worthy of my master's vision? Was I seeing what he invited me to see? Or was I blind to what he had intended and my most minutely accurate reproductions merely a further encrustation of the surface?

The differences were palpable. The oculus and broken tympanum of his photograph was now partially concealed by the umbrella of a stone pine. Television aerials clustered along a formerly vacant roof.

Other differences were more ambiguous: a formerly pristine façade now under scaffolding, a sign removed, a shop closed suggested history's reversal.

But what was most worrying were pairs of images that far from displaying differences were identical. Of course there were differences – a pigeon flying across a scrap of azure, a different distribution of shadow – but the substantial relations were in most instances unaltered.

Was this his discovery? That architecture and history are fundamentally opposed? Or was it more scandalous still – that history is an illusion, an ideological device designed to give spurious depth to everyday appearances?

How was I to represent this? It was clearly a question of choice whether or not I waited for conditions in which my image would imitate his most closely, or whether I sought instead to emphasise differences.

Should I wait for the washing to be taken in, for the church doors to open? If I loitered long enough, would they replace those bowls of geraniums?

There was no way of knowing and besides – this is the source of my guilt – I felt a certain reluctance to reproduce merely what the master saw.

I felt an egotistical need to make a point, to demonstrate the difference of my own point of view.

I strove to give my images an eventfulness missing from those of the master.

A vehicle trapped in a doorway, a passer-by looking towards the camera, a chance reflection in a window. By these subtle means I wanted to suggest the passage of time and the relativity of knowledge.

'Do not be surprised if at first you can make nothing out,' she resumed, making up her face. 'I am reminded how in the early days of cinema many misunderstandings arose. People complained when the lights went down that they couldn't see anything.

'And when the screen suddenly came alive, they were completely non-plussed. The catatonic stutter of black and white made no sense to them.

'They were impatient for the screen to be wound up out of sight so that the film could begin.

'The agitated monochrome sea hovering in front of their eyes struck them as an unconscionable intrusion, making them more impatient than ever for the action to begin.

'It often happened that the projector broke down, leaving the audience in a cavernous gloom only lightened by the low incandescence globes in their scallop-shell wall brackets and, occasionally, by a sudden shaft of light from a door opening at the back.

'Reflected on the screen, and partially absorbed by it, these dots and circles of light assumed a dreamy vagueness, a soft abstractness suggesting a hitherto unknown order of reality.

'A few, and amongst them the leading avant-garde spirits of the day, were enraptured by these chance effects and when, at length, the film was rewound and the projector began again to clatter, walked out in disgust.

'We should not smile at their misapprehensions. These were people who dwelt on the surface.'

✾

A further doubt assailed me. Perhaps the monumental calmness of the master's images was deliberate, the result of a conscious effort to evacuate the city of all trace of himself. His lack of egotism seemed to reprove my own self-centredness.

But then again: wasn't there something narcissistic about this self-effacement? Wasn't this the supreme Baroque gesture: to draw attention to oneself, not by plumbing the depths of personal psychology, but by an elaboration of the surface.

The Baroque personality substitutes outwardness for inwardness, fleeting appearances for architectural structures. But it is driven on, not by a new confidence in the objectivity of appearances. On the contrary, it is obsessed by an Aztec horror vacui.

I began to understand the Baroque sensibility informing the camera profonda: its obsession with detail, its passivity, its willingness to reproduce appearances over and over, was not a sign of its empirical bent.

It bore witness to the contradictory scepticism informing its hunger for images, its lurking suspicion that after all there was nothing there. Or that what could be seen had no meaning.

Grazioni had recognised this. He had grasped with his instrument the Baroque paradox of seeing, that to see is to see nothing and that to see nothing is to abandon the eye to the ocean of fleeting appearances which, in the absence of freedom, must pass for reality.

'Why,' she went on, all the while rearranging her features, 'only last week there was a similar occurrence at the meeting of the Circolo.

'Our guest speaker, a nice young man from A—, asked if he could show some slides. We were at a loss for a screen until Mr Piano, a camping enthusiast, offered us his plastic awning.

'The men managed to suspend the sheet across one end of the hall and the talk began. The awning, now rigged like a sail, swelled and sagged in the draught. I couldn't take my eyes off it.

'The quadrangular creases where it had been folded were clearly visible and, as I looked more closely, I began to notice inside their shadowy latitude and longitude wedge-like creases resembling geese in flight, finger-shaped outlines suggesting the pale breasts of sandbars sinking into the sea.

'In another part a crowsfoot of wrinkles and its mirror image perched equidistant to left and right of a valley. They looked like hands pressed against a wall.

'Yet other parts resembled crumpled suits of clothes, as if hastily buried men and women were coming to light.

'Yes, and the light. For there filtered through the end window enough light to cast a shadow of the chandelier on the screen; and this shadow of light, surrounded by light, resembled nothing so much as Christ hanging on the cross.

'Afterwards, the nice young man congratulated me on listening so attentively.'

'The ground storey capitals and entablature of Sta. C— feature an array of partially naked figures. Their nudity is avoided – or per-haps revealed – by a variety of devices.

'A doughy-breasted damsel is snapped half-born in a capital: a fringe of out-turned acanthus leaves decently hides her lower limbs. Above her, presumably naked angel boys struggle to hold before them a beach-towel-sized cartouche bearing the church's Latin dedication.

'Higher still gryphons and other semi-mythical beasts alternate with African slaves in shouldering the weight of the balcony ...

'It occurs to me that concealment of the surface, the intuition of a third dimension, is associated in this façade with labour. The figures who stagger under the weight of its words, who kneel in Purgatory under the intolerable burden of its overhangs, who are pressed spreadeagled against the stone by the chain-like wreathes they are charged to hold aloft, are figures you might meet with anywhere.

'They are taken from life: from the new wife concentrating to balance a water jar on her head, the arthritic fisherman straining to keep his feet as he hauls in his nets, the stonemason's underfed assistant inwardly crying as he lifts another scaffolding board into place.

'The torso's controposto, the hollows of the bent knee and the crushed stomach, which in Rome signify the flesh's spiritual aspirations, are interpreted here more literally as signs of servitude, indicating the way the vulgar live.

'Surface, serenity of countenance, clarity of articulation, these are class characteristics rather than determinants of style. It is despicable to affect a disdain for the straining folds of the working classes ...'

Listening to the Contessa's harmless anecdotes, I began to become curious about the person who lurked behind the voice. How much of it belonged to her? Or was she her deceased husband's parrot?

I observed her nervously touch her hair, and the tiny explosion of powder this precipitated.

I was suddenly glad I cast a shadow, I rejoiced in the ordinary people, whose daily journeys through the streets I now saw in a new light. They were not intrusive movements disturbing the pristine space but the woven and rewoven strands of a collective consciousness.

Without their web of mutual self-interest the urban fabric would fall apart and collapse.

It was foolish of me to imagine the city without its builders, to treat its architects as mobile phantoms, angels untethered to the earth and independent of time. They had their accidents as I did, their strained backs, their ruptured groins, their broken limbs.

The façades about me registered the sweat and strain of their labour. Who could contemplate their intricately chiselled reliefs without feeling the sharp prick of dust collecting in the corner of the mason's eye?

Who could doubt that vertigo was their companion and that it was not only sparrows that fell from their nests but builders foolish enough to look down?

I observed the Contessa visibly wilt, as if overwhelmed with tiredness. I felt compassion for her. I wanted to touch her, to stroke her tired, pomaded cheek. My other mother.

Trying to rise to my feet, I once again felt dizzy and had to sit down.

I went in.

It was as I would have predicted: the façade had been a mere façade. Nothing in Sta. C— 's surface decoration prepared for me for an interior so unpredictably predictable, regular, linear, free of Baroque self-regard.

Except in one significant detail.

The side altars and the high altar beyond the crossing were fringed with spiral columns. The undulating surfaces of these – what Baroque-haters would no doubt call 'barleysugar confections' – were covered with the gold-leaved tendrils of a climbing ivy.

Looking at these flamboyant ropes in stone it was impossible to locate the beginning or the end; to say whether the ivy moulded itself to the stone or the stone to the ivy.

It was difficult to say whether the columns consisted of two convex mouldings spiralling upwards on either side of a concave trough.

Or whether what one saw winding ambiguously up and down was a single rounded ridge flanked by two glacial valleys.

It occurred to me that this double spiral was a way of giving depth to the surface. As the light struck it, the columns seemed to revolve like a barber's pole.

Squinting, you could almost believe you were looking down a street where, here and there, dazzling passages of washing hung out, or a door was opening into a shadowed courtyard.

(I am only trying to make you see it.)

The alternating pulse of light and dark, the stately dance of un-dulations, never punctured the surface. The column was not a peepshow or a doll's house concealing miniature interiors (mini-ature churches).

It attained its effect by magnifying the surface, as wind does when it plays on the surface of the sea folding it into crests and troughs.

Looking into her face, which all the while was changing hue and growing ever more densely cobwebbed, I realised that there was no end to the stories that might be found there. The skin's mobile network represented a history of the environment.

Her squint signified the slow deposit of sunlight over decades, the filigree of veins on her cheek, the strength of the prevailing wind.

Her fissured brow, as minutely reticulated as a fisherman's net, was a miniature city of directions contemplated and taken, contemplated and not taken.

But as I studied her, a shadow came into my seeing. It seemed to me that the more I focused on the details of her face (and there was little else to do while I lay there on the couch) the more I reduced it to a lifeless mask.

In order to comprehend her facial history more fully, I was behaving like a camera, in advance of her dying preparing a death-mask.

This was the price of my clearsighted Realism, my refusal to flinch from a comprehensive description. The light in her eye was going out; her tongue was growing wooden, her hand as frigid as marble. Frozen like a country in a map, her face was open to exploration at my leisure.

But at what price?

No, to see as the Baroque builders saw, it was necessary to see Realism's mask for what it was – Death's disguise.

To complete Realism's examination of the skin would take eternity.

And what would be the gain?

A novel of Proustian proportions.

A universe whose infinite largeness was inversely proportional to the infinite smallness of its constituent parts.

To discover the Baroque outlook in the face of its people, it was going to be necessary to see differently, as Grazioni had, to develop a different style of seeing.

Instead of treating the eye as a lamp or a mirror, it should be trained to behave like glittering water, cultivating oblique lines of flight.

It should imitate light's reflection, its instantaneous ricochet off stone, metal and polished wood, its imaginative connection of unlike surfaces.

To make any sense of her time-chiselled visage or her forebears' lively qualities long sepulchred in stone required the lightness of light, the insouciance of a style that kept to the surface, treating it not as a ploughed field laboriously to inspect for sherds, but as a moving body of water to cut without cutting, as the shearwater keeps to the trough of the waves.

One needed to do away with the elaborate enclosures of subordinate clauses, with the architectonic structure of paragraphs, with their palatial openings and exits.

A better style – one that imitated the eye's restless movement, its continually provisional alighting here and there, the incompleteness of even its most complete knowledge – would abandon the scaffolding of syntax, grammar and tense.

Fragments of speech.

Lists of nouns.

Phrases in associative chains meandering on, petering out.

If only I could stand up …

It occurred to me that these mirage columns wavering in their cool sanctums might be a way of describing my experiences differently.

Imagine, I thought, two alternating histories winding round one another. Theirs is not a dialectical struggle: one does not try to strangle the other in order to gain supremacy.

They consciously avoid meeting and, like dancers circling, shifting across the floor, strive to keep their distance.

As the column rises, one whispering line pursuing the other, so their interwoven histories shift ground, travel on, keeping pace with each other.

One story is not the echo of the other. There is not the tedious symmetry of Yes and No but the dreamy awareness of the other found in dialogue.

Dialogue is like a double winding stair: the footsteps we hear are neither ahead nor behind but adjacent, accompanying us however many disguises we put off.

They are the might have beens that continually peel off as we take one route rather than another; they do not disappear: never having happened, they never pass into History; growing in parallel with what has occurred, they stay in mind as memories growing ever more Baroque.

On days like this there is no end of going south.

And I stood up, and although the Contessa had withered beyond all recognition, I placed my arm around her waist, and
gripping her right hand firmly, waltzed her across the floor.

There was nothing to her. She was skin and bones, angular,
nosy; a ruined anatomy, incomparably ancient, papery, transparent, equipped with wings.

A marionette on strings, she pulled after her my feet, my legs, so
that it was unclear who was Time, who the prestidigitateur of
Time.

I noticed the chamberpot grinning at us like a vacant skull; I
observed the scythes, their great toothless grins, leaning against the
wall.

But despite the portents we went on dancing to nothing louder
than the swish and hush of our own to and fro and a palpable
breathing.

Her wig slipped sideways, rolled to the ground; her face began
to unpeel, disclosing an unsightly beard; her frock slipped from her
shoulders exposing where her breasts should have been a carcase of
wind, a vortex of air.

And still, as I began to retrace the photographic journeys of the
master, we went on dancing.

And although there was no-one there to record it, the clatter of
bones on the shiny floor curiously resembled the camera giving
birth to a photograph.

Clack, click. Click, clack …

Martin Magellan's Theory of Types

It was, I remember, my first day out. The day long longed for. The beginning of my homecoming.

While others were sick, vomit-stricken countenances by turns green and white mimicking the foam-flecked surface we strode upon, I was in my element.

The prow rising and falling, hesitating, gliding swiftly on, was, I fancied, a chisel carving an undulant line in the swell. I was its sculptor: like the helmsman of old leaning left or right on the tiller, as the deck heaved and pulled beneath my feet, I sculpted a passage through mountainous passes.

The seething sea, I said to myself, is a crowd of uplifted hands eagerly vying for the honour of carrying us forward; as the foremost grow tired, falter and stumble, fresh runners step up and, hoisting aloft the precious burden, hurry us on.

How far this is from travel on land, where the ground lies sullenly still, roaded and levelled, neither greeting the foot nor rebelling against it. Such servility binds the traveller: what pleasure is there in footing it with a dead partner?

Where in a metalled strip hooping the horizon is the invitation to frolic and jig?

Here travelling is a dance. O drunkenness of decks where to balance is to describe a figure of eight and equilibrium depends on adept arabesques ...

Where the mere transport of a cup of tea becomes a grave and sensuous sarabande and where old and young alike sink into a mazy trance-like motion, as if they inhabited a film or moved backwards over half-forgotten ground like dreamers following a thread or sailors hearkening to a siren's call ...

Which was when Martin Magellan, leaping forward, caught me, and draping my arms about his neck steered me to a nearby deckchair.

2

Von Economico, it may be remembered, had brought out the final volume of his official *History of L—* and against my better judgement I had agreed to review it for the Proceedings of the Infuriati (edited at that time by my dear friend Highberg).

It would have been better perhaps had I stayed my pen; my silence and the silence of generations before me (those thoughtful men and women whose internal events find no recognition in Von Economico's annals) would have demonstrated more eloquently than words the shortcomings of his history.

Or having elected to write, I might have disguised my motives more proficiently. Instead I brought upon myself a public opprobrium which, it is no exaggeration to say, put an end to my career.

I who was once a scholar, a rising star seriously talked of as a future cardinal, am now reduced to this: an albatross of the high sea looking for a character on which to hang its fate.

A few quotations will convey the drift of my remarks.

'Our learned author refers to our justly famous façades. He analyses our human face, demonstrating beyond a shadow of doubt the migrant genius of our people ... But where is the sound of their voices or Sunday's gallimaufry of bells?

'... He lists L— 's founder builders. But what does this tell us about the buildings as they are, their daily drama of light and shade?

'... Will his chapter on dialects diminish domestic misunderstandings or contribute to a decline in juvenile graffiti or to better spelling?

'... He has mapped our sewers; he has surveyed our drains – but can he tell us why the oldest stone pine in the Vicolo della M— is dying?

'... Those curious to know the relative volumes of black and white wine pressed on the estates of the Conte de V— in the exceptional year of 18— will not be disappointed. But what of the pleasures of drinking?

'... He takes a hammer to the surface of things and, unearthing fragments of his own creation, declares these to be the true facts! His city is not our city but a mausoleum of his own imagination!'

His familiarity surprised me, but he told me not to be alarmed. He was sure he had seen me somewhere before. He reminded me of a character in one of his stories ...

'You see,' Martin explained, 'I live by travelling round the world, sailing from one port to another, writing stories about the characters I meet on board.

'You must not suppose, Nostalgia,' he said, apparently knowing my name, 'that this vessel plies only between the places on your ticket. In A—, where you embarked, others disembarked. In L—, where you leave the ship, others will take your place.

'And so on, round the world.

'As we sail north, some will leave the ship earlier than planned. Others will modify their arrangements in order to stay on.'

At first, he told me, this uncertainty made writing difficult.

If some passengers disappeared leaving their life-stories half-finished, others stayed on after their lives had been written.

It was impossible to write well-rounded stories at sea. At sea lives were always too short or too long.'

As if I had nothing else to do but listen, he went on.

'The lives of those who departed early reminded me of bubbles of foam squeezed to nothing in the troughs between waves.

'The lives of those who stayed on reminded me of the same bubbles climbing to the wave's crest and extending themselves into archipelagos.

'Where did the truth lie?'

Why did he take my stifled yawns as a sign of interest?

'It must not be supposed that the stayers-on provided me with a welcome opportunity to check the accuracy of my facts. No sooner had they changed their minds than they began to talk about themselves differently. They began to invent a new past consistent with the new future they had mapped out for themselves.

'And, if this was true of those who stayed on, what about the early-departers? Presumably they, too, left nothing behind except their stories, the parts of them that were no longer true.'

I rose from the deckchair; I tried to wave goodbye, but he thought I was beckoning him to come.

♪

A few further remarks may not be out of place.

'"Every day things happen in the world that cannot be explained by the physical laws we know and have to be forgotten because they cannot be explained."

'I have often thought that our historians should be obliged to print this remark of Ernesto Cairo's at the front of their books. It might make them more circumspect about the laws of evidence.

'Pausing to ponder the narrowness of their deductions, they might notice how much of everyday life they leave out.

'If one event leads to another event, what does this prove except the existence of mere coincidences?

'The laws of deduction rest on a simple assumption: that the hybrids of time and space are fertile and give rise to offspring of their own.

'A genealogy of coincidences: that, my friends, is what History adds up to. Nothing more, nothing less. What can its laws of deduction tell us about the rest of the world, where appearances do not coincide but stand side by side, having nothing to do with one another?

'The odd liaisons in which History specialises resemble the meetings of tourists in a foreign city. Thrust out onto the green sward of fate, like billiard balls, their trajectories briefly coincide –

'But from their passing kisses, their exchange of addresses and personal histories, what can be deduced about the city?'

As Magellan talked I took the opportunity to inspect him more closely.

'It began to occur to me that characters at sea might have a different shape from those on land.

'People on land are proportioned to the horizon. They conceive of the pilgrimage from birth to death like the sun's diurnal passage across the sky.

'Their stories begin with a door bursting open and the sounds of a child crying. They end with the traveller departing to cross Death's mountain-pass.'

His double-breasted blazer might once have been worn by a naval officer but now hung in folds off his shoulders.

'In the old days stories were proportioned to walking. The number of feet a poem possessed corresponded to a graduated line drawn across the landscape.

'In mountainous countries where the horizons were nearer, poems were brief, elegiac. In the deserts they wrote encyclopaedias.

'As methods of transport changed and it became possible to travel more quickly, poems became shorter; as planes approached the speed of sound, the longest plot could be written on the back of a postage stamp.'

His paisley cravat, which he had evidently slept in, had slipped to half-mast. His twill trousers were stained ... what did he suppose we had in common?

'The people of those countries, it occurred to me, inhabited a convex world. They were Mound-dwellers whose dignity depended on the horizon in every direction bowing down at their sight.

'Their stories fitted the visible landscape exactly; and, where it disappeared below the edge, they too passed out of sight.

'But at sea, you see, it was different. We passed our lives in crossing the horizon.

'Or, better,' Magellan went on, taking me by the arm, 'for we must not burden ourselves at sea with landlubberly metaphysics, we surfed a horizon that travelled with us.'

And he turned and tried to look into my eyes.

His shoes once spórted a double fringe of quatrefoils around toe and heel and fanciful chevrons like tiny battlements puckered either side of the tongue, but now the leather was scuffed and faded ... who did he think he was talking to?

And when I did not look back, he resumed talking, walking.

'The surface we traverse is not flat. It resembles the frill of surf peeling back from the roller as it ramps on the Pacific shore.

'Riding the rondure of the earth, we turn the world's skin inside out.

'The surface they land-dwellers think flat – which their science declares convex,' Magellan exclaimed, stroking the inside of my wrist, 'we know is concave!'

And what to say about his nose, whose hairy nostrils resembled nothing so much as the reed-fringed tunnels said to lead down to Hell?

⌇

'The memory of architecture is not like ours. Buildings house more than human meetings. There are corners of brooding air the wildest orgy never disturbs, extracts of architraving the fiercest fire leaves intact.

'Cornices that go unvisited, undersides of staircases, the inter-stices of floors: these symbolise the might have beens of History, the spaces whose fate History has no use for.

'Look, a city like ours entertains neither presences nor absences. A congregation of emptiness, it has no need of births and deaths to complete its form; it does not wait on events to lend it a sense of purpose.

'Those who, like the Marquis of L—, insist on straightening out our winding streets misunderstand their logic.

'To stretch them out in parallels, imposing on independent façades the tyranny of a common vanishing point, is to overlook the intrigue of the surface.

'The horse-shit, the hand-polished bollards, the shadow advancing into view ahead of its owner: to what end overlook these incidental histories?

'To the end of seeing at once the end of things, eh? '

❧

I pulled apart. I made to walk the other way. But he beseeched me not to leave him. He was curious to find out who I was, he said. And nodded his head as if I had spoken his words.

'It occurred to me,' Magellan resumed, 'that I could be certain of nothing except their coming into view.

'Passengers were constantly descending the companion-way or rounding the corner of the forward lounge and weaving their way towards me.

'I did not know when they had come on board, how long they had been sailing or when they would depart.

'I could catch their eye, beckon them to sit down, take out a notebook and begin. But beyond the beginning anything might happen.

'Writers on land, I reflected, occupied themselves with origins. They thought of voices as the outsides of characters; and characters as the foliage springing from the twin roots of Childhood and Place.

'But here, where people were born when they stepped aboard and carried their birthplaces with them, treading them everyday – here it was different. We were like ship's masts and any pretence to depth was as hollow as the sails ballooning out.

'The vital force of that billowing concavity appealed to me. Its invisible animus always swelling or dying away to nothing was the same breath giving life to the voice.

'What was needed at sea, I reflected, was a literature corresponding to the wind. A style as unpredictable as the directions, durations and dynamics of the breeze.

'A literature capable of billowing like spread sailcloth to register the sensation of first contact, the initial susurration of syllables improvised between people with nothing more in common than a desire to stay afloat.

'A literature, not of origins, but of endless beginnings.'

A literature, I thought to myself angrily, of meetings that might have been but which never came to pass because one of the parties talked incessantly.

What was I to him but a page on which to write his theories about the world? His fiction depended on never listening. To live up to his 'Nostalgia' I must say nothing at all.

But I was another Nostalgia and would have nothing to do with his past, his future.

ʃ

'Better by far to steer, as the blind man steers, by cantilevered stones and unseen canaries swinging in their cages, by axle-scored corners and alternating cantons of coolness and heat …

'Our city is composed of might have beens: if the potentialities of meetings, those hidden forces that converge on what history calls events, did not veer away from one another, we would not have our radiating streets.

'Time that in History exercises a power of attraction, creating unforeseen collisions, works in the city as a force of repulsion.

'The crowd is composed of countless individuals, striding in every direction, criss-crossing each other's paths. But never once do they collide. Instead, obeying a mysterious law of mutual repulsion, they swerve left or right, subtly accelerate or retard their pace …'

➤

'If you cannot stop talking,' I said sometime later, a Manhattan Snowball in my hand, 'can you at least stop talking about yourself?'

He smiled, as if he welcomed the sarcasm as a sign he was on the right track. As if, I reflected, I had said the kind of thing Nostalgia used to say.

'When I began to submit my stories to newspapers, they returned them, if they acknowledged them at all, saying that the lives I described could have no possible appeal to their readers.

'My stories, they said, lacked depth. My characters seemed, in the words of one editor, "to float outside history."

'This last remark irritated me as it must upset all ocean-dwellers. We strongly reject the criticism that, because we dwell on the surface, our lives are superficial and useless.'

And here Magellan held up a hand to indicate that he had not forgotten what I had said.

'Evidently I needed to explain the history of our movement: if those on land were to take us seriously, they needed to understand where we came from.

'This was how I came to take an interest in Christopher Column.

'You see,' and here he leant over and gently took my hand, 'Christopher was the first to extend the surface and to contemplate its pure extension.

'He was the first to travel for the sake of travelling. His islands, Sternatia, Egnazia, the rest, were like footsteps, fulcrums giving him a leverage on the globe.

'Christopher,' and here I felt his hand slide closer, 'desired to put off the ending. He voyaged towards a place he could never reach. Others viewed the earth's convex shield as proof one could come back from the other side.

'But Christopher, who had no home, did not want to get home. Had he reached his much talked of Cathay it would have been the death of him.'

His hand slid under my arm. His fingers moved towards the underworld of my breast.

'Christopher did not find the surface of the earth dropping away. He did not regard it as a level expanse.

'Towards the New World, he said, it tilted upwards. It was as if, he said, he sailed up the slopes of a woman's breast towards her nipple, Nostalgia.'

It seemed odd to me that Magellan could only navigate the body of me in the name of another. Removing his hand, I might have been removing the hand of any man who, having put to sea, did not know how to come home.

'Christopher inhabited a concave space,' he went on transferring his fingers to my lips, 'His sea was always rising to meet him. No matter how skilfully he navigated towards the upper rim he would never reach it.

'He knew that the nearer he drew to the edge, the more tightly it would coil above his head.

'He knew that if he ever glimpsed the beyond, the horizon would rise up and break over him like a wave.

'He imagined that he would have the sensation of dying as he rolled over and over in its mothering maw ...'

And here, as he leaned over to kiss me, his high stool overbalanced and he crashed to the floor

♪

And without extending these remarks unduly –

'Earlier today I was working at my desk when I became aware

of a noise in the street outside. At length unable to endure it any longer, I stood up and strode over to the window intending to close it.

'Whereupon, leaning out to release the shutters, I happened to notice my neighbour opposite doing likewise.

'When I had put my hands to my ears he had put his hands to his ears. As he had risen from his seat, so I had risen from mine: as a result we now found ourselves leaning out of our windows like two puppets controlled by a single puppeteer.

'But what had brought us together? Not Historical Design but a common carter down below mercilessly beating his donkey. The poor animal's load was wedged irreversibly between two bollards. The creature could go neither forwards nor backwards and brayed piteously as his master lay about it with his whip.

'At that moment, catching each other's eye, my neighbour and I were never further apart. We were embarrassed to have acted involuntarily as one: and now, when we might in all conscience have acted voluntarily as one, we were constrained by a need to assert the independence of our actions.

'Had someone not intervened, we might still be there, immobile as the donkey and, more asininely trapped, unable to decide whether to call out or not to call out …'

❧

'Ass!' I said, climbing off my stool and smoothing my skirt.

'I have left behind a country that tunes its radios to stations that cannot be heard.

'I have left behind the bungalows capped with scallop-shells … the pavements patched with afterthoughts … the fire-engines nightly breathing flames …

'I have said goodbye to my father because he refuses to listen to me, insisting my name was a joke.

'A Miss Diagnosis, he would say, taking me on his lap and patting my nose; and he would burst out laughing.

'A world so thin names were like street signs and seen edge on signified nothing.

'Now can you see why I love the sea? It is fat, it harbours mothering forms; it hatches children of light and folds them up to sleep.

'It takes me to its heart. It listens to the pattern of my dreams. It assures me that the roar in my ears is the premonition of homecoming.

'I refuse,' and here I stepped over his slumped form and marched away, 'I refuse to be the offspring of your nosiness, another nostalgic projection of Martin Magellan!'

♪

'Later ...

'It is a fault of mine to go on. I frankly admit it. Allow me to finish this anecdote and I am done.

'Later, as luck would have it, he stepped out of his house at the very moment I stepped out of mine.

'"These carters with their whips make a peaceful life impossible," he said, "no one with anything like an idea in his head can avoid a feeling of physical pain at the sudden, sharp crack. It paralyzes the brain, rends the thread of reflection, murders thought ... Good day to you."

'And he strode on.

'Watching him depart, I thought: here I differ. But for the snap of the carter's whip and the braying of the donkey I might have gone on with what I was writing before.

'But when I went back to my desk, I found I had forgotten what I was going to say: the words on the page before me brought back nothing. They might have belonged to someone else ... so hard is it for me to collect my thoughts ...

'Which is why, giving it up, I donned my beret, took my white cane, and descending the stairs which lead to the street, found myself bumping into my neighbour ...

'But for this little history of coincidences leading to his parting words, I might never have turned back, climbed the steps to my room, hung up my beret and cane and, recalling the words of Ernesto Cairo, sat down at my desk to begin compiling these words against History.

'Which I am thinking of calling *Baroque Memories*.'

♪

'I wouldn't want you to think, Nostalgia,' he began, when I visited him in the ship's hospital, 'that I was only interested in Christopher for his own sake.'

I didn't mind visiting but I was not prepared to mortgage my thoughts to his interminable chatter.

I stared fixedly out of the porthole, watching the twinkling waves slide by.

'It occurred to me that Christopher's desire to put off arriving might be the key to a different way of telling stories.'

Every army ever filmed with flashing ranks of helms and shields was gathered there and charging me burnt itself into my eyes.

To cool my eyes down I turned them inwards, where Magellan lay, his leg encased in plaster. It was incredible that a man so in love with nostalgia could go on the way he did, as if nothing had happened.

'Why should stories any more than journeys have beginnings and endings? The movement was what mattered, the sensation of water slipping under the bows.'

The portcullis of the lids slid down but the lancers were already in, throwing themselves against the inner keep ... his talk was a way of forgetting, yes.

'There was no reason why a fragment should be less than the whole. Even a well-rounded novel is only a sliver of the whole. Why, language itself is but a minute in the hour of reality.

'Christopher taught me that empires of meaning could be founded on the simplest of recognitions, the most banal of repetitions.'

Their painful jabs I seemed to see projected forwards onto the eyeball's curtain wall as a darkness pierced here and there by shearwaters milling above a moonlit sea ... keeping me before his eyes was a way of turning his back on the future ...

'The essence of this new world is not the word but the dance: the dance of the tongue and the finger tip, the everyday repertoire of gestures and sounds we unconsciously use to engage one another.'

And here he leaned over and took me by the hand.

Within the aqueous humour tufts of light began to sprout. The shadows gathered into rows and in-between them bands of light began to glow – as if through silhouetted shutters one suddenly glimpsed a whitewashed wall.

'The mazy motion of couples walking the deck ...'

The pulse of blood turned into feet, the middle-distance cry of gulls to squeaking wheels on hawkers' carts.

'The play of light and shadow ...'

And letting his cold hand lie there, slipping into reverie I emerged from a cool archway into a sunlit square where pigeons hurried from my feet.

꧁

So much for my review which, looking back, I readily admit wandered somewhat from the point.

I will not repeat what Von Economico (God rest his soul) wrote in reply. Suffice it to say that he returned my argument with interest.

Where I had stated my reservations plainly, he enlarged upon them; until, magnifying the details of my argument, he found in it implications I had never dreamt of.

On the modest foundations of my remarks it is no exaggeration to say that Von Economico erected a veritable city, whose fabulous views went far beyond anything I had ever imagined.

'If,' he began his reply, 'we were to take The Gadfly [for so I signed myself] at his word, where would it lead us? The Gadfly asks us to entertain a history of inexplicable appearances. He invites us to take things as they come, to dwell on the surface of phenomena ...

'The truth is: he cannot decide what is significant, what insignificant. His sensations assault him from all directions at once. Unable to decide between them, he perceives himself constantly standing at a crossroads.

'His praise of wandering disguises an actual immobility. He wishes he could take all routes at once. Not being able to, he imagines a host of characters like himself in whose multiple disguise he can explore left and right, before and behind ...

'Only there is no end to this duplication of selves: for as every road has other roads that lead from it, so every self must bifurcate, producing other selves ...'

Whether it was the interruption of his voice that wakened me (or whether it was his voice that put me to sleep), I became aware that I was alone.

He must have seen I had fallen asleep. To avoid disturbing me, he must have heaved himself into his wheelchair and quietly withdrawn. Had he been offended to discover he was talking to himself?

Perhaps Nostalgia had been in the habit of dropping off whenever he began to discourse in the sun. What if my falling asleep did not make him go but bound him to me more closely than ever?

I regretted I had not stayed awake. Perhaps I should have understood better how not to be Nostalgia but somebody else.

As I went up on deck a new lightness had come over me. The concentration needed not to be Nostalgia had helped me to bring the city of my dreams more clearly into focus.

I was almost prepared to say that Martin Magellan's mis-recognition of me had helped me on my way. The after-image of my reverie remained clearly in my mind.

If anyone had asked me where exactly that city lodged - was it the fruit of personal experience, a tapestry woven of family photo-graphs or an impression derived from certain stray remarks? – I doubt if I could have said.

Never again was the city so clearly etched on my mind. Never again was I so sure I would find the place as I had left it, that it would correspond so completely to the sunlit city I carried with me in the darkness of my head.

And feeling I had left Magellan behind me, I began to feel more warmly towards him.

♪

'What do his "perambulating presences" amount to but the au-tomata of his indecision?

'What would his history of the city be beyond an anthology of diaries kept in parallel, whose authors occasionally meet as they cross from one street to another, before passing back into their solitudes?

'And who would these anonymous authors be? Eternally perambulating, gypsies without genealogy, they would be indistin-guishable from one another.

'Except for a difference of an inch or two in height, of a year or two in age, they would all be aspects of the author himself.

'One wears a furrowed homburg, another orders an amaretto with his coffee, a third boasts of land in Andalucia expropriated by the government, a fourth addresses poems to Julian "The Apostate": they are all the many paper-thin disguises of one alone …

'What community can come of this?'

❧

I could not help smiling to myself. I felt grateful to Magellan. I felt suddenly tender towards him, his dandyism, his absurd pretence of being younger than he was, aroused in me now compassion.

I imagined stealing up to him wherever he was taking his lonely siesta, lifting the silk handkerchief he had draped over his face and planting a daughterly kiss on his brow.

I felt tears rise to my eyes and whether they were tears of joy, flowing from the thought that I had a story of my own, or whether they were tears of pity, I could not say.

Such are the springs of tenderness that flow in absence: but no sooner did he wheel himself into view than I felt them begin to dry up and the glaze returning to my eyes.

'You see my dilemma,' he started, as if we had never been apart, 'A literature descriptive of people meeting and departing is scarcely remarkable: the theatre is founded on this idea.

'What is a play but a device for organising random arrivals and departures into a semblance of order? Actors converge on the spot-lit stage and hurriedly talk to one another before diverging again into the dark. Their sole object is to persuade us their meetings have a plot and are not a matter of pure coincidence.

'But I was confronted with a stage, a rolling deck, where folk were constantly meeting for the first time – where as yet there was no common History to be unravelled and no explanations were needed.

'Beyond the physical motion of the surface itself, what laws of attraction or repulsion could be invoked to account for their un-foreseen couplings, their unpredictable estrangements?

'It was these laws I set out to discover: I had no desire to demonstrate the effect of the sea and the wind and their endless coupling on the period and amplitude of the deck's dip and lean.

'The convergence,' Magellan took my hand, 'and divergence of travellers at sea,' he went on as I removed it, 'demanded a human rather than a natural explanation. What was it that brought people together, that made them mutually attractive or repulsive?

'If I could answer this question, I thought, I might place story-telling on a scientific footing – which reflections led me to develop my Theory of Types.'

꒡

It would slander History were I to give the impression that every-one took Von Economico's side. Our public parting of the ways aroused partisan debate on both sides.

A young man by the name of Ramblas, who had won many prizes for his poems, published the following anecdote about his first meeting with me.

'I had woken up with a line going round and round in my head and had spent the whole morning trying to recapture my first care-less …

'In short, I was in no mood for listening; so when, issuing out into the sunlight, I accidentally bumped into my neighbour, I confess to feeling annoyed: our polite pretence of meeting voluntarily must, I thought, spell death to my poem.

'But it turned out differently: sensing my thoughts were elsewhere, he steered me to a table, and without a word beyond ordering the coffees, signalled to me to close my eyes and listen.

'At first I noticed nothing except the sound of my own voice mildly protesting.

'Then suddenly it burst in, the noise I mean. I heard starlings squabbling in the plane trees overhead, pigeons crooning between the chair legs, jet planes coming in and the oceanic roar of traffic.

'The clatter of cups and saucers, brakes squealing, coughs and laughter … and then the sound of voices.

'I could feel the poem draining away but it was too late to recall it.

'All round us conversations were going on and, so exquisitely had our master of peripateia positioned us, we could hear them criss-crossing one another, rising and falling, as if they were one.

'Voices which, taken individually, would have been insufferable became, when woven together with other voices of which they were unconscious, numinous with poetic possibility.

'The chance conjunction of sounds translated meaning into music; and the music, an ocean of syllables glittering, folded over and broke on my ears as a poem that resembled nothing so much as a city slowly revolving on its axis, an umbrella of noise sweetly harmonised.'

Some, reading Ramblas's story, interpreted it as evidence of the correctness of my historical thesis. Others drew attention to his final sentence: 'When I opened his eyes, my host had departed, leaving me to pay …'

🐦

'I reasoned that we carried around with ourselves a multitude of others. If we carried a single other, we could envisage an end to our journeying, a perfect reunion; but since, in my observation, this never occurred, I was forced to conclude differently.

'We were host to a city of beings, none of which inhabited us wholly but one or more of whose distinctive features − a nose, a phenomenal memory, a gift for singing − we bore.

'When we seemed to recognise one we were looking for in another's face, we were drawn not to one but to many others; it was our neglect of this fact, our failure to acknowledge the multitude of others seeking our attention, that led to resentment, jealousy and estrangement.

'This,' he said, attempting to nestle his head in my lap, 'was my first sketch of a theory of attraction and repulsion, but it failed to predict individual events: why was one person attracted to another but indifferent to a second? And how was it possible that affection on one side was not returned?'

I gently pushed his wheelchair away.

'A face assembled from features drawn at random from the common run of human kind was more likely to be bestial than angelic. One had to imagine, I reasoned, that there existed certain universal types.'

I got up and began to walk.

'Perhaps they were related to the descendants of Noah's sons; perhaps they were to be identified with the long-heads and the short-heads beloved of the old Aryan apologists. I could not say. But this much was clear: wherever I looked I began to see evidence for the dispersion of certain original types.'

He bowled his wheelchair along behind me.

'It was this dispersion that motivated our lifelong travelling and searching; and which also explained the mechanism of those meetings which people described as "falling in love".'

I lightly stepped down two steps but he miraculously hopped down after me.

'In these instances the individuals belonged to the same family type: in uniting themselves, they sought to harmonise their partial features, thereby recovering, albeit approximately, the original type whence they sprang.

'In this way their offspring would not further dissipate the original kind but begin the long uphill journey back towards it.

'In this sense the truest sons and daughters were those that resembled most closely the Great Father and Mother.'

Triumphantly I grasped the rails of the gangway and began climbing to the upper deck.

'This was my discovery,' he called up to me hoarsely, 'at sea there are no first meetings. Those meeting for the first time are drawn to one another because they dimly discern they are complementary types.

'Like Christopher drawn to Nostalgia, or to that part of her he called Paradise, they see in each other not a new world of novelty but an image of homecoming.

'The image is not complete for no one now completely embodies the original type – and if they did we would probably take them for an angel.

'But a mildly concave cheek, a freckled wrist, a neck archly arched,' and here he vainly extended his hand to me far above him, 'these fragmentary surfacings of the old type are sufficient to discharge a spark of recognition.'

I walked along the upper deck and he, on the lower deck, kept up with me.

'They exchange glances,' he called up to my shadow, 'they find a way to cross each other's paths: they sense a common inheritance that extends beyond what either can remember. They fondly imagine they can piece it together, by this means finding a way home.'

I leaned over the rails. I looked down where Magellan in his wheelchair looked up at me, dishevelled, flushed, struggling to get his breath. His fingers, rubbed raw on the wheel rims, bled.

I noticed that the wisps of hair behind his ears were of the same auburn hue as mine, his eyes the same oceanic green as mine.

♪

Others were more critical of my remarks. The Union of the Legless, for instance, published with the help of the Migrants' League, this denunciation:

'Have you ever seen a man just released from chains?

'After twenty years or more dragging an iron ball at his heel he cannot walk normally.

'To take a step forward he exerts the force he needed to drag a hundred pounds of inert iron across the cobbles.

'The result is laughable. Instead of advancing steadily, he moves in grotesque leaps and bounds.

'Dodging to avoid a vehicle, his forward foot swings up in the air, he collapses on his back.

'Turning to return a greeting, he revolves like a spinning top.

'When he thinks he is advancing with military precision, the casual observer perceives a man who looks as if he is trying to keep his balance on a rolling deck.

'The man is a clown, a puppet moved by invisible wires. But the people take his buffoonery to their hearts. The bourgeoisie praise his subtle, untutored artistry. He has, they say, endowed comedy with a new depth, a profound tragic pathos. It never occurs to them that his movements are involuntary, that the pain on his face is private not public.

'This is what Baroque taste boils down to: heartlessness disguised as refinement. Tyranny has debauched judgement to the point where it cannot recognise freedom except in its parodic imitation.'

❧

'This is the motive of our sailing: to locate individuals of the type answering to our desire, that little by little we may put back together the shattered mould of her form – a form, which I hasten to add' – and here Magellan moved by his own voice tried to stand up – 'may not be a woman's figure at all but a community of men and women, a radiant and radiating city …'

I stopped him. I turned back, descending the gangway. As he tottered, dragging his leaden leg behind him, I caught him in my arms.

And he, instantly yielding, looked up at me and said, 'Your nose, allow me, please, to touch your nose.' And I nodded.

He placed one hand after the other over my nose gently, like a blind man fingering a difficult passage, trying to distinguish the salient features.

Like a water diviner tuning himself to the vibrations of the earth's many-surfaced membranes.

A mountaineer dreaming of the peak he will climb which, though no larger than a photograph, seems to him to dominate the whole horizon of his life.

Like a sculptor who hopes that the surface will transfer itself to his hands and become, like the convex fan of the sea embaying the land, a physical memory of space.

His finger-tips emitted a bitter ferruginous odour where he had been gripping the rusted side-rails of the ship.

There issued from the north-west region of his wrist the faintest suggestion of eau-de-cologne mingled with sweat.

I became conscious of a corresponding odour surfacing within the inner linings of the nose itself: as if his minutely grooved fingers stroking the tip of my nose induced a sympathetic olfactory current to flow up and down the tiny tunnels of my nostrils, releasing crowding memories.

'We have concentrated our consciousness of touch so exclusively in the finger-tips that we underestimate the power of other extremities to communicate the tactile qualities of things,' he said.

Under his fingers I became aware of my nose as a fifth finger exploring the surface of his palms. I raised it insensibly to trace the lines there, to explore the roads and crossroads laid out in miniature there.

As if my nose were a medium of cheiromantic revelation and could deduce from the history of the hand the character of an entire people.

While he, the tactile photographer, sought to record my face for posterity and to make my nose a form of knowledge, I, half-suffocated by his jacket's woollen cuffs brushing against the soft hairs at the nasal entrances, and dilating my nostrils vainly against his thumb and index finger as they pressed gently up and down the organ's length, fell into a sort of waking dream.

The nostrils were twin gateways to a city whose smells wafted to me on the wind. As I entered, breathing in deeply, I became aware that the scents around me were dark or light, cool or warm, and that from these qualities I could deduce the proximity, size and shape of the buildings that flanked me on either side.

A cool breeze, flecked with fountain-spray and the scent of lemon-blossom issuing from a gateway, was the perfumed ghost of a pleasant courtyard. The merest hint of cinnamon suggested the Baroque entablature and its sentry pigeons gathered over the entrance.

In another direction the dust of dessicated dung mingling with petroleum fumes unmistakably outlined an avenue of stone pines flanked by apartment blocks, the vengeful daggers of television aerials plunged into their palpitating rooftops.

And by the other gateway, passing out, I thought I observed a venerable Jew explaining to his son, 'All knowledge, my son, begins with this,' pointing to the nose, 'in acuity of smell. It is not by chance that the ancient word for mind is the same word we use for the organ of smell: nose …'

And the pun being the mechanism of dreams, I did not find his remarks in the least far-fetched.

And then passing on beyond the city lights I came upon another figure, a woman at the side of the road, her head covered in a black mantle, as if she were deep in mourning, who, when I spoke to her, unveiled herself, looking at me with a face like mine and who, when I said 'Mother', replied 'Nostalgia'.

Shortly after which the ship docked at L— .

♪

Which is why, feeling at sea at home, wafted hither and thither by the storm of criticism my modest review precipitated, I, Martin Magellan, put to sea.

If I could not find L— at home, then I must seek it in the element most akin to it: the evolving surface of the sea.

Some criticise me: they say I mistake faces for islands. They say I base my diagnosis of the human condition on too narrow a foundation. As if only continent dwellers can be sure of their reason while we denizens of archipelagos are condemned to live at the mercy of the tides.

But I disagree: I find in the glitter of the turning surface, in the cinematographic stutter of my characters back and forth across the deck, in the shadows dancing in the heart of light, an apt image of my former life.

Where, as now, the mere coincidence of forms is all we have to guide us, the chance convergence of cones in the eye and the tripod of shadow the walker subtends.

And who is to say my experience is eccentric or narrowly-based?

Having no address to which letters can be forwarded or stories returned, I have no way of knowing whether or not my stories are read.

I like to think, what is surely reasonable, that a day will come when every newspaper in the world has printed one of my stories.

And if by mere coincidence every newspaper in the world published me on one and the same day, surely I would pass for an historian?

The Afternoon of a Park

What goes first on four, then on two and finally on three legs, the Sphinx of Thebes used to ask. And the story goes that Oedipus solved the riddle. Man, he said, citing the crawling baby, the up-standing youth and the white-haired old man leaning on his stick.

I find it hard, though, to believe so indefinite a reply could have jinxed the Sphinx, forcing it to avert its baleful gaze.

Leaning over my camera, preparing to take a shot of whatever comes into view – lovers, grandpas, mothers with prams – I am in no doubt that what goes on three legs is the camera on its tripod.

And going back, what crawled on all fours was not the mewling infant but the city itself which Grazioni attempted to plumb with the camera profonda. It is the windows and doorways of the four-square buildings that slowly revolve and appear to migrate in the eye of that machine.

The camera that walks on two legs is not a riddle. It is ourselves, balancing our two-eyed heads aloft, like balls on sticks, adroitly nodding them left and right.

The Photographer: that was what Oedipus should have said. Who else was powerful enough to outstare that monster?

Besides I dare say the Sphinx foresaw its fate. Why did it leap so precipitately into the river Ismenus if not to join its image?

Its splash was the sound of the camera, breaking its fast to take a photograph. This is the destiny of sphinxes, to want to be remem-bered, to find nothing of themselves remains but the stare …

But where was I? Bending over my other eye, about to release the shutter, I wanted to say: it should not be thought we photo-graphers are indifferent to the sounds about us.

They press upon us as loudly as the crash of water breaking upon the ears of the Theban Sphinx.

❧

Why are the children's calls so shrill?

Is it because we raise our voices to speak to them and they copy us, learning to associate the lower tones with the moans of aeroplanes?

They sound like their mothers: permanently surprised.

Perhaps they are like parrots which fly at one speed and scream through spaces in the twinkling of an eye. They would like to alter pitch and sink to earth but they lack the gravity to slow down.

The first protesting squeak of the bell in the bell-tower, as it begins its slow upward swing, preparatory to striking the hour, awakes my ears.

Listening for what must come to pass, I hear the musical madness of what is.

The playground's clamour is amplified. The drugged circulation of traffic is another surf. The park is an island where every tree of insects seems hung with tiny radios on heat.

The hush and rustle of the bamboos signifies batons of air making of the cicadas' sharpening knives, the squeak of swings, the hissing hair of the fountain, a sort of symphony.

Upswinging, the bell of Sta. C— , and out of its throat, before it can speak, those terrorists of dreams, swifts, streaming.

But where was I?

I had harboured the hope of reunion.

I had half expected an unknown face to burst out of the crowd, and running towards me to exclaim: 'Nostalgia!'

If we came originally from this region, it was not unreasonable to expect a family resemblance to survive.

Even if they could not put a name to my face, there was every likelihood that we would eventually find we had a forbear in common.

She would identify my photographs and I would be able to fill in the story of hers ...

But instead a flotilla of tourists sailed, umbrella-ensigned, into view. A—ns, like me, they took me for one of them: they plucked me by the arm, they pressed me to go with them, they surged ahead ... There was no time for explanations, protestations: Sta C— , L—'s architectural flagship, was about to close ...

Already the bell was straining upwards, about to fall, about to chime.

There was no time to spare: they had to get in ...

They were too late. Despite their gesticulations, the wall closed before them. As the mighty door cleaved to its frame, it was only with difficulty that our tour leader was able to withdraw his umbrella, ferule-fractured ...

Too late! Again, too late, the A—ns protested: under the bell's blind mouth, clanging, slanging, all hell threatened to break loose.

But where was I?

First meetings are never first meetings; they are always a kind of return.

Aware of my recent indisposition, the inhabitants of L— come up to me when I am taking photographs and address me as if I were a child. They gesticulate; they take me by the arm; they nod enthusiastically, pointing out objects of special interest, offering to guide me round the park.

What is your name, they ask; and when I reply 'Christopher', they laugh, seeming to say I have mistaken myself for another.

From which I conclude: I have been here before. Or if not I, then another very like me. My father, say, or a brother.

In me they address a family resemblance, the necessary ghost whose departure alone explains my return.

I am, as it were, the photograph of an original, the soul of a former presence who for whatever reason left, dissolving into air.

Whose death mask was not a lasting statue but this pitted face of stone, which in these parts is forgetfulness's eager adjutant, outstripping decay in its eagerness to model nothing.

So far as the natives were concerned, I was the son of the camera, the little offspring of its potent magic. And if, Aeneas-like, I slung my father round my neck, it merely proved the piety of my ancestor-worship.

When I attempted to explain that I had an appointment with Nostalgia, I can see it was understandable that they should break up laughing.

They threw back their heads and roared, and in dreams afterwards their mockery returned to me as a flock of teeth fluttering from their uvula-quivering, gaping jaws, fanning out to perch on every echoing balustrade, and shitting on me as I pushed past.

❧

Playtime's nightmare. Voices as mirage. The schoolyard as the Void. This comes to me over the wall.

It is another thing I hold against my father, that he could write, 'I do not know what they have against noises.'

Their little voices are cruel fireworks, twisting open the sky's blue fist, releasing a hundred black parachutes of darkness.

Sharp as bull-nosed telephones come their impish rhymes, pulling at my hair, jostling me, insisting I take notice.

Their little finger-tipped noses.

Hearing them I see them: this is the schizophrenia of being at home, not being at home.

There they are, no bigger than ants, marching down the path, twirling aloft what seem at first sight to be laurel leaves.

But which turn out on closer inspection to be severed ears.

This is the sacrifice we make when we hear only the sounds we recognise. Familiar languages – ringing bells, parrots in their cages, the radio imp – represent a kind of deafness.

Is it to be wondered at that our ears cry out against the silence with which we surround ourselves, and thirst to let the noise back in – which to them is flesh and blood?

Is it surprising that they resent our treatment of them and, whenever they can – in unfamiliar cities, say – take their revenge, filling the air with a mirage of sounds in-between, shrieks that lie on the border between ecstacy and torture.

I open my mouth to make the only scream I can, a silence as open as the neglected park with its armless busts, its dead fountain, its gaping gates: a silence that might release the clapper, waking the bell from its upward drift towards sleep.

But where was I? Ah! Philophilus!

What is a Park? It is the Piazza's other ear, the neglected hemisphere of the brain.

It is the report of what happens there.

It is Nostalgia.

It is the form those memories take that by their nature leave no trace behind. Memories of walking, say.

The armless, trunkless busts of old Academicians which flank the formal walks symbolise the decay that remembering suffers when it is transferred to the memory.

The Memorial Park reminds us that there must be other places where memories live untruncated, where they retain the grace of arms and limbs.

I like the juxtaposition of deserted avenues and high-walled schoolyard, the dry silence and the disembodied mob.

They may be said to mark the extremes to which the body will go to rid itself of the labour of listening.

I can understand their panic: at first it is frightening to have no thoughts of one's own, to be a prey to every passing klaxon, every casually ringing telephone …

But at length the pleasures of the Piazza, of lying prone as an ear, become apparent.

But where was I?

The tour party turned on Philophilus. They surrounded him, jostling him – with difficulty did he maintain his bent umbrella aloft.

The journey from A— had been, they said, full of the usual delays and discomforts, but this would not have mattered had L— lived up to expectations.

But according to the oldest of them, those who remembered it best, the town had changed beyond recognition. Except for the children who, like busts, are immortal, nothing struck a familiar chord.

Philophilus tried to explain: depopulated a hundred years ago when their own forbears departed, L— is now occupied by folk whose memories go back no more than a few years – in some cases no more than a few days.

The older families have all been forgotten; their houses have been so changed that even those with photographic memories occasionally find they have been transported from one street to another ...

Philophilus's flock would not be appeased: they resented being treated like strangers or nouveaux arrivistes. They felt they had a better claim to belong here than the city's present inhabitants.

Why are we here, some began to complain. And others, children taking up the refrain: why did we come back?

But that was earlier. And here?

A tiny cloud hovers in the eye of the sun, insensibly calming the children down. The swish of the fountain's horsetail; doves of no particular species crooning among the tombs.

※

I have had the oddest sensation. Earlier, walking through the gardens I had the distinct impression I was about to be recognised.

I had the strangest premonition that someone whom I only half-remembered, who meant very little to me, was about to spring out from behind the flowering oleander on my left and confront me on the gravel walk.

He was going to greet me warmly, I knew it, and instinctively, I drew back; and rapidly, turning on my heel, I made to go back the way I had come.

Call it a quirk of personality but this breed of easy welcomers fills me with loathing.

When they slap you on the back, it is their own wide-armed hospitality they congratulate.

They take advantage of your absence to pretend that you have never been away.

Their easy conviviality disguises the sense of superiority they now feel; possessing a knowledge of the time in-between, they can at a single blow destroy your expectations.

And yet, despite myself, I found myself turning back.

Which is why I find myself seated here in the Park where, except for a distant woman similarly seated, I may be said to be alone.

❧

Poor Philophilus! He raised his hands to his ears. He refused to listen to their complaints. Over their voices he began to speak, some say to rave.

'I do not find myself in other people's childhoods. Their earliest memories are not mine. I do not share their fond recollection of the village or the street with its cast of quaint grown-ups.

'When I try to remember my infant surroundings, a rich tapestry of brooks, railway cuttings, limestone caves and Regency attics does not come into view.

'Nothing comes into view.

'I remember nothing.

'My past is a Void.

'Or: I do not seem to remember as others remember. They remember with the eye, with the ear and the nose.

'The knap of velvet, grandma's lavender water, the blacksmith's hammer, the drawing room's flowered drapes: these details represent for them the texture of that former existence.

'They are no more. History has seen to that. But they cannot bear to confront History. Father History's murderous, open maw is too horrid to contemplate: the incestuous step on the creaking stair.

'They pull the blankets over their heads and whisper their pitiful prayers to his daughter instead, whom they call Nostalgia.

'If they could do away with History, confronting the Void, they would not identify with the past ...'

Which was where I, in an effort to distract him, began cutting off my hair.

※

I would like to find a rational explanation for my behaviour. Suppose, as the natives suppose, that I have been here before.

As I advance down the gravel walk this morning, I find myself approaching the very place where, ten years ago (perhaps to the day), I took a photograph of the Park.

Briefly, I have the sensation that I have ceased to see for myself; that I am seeing with another's eyes.

And this other, instantly recognising my point of view as his own, is about to step out into my path and greet me as a long lost friend.

Reasoning like this, don't you see how the whole city might begin to appear differently?

Imagine the plight of a man trapped forever in another's remembered city, waiting, perhaps a lifetime, for him to come back.

He is like a face carved in stone. Is it not my duty to come back and, witnessing the erosion of his statuesque outline, to free him back into the everyday traffic of things?

❧

'My mother,' Philophilus continued, 'was not the earth-mother type. She was an advocate of air.

'She said to me: "I distinguish two kinds of flier: the aviator and the pilot.

'"The aviator lies down to fly; he attaches wings to his arms and pushes off into the atmosphere's turbulent ocean.

'"The pilot stands up to fly: in his pressurised cabin, he remains the child of Wilbur Wright, absurdly cycling over the abyss."

'When she was dying, she said to me: "They fill my lungs with oxygen, I climb to 33,000 feet and know I spent a lifetime not flying. But it was not always so.

'"There was a time when I had only to draw in a deep breath and I glided halfway to the ceiling and, veering from one pocket of cool air to the next, steered my sheet from room to room."

'And I knew what she meant.

'When I was ill as a child I amused myself by imagining lines projecting out of my eyes. Striking a surface they rebounded, striking another surface, they rebounded again …

'I wiled away the time weaving a thickening cobweb of space substantial enough to support me.

'And among these airy lattices I liked to imagine myself sitting disarming mirrors.'

By now my tresses lay in coils about me. I began to shave my skull.

The doubles in which we photographers invest do not straitjacket us. On the contrary, populating the world with them, we use them to take us out of ourselves.

The interruption I feared opens a gate.

The figure I have described standing in my path may be another photographer. It is not beyond the realms of possibility that he aims a camera at me.

Perhaps he is resentful; perhaps he aims to make me suffer as he has ten years of photographic enclosure.

I prefer to think otherwise, focusing on the mere fact of his interruption − which, I now see, releases from me from the tyranny of repeating myself.

It is a mistake to characterise the photograph in terms of what goes on inside the camera's head. Enemies of its seeing complain that its little guillotine is a form of death. They insist its picture of reality is but a truncated fragment of the luminous whole.

I beg to differ: what they leave out of the picture is the before- and after-life of the photographer, a man who, but for the little coitus interruptus of the shutter, would find no escape from the reverie of seeing.

It is this momentary blindness when he becomes vulnerable to voices not his own, when like some underwater swimmer nosing along a coral strand he becomes aware of the world flooding back in, that marks his advent.

The Park, I fancy, is photographing me from every side; and it is not the glittering laurel leaves, the scintillations from the shattered bottle or the greased filaments of the water's plumes that betray its Argus-eyed intent …

But the noises, the surfaces vibrating, distracting me from any thought I might have had of coming home.

'"Why" is the root of your self-delusion,' Philophilus, went on, haranguing the growing crowd. 'What is the meaning of "why"? It is that the answer is not obvious, that the answer lies hidden, that the answer lies elsewhere.

'This is the secret motive of why: to make you imagine another place, to trick you into nostalgia.

'They say the knowledge-loving Greeks taught us to ask why. No, the first people to ask why were migrants.

'Why is the name of the home none of you ever had.

'While you ask why you are here you remain neither here nor there.'

He said, as I steadily undressed.

'I am tired of your uncomprehending stare.

'Why do you imagine behind these façades another city?

'The depths you imagine reflect where you stand. If you stood inside, not outside ...'

I removed my underclothes.

'But there is no inside.'

I turned out the contents of my handbag.

'Look at our walls. Fragments of angels wings, rose petals, pan pipes, garlands of acorns and low-relief arquebuses assemble there. Nothing is rounded, nothing complete.

'They correspond to your memories. What do your memories add up to? A scrapbook of folklore, sherds of vernacular, a snapshot of grandad in uniform taken against a Tyrolean backdrop, a Bulgarian cap with tassels, a zither with half its strings missing.

'Our city is exactly as you remembered it, a Baroque arrangement of fragments.

'Why else do you think its inhabitants, your ancestors, left? They were looking for the country you now inhabit, a land of unfractured plains and unscored horizons.

'A land resembling their own country when they first arrived.'

Perfectly naked, I finished cutting up my photographs, my scarfs, my tickets.

'Many of them mistook the sea for it.

'They transported their nostalgia with them, scoring the surface with wakes, with wheel ruts, with ploughshares and the report of guns.

'Trying to get behind the Baroque façade, they built a new country that surpassed the old, that tried to revive its original appearance.

'But each migrant had a different view of the past: no two houses grew alike, the effect was fragmentary.

'They constructed little boxes on stilts, decorating them with dragon finials and lacework verandahs, with sunrise aediculi and scallop shells.

'And scattered them across the plains.

'These ornate additions to the landscape were more purely Baroque than the shells they had left behind ....

'Do you not see?'

I did not break into a dance; I slowed down, coming to rest, assuming the attitude of a statue.

In which position I might have remained until all trace of my former self had fallen away, had Philophilus, overcome by the vision of loss he had conjured up, not fainted.

When, leaping forward to catch him, I instantly gave myself away.

�ıж

Think of the other man as a sound: not a statue, a revenant of ten years' vintage, but a living presence surrounding you on every port.

Only intangible, porous, continually passing into another state.

The Park this afternoon is empty. But it is full of such presences, Piazza-echoes, walking arm-in-arm through the flickering shade.

The light dapples their shoulders, taking photograph after photograph of their flowered frocks, their black-ribboned panamas, their spats and poodles.

The air is in continuous motion and the rectilinear certitudes of the Park's design splay out. Straight lines wind back on themselves, discovering ear-like whorls.

The place is an endless distraction and if you ask what lives here, it is the voices that are quietened when we insist on listening intently to the inner voice.

Gathered here are the outer voices which the camera's shutter releases, and which, if we let ourselves dream, we would hear talking among themselves on every side.

Not fragmentary because free of nostalgia for the whole; and in this sense the camera's true other.

➤

Poor Philophilus. I drew him out of the sun. I bathed his brow. I settled myself, a bald-headed madonna, to await his coming round. I suffered myself to don a borrowed shawl.

Coming to, he did not rest. Was it to cover his embarrassment or my shame that he laid his head in my lap?

'From the beginning,' he said, reaching out towards my face, 'I passed over surfaces lightly.

'I did not pause to count the annular rings splayed out like speech patterns in the table leg.

'I do not remember putting my finger in the strawberry jam cooking in the pan.

'The sensations concealed in the depths of things held no appeal for me.

'I beheld my surroundings as an assembly of surfaces, as edges of space where space turned back on itself.

'My first perception of surfaces was temporal. I grasped them as a sequence of positions.

'The eye was like a dancer's foot springing elastically from one surface to another.

'Differently shaped surfaces corresponded to different pressures of the foot and different amplitudes of intervening arc.

'The table, the irregular faces of the stones in the wall, the flag-pole's slender cylinder were grasped not as the exteriors of volumes but as angles of reflection.

'They lent interest to the flight of the eye, as they revealed an infinity of lines flowing between objects.

'The geometry of these flightlines was not reversible. It resembled the topography of the labyrinth.

'The last step determined the next. There was no turning back. Yet the next step and the next step after that remained unpredictable.

'It was a world where nothing could be repeated.

'A world in which attachments suggested the nightmare of a man whose heel is caught in the groove of an escalator.

'Where straight lines spelled loss of balance, collapse and death.

'Where vanishing points signified nostalgia.'

※

It would be interesting to know what kinds of books are written by the outer voices: with the Histories penned by inner voices we are all too familiar.

I imagine they would be very much like the photographs of Grazioni, who, if he had ever written his autobiography, might well have entitled it *Memoirs of a Sound Photographer.*

What we can say is that the books of the outer voices would not resemble those with which we are familiar: it is these latter, cut, pasted and bound, that truly fragment the world.

How can their little slices of life pretend to represent the truth?

Perhaps it is their own thinness they fear in photographs: perhaps this is why historians hate them so – they see mirrored there the superficiality of their depths.

They know that, turned edgewise, they would all but disappear.

No, our books would resemble cities. Or more exactly the open ears of the city where no two apertures produce the same melody, where no two balconies overhear the same conversation. And reading these books would resemble opening a door and issuing out into the street ... or opening another door and issuing out into the street.

It would be indistinguishable from the mazy motion of the crowd where individuals move like threaded needles, nosing in and out of each other's wake ...

Feeling my skin, Philophilus said, 'I do not seem to see as others see.

'I do not see, for example, the clear distinction they make between the visible and the invisible.

'I see many things that are invisible.

'The tunnel between two trees that suddenly blossoms in the tracer-like passage of a bird.

'The airy arch bounding an acre of air as the ball catapults from my hand.

'The ground ahead as a metrical pattern of beats and rests. There is a pebble on the road ripe for kicking. It is twenty, thirty yards away. I know at once whether I shall meet the pebble in mid-stride.

'Balancing a ball on the tip of a stick, it would be useless to analyse its movement cinematically, letting the eye lag behind its fall.

'To keep it there means spinning a space for it, imagining a vortical ground where it is at home and hangs like a globe.

'I see the air. I register it on my face and hands as a Gulf Stream imparting its own motion to the motion of things.

'The swallows hawking distractedly by the fountain, the mayflies dancing under the stone pine: the vagrant gust that blows the swallow sideways also balloons the mayflies apart.

'Recovering their balance, predator and prey carry on mapping events of equilibrium.

'Where turbulent surfaces meet, they begin to buckle and warp. The momentary balance of contending pressures creates grooves of rapid transport down which the poplar's cotton seed-clouds, doors left ajar and circling hawks accelerate.

'None of these things can be seen but they are clearly visible.'

But I can sense that I am dropping into a wellworn groove – I am reminded of Von Economico's searing attack. And he is right: what drives these perambulating presences? What prevents them from becoming dream-walkers? What makes them useful citizens likely to contribute to the prosperity of the city?

The distractions I have referred to cannot be reduced to occasional discrepancies in the appearance of things. They cannot be likened to bomb-scares or the inexplicable subsidence of ancient stairs.

At the same time they are not a permanent feature of the plain. They do not correspond directly to the stone pines or the statues in their cuirass of stealth.

We might think of them as the principle of interruption, whose motive is elaboration, continuous departure from the straight and narrow.

The asides they steer us into are not supplementary to History; they are the might-have been's that continually shadow us when we walk in the sun.

And they aspire to an orderliness of their own.

Imagine how it would be to live as the camera does – in a Baroque city where no two views are alike, and where no metaphysical position can be found completing the picture.

Our progress would occur differently – as if the camera shutter were endlessly clicking in time to the click of our heels.

We would inhabit a world which operated according to the Law of Continuous Substitution.

This is the condition the stones aspire to as they surpass the sculptor's fantasy on the way to the Void.

'Flying birds,' he said, his hand sinking towards my cleavage, 'obey the same physical laws as the washing midway between stone and air.

'The swifts gliding low over the festooned turrets eye the upside-down shirtsleeves intelligently, on the look out for indications of updraught and eddy.

'Their sympathetic motion manifests the Baroque. The Baroque is the form air gives space.

'In my philosophy,' Philophilus looked up at me, 'there is no gap between the planets: the airless intervals said to extend between them are unthinkable. They are the thin and deadly artefacts of Newtonian nostalgia.

'I adhere to the Void, that turbulent vortex whose continuous unwinding is the origin of all matter and motion.

'Air is the body of space and shapes the things that grow there after it. So thunder clouds resemble tree-tops.

'Space lends body to the eye.

'Without the airy inclination of space to imagine more surfaces that we can see, the eye would remain as weightless, as lustreless as a camera lense.

'It would have no reason to travel, to move beyond what it can see.'

And here, his hand upon my breast, he once again swooned and fell unconscious.

The seething playground is emptying. Or the fountain ties itself in knots. Or a statue of a cavalier on horseback suddenly appears to rear up, steam issuing from the animal's nostrils.

Or very high above the cobweb of wires the swifts, unable to slow down, are mating. To birds as thin as these the television aerials flashing far below are as fat as minarets.

All about us the operations of Continuous Substitution are apparent: nothing is ever left behind to mourn the disappearance of the camera's eye.

Everything is on its way to somewhere else: even the woman over there, writing a postcard and one might easily imagine weeping as she writes, is not the alma mater of absence.

Unless I am mistaken she is listening to the hollow which the children's voices have sculpted in the air.

There are some, I know, who, in the name of the family, will condemn my Principle as a foreign aberration. They will lobby for the restoration of organic metaphors. They will take a hammer to my surfaces.

But, I humbly submit, they have misunderstood the nature of the change I advocate. In seeing Death's mask firmly riding the visage of Life, I bring to the surface a natural principle.

I refuse to consider the mouth a marble tomb, a painted pool, its toothy integument prefiguring the bone-lined coffin. I want to live in-between the breathing mouth and the listening ear in a different circuit of space.

In the playground between the Park of Memory and the Piazza of Forgetfulness where other people live.

But where was I?

This is the letter Philophilus dictated, preparatory to suggesting we live together.

'To Doctor Duende, L— , 19—.

'This has been the pattern of my life.

'Always to be out of step with my surroundings.

'Always to be gathering up fragments of the past and putting them in order in another country.

'Always to be constructing memories as if I had no past, as if Memory was always another place.

'And that other place could only be known, only truly known, by remembering it somewhere else.

'Not rebuilding it stone by stone but adding on to it a façade of subsequent experiences.

'What is this place to me except another place where I have not been born?

'Another city where I would have liked to have lived?

'Where, in another century, I might have felt at home.

'This is the fate of the migrant, to build on nothing.

'Greetings from home.

'Nostalgia.'

If, my sphinxlike other, you did come out of the shadows and stood there, a living tripod, a hooded vanishing point, what would you say?

You would say, gesturing to the ghostly plain of light spreading round us, 'These unseen prospects and untaken roads also belong to the realm of Memory.

'Before a choice can be made to go one way rather than another, both avenues have to exist as possibilities in the mind; if the mind did not contain ideas of both, and of the different consequences attached to both, it would not be in a position to choose between them.'

But having chosen between them, you would ask, taking me by the arm and encouraging me to perambulate: 'What happens to the untaken choices, the unfulfilled events?

'They do not disappear, although they make no immediate impression on the surface of History: rather they accrue as unresolved impressions in the Memory.'

And seeming to be engaged in conversation, we would perhaps in this way approach the woman on the other side of the Park without her taking any notice of us.

❧

That was the letter he dictated. Taking over my inner voice, he should have foreseen what would occur.

He believed he would draw me into his power; make me his ventriloquist; his other, shielding him against further humiliation.

But the opposite happened: free of the burden of listening to myself, of copying the same old habits of regret, I walked out into the sunlight and, turning the corner, made my way to this deserted park.

As I wrote, his shadow on my shoulder, I grew conscious of unravelling the joined-up writing of my former life. As I covered the page, it became barer and barer of marks. Until when I had finished there was nothing there.

But what was unravelling here was winding itself on to another spindle belonging to the future.

I am reminded of my mother who, as she grew older, began repeating herself. The same anecdotes in the same mechanical phrases.

At ever shorter intervals she would repeat what she had already told us – about her son who was a writer and lived at sea and might as well have drowned, seeing he never wrote.

Sounds had never solaced her; words were as paper meat to her. She was too old now to take the plunge: speech was a receding tide, she a rock pool gazing vacantly, open-mouthed at the sky.

When the intervals between repetitions became so brief that it was impossible to tell utterance from echo, a strange thing happened: the two coincided, original and copy.

I remember she stood up from her rocking chair and broke into laughter: it was the first time she had heard herself speak.

That was my mother. And you, Philophilus, like every other man, supposed I came back here looking for you!

'Properly understood the true life of an individual is preserved best, not by a biography of external events but by an account of that shadow-world of non-events that, never coming to pass, remains present to the Memory as potentialities ...

'If true Memory occupies itself solely with what might have been, then, logically speaking, the choices we take represent forms of forgetfulness.

'We have all,' he would say, as he steers me round the flower-bed, 'had the sensation of reaching a place of which we have previously formed an image, only to find the image bears no resemblance to reality: choices taken usually oblige us to relinquish a part of ourselves.

'To recover what never happened, what was, and is, continually lost along the way: this is the traveller's responsibility and explains why he carries a camera ...'

But at this moment, as I or a part of me drifts towards her, the bell hurtles downwards.

She is replaced by the statue of a naked muse – it might be Mnemosyne.

As I erect the sharp nose of my tripod, preparatory to taking her, the bell's irresistible clangour slowly topples her from her plinth, shattering her on the walk.

I release the shutter again and again but it is late, far too late.

Black clangour, and the white echo, her ghost of powder, rises to go but it is far too late: the children burst out of the schoolgate, surging towards me. They waft the wraith of her up to the roofs, up to the stressed, vibrating sky.

An open umbrella which in their wake miraculously rises, lodging itself in the fork of a plane tree, looks for all the world like a hook-nosed parrot raising its crest and crimsonly looking down.

While on the walk below a faded wreath of gillyflowers proves to be the inside-out of a discarded wig.

The wheezing in-rush of the bell poised to ring: is it going forwards or backwards? Has time passed? Or am I growing younger?

Scaffolding is associated with the oldest buildings, while the newest sections of the city look as if they have been restored.

This is the ambiguity of appearances here.

Other mothers than mine gather beside the sand-pit while their little architects set about the daily task of destroying what they have built and beginning again.

The girls on their swings climb up to the rooftops. Their petticoats release hems of light that ten years on will be associated with fireworks, ejaculations of Baroque foam.

It is ten, twenty, thirty years ago, and look, listen, the school gates shake out a hundred shrill voices, satchels-bobbing, white-bibs on black smocks, a rippling tide breaking, laughing, scrambling up the path towards me.

Where a man and his shadow, like a bird on a rock, is engulfed, exploding into a halo of light.

I am my mother. And he? He is perhaps another future I left behind.

And yes, the mighty down-sweep of the bell begins. The blackness of sound. Repetition's clangour.

Reveries of a Library

'In the eighteenth century when the city was founding itself again, there naturally arose (once again) the liveliest debate regarding the city's traditions.

'Some, like the Conte de L— , wanted a return to the city's classical form, advocating the extension of straight streets; others, insisting on an indigenous building tradition, clamoured for the preservation of curves.

'Others, notably the merchants, considered this backward-looking perspective morbid. They reminded citizens that the wealth of the city had come from trade – from looking forwards and refusing to be tied down by precedent.

'And yet others said things should remain just as they were. If it was true, as the poet said, that sub imagine eadem nothing endures for long, renewal was merely a matter of going about one's everyday business: decay would occur in its own good time and out of ruin new forms emerge.

'These debates created the widest interest and became so heated that the wealthier philosophers hired handsome youths whom they armed with lances and blunderbusses to defend their positions in the streets.

'Public security deteriorated to such a degree that the government decreed no further discussion should take place in or about public places.'

'In this room are conserved all the books for which there were no authors.

'These were the books that were composed in dreams, written simultaneously in every language.

'These were the books that authors occasionally glimpsed when they looked up from the page, momentarily letting the light of day back into the underground passages of their thought.

'When they momentarily caught the real resemblance between the clouds and life.

'At such times all the connections their linear tales prevented them from making became apparent.

'Previously cloudy arguments appeared to them as gloriously

shaped figures – crimson tetrahedrons and lapis lazuli lozenges – that suddenly fitted together.

'And from every direction, like parrots out of a tropical sky descending to feed, they had the sensation of shattered Reality reforming itself into a single whole.

'Here are stored the books that books made impossible; the books whose pages are stuck together; the books whose pages are transparent ...

'The books so finely attuned to the voice that they shrivel up and die if left behind in unoccupied rooms.

'The books the birds write, which some say resemble musical scores but others contend are most notable for the nodular irregularities of the surface.

'The atmosphere of this room is not lyrical. For instance there is no place here for books that have been left out in the moonlight.

'As one curator remarked, "We do not believe the moon wears spectacles."

'But it is undeniable that a certain nostalgia for the might have been's of time pervades the air.'

'The birthplace of Mnemosyne, like that of Homer, is much disputed. On the face of it this building here has the slenderest of claims. A speculative glass cube which from certain angles, and but for its consumption of clouds, is indistinguishable from the sky, it clearly postdates the Baroque.

'Nevertheless,' Philophilus went on, 'my researches show that it stands on the site of what was once the headquarters of the most radical of the Memory Palaces.

'The group occupying this edifice became notorious as the originators of the cult of Agnaiology. The past, they said, was an illusion and the images of it proof of a collective neurosis, which needed to be purged if we were to realise our full potential.

'In the interests of therapeutic forgetfulness, they devised many strategies. They developed, for instance, special techniques for meditating on the surface.

'They are remembered, if they are remembered at all, for their "Proposal for the Rational Displacement of Populations" which, it has been argued, did more than any other single document to precipitate the Industrial Revolution and our contemporary migrant culture.

'Angered by the anti-civic cast of their arguments, the fathers of L— expelled the Agnaiologists from the city, but not before these terrorists of time had succeeded in burning down their own palace.

'When the building you see before you was built new environmental guidelines existed. The architects were required to respect the historical associations of the site and to preserve the view.

'One of our best known daily newspapers is now produced on the upper floors formerly occupied by the Contessa Von Economico, the last surviving descendent of one of our city's best known Academicians.

'The tenants on the ground floor include a barber, where you can hear all manner of snippets of gossip; a consultant in facial uplift, a travel agency and a very successful pet shop specialising in parrots that talk.

'A second-hand bookshop operates from the basement.'

'This room contains the dreams of a historian who went mad.

'Here is the mappa mundi he engraved. Through a looking glass you can still make out the names of the islands he invented, together with their epithets, although it is sometimes difficult to tell coastlines and calligraphy apart.

'"Euclidia, where charts were invented ... Sternatia, where once a year they pretend to lie ... Sternutia, where they take it in turns to sneeze ... Sympatia, where they walk hand in hand ... Lascivia, where they never get up ... Euphoria, where historians are condemned to death ... Eugenia, renowned for its slaves ... Nostalgia, where they steer by mirrors and drown at sea ..."

'Over here is the imprint of his hand, which, together with a profile of his nose, was all, he said, of his that he wished to leave behind. The minutely grooved surface of the former resembled, he said, a gramophone record; the latter, a kind of stylus; he asked that his requiem be the sound of their playing.

'But the largest part of this room is given over to the drafts of an opera, dedicated to the story of a man who set out to go back and who, finding his echo everywhere, remained unfinished to the end.

'This fan, believe it or not, he referred to as his pen. The wind it causes is, he explained, merely an amplification of those little perturbations we humans create when we open our mouths and begin to talk.

'Its indifference to sounds and its mechanical reliability made it, he said, no different from other people's writing.

'And he was in the habit of letting it play over the pages of a blank notebook, to all intents and purposes reading it.'

&

'Forced to give up their porches, their piazzas and beaches, the major parties retired to the palaces of their sponsors, where they established Academies to propagate their views.

'At the height of the debate, the city boasted no less than seven societies dedicated to the cause of Mnemosyne. But, just as the philosophies of the different Memory Palaces (as the buildings they occupied came to be known) sharply differed, so did their physical structure, their social organisation and the character of their propaganda.

'These contrasts are of such interest,' Philophilus went on, warming to his task, 'that I feel compelled to describe them.

'However,' he went on, 'we should not forget that the historical reconstruction of that period is difficult. Not agreeing about the nature of Memory, the Academies did not agree about History.

'Some denied it altogether and behaved as if the other Academies did not exist, while others, pretending to take a comprehensive view of events, looked upon their rivals as Catholic apologists looked upon the priests of Mexico and Peru, as providential proofs of their own superiority.

'Whether advocating amnesia or anamnesia, the superiority of dreams or the reason of documents, each Academy naturally claimed to be the first.

'Thus, from the start as it were,' Philophilus smiled, 'I have found myself frustrated in my efforts to establish their chronology.

'About one thing, however, there was no dispute. As even today's tourists can see for themselves: the seven palaces occupied different sites. However profound their quarrel about time, about space, it seems, they agreed to differ.'

&

'In this room are kept all the books which were finished but which no-one had time to read. The *Proceedings* of the most illustrious Academies line its walls.

'Here, for example, is a treatise dedicated to the understanding of caves. It is remarkable for its inflatable models and for its proof of the philosophical significance of their spaces.

'The extension of surface represented by caves, together with their infolding of space, constitutes, the author says, a forthright challenge to the way we live and think.

'If we were to live in caves, he says, think of the space that would be made available for thinking.

'The irregular floors and nose-hung ceilings would entirely alter our view of the world; and surrounded by the echo of our own affairs, nesting, as it were, in the ear of the ground, we would be saved the trouble of remembering.

'Of this book all but the title has been eclipsed – which may explain why more scholarly attention has been devoted to it than to any other volume in the room.

'Some suppose *Aluna* was a conventional paeon of praise to the moon. But the balance of learned opinion favours the view that the anonymous author intended something more radical: a lunarless history of the earth.

'According to the fullest reconstruction of the lost text – which might be compared, not altogether fancifully, to the face the moon normally turns away from us – the author tried to imagine the form a moonless civilisation would have taken.

'The outcome of his lucubrations is pessimistic. Without the moon, he contends, humankind would never have conceived the reflective faculty.

'The sun, creation's primary force, is a vast stream of energy in whose turbulent current we are thrust out. We face away from it, we are inseparable from it, emanations of its unity, we are monads of its monarchy.

'But the moon is not a propulsive force. It has no self-evident Reason or Logos. It is a supplement or addition, a counter-image that, rising through the trees, faces us calmly, quietly, questioningly.

'The moon instils in us an intimation of unutterable otherness. It seems to eye us, but with no distinct design or purpose: it neither warms the earth nor colours her productions. It seems to hang there questioning our motives, our customary way of looking at things.

'A confessor, an innocent eye, a conscience – but for the moon bidding us to explain ourselves, doing away with too easy shadows and palpable masks, dialogue, the idea of a silence to be met, might never have occurred to us.

'We would have gone on talking to ourselves, never turning round, our slumbers undisturbed by dreams. That tongue, whose cry creates a clearing in the forest where the moonlight lightly steps, would never have begun to vibrate, to oscillate between tidal poles of attraction.

'She wakes us to a vision of our darker side – and this while flattering us with her luminous cyclopic gaze that we are the only children of her contemplation.

'In short, without the moon we might never have thought of cities.

'And without her cratered face to guide us, the design of their physiognomy would have remained a mystery.'

❦

'It has occurred to me,' Philophilus continued – and here I must acknowledge that some of us began to fidget, wondering if he would never come to an end ...

'It has occurred to me as I have watched the visitors ambling underneath our old arches, pausing to contemplate a flaking façade or even peeling an orange beside a fountain, that a peripatetic mode of discourse might be the key to one of the most famous episodes in our past.

'At least it would let us appreciate the differences; and perhaps, it has dimly occurred to me, their history lies not within (behind dusty curtains and inlaid panels) but outside in the spaces in between.

'This is why I have been visiting the Library more infrequently and, buying a comfortable pair of sandals, taken up walking.

'And even, as the occasion arises, acting as a guide.

'I would go so far as to say that today, in comparison with the much disparaged ritornello of the tourist, the operatic homecoming of a Ulysses is as nothing.

'To my way of thinking the true historian is but a stylus in History's great groove' and here Philophilus drew the ferule of his umbrella left and right down the cobbled interstices of the cobbles at his feet.

'The challenge is not to leap out of the ruts that surround us. On the contrary: it is to demonstrate by the nimbleness of our movements the continuity of their surfaces.'

❧

'There are many more rooms beyond those we have visited, and we have still to see the Memory Palaces.

'Permit me, though, to draw your attention to the single book kept in the room facing you – a room remarkable for its floor composed entirely of upturned nails designed to repulse burglars …

'And which, some say, also accounts for the general ignorance surrounding L— 's origins. I believe it will clear up many of the doubts you have expressed about the historical reality of our city.

'*The Celestial Nose, Or, The Art of Simia Applied, Being a short facial history of L—* maintains that the builders of L— originated in Thessaly or possibly Epirus.

'The forefathers of the city's architects, it says, referred to themselves as the Piridae.

'According to some the name indicated they were tributaries of King Pyrrhus (an argument in favour of their coming from eponymous Epirus).

'Others, deducing their name from the Greek pyre, said that they must have been fire worshippers.

'Yet others, who connected it with the Persian peri, argued that they were fairy folk, their semi-divinity being a sign they brought from the East a superior technology.

'For his part the author of our facial history thinks the name proves the people had pear-shaped faces.

'The Piridae enjoyed from the very earliest days a great reputation as builders. Not only skilled stonemasons, they also designed the buildings they erected and whose forms were said to be without parallel.

'Consequently, when they received a summons to work on the Tower of Babel, they were much offended, responding haughtily that they would not work to anyone else's dictate.

'This was how they avoided God's wrath when it fell upon Babylon – why, when the rest of the world lapsed into language, growing deaf to one another, they continued to communicate in the prelapsarian way.

'Indeed, right up until the time their country was invaded and they were forced to flee as refugees to these shores, L— 's ancestors communicated entirely by way of physical gestures.

'They did not use speech as other races did but expressed their meanings with their arms and faces, through a kind of mimic dance.'

'This building,' continued Philophilus, as we shuffled into a court-yard in the full heat of the sun, 'was originally the headquarters of Historical Memory.'

We shaded our eyes with newspapers, we waited ...

'There is an interesting little story associated with it.

'Before they were banished indoors, the civil servants who formed a powerful element within this group, stripped the public archives of their most important historical documents, arguing that they alone were qualified to preserve them for posterity.

'But their new palace was by no means large enough to house the many scrolls, paintings, Renaissance memorabilia, Byzantine coins, sarcophagi and the like that daily poured in.

'The civil servants were convinced that cataloguing would reduce the artifacts to order, but in what came to be known as the Palace Coup of the Narrators, they were overpowered by a progressive group composed mainly of students.

'These Narrators argued that it was more economical to organise the spoils thematically: instead of cataloguing a thousand titles, they should look for the common thread running through them, and preserve this. In this way, they maintained, it would soon be possible to jettison much material that had no historical significance.'

❧

'Some say the name of these people has its origin in an ancient Greek war dance known as the Pyrrhic "in which the motions of actual warfare were gone through".

'But our savant explains that the resemblance is pure coincidence, based on a confused recollection of a real historical event – the first confrontation of the Piridae with an outside race.

'When the Romans came into view on the crest of the hill, the Piridae proceeded to behave as they always did when they wished to open a dialogue among themselves: facing the armoured infantry, they began a mimic dance.

'Their diplomacy did not, though, produce the desired results: seeing themselves so truthfully mirrored, the foreigners supposed a hostile intent. Instead of falling into step, they opened their mouths and giving a deafening cry began to charge.

'At which the Piridae broke up in terror and dispersed ...

'Our author clears the Piridae of any charge of cowardice: the satellite spears did not make them turn tail, but the unprecedented phenomenon of a human face they could not imitate.

'When the Roman soldiers opened their mouths and bellowed, our people saw the very ground and foundation of their society crumble.

'The supple surface of the lips had horribly distorted and caved in: where feelings had passed as lightly as clouds over grass-covered slopes, casting their temporary shadows, a gaping void confronted them. And to compound their confusion, they could hear what they had formerly seen: clenched hands, wrinkled brows and wistful smiles reduced to syllables, the terrible murmuration of ghosts.

'A yawning hole had opened up, revealing the surface as a mere façade: it is curious to think, our writer adds, that the origins of doorways and windows may go back to this occasion when the Piridae encountered for the first time the hollowness of the surface.

'At any rate it would explain the elaborateness of their façades. What is the function of their endlessly self-dividing surfaces if not to ward off the evil of the Void? If not to persuade the eye that beyond what it can see lies nothing but windy rhetoric?'

'These were the circumstances that lay behind the attempted Burning of the Books – which, the palace Cataloguers maintained, was essential for the survival of their practice, and in fighting which the renegade Narrators were equally resourceful.

'Seizing the burning incunabulae the Narrators flung them into the streets below – where antique dealers eagerly loaded them on to their wheelbarrows and hurried them away.

'By one of those pretty twists of history, their subsequent dispersal into private hands keeps the Cataloguers employed to this day.

'Later, being custodians of other people's memories, the Narrators lost any identity of their own. As you can see for yourselves, their palace became the headquarters of the government's Deaths and Duties Division.

'Occasionally there is friction between employees that can be traced back to the ancient feud between Cataloguers and Narrators but, generally speaking, you cannot tell one from the other.

' "How, the Narrators complain, can we perform our duties without desks, without blotting paper, electric lamps, telephones and rubber stamps?

' "And what are we meant to do, the Cataloguers reply, without ladders to reach the shelves and with a roomful of stuffed parrots?

'Yes, by all means, look inside …
'Yes, for a building so rich in history, its emptiness is remarkable …'

✬

'Turning from the early history of the Piridae, our author gives us a wonderful picture of their culture.

'The Piridae made do without writing materials and telephones. They expressed themselves, as we have said, through their faces and hands.

'In many ways theirs was a superior form of communication to our own: as no two individuals were physically identical, each person conveyed himself in accents entirely his own. Indeed in those days the individual differences between folk constituted the reason of communication.

'It was the felicity of intercourse in that country that, as no two faces were the same, instead of having to travel to the ends of the earth to satisfy a taste for novelty, it was enough to gaze into a neighbour's eyes.

'Compare this satisfactory state, our author adds in a footnote, with our own tireless efforts to get beyond appearances, to mould our thoughts and tones to those of our interlocutor.

'Compare their naked speech of silence with our elaborate wardrobe of self-effacing masks, cloaked meanings, ironic disguises and velvet-gloved misrepresentations.'

✬

'This building on your left was originally the Palace of Fiction.

'So great has our progress been of late that the tower is, as you can see, largely ruined. Only a few decades ago, however, its library rivalled Alexandria's in the speculative histories it inspired.

'Among the best of these was by our own Rinaldo Rumore, many years Chief Librarian, and the first man to bring some kind of order into the collection.

'Rumore arranged the rooms of poetry, history, belles lettres, biography – all of which he called fiction – not by author or subject matter, but by style.

'Arguing that the history of L— demonstrated an increasing stylistic elaboration, he began with the simplest words scratched on potsherds, proceeding by way of ancient graffiti, inventories of

smoke trails, catalogues of medieval traceries to the fullest exfolia-
tion of this tradition in the nodular surfaces of the city itself.

'This, he maintained, provided the best index to the literary
productions of the place and an infallible means of distinguishing
the bumpily local from the smoothly foreign.

'It was no accident, he pointed out, that L—, alone among the
great centres of civilisation, had from the beginning designed its
books with blind readers in mind.

'Rumore intended his own work, the ruined-tower you see before you, to be the culminating masterpiece of this upright tradition. He left money in his will to have the bells in its steeple tuned
to play daily a musical arrangement of his name.'

'I shouldn't give the impression, our oddly modern author goes
on, that the Piridae were without a facial grammar or conventions
of reading.

'Individual faces were regarded as exquisite variations on a universal face.

'The universal face – of which the celestial nose was the most
prominent feature – expressed in its countenance every conceivable human feeling; and, to aid in its interpretation, the different
feelings were located in different regions of the face.

'Once familiar with this temperamental diagram, it was possible
to read a person's character in his physiognomy.

'A pronounced curve in the profile, like a road turning out of
sight, signified a love of travelling; its absence, or a weaker curve,
revealed a sedentary disposition and, when allied to a tendency to
purse the lower lip like a portcullis, a pronounced affection for
home.

'Those with a nose for it could distinguish the combative nose
from the executive nose, the economical nose from the mystic nose.

'Let a woman cast the shadow of her profile on a wall and the
skilled observer instantly knew whether she loved the motion of
the sea, had a fear of heights or was easily led astray.'

'Visitors who come to our city across the plains,' Philophilus said,
fixing us with his sphinx-like eye, 'are often take aback by the
luxuriance of our architecture.

'They find it hard to reconcile the flattened minimalism of the countryside, with its depressive stone wall ideograms, its calligraphic olive trees and blankly walled police stations with the El Dorado of visual delights that greets them on passing through the Porta N— .

'Rumore maintained, however, that this contrast was apparent only and in any case the most natural thing in the world.

'Our exuberance as a people, he said, was a consequence of the freedom we felt on entering a country that had not been written over. It was as if we had escaped the curse of Babel and, freed of the necessity to represent our meanings, could sculpt our presences directly, physically.

'Unconstrained by the need to describe what we saw – for in truth in those days even the stone walls did not exist – we invented freely …'

We shuffled our feet, we prepared to move on; and besides, having used up all our film, I think I speak for all of us when I say that lunch was uppermost in our minds …

But not in the stratified tumulus that was the mind of Philophilus, who proceeded to all appearances undaunted.

'Others argued that Rumore had sentimentalised the situation; that the Baroque was an expression of despair, disorientation, a kind of architectural virus that reduced the reason of building to rubble.

'But Rumore did not see that this undermined his argument …'

'The shape of the face was no less significant.

'The three great divisions of face originated, according to *The Celestial Nose*, with the three sons of Noah: Cam, the Round-Faced, Shem, the Oblong-Faced and Japhet, the Pyriform or Pear-Shaped Face.

'In these latter, thoughts are quick, the senses acute, the imagination lively.

'The pyriform face is the literary, the artistic, the poetic form and, as our writer doubtless knew when he deduced the shape of the Piridae's face from his name, the architectural form.'

'It may comes as a surprise when I tell you that this very substantial edifice with its two doors of (imitation) ivory and horn was originally the Palace of Dreams.

'It's the first time I have seen it myself – until a week or two ago it was swaddled in scaffolding.

'The complete reconstruction was ordered by the Department of Culture and Antiquities to coincide with the anniversary of the city's foundation – the reason why presumably the date of completion has been put off so many times.

'After a long period of desuetude,' Philophilus continued, getting into his stride, 'the original palace had been commandeered at the beginning of the Long War by the Department of Defence.

'Its labyrinthine underworld, they said, made it an ideal strategic headquarters and bomb shelter and they proceeded to occupy it, extending some of its underground corridors, it is said, as far as the sea.

'The war ending, it was decided to restore the site to its original splendour. The Army had, however, destroyed the labyrinth's plan and (it was rumoured) blown up substantial portions of the oldest tunnels, burying many interesting documents relating to the conduct of the war.

'The predictable debate erupted.

'Some were for digging down and exposing the deepest layers of the site.

'Others pointed out that these were likely to be the newest not oldest tunnels and a complete red herring in trying to recover the palace's original form.

'A letter to the newspaper said that, as it was in the nature of labyrinths never to let you out once you were in, it would be sufficient (and cheaper) to repaint the city's stock of one-way signs.

'The writer had spent, he said, five years trying to drive to the city centre but, however closely he followed the signs, by sunset always found himself once again outside the city walls.'

'But where was I?

'Unable to resist the storm of syllables, the Piridae, like those unhappy inhabitants of the New World whom Christopher Column insisted on addressing in his own tongue, quickly came to adopt their conquerors' mode of communication.

'At the same time they did not wholly forget their former facial discourse.

'The refugees of that fearful advent of noise made their way painfully to these shores and, although they now spoke, they had by no means lost their traditional skills.

'Their adopted country was as level as a table and composed of friable limestone. They were naked on the beach, a prey to every enemy. What could be more natural in these circumstances than to turn their skill as masons and architects to defensive account?

'And, in designing the new dwelling places, what could be more obvious than to employ the old physiognomical techniques?

'The ancient facial diagrams had divided the face into upwards of nineteen horizontal bands.

'Each of these bands or bandages contained approximately nineteen oblong divisions – the hilly nose bands traversing a larger surface area having a higher number, the level bands moustaching the upper lip rather less and so on.

'Individual bands corresponded to individual classes of mental faculty and the divisions within them identified the many species of feeling appropriate to each class.

'While intellectual qualities clustered along the brow, the passions made their home the chin and lower lip.

'The moral virtues populated the lower slopes of the noses, while the vices of dissimulation and subterfuge disguised their true nature by inhabiting the open prairies of the upper cheek.'

⁂

'The Commission for Leisure held a competition inviting members of the public to submit dream buildings. The only condition was that evidence must be provided to show that the dream building had been dreamed – not simply made up.

'The winning dream was a triumph of technology, submitted by a dear friend of mine, Nostalgia.

'Nostalgia recalled a dream in which she had found herself in a room watching a film. The room was by no means blacked out and she quickly realised that the film she was watching had been filmed in the very room where she was now sitting.

'It was this that made her certain that she had found her way into the Palace of Dreams.

'The room in which she was sitting was occupied by a group of men. They wore combat jackets and self-consciously rolled their own.

'She was also aware of a parrot swinging in a cage.

'The window looked on to a walled orchard – the whole building resembling one of those fortified farmhouses so typical of the district and in which, as children, we used to play.

'The chief of this group of men and women seems to talk of nothing except Baroque architecture and some of the most animated scenes concern the rival merits of local churches or disputed dates of foundation.

'She decides that this Baroque talk must be a kind of code designed to conceal the details of their terrorist campaign from outsiders.

'She becomes aware that one of their number – the young man who wears spectacles and a beret – is a traitor: his furled umbrella gives him away.

'At the climax of the film, when the whole group has been rounded up at gun-point, it is he who runs across the room, and in full view of the friends he has betrayed, kisses his commanding officer on both cheeks.

'Whose face beneath this rubbing of noses begins to fade into a flicker of dots not unlike a crocodile of black-and-white habited nuns threading the sunlight of a colonnade.'

'Exiled from their former home, the migrant Piridae now built as they had formerly lived.

'They quarried and dressed the stones, selected and assembled them into walls just as they had formerly read each other's faces.

'The nineteen horizontal bands became nineteen courses of stone and the oblong divisions composing them individually faced limestone blocks.

'In this way they not only created imposing walls and public buildings of singularly dignified aspect but surrounded themselves with an infinite variety of expressive surfaces.

'To outsiders the care lavished on surface details suggested superficiality. But this merely showed that they lacked the depth to read them.

'With typical migrant ingenuity, the Piridae prospered in their adopted country. Constructing for themselves a silence that was eloquent, they projected an air of nostalgia they did not feel.

'Concealing their foreign interest in surfaces as a muted reminiscence of forfeited depths, they rendered their own presence acceptable and, under the guise of being superficial, made the depth of their subversive attachments invisible.'

'Knowing that the judges would find her story far-fetched, Nostalgia contrived to film her dream.

'The footage she submitted captured so accurately the architectural structure of the place, even down to details of window fastenings, flaking plaster over the fireplace and the number of floorboards, that the Commission for Leisure felt confident that an accurate reproduction could be built.

'Which is why to this day the city boasts not one but two Dream Palaces, each with its own doors, windows, façades and interiors.

'That you see on the left is the scale model which Nostalgia built in order to make a film of it.

'That on the right is the official palace erected after careful examination of the film.'

※

'We must be getting on. But before we depart I must not omit to mention, a curious postscript appended to *The Celestial Nose*.

'"Some," it commences, "may regard the story of the Piridae as a fiction because it satirises History's obsession with origins. But if so it is a fiction that keeps to the facts.

'"Historians explain the city's infinitely inventive surfaces by appealing to a reality behind the surface, a common principle which they mimic or represent. This metaphysical principle, this deep convergence on a common origin, is, though, a fiction.

'"Which is why I have invented a fiction: in order to keep to the facts. And the fact is that the city is composed of manifold surfaces.

'"In creating a supplementary historical surface, one that has no precedent in History, my little story imitates the spirit in which these facades were improvised. For the idea was never to build on the past: no nostalgia for foundations afflicted the stonemasons, carvers and architects.

'"The impulse was worldly and forward-looking, to treat the wall not as a metaphysical line dividing empty space from solid matter but as a permeable membrane continuously evolving new forms.

'"There is no use in looking behind appearances for the true story. No amount of library-searching will enable you to penetrate beneath the facade to unearth the authentic history of the Piridae.

'"They exist only on the surface as necessary fictions, as points of departure.

' "Their story unfolds in the same direction and along the same temporal curve as the arabesques of the Baroque sculptor's chisel. It is motivated by a desire to evacuate the past of its metaphysical depth.

' "It imagines a history that harmonises with architecture, an architecture unaligned with history.

' "In short ...

' "A building." '

'Although they have only been open to the public for a week or so, some important differences have begun to emerge.

'It had been predicted that confusion would be created by the existence of two identical palaces side by side, but as one wit remarked, being indistinguishable it made no difference which steps one climbed, which doorbell one rang.

'Another Bollettino correspondent observed that their deft juxtaposition might have a civilising effect on the local economy: if the trading of goods presupposed gain and loss, here business died – what could equals exchange? And if they did exchange what they had, who would be able to tell the difference?

'The public reinforced this view: a telephone survey conducted in the first three days of the palaces' unveiling revealed that ninety-three per cent of those interviewed refused to believe a second palace existed even though they had seen it with their own eyes.

'All of which says something about the dreamlife of our province, and raises a pretty question: if our waking experiences exactly reproduce our dream impressions, who is to say we are awake or asleep?

'But I must not go on. It is a mistake of mine to go on.

'Suffice it to say that only today this mirror state, if such it was, has been rudely shattered.

'In their calculations neither Nostalgia nor the Commission had considered the behaviour of the parrot.

'It might have been supposed that two natural mimics swinging in adjoining windows would have been content to imitate each other. And this was indeed the case – all day long they happily echoed each other's clicks and squawks, the snatches of bureaucratese, the bell chimes, without any appreciable exchange of sense.

'What had not been imagined was the unrest this regime of echoes, this stereophony of nonsense, which others call "noise", the public disquiet it created.

'Within an afternoon or two employees of both establishments were seen staggering out into the street, hands clasped to their ears, shaking their heads.

'When they had stopped launching themselves into the air, furiously paddling their arms and whistling, when they had come back to earth and could be questioned, they said that, until they had heard the echo coming back, they had not had the slightest inkling they might belong elsewhere.

'They felt, as one put it, that their inner voices had flown the coop and in their place they were thronged with nightmares of other people just like them, duplicating their work, picking up the other end of the telephone as they picked up theirs ...

'But I must not go on ...

'Suffice it to say: this is the odd effect of Baroque repetition: against all expectations it produces the breakdown of mirrors, the madness of difference.'

'As to the author of the Postscript, there are various theories.

'Some, noting that its style is no different from that in which *The Celestial Nose* is written, conclude that is by the author himself.

'Others adduce the same fact as proof that it was written by another, whose secret object was to impugn the author's motives.

'Yet others reject both interpretations, regarding the Postscript as an affectionate parody.

'While most recently, I see that someone has asked whether the entire treatise may not be described in the same terms.

'In which case who is the author so brilliantly mimicked?

'Such is the ambiguity of appearances here.'

Grazioni on the Beach

It was about this time that I found on my answering machine a message from Nostalgia.

She had seen me in the street photographing, she said, and was anxious to find out more about my work. She had already incorporated some of my images into a film...

Flattered by her interest in me, and not immune to the charm of her voice, I responded, suggesting an appointment that afternoon.

While I waited I wondered how I would recognise her. I took another look at the photographs which I now kept in my pocket. There were women in them ... insensibly I found myself identifying the voice with the most attractive among them.

When she opened the door, it came, I admit, as a surprise to find she was bald, to find that the voice was only another appearance.

My embarrassment seemed to please her.

'To come to the point,' she said, 'it is so difficult to meet; so many expectations, prejudices and fashionable ideologies come between us.

'It is best to be honest – and embrace our images at once, wrestle them to the ground, strip them of their mermaid's tails, their ginger tresses, their island breasts...'

I asked her to sit down.

'Unless we begin as complete strangers, I do not see how it is possible that we shall ever find out anything about each other.'

And it was true: already her voice was beginning to change.

'Apropos of the voice,' the Contessa remarked one day, 'are are you aware of Grazioni's experiment? Von Economico refers to it in his *Golden Age of Anatomy*.

'Two philosophical visitors from England passing through L— in 17— furnished Grazioni with an opportunity to carry out an experiment.

'Grazioni noticed that their balanced either-or's, their disinterested reasonableness, was belied by the manner of their speech – which, far from maintaining an even pace and tenor, tripped and stumbled, now inexplicably accelerating so as to swallow up whole syllables, now as mysteriously pausing to draw out a vowel into inordinate length.

'It was as if they pursued their thoughts through mountainous territory, here rushing down into a secluded valley, there labouring to attain a lofty peak.

'As if they read the book of the mind with a magnifying glass, here amplifying a phrase, there warping it into insignificance.

'Consonants on the verge of pronunciation would be sucked in and disappear into the innermost keeps of the nose; while simple vowels would find themselves attached to the maxillary muscles and involuntarily stretched into a sneer.

'Recalling how men who in the third stage of Venus's disease stagger down the street, now marching stiffly, now ambling, now shuddering to an indefinite halt, Grazioni was convinced their uneven delivery had a physical root – which he determined to locate.

'The abduction of the younger of the two men was simply enough arranged – a glass or two of claret and the wiles of a charming young lady did the trick – and the operation itself proceeded along strictly scientific lines.

'Grazioni had hypothesised that within the young man's throat there must exist an organ that functioned like a see-saw, now opening the vocal passage and now closing it.

'Seeing that this was the role played by the larynx, he fully expected to find what he was seeking in this region and proceeded with his knife accordingly.

'Nor was he mistaken for he rapidly came upon a glandular excrescence previously unknown to science, which he duly excised.

'The young man's murmurings on recovering consciousness fully confirmed Grazioni's surmise. All trace of sweet reasonableness had gone from his discourse.

'He babbled, he cried, he swooned. So like a politician had he become that Von Economico reports Grazioni almost regretted the operation, wishing the missing organ could be replaced.

'But alas this lay beyond Grazioni's powers. And besides shortly afterwards the Englishman expired.'

✳

'But where was I?' continued Nostalgia, laughing, running her fingers over her scalp. 'We need an account that is not backward-looking, that does not attempt to reunite image and original.'

'I see.'

'You see, the original itself had eyes and carried a mirror with it.'

'An account that looks forward, that runs in the same direction as life ...?'

'I would like to make a film about going back ...'

'But...'

'A film that showed how each image was changed into something strange by the nostalgia with which it was viewed. It would emerge that the past was nothing more than nostalgia's inability to see what lay before its eyes.'

'The surface, the skin...'

'The film. I can imagine a film which focused on the surface, that revealed absolute space and absolute solidity as the complementary propositions of one mistaken metaphysics.

'The crumbling wall with the door set in it is coming closer ... Surely it must open and out of the interior, backlit by a kitchen door, surely my former self must come towards me

'But it does not happen. As the camera closes on the surface, the surface reveals details that are unfamiliar, graffiti, blood stains, bullet holes.

'Is this the same door, the remembered portal, or another one – the door towards which the past was going to open.

'What is the meaning of these unremembered portents?

'If they are signs, their meaning remains to be assigned.

'I would like a film that, dwelling on the surface of things, displayed arrival's endless deferral.'

'The camera profonda,' the Contessa remarked one day, 'was by no means the only machine attributed to Grazioni. In his own day his reputation rested chiefly on the capillarimeter, an instrument for measuring the force of attraction lovers exert upon each other.

'Beyond the fact that the apparatus was attached to the hair, little is known about how it worked. Of his treatise, *On a New Instrument for Measuring Human Attraction*, only the following snippet survives.

'"Barbers suffer from a peculiar malady. However nimbly they wield scissors and razor, they cannot keep free of hair clippings. Minute specks of hair fall constantly on forearm and wrist and lodge among the barber's own body hair.

'"Hair-coloured snow avalanches off the customer's lap on to the floor, attaching itself to socks and shoes. Barbers unwise enough to wear sandals find by the end of the day they are walking on pads of human hair.

"'If not carefully removed this insurgent pelt works its way into the pores of the skin and disappears inside the flesh. The pain this causes is intense – barbers always carry with them a pair of tweezers and a magnifying glass.

"'However minutely the skin is inspected, a few hairs always escape detection. These burrow in and eventually create felt-like wads under the skin which resemble bunions.

"'In some cases his hairy ingestions cause the barber's death. I have been present at post mortems where the cadaver could have been mistaken for a teddy bear.

"'A colleague of mine told me of a sexton who, noticing a swelling in the level sward of the churchyard, decided to investigate. Levering back the sod he revealed a man completely fabricated out of felt – which on closer inspection proved to be the mortal remains of a well-known local barber.

"'The seasonal rise and fall of the hummock as the felt man becomes airier or more waterlogged is, I believe, a tourist attraction."

'Although what this has to do with the capillarimeter remains unclear.'

⁕

'What is memory?' I said in desperation.

She laughed: 'In this at least Memory is honest, that it refuses to be remembered.

'Memory,' she said, 'is a village of whitewashed houses reached by climbing a long track through olive groves, flanked by oleanders in bloom, and the gurgling descant of nightingales.

'Memory is the street with the donkey still tied up, where the shutters still slumber in the mid-afternoon heat. It is the radio still broadcasting the Dictator's voice.

'Memory is the little room where, pushing aside the bead curtains, you see a bed big enough for a doll and against the wall a shelf with schoolbooks from the Fascist era.

'Memory is the lemon tree still dropping its delusory fruit into the fountain behind the rail.

'The plume of vapour that aeroplanes left behind in the 1950s.

'The father who rocked on his heels and at length went away; the pitchfork he left in the outhouse, there to this day.

'And those critics of departure, the doves mindlessly cooing, still feeding off what we left behind.

'Don't you see?' she said, beginning to weep, 'this postcard nostalgia will be the death of us.'

☥

But to come to the point. Out of these regular appointments with the Contessa a clearer picture of Grazioni was beginning to emerge.

Besides producing a slim volume of elegiac poems, he published a monograph on the cultivation of the olive.

He contributed notes on the language of the peasantry to learned journals as well as penning (pseudonymously) an essay on the application of Natural Law to the amelioration of the contadino's conditions.

Not a man of action, he nevertheless stood for the Senate twice, but was turned down (twice) – on both occasions to his mingled relief and regret.

A gentle irony informed his work, as if he was mildly conscious of being out of step with his time.

Aware of his solitude he founded a new school of thinking that all were free to join.

'The new goal of thinking,' he wrote, 'must use the scholar's traditional method of comparing and contrasting phenomena but put it to a new purpose.

'Instead of comparing different things in order to demonstrate an invisible historical process, it is necessary to dwell on the differences.

'Historians with their paradigms of human motivation are,' he explains, metaphysicians who have succeeded in finding themselves employment.'

After his second failure to enter the Senate, he designed a poster of antitheses.

He paid the Government Printer to produce a hundred copies, which he attached to conveniently-sited notice boards, bathing huts, telegraph poles and oak trees.

Language v. Dialect, Passive v. Active, Two Dimensional v. Three Dimensional, Local v. Foreign, Visible v. Invisible … and at least one other which I now forget.

The people mistook it for an election poster – you must remember that there had not been elections for a hundred years – and wondered how politicians got their names.

That year every second boy was christened Three Dimensional

or Invisible – until the priests jacked up and locked the fonts.

Grazioni used to say that no man could claim to be a philosopher unless he could dance the sarabande without sensuality.

Grazioni was a great enemy of dialectic, which he regarded as a barbaric foot-chain on the mind's natural movements.

'Most philosophers,' he said, 'are like clowns on stilts: their arbitrary either-or's are admired much as we admire the jerky left-right of stilt-walkers.

'It is not that their progress is any more elegant than our own earth-bound progress, but the difficulty of it is undeniable, the useless dexterity.

'But take advantage,' he said, 'of that unbalanced moment inbetween when one giraffe leg sways ahead poised above the ground, to push him – and all at once the garish edifice collapses, the baggy pants of rhetoric, the top hat of faith …

'The symmetry of their zig-zag logic cannot conceal for long its fundamental lack of balance.'

Grazioni founded an academy of the Non Se Non Che. Its members agreed to abide by one rule: that nowhere either in their conversation or in their writings would they fall back on the dialectical convenience of 'Nevertheless …'

As we became more intimate, Nostalgia told me many things concerning the origins of L—.

One day she said, 'The breast has a long history but to understand it you must be aware of a bifurcation early in its development.

'Before our city assumed its present form the site it occupies was held by the Mound Dwellers. These people worshipped the breast, in whose form they fabricated their own houses and temples.

'Forbidding right angles, they laid out the town in the form of an oval. By this means palaces were always viewed obliquely, even flat facades seeming to turn towards the viewer.

'In this city - you can still feel the effect - attention constantly passed from the surface of things to the narrowing cleft between.

'Nevertheless this vision of the world was challenged.'

Grazioni said that the philosopher's 'nevertheless' signified the failure of his discourse to explain all the facts.

His 'nevertheless' was a falling short which masqueraded as a ladder. But let him explain.

'Nature,' wrote Grazioni. 'does not think ahead. It never experiences self-contradiction. Nothing underlies nature except the principle of manifold difference. But human reason thinks differently – in this proving itself but another natural manifestation.

If human reason followed infinite nature to the end it would abandon reason; but it has no patience.

'Generalisations signify the impatience of reason; and the same impatience leads reason to rebut its own generalisations with new ones: thus does reason transform its shortcomings into a Baroque edifice of self-reinforcing contradictions.'

📎

'There arose within the town a body of opinion that argued for a different interpretation of the breast.

'The massy domes and sagging overhangs of our ancient balconies were, it was said, indications of decadence.

'They were the result of fetishising the breast as flesh.

'It was necessary to define its appeal differently. In what did it lie? In the memory of a physical sensation, in the child sucking at the nipple, or in something else, in the outline of movement?

'These people argued that the dome was a partial and misleading idealisation. The universal feature of the breast was its double curve, its concave upper reaches, its convex underside.

'These two curves, replicated throughout nature, in the profile of waves about to break, in lanceolate petals, in drifting clouds, constituted the breast's claim on our attention.

'The primary reference of the breast was not to Birth but to Death and Resurrection.

'The sarcophagi of our Roman ancestors, they said, were invariably grooved along their sides with an "S" design incorporating the double curve of which we speak.

'The design alluded to the double movement of life through Birth to Rebirth.

'To dwell on the mass of the breast, to succumb to a childish desire to hold and mould it, is to flirt with extinction.

'Revere instead the outline, where curved space reveals the promise of return.'

☙

To the colonial administration Grazioni's political views smacked of dangerous radicalism. The peasantry regarded him as a harmless antiquary.

He despaired of awakening his neighbours from the slumber of habit but did not neglect to tie up the japonica on his balcony and to water it regularly.

He found consolation in the nobility of his surroundings and was filled with nostalgia for the liberal society it had promised but which had never bloomed.

As he grew older he became more conscious of his own solitude; the more clearly he realised that the past he longed to revive was a future he had missed taking.

The more ardently he imagined it the more impossibly remote it became.

The more it resembled a decaying façade.

As we became more intimate, stripping away the many surfaces of our disguises, our conversation took a personal turn.

'And what was your own feeling?' I asked one day (alluding to the ancient division).

'That desire resided neither in the ideal outline nor in the naked fact but somewhere in between.

'In the oblique curve disappearing into shadow.

'It is not the breasts that attract – breasts as mobile in form as the vowels of our speech – but the concave contours between them.

'It is this secretion of the surface,' she went on, 'this vortical infolding of the cleavage that signals the centre of desire.

'For here the surface is maintained but promises always another aspect that can never be realised.

'It is not the breast fully revealed that turns towards the eye.'

'No,' I said, 'no.'

'But the breast half concealed.'

'Yes,' I said, 'yes.'

'The explorer does not prize the unambiguous caerulean.'

'No,' I said.

'He focuses his longing on the globe sinking towards sunset and, like a necklace on the throat of the west, the wedge of birds flying into the bosom of night.'

'Yes.'

Grazioni was a philosopher of the beach. He delighted in contemplating the meeting place of two elements as different as water and earth.

He used to say: 'If we could understand the mystery of their reconciliation we would have no need of philosophy. We could do away with priests and marriage counsellors, with notaries and prostitutes.

'Let us admit,' he used to say, 'that the world consists of infinite planes and that each plane is unique and infinite. The question is: can these planes ever meet? Is it possible to cross over from one surface to another?

'And, if it is possible, in what plane does it occur? Must we invent a third dimension that accommodates difference or is there another solution?

'Here,' he used to say, pointing to the saturated sand shining like a woman's cheek, "is one plane, and here," pointing to the lace ruff of the waves momentarily mounting the sand's fair bosom before dying into it, 'is another plane.

'They meet,' he said. 'They melt into each another. But where? Neither above the surface nor beneath it.'

There had been spells of fine weather in the past when Grazioni had felt certain of the answer.

There had been delicious mornings when he had strode triumphantly off the beach sure in his mind he had glimpsed the truth, when he had been ready to write at once to the Academy of —, announcing his discovery.

But the beginning had always defeated him. The rhythm of the argument abandoned him when he sat down. He found himself rehearsing dead authorities.

'The author of the *Metamorphoses* was right to link the decadence of the golden age to the advent of mining. The answer is not to be found underground, in the earth's geological history.

Or: 'Legend has it that Alexander the Great ordered a bathysphere to be built for him in which he descended to the ocean floor: whereupon his servants let go of the cord and left him to drown. This is a parable about the futility of plumbing the depths in search of the truth …'

If only he could write as he walked, Grazioni reflected.

As we became more intimate, the shape of my desire could no longer remain invisible.

She wanted to bring it out into the open.

I remember the time she first pressed herself against me. 'In comparison with this,' she said, gently pressing her hand into my crotch, 'the breast is a phallus.

'You must not misunderstand me. I have no wish to impugn your manhood, but look …'

'Not here,' I said hastily.

'The statuesque rigidity you aspire to, seeking to immortalise desire, falsifies it.

'I am not interested in tracing the imperial veins that network its leaning column. I am not interested in seeing its single-eye at length procreate a single tear.

'It is the coming and the going that is admirable.'

'Not here,' I hissed, breathing deeply.

'Then where?' she replied, relaxing her grip. 'In the picture-house?'

If only the whole world were a breast, I thought, an endless surface, these difficult conjunctions and fraught interpenetrations might be avoided.

'Apropos of the film,' I said. 'You are mistaken in thinking it can remember forward.

'Its subliminal stutter of images imitates people walking, horses and carriages turning the corner, puffs of steam emerging above the station roof.

'But it is an illusion: the people moving so confidently across your screen are blind to the future.'

Nostalgia for my former tumescence did not prevent her withdrawing her hand.

'The film image may mimic the direction of lived time, but it is mimicry only.

'The man who walks forward has no choice but to continue walking forward.

'On film the future has already been remembered for him.

'His submission to his fate is, if the paradox may be allowed, a form of backwardness.

'In truth he walks backwards into the future – not seeing, not needing to see, where he is going.

'The contingency of the future, the way in which memories create a past different from the past, is best caught by running the film backwards.

'Why do we laugh at the locomotive jerkily ingesting its breath, at the window reassembling its shattered glass, at the man backing into his house like the claw of a crab withdrawing into its shell?

'I will tell you.

'Because we know the past was never, never remotely like this, whatever the records may show.'

I tried to catch up with her but the faster I ran the faster she seemed to retreat from me.

It was as if I were pursuing my own image in a mirror but the image I pursued was reflected from a mirror behind me.

There could be no doubt about it, Grazioni reflected wiping his eyes, the winds had been getting stronger of late.

Like a marionette which, by some quirk of upside-down logic, is stringed to the underground and, instead of dancing nimbly, threatens at every step to sink up to its waist, so Grazioni soldiered through the sand.

A woman on the beach turning to upbraid her son for throwing sand over her oiled behind discovered the cheeky wind peppering her.

A beach umbrella slipped its mooring, bowled across the beach and took to the air; cleared the palm trees, wedged itself in a hotel window, a crinolined marionette up-ended in a well.

The winkle-collectors, up to their knees in mud, had drawn their hats down low, substituting matted orbs of felt for faces.

Gale-sharpened swifts were dodging through the streets in gangs. The flags streamed out stiffly like a revolutionary's daydream.

There could be no doubt about it, change was in the air.

The rains this spring after the longest drought in living memory had not marked a return to the normal pattern of things but the initiation of a new climatic regime.

The priests were taking advantage of the unsettled state of things to bring forward the Final Judgement. Trade in tombstones, in penances and pardons, was flourishing.

The fishermen – whom Grazioni, himself a fisherman of sorts, trusted more – were saying the same. They blamed their torn nets and poor catches on the 'brutta mare'. This spring, they said, more fish had been freely cast on land than they had caught in their nets.

On land the season had been so inclement that the peasants had retired to their huts, where they passed their days in tourist handicrafts and roof repairs.

Out of the wind and sun their ruddy countenances had begun to acquire the pallor of porcelain. They were frequently mistaken for their masters and mistresses.

On the Conte de L—'s estate the servants recently occupied the palace; for a whole winter they entertained so handsomely that no one could tell the difference.

(Their generosity at length gave them away.)

The rising tide was sucking the sand from under his feet. Feeling the imminence of his fall, Grazioni could not avoid the conclusion that the world was topsy-turvy.

After that I went back to taking photographs.

Until one day my telephone called me. I ran to it, cradling it to my ear. I encouraged it to speak.

'I have a friend,' her voice said, 'who remains perfectly reasonable on every subject except this: the constitution of the world.

'He has collected a library of authorities to prove that the globe is concave.

'Under our system of government,' her voice went on, now imitating mine, 'the phenomenon is all too common.

'A man of undoubted abilities denied the road to self-advancement turns in upon himself and becomes prey to Baroque fantastications.

'His dwelling,' she said in her own voice again, 'is formed after the sky.

'Its overarching walls are hung with trophies of his enquiry.

'Beautifully tooled curved chair backs, cups and saucers, coruscated thimbles, tooth fillings.'

'But how,' my voice said, 'can you bear his company?'

'He says,' she said, changing voice once more, 'that a powerful union of convex folk has conspired to prevent the recognition of the world's true nature.'

'How can you take him seriously?'

'Philophilus? He has made moulds from my breasts.'

The import of this Baroque display was obvious.

I was the fantastic philosopher she satirised; only unlike him I never descended from the metaphysical to the physical.

I felt the colour rise to my cheeks.

I was ashamed. But also angry: I was not the person she thought I was.

Only pausing to grab a beach towel and shades, I set out for the beach.

⟡

If only he could walk as he wrote, Grazioni reflected.

The thought depressed him. But more depressing still was the thought that he had had this thought a thousand times before.

Depression suddenly gripped him, like a rain-sodden cloak.

His mind was a Baroque masterpiece which due to some chemical reaction of the glaze with the environment was becoming prematurely crepuscular, hierophantic, suicidal.

He turned and started to stride out into deeper water.

Yes, and closing my eyes I had an even clearer picture of him; and it was not an engraving in a book or even an ancient photograph.

I had an impression of a strummed sea, dark bands like the strings of a harp hovered horizontally there and seemed to fire into the cornea a ceaseless rain of arrows, whose after image was a flock of white fishing gulls, glued to the grainy waves.

And at the centre of this, like a black lighthouse, like a velvet pyramid – I am only trying to make you see it – a cuneiform cavalier stood; and, as the air drove round him, swarming, swelling, licking his outline, threatening to make him the shadow of a hulk, he staggered into motion …

🐛

'You need,' she said, turning over, 'a theory of the groove.'

I glanced away.

'Otherwise how can you give a satisfactory account of the surface?'

She beckoned me to lie down beside her.

'The surface is a skin by virtue of the fact that it conceals depths.'

Belly to the sand, head to one side, I said, 'But the depths – this is the Baroque insight – are not a solid interior. The surface is not wrapping paper supinely enclosing a Platonic essence.'

She got on all fours, she squatted on her haunches, greasing her hands.

'It is the expression of natural forces, those powers of attraction without which the elements could not coagulate and separate themselves from space.'

Her shadow fell across my shoulders.

'You have in mind something like Leonardo's studies of turbulent water ...'

'"I am a great friend of rivers: they do my spirit good," said
Bernini."

Gently, she began to massage my back.

'The surface, the bland face of marble, is not enough.

'Clouds would tell us nothing about the state of the air if they
were not pummelled, woven and unwoven.'

Desire raised the surface and then shrank back.

'Apropos of which,' she said, resting her hand lightly on my
other nose, 'it is not the face of stone that speaks but the gesture in
the surface.

'There are those,' she said, penetrating the little tent between
my hips, 'who would represent desire like this but,' she said, 'I am
a builder of a different kind, valuing the relaxation of the surface.

'Look,' she said, her fingers crawling through the open flaps, 'a
principle of continuous substitution operates here ...' and she
tugged at the pole until the tent dissolved into a rainbow-hued
umbrella, opening, opening ...

And after the rain, furling, folding, falling asleep.

As I closed my eyes there floated across my imagination not the
after image of nipples but the squeal of seagulls and the oral lap of
water.

Half a mile further out his face was unrecognisable but the water
had barely risen above his thighs.

'No wonder,' he reflected bitterly, 'death by drowning is unknown in our country.

'Ours is an environment of surfaces, of horizontal planes, deep
wells of despair.

'The profondeurs of the philosophical deep are unknown to us.

'We are soft here, sharp edges are rapidly worn away.

'Without strong opinions, we incline this way rather than that,
much as a sail to the wind.

'We are all provincials here and our magnanimous tolerance of
difference is proof of the lightness of our attachments not the depth
of our philosophy.'

Grazioni shivered. Was it the chill of his own irony or the temperature of the water, he felt?

Perhaps this was how Death began. But, if so, it was worth observing that, as the body slipped beneath the surface, the mind was flooded with thoughts. The ecstacy of the writer who finds a reader must be like this, he thought.

Amphibious, swimming, drowning.

Grazioni staggered back on to his feet. His vision suddenly possessed the clarity of a camera.

The waves scudded in under the strengthening westerly, breaking like rapid heartbeats against his breast.

He noticed for the first time the resemblance between their crinkled breaking crests and the waves of foliage slapping up against altar columns and curling over tympana in the churches of his native town.

The waves were growing in strength, falling one upon the other more rapidly.

The little hems of foam were widening into pinafores as intricately worked as any produced by the good ladies of Alberobello.

Why, the mighty breakers of Ulloa's Pacific could not boast a more elaborate display.

It was wonderful that water so shallow, flowing over a bed so sandy and quiescent, should rise to these giddy heights, produce these Baroque ejaculations ...

An idea surfaced in Grazioni's mind and once he had glimpsed it he found it hard to imagine why it had not occurred to him before.

Coming to I heard.

'The groove is neither above the surface nor beneath it.

'That is the difficulty with your bland application of the term "surface".

'In imagining the surface as a visually-telling plane, you remain detached from it, hovering above it.

'It is your distance from the surface that makes you idolise it.

'The groove does not destroy the surface: it does not penetrate to hidden depths.

'Indenting the surface, introducing a valley into its plain, it increases the surface area.

'The groove demonstrates that the surface is the other side of touch.

'The more a material is moulded, incised, drawn out, folded over and extended the more surface it displays.

'For the sculptor the whole stone is a potential surface.

'She is not interested in hidden depths but nor does she fetishise the skin.

'She is a friend of tattooists and cicatrizers.

'The economy of the skin does not resemble a globe but a coast-line that can be analysed into ever more intricate coastlines.

'The surface is not the imitation of a platonic form, it is the miniaturisation of the world.

'The architect or sculptor who works the surface reveals the equivalence between shells and stars.'

She leaned back on her haunches and, wiping her brow, flexed her aching fingers.

In a lifetime devoted to the explanation of his city's architecture Grazioni had never considered the possibility that its peculiar zest, its paradoxically orderly rebelliousness, reflected a change of climate.

Yet it was well documented that during the golden age of his city's building the summers had been cool and blustery, the winters grey and cloudy, autumn and spring prone to tempests, storms, typhoons and cyclones.

'However speculative the origins of our cherubs and whirlpool columns in the jungles of the Yucatan,' he thought to himself, re-hearsing a beginning he had once made before, 'in the fantasy of a Bernini or a Fanzago, this much is clear: our buildings illustrate the wind-bent trees, the gale-driven flowers and plumage of birds, the overturned seas ...

'In short the dislocation of natural things from their ordinary places.'

Could it be that the local stonemasons – folk long used to feudal oppression – saw in this a natural authority to overthrow the classi-cism associated with imperial tyranny?

Looking at it the other way, dated works of art might be used not only as a political barometer but as a meteorological record, a mirror of the changing state of the weather.

We touched on many things that afternoon, until well into the evening.

'The men are revealing their buttocks,' I said. 'They have

hoisted up their swimming briefs to reveal concave curves.'

I felt a wave of sadness break over me.

'The women are reduced to G strings.'

Gazing out from underneath my straw hat I could scarcely contain my disappointment.

'The more they reveal their skin, the more ingeniously they confine their genitals inside a strap or pocket of fabric, the more lacklustre I feel my desire.

'Desire is physical but the flesh revealed here is metaphysical.

'A flesh rendered more naked than nakedness itself, it exists only in the eye.'

But this was not enough to explain my depression.

I regarded the bathers with something like compassion.

'They have found that the surface is not the seat of desire but do not know what to do.

'The strips of silk slung across nipples or grooving the perineum do not preserve decency.

'They are subcutaneous weals, swollen organs threatening to split open the body wall like a pomegranate rind.

'Soon,' I reflected, 'they will have to strip off their skin to keep our interest.

'To preserve the illusion of another surface behind the one we see, they will need surgery to expose their interior tissues.

'Before long the only eye that can see them will be a monocular catheter reaching into rectum, vulva and penis in a vain attempt to penetrate to the centre of desire.

'This is the blindness of their appeal to the eye: not to see that appearing they disappear.'

Breathing deeply an irriguous wind which now seemed to fit him as closely as his skin, Grazioni experienced the dizzy sensation of a dancer who, leaving the ground, sails through the air only to return safely to his place again.

The same wind that beat on his face raised the water into images of stone …

The same wind that brought tears to his eyes also eroded images of stone, reducing the proudest statues to brainlike masses resembling a field of bubbles bursting in the wake of a broken wave …

The air was not empty. It constituted the surface of surfaces, the place without planes where all planes met.

Grazioni turned his back on the horizon.
Grazioni spread his cape like a black sail.
Grazioni began wading inshore.

I looked down at the naked figure of Nostalgia lying prone beside our beach umbrella.

I remembered how another time – it seemed like centuries ago – she had lain decently clad at my feet.

I had leaned forward then and wordlessly begun to stroke her stomach.

My insides churned at the memory.

Now she reclined there remote as a rock, the trickle of water from her wig devoid of symbolism.

Time to take a stroll.

I began to lever myself up from the deckchair.

Was it the heat of the day or the candour of my meditation? The beach turned white, then black.

I felt myself falling, floating away.

As the wave closed over me, I heard the unmistakable notes of nightingales calling 'Christopher! Christopher!'

I knew why I was dying.

I had been here before.

Duende imagines the Piazza

Duende did not die that day when for the first (and last) time he knew what it was to feel at home.

He went on living, refining his practical art of memory until one day he felt ready to begin his Memoirs.

He took his fishing rod. He went to the country. A student of noises, he fully expected the sounds of the bush to stimulate his recollections.

The river sliding by his feet might easily be taken for a recording of the old piazza in L— where he used to meet his friends. Their voices played back at half speed might bubble and gurgle, groan and hiss exactly like this.

And then there were the ventriloquial parrots cavorting among the flowering gums overhead.

And what of the limestone cliffs opposite, whose sculpted features resembled nothing so much as a Baroque façade?

Casting his line into their dazzling reflection, winding in, casting again and winding in, Duende recognised that nothing essential had been lost.

What he had needed he had brought with him. Not a freight of memories but a way of walking about the world, of slipping sideways between events, those theatrical sets which others took for History.

To begin again was simply to continue perambulating. It was as if –

And here Duende, making himself comfortable against a tree, closed his eyes to the glitter.

As if the past was like a crescent of buildings fronting on to an open space, whose surface was cobbled, populated with pigeons, walking feet, puddles, tyres, bollards and steaming shit …

Duende allowed his notebook to slip from his lap … there is the fountain where two strangers have arranged to meet, the cafe frequented by journalists from the *Bollettino*.

Over there on the wall, just where The Street of the Mimic enters the piazza, is the famous plaque: 'To the Memory of Doctor Duende, harpsichordist, designer of kites, L— 's Homer, 1685- …'

And over there, above the Barber's shop, is where the Contessa continues to hold her little salons.

It is all around me, Duende thinks, all around me. As he falls asleep.

• • •

'What? You never heard about Forgotson and his *Polyphony for a City*? I'll tell you how it came about.

'On the strength of his *Souvenir di Viareggio* (Opus 220-222) Forgotson was invited to compose a work to celebrate the —th anniversary of our city's foundation.

'When the Anniversary Committee invited Forgotson to tour the city, I covered the event for the *Bollettino*. Forgotson, I remember it as if it was yesterday, was struck by the difficulty of getting on.

' "One is continually subject to blockages and delays … Scarcely a market day goes past but a cart, laden high with melons, sheaves of wheat, Rubenesque daughters and half-buttoned pomegranates, unhitches a tail-board or breaks an axle, casting its contents like Pomona's cornucopia across the street," he said to me.

' "An interruption, as I wrote in my piece, not only to the tread of feet but to the feat of trade."

'Anyway on the basis of trying to walk round the city Forgotson withdrew his original proposal – a waltz entitled *Memorie barocche* – conceiving an altogether more ambitious scheme.

'Observing how folk at once fell in line when the band struck up one of his polkas, Forgotson proposed that the city's congestion could be overcome by orchestration.

' "Provide dance tunes for every piazza and street," he said, "and it ought to be possible to regulate the movements of the traffic in such a way as to facilitate the maximum harmonious flow back and forth."

' "Melodically memorable compositions, keeping a clear beat and avoiding rapid alterations of tempi, were," he thought, best adapted to the purpose: "they minimised the confusion that arises even on the dance floor when a rapid transition or syncopation all too easily spreads down a line of dancers tripping them over one by one, as if they were a wave of cards."

'Forgotson flattered the city elders that the citizens of a city so musically-minded would rapidly learn the different tempi demanded, while those who had forgotten had only to imitate their neighbours.

'As for foreigners and peasants, unused to these civilised gestures, a strolling band was to be employed at their expense on market-days and high-days to keep the time.

'It is odd to recall how warmly Forgotson's scheme was welcomed. Von Economico, I remember, wrote an article stating that such a system might contribute to law and order. Political movements – a group of disaffected workers gathered on a street corner, say – would be unable to resist the foxtrot's galvanising tempi.

'Before they know it,' Von Economico predicted, 'they will be dispersed, strung out like filings in a magnetic field, aligned to the dance of civic progress.

'As a system of administration, Von Economico thought, it would be without rivals … 'Cannons, firearms, lances and fingerscrews can be done away with: the city will be ruled by hautboys and fiddles, tambourines, whistles and drums ….

'In the event Forgotson's early orchestrations proved grotesquely impractical, although they were not without theoretical interest: the sight of a whole suburb winding through the Porta N— under the influence of his *Souvenir di Viareggio*, and attempting to drown itself in a field of stubble, which it took for the sea, remains one of the more colourful proofs of the locomotory basis of taste.

'As for the orgy that ensued from his promiscuous conjunction of well-known polkas – *A bocca dolce* (Opus 308), *Baci ardente* (Opus 236), *Bocca baciata* (Opus 271) – this, it was subsequently rumoured, had been fully foreseen …'

Here, seeing their editor ambling across the Piazza towards them, the journalists hurriedly called for the bill, and grabbing their hats, issued out into the sunlight.

Taking one last turn around the Piazza, Christopher decides that Nostalgia has forgotten their arrangement.

Or else, he reflects irritably, one of us is a day, a week, a month, even a year early.

He turns in to the familiar courtyard, past the Barber's and up the steps where, knocking on the door and entering, he finds the Contessa in the act of pouring a cup of tea.

'You must understand,' the Contessa begins, starting where she left off yesterday, 'that there are two Baroques.

'If there were only one, its history could be left to historians. But there are two and as their resemblance to one another can only be imagined, their story must be left to those epigones of nostalgia, the writers.

'As regards the first Baroque, you have already read Grazioni's biography,' and she waves a hand in the direction of the piazza, whose hubbub floats up to her window.

'In its light you may understand this better' – and pulling a much-yellowed and dog-eared newspaper article from an ox-hide phylactery hanging beside her, she hands it to me.

'We were young then,' Christopher reads, resuming his window seat, one ear on the Piazza, 'arrogant no doubt. We rebelled against windy orators and their syntactical lackeys; their sweetly-rhyming words without substance sickened us.

'We were not Baroque: we were against the Baroque.

'We wanted language brought back to earth. Could the currency of communication be cleansed, its natural signature might be read, its heavenly minting shine forth.

'But things worked out differently: as we inspected nature more minutely, we discovered plants and birds, rocks and stars, whose names were unknown ...

'Microscopes and telescopes revealed amoebae and galaxies formerly undreamt of ...

'We were dumb where we looked to be eloquent ...

'Some ransacked ancient vocabularies, creating a new class of scientific names adding mightily to the inflation of the tongue.

'Others, like the remarkable Doctor Kuber, improvised private vocabularies, which could only be used once.

'Yet others, like Doctor Duende, seeing the impossibility of telling the truth, took up History.

'To keep to the plain surface of things,' Christopher continues, translating as he goes, 'was, we found, to copy infinity: whatever track we took, we crossed other tracks; if we came to the edge of one field, we found another coming into view ...

'We had imagined worshipping in the temple of nature. We found ourselves lost in the labyrinth of botany, geology, numismatics, cryptography, aesthetics ...

'In worlds without end, words beyond number.

'In short, and not to elaborate further, we soon out-Baroqued the Baroque ...'

🙊

'L— owes its identity and civic consciousness to a miraculous event associated with a palace that used to occupy what is now the main Piazza.'

The palace had lain dormant on the site for centuries, no one going in and no one leaving, when suddenly one spring morning it began to erupt.

First one pair of shutters, then another, swung open, dislodging puffs of masonry – confetti which was as nothing compared to the chalk cannonade that soon began exploding from the windows and which, by lunch time, covered the surrounding streets and roof tops to a depth of six inches.

The white layer, popularly dubbed 'the winding sheet', consisted of legal documents, contracts, bills of sale, title deeds, covenants, wills and other memorabilia of mortality – but, as every paper had been shredded into tiny pieces, it was difficult to identify them or the motive of their dismemberment and disgorging.

(Some afterwards claimed that at this time they had seen white arms holding on to the waste-paper baskets that up-ended themselves from the windows, but soon even this sign of human agency disappeared.)

As the afternoon drew on the city's historical foundations assumed a more motley character: torn-up letters, fragmentary drafts of poems, postcards, bus tickets, concert posters, advertisements for meetings, advertising catalogues, fashion magazines, photograph albums, holiday brochures – caught in the vortex of the building's self-destruction, spiralled out of the high windows with terrifying force.

Their rain cast over the city a premature twilight: birds went to roost; the traffic in nearby streets came to a standstill – and everywhere an insidious hiss of paper sliding out of the sky and blocking up the conduits of life.

After the false dawn of history's end, as Duende later put it, the true dusk of nature brought no relief. All night long a heavy artillery of vellum-bound volumes fell on the surrounding suburbs, shattering windows, blocking up alleyways, terrifying children ...

By the following dawn, our streets presented a weird spectacle: the rarest and most precious productions of the human mind plastered every surface.

There were medieval charts displaying the roads to Samarcand.

Here the ventricles of the heart were displayed.

Here genealogies of the human race from the rarest presses of Ulm and Venice lay mired in the mud.

Nor did the battery leave off there. All morning the palace disgorged its past until it seemed that the very core of Memory must have been excoriated: astrolabes, canoes, quetzal tiaras, rifles, bearskin lampshades, assagais, organs preserved in bottles, packets of biscuits, stamp collections, cartridge belts ...

And before anyone dared go treasure-hunting – a yet heavier artillery of bookcases, chandeliers, mahogany tables, fire-guards, Mantuan mantelpieces, ormolu vases, credenzas and colourful ottomans …

By dusk on the second day the city fathers had begun to entertain fears for the future of the building. Some were for entering and arresting the ransackers; others tortured themselves with images of the owners gagged and bound in the cellars.

Yet others – the bookbinders among them – greeted the despoliation as a preliminary to revolution.

So begins Doctor Duende's remarkable *History*. If you shade your eyes you can see over there a memorial plaque which commemorates him as 'L— 's Homer.'

The man in the white suit over there, standing in a nose of shadow, is Philophilus with his umbrella.

Let us walk across and hear what he has to say.

'But the most remarkable Academy of all had its headquarters here – where, as you see, no physical trace of a building remains.

'The Academy of Walking was not, as you might have supposed, lineally descended from the Peripatetics. It was not that its members philosophised as they perambulated …

'Rather – and here I sometimes imagine a pair of them turning about and beginning to retrace their steps – they understood walking itself to be thinking.

'To think better was to walk better, and to this end they attended to the different forms of perambulation available to man.

'The younger among them insisted on walking on their hands; others measured out the world in cartwheels; yet others confined themselves to hopping, modelling their practice on the reported antics of the Monopods of Cathay …

'How, they said, can we ground our philosophy properly unless we master every branch of pedal locomotion? They offered classes in stumbling, in hopscotch and backsliding.

'They were specialists in sidestepping the issue. They sold unguents for the sole which were also said to be effective in relieving tickling heels.

'But to say that no trace of them remains is perhaps misleading. It may be that this Piazza is the outcome of their openmindedness. Certainly, early plans of the city show a palace here: could it be that its erosion and eventual disappearance are due to centuries of walking?

'Could it be that the original Academicians of the eighteenth century were roof-dwellers and held their colloquies among the chimneys?

'This would explain their familiarity with the stars, their deftness in negotiating abysses. It would also account for their sense of vertigo and their obsession with reaching the ground.

'The mildly undulating space in which you stand flows hither and thither; minute depressions we call paths appear, gathering to themselves the click of heels, the flow of conversation.

'Until, almost unaware of itself, the Piazza organises the noise into winding lines, whose dance resembles the murmur of a waterfall breaking into light or the rumorous impression of a distant crowd weaving in and out of the sunlight.

'Unless, of course,' Philophilus concludes, furling his little hat of Void, 'the ground underfoot is but another roof ...!'

*

'What would have been the consequences for psychoanalysis if Doctor Fraud had left Vienna behind settling in that opposite Austria in the south, A—?'

Scanning the Piazza in vain for Christopher, Nostalgia recognises the upward inflection of her countryfolk.

Despite herself she cannot help being drawn to what they are saying.

'Suppose he had accepted the invitation extended to him to preside over the clinical health of the miners on the gold-fields.

'His genius would not have deserted him but it seems to me unlikely his notion of repression would have surfaced there, where we say next to nothing and are too modest to boast of our dreams.'

She is reminded of her father.

'I agree. How would Doctor Fraud have persuaded melancholy miners that gold lay underground if they were but men enough to find it?'

'Had they not moled their way from reef to reef without finding anything worth bringing to the surface?'

She sits down at an adjacent table, her back to the voices.

'Exactly. And had they found what they were looking for, would they have attended his clinic for the missing?'

She signals for a coffee.

'What does his theory of verbal wrongturnings add up to beyond a muddled recollection of Italy?'

'Listening to his patients, he tried to tune into a radio broadcast from the south ... But our names are born of mishearings and reveal nothing except their lack of paternity.'

'To avoid the charge of living up to his name, I think he would have had to concentrate on appearances, developing a psychopathology of surfaces.

'What could be more appropriate in a district dotted with mullock-heaps, mine shafts and sunken leads, whose original appearance is changed beyond recognition?'

She takes a mirror from her handbag. She pretends to adjust her hair.

'Yes. I can imagine him resuscitating the lost art of phrenology and placing it on a scientific, which is to say, a topographical footing.'

'In a region like ours, where the surface is continually shifting, a haruspex of specks would be favourably received.'

Nostalgia's coffee arrives.

Taking another turn around the Piazza, Christopher decides that Nostalgia has forgotten their arrangement.

Or else, he reflects irritably, one of us is a day, week, a month, even a year late.

He turns in to the familiar courtyard again. It is late: the shutters of the Barber's shop are down. Up the stairs, the door opening, he finds the Contessa in the act of pouring a glass of sherry.

'It was the same in my husband's day,' the Contessa resumes, as if Christopher has never gone away, 'we were in revolt against the Baroque.

'In the salons and studios of Europe's capitals the Collagisti held sway – men who, seeing how commerce and the new technology yoked together terms formerly kept apart, creating metaphors more poetic than poetry's, determined to surpass them, advertising themselves as specialists in the dislocation of dreams.

'They published booklets on the management of the unconscious.

'They organised conferences to discuss the design of smoke.

'They rode motorcycles.

'They patented proposals for the dissolution of distance.

'They invented Larmalene, a cure for noise.

'They eavesdropped on the mispronunciations of the *mec* which, quaintly remixed with Confucius and Kant, they declaimed at tea-parties overlooking Capri.'

'And did you,' Christopher says, stooping to pick up her wig and return it to her, 'did you have nothing in common with them?'

'We sympathised with their despair. Our Titanic was the novel, split asunder and sunk by an encounter with "the people", a dispossessed majority whose mass movement nothing could resist.

'Waterlogged heirlooms and objects of personal significance could still be found on the surface – I remember the Nostalgisti, epigones of what had gone, made one last desperate attempt to salvage a heroic myth, but their attempts at irony cut no ice.

'The Progettisti, more abreast of the times, insisted on displaying the jetsam in pawn shops, while the Collagisti, with necrophiliac fervour, put on short plays with characters called Iceberg and Scream.

'But no, this was not to our taste. Like great-grandfather Von Economico, my husband felt he confronted an ocean of language, whose glittering surface contained nothing more solid than clouds, whose distorting mirror made manifest the Collagisti's residual naturalism ...

'I recall him saying: "It is futile to number the pulsing scintillae bursting on the eye; pointless to pretend that beyond the horizon the old sailing ships of Character, Motive, Property and Inheritance still voyage southwards.

'"We must attend to the surface of consciousness contemplating its own defeat.

'"We must focus on nothing, allowing our eye to glaze over like a photographic plate.

'"We must free ourselves from all physical attachments."

'"Instead of walking out each morning, bold, ambitious," Von Economico said, "the modern artist must train himself to stay behind with his dreams and lingering at the window let the shadows of urban trees in bud dapple his face."

'"He must resign his youthful enthusiasms for the workings of nature, his intricate train sets, his anatomical diagrams, his books filled with telephone numbers, his amorous connections and the broadening experience of a spell in the colonies.

'"He must make his vocation a provincial schoolroom or mercantile office where, matching his expression to the blank faces about him, he is free to plumb the Void."'

⌐

'Did you never hear the story of Rodrigo Ramblas?'

Returning to the fountain Nostalgia is surprised to hear a familiar voice.

It is Magellan in his wheelchair: 'Thought I would take a turn ashore,' he smiles disarmingly, 'unless of course we are all at sea ...'

He lights a cigarette. He watches its wraith of smoke warped by the spray.

'Rodrigo Mamblas,' he begins, adjusting his cravat 'was blind but he never stumbled.

'With his black stick he unfailingly located the potholes and hollows of his native city's decaying streets. He took an undisguised satisfaction in his mastery of the city's crumbling surface.

'Mamblas tried to avoid walking on pavements, preferring instead to tiptoe along the kerbs.

'He was an outspoken critic of traffic lights, which he likened to a form of collective coitus interruptus.

'He insisted that he could conduct himself safely from one side of the street to the other simply by listening to the ebb and flow of the traffic – and rambling.

'He explained to me that those who were attuned to it could discern the ancient music, a grave danza bassa that continued to cast its subtle influence over modern movements, including those of the motor car.

'It was enough, he said, to harmonise one's footsteps with the rhythm of the dance.

'He attributed the rising road toll to the increasing volume of tourist buses which, of course, originating elsewhere, were deaf to his city's civic traditions.

'Mamblas liked to ramble, as I think I have said. He enjoyed nothing so much as a conversation that led nowhere.

'If, as sometimes occurred, he noticed his friends settling into a groove of reminiscence, he had a surprising repertoire of devices for drowning out the drone of their voices.

'He would put on a recording of a kettle coming to the boil. He would turn on two radios at once.

'At certain times of the day and night he created the same effect by opening the window.'

Nostalgia, pretending she needs to consult her watch, gently removes Magellan's arm from hers.

Involuntarily she looks up where, over the Barber's shop, a window is opening.

Where, if she is not mistaken, an arm is beckoning her urgently to approach.

'No one was prepared for the events of the following night.

'About midnight the inhabitants of L— became aware of a lull in the ligneous onslaught. The disgorging apertures were seen to glow like the throat of Hell and then, as if their evacuation were complete, to grow dark and cold.

' "It was," Duende's *History* remarks in a memorable image, "a false dawn, this darkness". Suddenly, without warning, the roof of the palace began to disintegrate. It was as if the tiles were iron filings and were drawn to an enormous magnet that sailed overhead down towards the sea.

'The interior walls of the palace were lit up by an intense magnesium flare – by whose cinematographic light one could make out the porphyry and coquelicot coloured tiles, the celadonhued and the cherry, climbing on ragged chains, like ribbons on a kite's tail, up into the clouds.

'The roof having evaporated, the ashlared walls were swift to follow; facades unhinged as easily as if they were torn off a doll's house; purlins and rafters shrivelled up like cobwebs …

'In the shocked light of morning, there was nothing left of the mighty edifice but a space, a shadowless plain, a whispering emptiness.

'Which afterwards became the Piazza.'

In the windowpane Christopher catches sight of someone waving.

'I have seen him sit where you are sitting,' the Contessa smiles sadly, 'and describe how he felt the space wrap round him like a skin.

' "The doorways, the patches of light, the report of ancient feet in the street, a fellow clerk clearing his throat, a classroom of incanting children – these objects of the senses," he said, "withdraw to the other side of space."

'It was as if he inhabited a new element, an intervenient ocean of moted air wherein he felt at leisure to dream.

'But not to dream,' she said, pausing.

'To let his mind go blank and wait without expectation the

pageant of phenomena as his century began the long, painful process of withdrawing its imperial horns and retreating snail-like to its ancient, crumbling capitals.

'He would not be alone: he could feel already a hundred shades – men and women without names – crowding into his emptiness. Refugees from "reality", they came to keep him company, to run his errands, to write his poems, to populate the interstices of time with stories.

'Differing from him only as a shadow differs from its master, they would be his calculus of otherness, by subtle gradations departing from him bringing him into contact with "the world", the convex sphere of bank cheques, horse races, suffragette women, ocean liners, necromancy and nausea which, in his unearthly vacancy, struck him as the signatures of nothingness.

'"This is the true Baroque," Von Economico said, "not like great grand-father Von Economico to build new edifices of words, but to stand quietly among their ruins contemplating the dust-filmed air.

'"Not to legitimate new families of names, but fraternally to fashion a sideways genealogy of ideal companions, a generation of other men, as anonymous, as ineffectual, as mask-like as myself.

'"Yes, to release them into the sun-baked avenidas and, letting them absorb the noises, smells, the poverty and the outrage, to gather up materials for another past, another future, which might only be remembered because it had never happened, which could only be lived now as it would never come to pass."

'This is the man,' the Contessa raises her voice, 'who likened his history to a sheet where, as it was folded, events that were formerly far apart were brought face to face.

'Who on the same occasion likened his mind to a Piazza of perambulating shadows.'

But it is not someone waving; not even the lamplit veils of the fountain folded and unfolded by the evening breeze.

Only a woman shaking out a cloth – whose image, as Christopher closes the window, slides out of view.

♪

'Did you ever hear the story of Syrian Bow?'

'Leave me alone,' Nostalgia protests. 'What can be more absurd than a man in a wheelchair pursuing a woman young enough to be his daughter round and round a deserted piazza?'

'You know those frogs that in times of great drought excavate chambers in the ground where they contrive to live until such time as the rains come again ...

'So with Syrian Bow whose existence was discovered when the last of the old Memory Palaces occupying the site was demolished and cleared away.

'At some time in the past – and exactly when became a matter of intense medical speculation – he'd stowed away inside the palace's massive walls and cooped up in his coffin of plaster and lathe had lived peacefully ever since.

' "When I first left home I was very poor. I rented a hotel room so small that I was forced to sleep curled up. It happened by chance that my window opened onto a Baroque facade, whose volutes (I use the technical term), slumped either side of the upper facade, remarkably captured the posture of my sleep.

' "It was as if, while waking, I could contemplate myself dreaming ... unless," and here Syrian always used to hesitate, as if advancing this delicious paradox for the first time, "I was the dream the white facade was dreaming – after all the objective existence of the facade could not be doubted – but as for me, a stranger, a migrant known to none – who was to say I existed at all?"

' "Shaped like the runners of a rocking horse and leaning steeply against the *aedicolo*, they reminded me of quarry workers backing blocks of stone onto rafts to be rolled away.

' "Yet their *controposto* breathed space, the *ozio* of a perfectly poised spring. (I use the technical terms.) Their abstract curves, so finely poised, so tensely attuned, expressed the equilibrium of spirit and stone, soul and flesh.

' "Here was a mighty face embodying the physical fantasy of their builders, that displayed the human anatomy of stone, I said to myself, and I began to identify with its forms, to want to live as they did.

' "At night, heels hard up against the flaking plaster, the creak of bedsprings in my ears, I imagined myself one of a hundred secret inmates concealed within the hotel's joints.

' "I peopled the bare right angles of my room with cherub-like brackets. I imagined under the lathe and plaster X-ray figures in low relief, the diagonals of thighs and arms holding open the expanse of wall as if it were a sail and they taut ropes.

' "At length I decided to creep inside the walls of my room. It was cheaper than paying rent and besides, once inside, I found I was brought into contact with the minutest vibrations of the ground.

' "I experienced what space-dwellers never feel …

' "The regular pulse of the Atlantic breakers.

' "The saurian dance of the earth's sliding plates.

' "The groans of bridges.

' "The highly-strung symphony of the city …"

Nostalgia is right: what can be more absurd than Magellan in his wheelchair, stuck in a groove, going round and round the fountain until well after midnight.

He is like a storyteller repeating the stories he has told before, until at length he falls asleep still mumbling to himself.

※

'As may be imagined,' Philophilus begins next morning, his umbrella in one hand, a small vellum-bound volume in his other, 'over the years Doctor Duende's account has been the subject of much debate.

'The glaring anachronisms it contains have led some to dismiss it as a hastily concocted tale for tourists.

'Others, more circumspect, have replied that anachronisms are a peculiarly modern preoccupation: Shakespeare did not shrink from dressing Roman senators in Elizabethan breeches.

'They have taken the conjunction of telephone books and astrolabes as proof of the antiquity of the legend; the overlaying of older words with new ones more familiar to the audience is a typical feature of oral literatures.

'Others, more scientifically inclined, are convinced that the story is not to be taken literally. It is, they say, the rationalisation of a primitive myth designed to explain the origins of land and sea.

'The volcanic allusions are obvious and they draw a parallel between the erupting palace and the opening of Pandora's box.

'Others read into the expulsion of the books a very different meaning. They see it as a parable of God's wrath, as a judgement on man's acquisitiveness. They jog through the streets chanting, "What a man has not can never be lost."

'This, incidentally,' Philophilus shouts, as his group begins to disperse, merging back into the crowd, 'is the pious fraternity that proposed that L— institute an annual burning of the books – a suggestion that, by one of those strange twists of fate, resurfaced recently in the inauguration of L— 's annual Second Hand Book Fair.

'It was there,' Philophilus continues, addressing thin air, 'that I

came across Duende's curious little treatise and the various interpretations of it I have noticed here.

'Anyone,' Philophilus says, thrusting Duende's *History* under
the nose of a passer-by, 'who has handled this volume will see
through these explanations at once.

'Look, his book is nothing more than an anthology of paper.

'Look! No two pages are made alike. No two adjoining
typefaces match.

'Look. Some attempt at consecutive numbering has been made
but it rarely adds up to anything.'

Philophilus staggers across the space. He accosts the book dealer
by his stall.

'Duende's book is no different from the other books on sale
here: second-hand, rebound, they are mimic books. They are the
puppets of books.

'You can hold them in your hands and turn the pages, pretending to read.

'But they make no narrative sense.'

And here Philophilus throws away the literary past in disgust.

⟡

'What can be more absurd than a tour guide who loses himself in
the labyrinth of the past?'

Scanning the Piazza in vain for Christopher, Nostalgia recognises the upward inflection of her countryfolk.

Despite herself she cannot help being drawn to what they are
saying.

'Following him is like walking through a city where one piazza
does not follow another but exists at the same time in a different
place, where the linking streets that bind the spaces together give
no inkling of what lies round the corner.'

'To read the book of his mind, you would need to pull it apart
and lay the individual sheets out on the floor, until a pattern was
discovered in their juxtapositions.'

'Turning them over, who knows but you might find the map of
a previously invisible city.'

But as she turns to see who is speaking, to put a face to the
voices, Nostalgia finds they have already gone.

A bell begins to ring and the insect castanets of cameras clicking
momentarily stop to listen.

⚜

'Do you mean to say,' Christopher asks the next day as he begins setting up his tripod, 'that the figures perambulating the Piazza outside might, in another time, have been notable philosophers?

'The tramp whose feet are bound in newspapers, who wears a cushion on his head, who drags a back-breaking spar along in place of a walking stick, who noses about the malodorous bags of rubbish ...

'That in another time he might have been the respected author of a treatise classifying stones according to their different smells?

'And in the other direction, the overweight bank-clerk who issues out every lunchtime clad in silk shorts and singlet under the impression he is exercising ...

'That he is in reality a historian of sport, a man who has devised a wonderful method for getting to the heart of those enigmatic rituals where History is suspended and Time worshipped as a form of Space?

'That the man I heard just now ostentatiously blowing his nose as if it were a valved instrument might in another time have been a favourite of Charles the Third, Baroque's foremost patron, a man renowned for the enormity of his olfactory organ ...

'Might have been the President of a court expressly charged with prosecuting citizens guilty of crimes against the Baroque ...

'Citizens who surreptitiously tried to restore balance to the hippocamps galloping underneath imperial balconies ... who could not see one arabesque without wishing to neutralise it with another ...?

'How could an emperor so powerfully, so peculiarly, endowed avoid looking askance at them, denouncing their symmetries as perversions of the truth?'

And as the Contessa smiles, Christopher takes her picture.

'That Nostalgia might stand for nostalgia?' he adds to himself.

❧

And in their place Nostalgia finds two newspapers raised like screens, catching the sunlight between the umbrellas, as they shake and shudder, they look for all the world like a film of something being read aloud.

'The Conte de L— is the patron of road surveyors and traffic controllers. In the interests of an accelerated circulation, he advocates straightening the streets,' says one newspaper.

'In the interests of an accelerated circulation, he might as logically propose a city of concentric rings,' the other replies.

'He would like to fill in the hollows where the rainwater collects. For my part I would water them everyday.'

'He would like to flatten the little hills and valleys the streets contain. But these are an index of age, seeming to steepen as we grow older until at length the whole city is ramped between earth and heaven.'

'I would design roads that aged. I would advocate youthful surfaces gusting up like carpets, and for the old, passages that dimpled like the sea and slowly wafted shorewards.'

'The Conte de L— would like to remove the cobbles. I oppose him not because I fear the students will be deprived of ammunition, but because of the sounds that will be lost.'

'Instead of narrowing roads we need piazzas widening. We could start with the roads, rendering them bulbous wherever we found evidence of a passing place or the inclination of traffic to eddy back and browse along the open walls.'

'I agree with my old friend Vincenzo: thoroughfares should be fanned out to form a single mazelike place. Houses should no longer be responsible for streets: let them move about and change their point of view …'

Here, seeing their editor ambling across the piazza towards them, the journalists (whose voices recall those of Philophilus and Martin Magellan) hurriedly fold up their newspapers, and grabbing their hats, issue out into the Piazza.

And Nostalgia, having consulted her watch for the nth time, follows them with her eyes.

'You photographers,' the Contessa Von Economico begins as Christopher hands her her photograph, 'have stolen our looks.

'You have made us stand still until we are worn out with posing. The once imperious eye develops a tic, the voluptuous lips shrivelling up like burst balloons.

'You have scraped away at the surface with your little scalpel, the camera's slick shutter.'

Christopher looks nervously at his watch.

'Like an archaeologist removing the make-up of millenia from a tiny figurine, you have cobwebbed our light complexions until only the ghost of a blush remains.

'You have raked the surface with more searching lights, discovering lunar features, craters, pocks and porous fissures – which you have proceeded to fill with blood released from the face's subcutaneous canals.

'You have shown no mercy. No depth.'

Christopher is distinctly aware the moment has come. He must seize it.

'But I ...' he begins.

'Desire,' she says, mishearing him and pushing a poodle from her lap, 'what can you know of desire?

'What did men ever understand about the Baroque beyond what they sucked in at their nurse's breast, beyond what they confessed laying their heads in our laps?'

And Christopher, feeling that the float of time hooked in the mouth of destiny is going under, tears himself away, and running to the window leaps out.

Shouting 'Mother!'

And she after him, 'Nostalgia!'

Whereupon Doctor Duende, slumbering beside some antipodean stream, became aware of something tugging at his toe ...

He opened his eyes, he tried to focus them on the glittering maze of the river's upturned belly.

Where that little nose of darkness, the float, was not to be seen.

He unhooked his rod. He stood up. He began to wind in. He was like a bell-ringer trying to dislodge a note.

In his head the bells of the Piazza were still faintly ringing.

Or was he in the Piazza still – the glittering surface before him the recollection of pigeons' wings, upturned feet and glinting cobbles?

He sat down again, dizzy. It was true. He could not tell the Piazza from a sheet of twinkling water.

He blinked.

Were they figures in a film weaving their way across the strung space or the shadows of fish in the gum tree's reflected reticulations?

Who was dreaming?

River light swarmed up the gum tree boles on the opposite bank.

The cliff was not a silent screen on which the water projected its angel wings, its lozenges, its tackle of light-warped ropes: nodular compaction of bones, anthropomorphically browed, Baroque relief of noses, skulls, nostrils and gaping sockets – it had designs of its own.

Duende remarked the eroded surface. My ancestor would have been at home here, he thought.

Calcareous deposit, precarious, erupting, on its way to becoming water. It is not that it lacks a sense of form: simply that it is free of Tuscan nostalgia.

In A—, he reflected, the Baroque wave continues to break. The marriage of air and water produces not molar stone but moving hills of sand, pluming estuaries of sand ... Had Leonardo lived here, he would have drawn his designs in sand ...

The pleasures of marble are not missed in A—: the diver in the dark river becomes one with the form of the water; he knows the pleasure of the statue sheathed in his silk of stone.

The water, chiselling light, pecking away at the sun-flecked surface, preserves the sculptor's essential pleasure – which is not to unlock the form in stone but to preserve its depths, matching his blows to the surface pattern, much as a pianist follows the score.

Churches were not needed here to suggest the monumentality of flux: it was enough for a cloud coming over the water to dislodge the angels from their balconies ...

Duende became conscious of something else: the surface at his feet was buckling, folding, rearing up and caving in.

It was as if he were observing a trampoline where invisible bodies cavorted.

Or as if he crouched behind a curtain in and out of whose folds a hidden crowd seemed to file and jostle.

He stood up afraid, and as the waterfall of blood cleared from his ears, the ground beneath his feet continued moving.

Only it was not turning to mud; it was not sliding away; it was not rejecting his weight.

He was conscious of footprints, marking the earth's taut drum, lightly striding towards him, as if along a gangplank which, as they approached, lightly rocked from left to right.

Duende turned: there beside him was a man who, in the Fascist language of an earlier time, would have been described as having a negative for a face.

Whose presence seemed to calm the bucking surface down, and who without further ado gestured to Duende to be seated, and idly drawing a twig through the sand, invited him to explain his lineage and his reason for being there.

'You must understand,' the native of the country began, 'the nature of the surface.

'The ground you tread is groundless. If an equal and opposite force did not push up wherever you went, it is not that you would fall through …

'It is not that underneath this sandy bluff there is a harder, more substantial rock that will not let you down …

'Falling in, you would remain what you are: groundless, like the river.

'Your passage though the land depends on the company of an upside-down folk who shadow your footsteps wherever you go, giving you the illusion you tread a cleared path.

'But for us supporting your weight you would have no existence here at all.

'As for us,' the black man continued, 'it would be false of me to deny that we are becoming tired of not being seen.

'We are tired of your saying the Void is empty: the Void is filled with voices.

'If the first inhabitants of this land were to take it into their heads to withdraw their support from you, leaving you marooned in the salt pans of your imaginings, those clearings our people call Death, I am afraid of what might become of you …'.

'A common way of travelling is needed,' Duende interjected, stumbling to his feet and swaying, 'a Baroque recognition that the ground never quietens down.'

'The ground,' his other replied, giving Duende his arm, 'is never given: it is the surface where differences meet …'

'The other ear of air,' Duende said, still dizzy, and looking up he was conscious once again of the stutter of light-filled branches, resembling nothing so much as a file of black-habited nuns threading a sunlit cloister.

Turning together they picked their way awkwardly down to the water's edge by a path Duende had not noticed before.

The ordinary other did not dissolve. He did not turn out to be a dream or a shadow's double.

As for Duende, he, too, stood where he stood.

A conflagration of light did not surround them like an aureole. It was true that the dark river sliding quietly between its white cliffs might have been mistaken for a piazza that had caved in.

But that is all.

Nostalgia's Nose

'Her nose! It is her nose. I have looked everywhere for it only to find it one spring morning under my own … Nostalgia's nose!

'Let me not lose sight of it. Let me not approach it bluntly.

'A profile so tenderly turned deserves something subtler, an approach resembling its own exquisite shape.

'Let me stalk it daintily, as if it were a butterfly.

'Let me not crush it with banal conversation but find a way of keeping it alive and breathing.

'What is a nose but the resolution of two curves, the miraculous conjunction of independent planes to form a single harmonious outwork?

'Let the convex propensities of the nasal bridge predominate: the face finds itself bridled with a parrot's beak.

'Let the outward-thrusting septum have its way – the stiff and unwieldy proboscis of the unicorn results.

'It is necessary to model my approach to her on the nose itself, approaching her along a curved path that by way of many detours eventually turns into hers.

'The place of our meeting must be as natural as a shapely bend where two old streets embrace and pass into one another.'

❧

'After so long at sea the sensation of coming home is not as I expected.

'L— seemed solid in our family album. In our photographs it looked as if it were built out of stone: its shadows were permanent; its clouds wore the aspect of marble.

'Here it is different. Its streets flutter and shudder beneath my feet; the well-polished cobbles glitter like sunlit waves. It is impossible to walk straight.

'I weave left and right and the winding streets wind with me left and right. I feel again the drunkenness of decks!

'I saw hidden depths in the photographs. I imagined myself diving into the shadowy folds between sharp-edged planes or where the middle-distance lost focus swimming towards a vanishing point of light.

'I expected my arrival would shatter the surface and, putting an end to the past, grant me a future of my own, sans père, sans past. But the opposite is true. Instead of disappearing into the tunnels of History I feel only the gravity of my appearance.'

※

'I must be careful not to speak of my Nostalgia. It has been a weakness of mine to want to go back, to begin at the beginning, to clear away the accumulated debris of upbringing, customs, region and tongue.

'These attempts to reach a clear understanding have the opposite effect. On the last occasion I met Nostalgia she said, "If only you had begun differently, every step backwards would have been a step forwards: but to begin at the beginning left us with nowhere to go."

'What am I to do? To meet her or not to meet her? Meeting her I risk another ending. Not meeting her, I keep alive a beginning.'

❧

'Instead of being lightfooted I feel myself rooted uneasily to the spot.

'It is as if my arrival has turned the buildings into cameras: the black archways crouch like photographers underneath their shrouds; and when the pigeons burst from the rooftop catching the sun, it is like a cannonade of flashbulbs.

'The buildings in the photographs disappear; they turn into eyes; and where in the photographs I once imagined my vanishing point, I see looming up an image of myself.

'My dark hair, my buttoned coat, my flared skirt, a pair of shoes: if the city were a face, I would be its nose!

'Only the rest of the portrait is missing.'

※

'The matter of framing is coming to obsess me. Positioning myself so that streets are framed between walls, I add another frame of my own: that of the photograph. The walls of my photograph frame the walls of the city.

'This doubling up of verticals recalls the composite pilasters beloved of Baroque architects. Even though I avoid facades, my photographs employ the technique of facades. To represent the idea of depth, I am obliged to build up the surface.

'The more I seek to portray the city's anti-Baroque spirit, the more I find myself falling back on Baroque techniques of deception.

'Today, no longer content with shooting streets, I commenced recording crossroads. To do this I had to assemble as many as four corners in a single frame. The result was a photograph composed almost entirely of sharply shadowed edges.

'Only by collaging fragments of the visual field, sections of signposts, overhead lights, scraps of cloud and kaleidoscopic architectural details could I accurately represent the deepness of the view –

'The infinite lines connecting all objects to all others, as Leonardo said ...'

'I feel as if I have entered a painting. Movement has a viscous quality here and at a brushstroke an entire street draws aside, as if a gust of wind ran through a field of grass.

'My shadow runs away and links up with wires overhead. I glimpse my nose and it is like a ship ploughing through the urban light. Small bruises mottle the cheeks of stone until they alter the cast of the sky and threaten rain.

'Shopkeepers draw back from me as if I swept by with a train of slaves and peacocks; and I cannot hurry up or conceal myself. I am as conspicuous as Salome with her beloved's head – which, attached to my ankle, drags behind me like an iron ball.

'There has been an unspeakable disaster; or it is imminent. Those in the know stare at me angrily, as if my ignorance is to blame.

'And it is true: I feel myself in possession of a memory that no one else here any longer has, a city composed of photographs that no one else remembers.

'They look to me to paint it for them; as someone who has come back from the dead.

'And it is true: I have the sensation that I am the only one who has always lived here. Everyone I grew up with has gone away or died.

'These faces that surround me are mere usurpers of the emptiness: they pretend to belong here, but they come from somewhere else.

'They are like extras in a film who wander the familiar streets forgetting they are on a set.

'They are like the tourists who gather at the street-artist's shoulder and stupidly gawp, as before them there unfolds a scene in which they have no part.

'I had imagined that coming home I would feel at home. It would be, "Nostalgia thought to herself", as if I already lived here. I had dreamed more than once that my double came out to meet me and guided me to a white facade.

'The friendly door was like a smiling mouth. I had gone in and when I turned to thank my hospitable twin, I found she had disappeared and in her place a wall of white dinner plates.'

✿

'A nose is a miracle of attraction. The bridge of the nose retroussé is bent on turning up: if nothing were to draw it down it would become a coiled-up spring, a trumpeting conch, attached to the forehead.

'But the little hedge of the septum firmly guyed with surface-raising ropes to the upper-lip draws it back to earth again; and the gently-billowing flanges of the nostrils smoothly tent it to the cheeks' adjacent fields.

'What mathematics can explain their merest coincidence, the nose's tip, where mutual desire turns inside out and outside in? O happy organ that understands by instinct the inwardness of outer space.

'Our sense of smell is but the meeting-place of what has been and what might have been – which, always drifting away from us, reminds us of what can never be.

'Nostalgia!'

➤

'Nostalgia!'

'The lightfootedness of the traveller is a myth! A man comes hurtling towards me. Were I more at home, if I were familiar with the local manners of locomotion, I might sidestep him agilely.

'Between our mutually circling forms a little jar of turning air might spring up, momentarily entwining us, mingling the flowers of each other's perfume.

'But as it is …'

'Nostalgia!'

'I do not know where to move; I sway to the left; he veers to my left; I sway to the right, he veers to my right; and although he understands the ground's coefficient of friction as only a resident can, he is wrong-footed and cannot avoid colliding with me.

'And so there is a physical conjunction …'

'Nostalgia.'

'A sudden buffeting …'

'Nostalgia.'

'A subtle in-curving of outcurved forms as shoulders jar and hands momentarily press against waist and chest. Yet we no sooner meet than it appears that we have not met, for he calls me by an-other's name –

'"Nostalgia."

'He has not bumped into me but into someone else.

'But if I had been someone else, Nostalgia say, familiar with the local laws of motion, our collision, I suppose, would not have occurred.'

'Call it indecision but in the magnet of your nearness all the other Nostalgias stubble the surface of my mind.

'When the first, whole Nostalgia left she did not disappear. It was as if she had been torn apart, and her individual features scat-tered throughout the world.

'Wherever I looked I was certain before long to come across a face or form that in one particular or another recalled her to me.

'It might be the angle of the chin or the exact outline of an eyebrow but more often the affinity lay in the relationship of parts, of one surface to another.

'After a while I had the distinct impression that she was looking for me; that she crouched in the dappled trellis of nature playing hide and seek with me.

'I began to identify her with the light-filled spaces in-between.

'But always, her nose eluded me!'

'It is his nostalgia draws him to me and my "Nostalgia", the name that is only a name, that repels him from me.

'I regret this and I do not regret this.

'I regret that he is drawn to only a part of me that he recognises from his past – and that, recognising that part, he recognises that he does not recognise me.

'I do not regret this because whatever part of me he recognises is not my own; singled out and framed in the moment of our collision, it belongs to someone else.

'But wait: what is Nostalgia?

'She is the feature of my face that projects me back into L—.

'The key that opens the door. Yes.

'She is the little fold in the surface that grows into a rhinoceros' horn and bursting through the cardboard wall propels me into a city composed – who knows? – entirely of noses!'

'I decided I must place my fleeting impressions on a scientific foundation.

'I attempted at first to capture the lineaments of her face, as they appeared in the laughing wave or the many-eyed grass, with a camera.

'I found I was recording massy objects instead, while the forlorn light that set them off, curdled, sepulchral, expressionless.

'Inspired by Nostalgia I took up the brushes and began to copy the lively textures of space; and to assist my memory I took to waiting where the ships come in and, whenever I espied someone alighting who possessed a fragment of her original visage, I made a point of meeting them.

'An ear, a pleasing nape, a nose-like heel or elbow – these were not fragments to be stuck together as I chose: I studied them as outcrops of Nostalgia's soul which, I firmly believed, lay concealed beneath the physical integument, as the outline of a breast may lie concealed beneath an additional fold of robe.

'And I would question these partial copies of Nostalgia for any recollection of her; and if by chance I found one whose auburn hair resembled hers, who also tossed her hair back as Nostalgia had, I rejoiced to think I was drawing closer.

'And I am drawing closer.

'O subtle in-curving of outcurved forms!'

'Until now I feared there were two cities: the city of oceanic movement which I inhabit – and from which it seems I can never alight – and the city of stone – which is the domain of photographs.

'But I am relieved to find I am mistaken: these two cities are but aspects of each other.

'The balconies foaming with galloping stallions, the cherubs hatching from ovoid columns, the coralline faces forming along the blank facades, the sinuous jib of the streets themselves testify to the fertile intercourse of one with the other.

'Their marriage is like the principle of chiaroscuro or an ocean prow carving back the surface of darkness to release a hidden light – a shining wake which, dividing in two, describes the history of their meeting.

'All along the widening wake holes appear in the lace of foam: one whirlpool after another hands on the little nose of space lest it drown.

'Like a line of dancers whose leader turns and weaves his way back down the line; and all the others follow, so that though the positions change, the space refolded remains the same.

'In some such vortical nose of space,' Nostalgia speculates, 'we find ourselves whenever we escape the statues we normally inhabit. In some such space we may come close and, yes, insensibly wind about another.

'And though these instances of coiling space may seem to be too insignificant to live by, they model the reason of the whole.

'The smallest granule I roll up and down along the whorled grooves of my finger and thumb is magnified in the gryphon's eyeball and the hippocamp's flaring nostril.

'These details of the façade are, if closely inspected, whole countries with cities sitting in their folds.

'The stone beneath my hand has two faces: one face is an image of the deep, composed of sedimented skeletons; the other is an ageing skin which, like the surface of the sea, continually evolves new forms without their like in nature.

'And one is only the magnification of the other.

'If my attachment to L— is amongst the most superficial, it is also amongst the deepest. For it is when we are least attached to the ground that we are most prone to respond to the turbulent movements of the deep.

'It is when we are light-footed that we are most at home.'

'Nostalgia, it is true.

'It is the judicious arrangement of the city that brings us by chance face to face; that propels us into the grooves of earlier lovers meeting for the first time; which is never the first time but always a return to what might have been.

'The city does not consist of walls and streets but of many scarcely perceptible surfaces which lie like glazes over the visible outline of things. These surfaces are not flat but subtly grooved and pocked; here and there nose-like elevations rise out of them like stepping-stones.

'The walker who inhabits these surfaces is not like the ordinary walker, who traverses the ground insensible to its subtle crests and furrows: he is a dancer conscious that the ground beneath him is alive and springs to meet his springing heel.

'The dancer does not tramp his shadow slovenly across dead space; he is a brush alive to the drag and slide of the ground; he surfs down salient folds; he pirouettes where dark meets light; he meets the other dancers in the street a hundred times without falling into step, without ever tripping.

'What is a city but a concrete choreography, a machine for meeting?'

·

'It makes me dizzy but I understand – the residents of this country travel at different speeds from us. Novel laws of motion govern their circulation.

'They inhabit a space that is naturally curved. A space that resembles a summer cloud: its coastlines are continually breaking off.

'It is as if a clan of Ice Age dragons stood round the fringes busily breathing out plumes of steam. Which, being the outsides of their columnar nostrils, might be expected to drift away as languidly as streamers until achieving metamorphosis as sandbars in the west.

'Instead they no sooner plunge into the oceanic blue than they begin to gather up their spreading veils, coiling them in delicate spirals – which, rolling back like breaking waves, are reunited with the mass.

'Like the elephant's proboscis or the chameleon's tongue, they wind themselves into ever tighter rolls – which they stack where they can among their mother cloud's ample and uneven folds.

'The clouds have neither surface nor depths, although they can cast shadows. Mother and offspring, though continually dividing, are as one; and the one is all a slowly rolling and unrolling surface.

'If the clouds entertain us with a thousand fanciful forms it is because they imitate nothing; if a thousand fragmentary images pass through their minds, it is because they cling to nothing and are content to go on conjuring the might have been's out of what is.

'If the clouds paint Nostalgia truthfully, it is because they have no nostalgia for her.'

'The more she departs from herself, the more she becomes Nostalgia – the more her nose comes to resemble a spinning top, a radio transmitter, a vanishing point, a little pyramid, original of glancing shadows.

'Do I make a god of her nose? Or is there a nosological science of cities, where it is shown that every nodal form, the crusted apertures, the circumcised bollards, the mushrooming cupolas, are symptoms of the nose?

'The nose is not an island; it does not lie in space like a chocolate in a box but like a high-ridged house commands the prospect of the face: it sees the twin pools of the eyes; it hears the ancestral breezes curdling in the ear; it contemplates the chrome locks coiled along the brow like skeletons of waves; it senses deeply the long slope of the cheeks and chin, the eloquent fold of the lips, minutely creased like deflated balloons.

'And, if the nose thinks, it thinks to itself: the world is entirely composed of faces. What we see we can see because it turns towards us. If we can see the clouds as clouds, it is because they face us.

'Can anyone honestly say they have seen the edge of a cloud?'

'And what is true of the clouds is true of L— ,' thinks Nostalgia, miraculously catching Christopher's drift, 'its inhabitants do not walk from place to place but ravel and unravel themselves, like yo-yos on a string.

'In other places, in other stories, films and photographs, we might have swum towards each other slowly until a world of time was swallowed up in our meeting lips.

'But here there is no end of meeting; and even though we should part and never see one another again, the form of our attraction remains grooved in the face of the city, like another wrinkle.'

'It is a mistake to suppose we own a single face. Every fragment of the surface is a face.

'There are faces parting the branches to stare at us in the tracery of our palms.

'There are smiles concealed in the folds of the crotch; and eyes look out at us from buttons and buckles.

'A portrait of the face need not represent the sitter's physiognomy at all: the face is to nature what the nose is to the face – a parting in the general tangle where the nature of reality is nakedly glimpsed.

'A comprehensive physiognomy must go beyond the little lexicon of the face, and the mere coincidence of meeting eyes, cataloguing the expressions that everywhere animate the surface.'

'The mere coincidence of meeting eyes, but …' Nostalgia hesitates.

'Look at me: are we meeting or not meeting?

'Why are you no longer looking at me? Why have you eyes only for my nose. I look into your eyes: you do not look into mine.

'The mere coincidence of meeting eyes would be enough to keep us circling round each other. But our paths are elliptical. Little eddies threaten the stability of our mutual orbit.

'I feel the weight of your looking away, pulling us towards division.

'Yet the more you do not look at me, the more your blindness draws me to you. I regret you should possess but one pair of eyes with which to see me.

'That column of turning air that springs up in the wake of our meeting: it begins to wobble, threatens to fly apart.

'I wish every part of you were a face, and that every face were furnished with seeing eyes; I wish your hands were stigmatised with weeping eyeballs.

'I wish you were a painter, and I your painting.

'An irregularity forms in the surface of the whirling vortex – an unanswered mass, which at first is no larger than the mole on a cheek, but whose little assymetry rapidly gathering centrifugal force warps the column ever outwards until it resembles a rope gyrating through the air, or a spinning top in its final throes.

'I wish my nose could see!

'Against the weight of History pulling us apart, I poise the counterweight of this desire.'

'I am not looking away. I am merely looking at more of you; at flanks and promontories which until now were blind to their own beauties.

'Look, mine is entirely an art of façade. The task of the artist is not to represent what the public calls Reality: it is to reconstruct the surface.

'It is, point by point, motif by motif, to put back together the face of Nature that too much seeing has worn away, until nothing is left but the sockets of sight.

'Let us suppose that Nature wears a single face: yet who has seen it? Everywhere we look it appears differently, as if one part had no recollection of another.

'Thus from the beginning the artist is bound to record the ruins of her visage. And haunted by Orpheus' fate, he scours the world for local details which he humbly sticks together.

'But the fragments scurry away before his feet − the glass-blower's bubble bursts before he can possess it, the shrike impales the fritillary's eye-taunting wing, the coiffeured clouds sail on leaving a bald sky.

'It is as if, where ever he turns, he disturbs little devils of turning air that bear away from him the leafy surfaces he strives to collect.

'So it is with every painted subject: it takes the form of nostalgia for a surface that has been torn and scattered like a storm-shredded sail to every corner of the globe.

'Which is why I dedicate myself to painting the face of the face-less, which I conceive to be an accurate portrait of Nostalgia.

'Which is why, painting a detail of you, I will paint more of you than anyone knows.'

❧

'There is no help for it, Christopher,' Nostalgia cries. 'Some force of History pulls us apart.

'And when, against its centrifugal strength, I lean towards you, growing closer I feel myself descending into a vortex in which I shall be pulled apart.

'And feeling myself sail away from myself, I begin to understand Nostalgia.

'Had she escaped History's counterpoise, had she yielded to the might have been of your desire, the equilibrium that held you in thrall, circling each other, must have collapsed; and spiralling in-wards like two sunless planets you must have smashed each other to pieces.

'She was like another Salome who, had she not ordered the Baptist's head brought on a platter, must have danced herself to death.

'I look away: as if by staring into outer space I can restore my fading mass; as if some passing comet can be drawn into my ken, lending me the weight to pull away, to keep my place.

'But it is beyond me to master the calculus of desire.

'I spy in the wall a fossil whelk the rain has leached into low-relief but it does not help me pull to port: in the colloid suspension of our double orbit, it begins to revolve like an all-seeing eye.

'It grows; it explodes; a nebula separating into stars.'

'I can see nothing else, Nostalgia; and seeing nothing else I see it all at once; how you must be painted.

'A candle flame shaped like a flaring nostril illuminates a recumbent face, a snowdrift of contorted throat, the bosom's fold and by your side a pallid hand, extended like a wave foam-fingered.

'Tides of darkness are drawn up your sleeping form, deepening the folds that lie across the hidden reefs of the lap, funneling between your breasts, emptying into your open mouth – which comes to look like a black new moon.

'Until the obscure tide crowds home where, like the spoor of the Maker's thumb and finger, the chambers of the nostrils stand, beetling and proud.

'Yes, and in your other hand, my lifeless head, sightlessly staring back at her.'

'I gently raise the wrinkled eyelids, to see if there is an eye at home, but find instead a schoolboy's marble floating in a blood-veined Void.

'I linger about the antars vast of his nostrils and license his lonely fingers to stroke the lesser noses of her ear-lobes and her breasts.

'My hand is my camera; my fingers lightning rods. When I touch his pallid temples a nightmare gallops across his sleeping eyes.

'In the little copse of the eyebrow a trapped nerve flutters like a limed bird ...

'His deathly aspect thrills me; his pallor brings the colour to my cheeks.

'O Christopher!'

'My dizzy head shaved of its superficial hair resembles one enormous marble eye.

'And you take it, hold it to your lips and prizing open the lifeless lids stare into them.

'And what you see is not my soul looking back at you but two tiny Salomes whose slender waists, whose out-hooped arms recall the septum and delicately flared flanges of your own nose.

'I am falling apart, going back to the Chaos from which I never really escaped.

'O Nostalgia –

'You may think these fancies far-fetched but they are the everyday argot of the Baroque and occur wherever the equilibrium of the surface is lost.'

•)

'Is this what our meeting must come to? A convergence so vertiginous, so shallow, so raked with melodramatic foreshortenings, that it scarcely seems to penetrate beneath the surface of appearances?

'Then I understand Nostalgia's desire to begin differently.

'How differently our story might turn out, if it began somewhere else.

'If, say, it were told from my point of view.

'If, say, trying to take Christopher by the arm, I turn into the Street of the Mimic and my eye is caught by a painting leaning against a doorway, the sunlight falling on its glass turning it into a mirror of the street.

'If, say, drawing abreast of it, the reflections slip off it and I see it is a Baroque production of the late eighteenth century, attributed to one M.E. Grazioni of L—, and represents, or apparently represents, the daughter of Herodias, Salome, swooning over the decapitated head of John the Baptist.

'To my eyes the face of the woman bears more than a passing resemblance to me; her nose, to be exact, is beyond a shadow of doubt the Duende nose.

'I am seized with the idea that here, perhaps, is the first tangible proof of the antiquity of our family's connection with L— .

'In her, it occurs to me, I may pass beyond myself; or, rather, return to that former self which was fragmented and cast to the winds when we left for another country.

'Here is the true Nostalgia!

'I bend closer, cocking my head like a parrot to scan the image sidelong, as if I expect the nose to leap from the canvas and stand up in sharp relief.

'And here is a place for you!

'As I draw erect again, casually shifting from one foot to another, I allow the sunlight in again. It strikes the glass and I see projected on the painted image the reflection of herself.

'I look again; sunlight floods the frame once more, turning the painting back into a blank, white canvas – except where the little feature of the nose, fortuitously shadowed, stands out, an archway in a plain of light.

'And I turn to find a photographer facing me, about to take my picture, and I recognise his hood as the image shadowing Salome's nose.'

⚸

'To see through your fancy, it is enough to try painting it. If Nostalgia bequeathed me anything when she left, it was an understanding of the fundamental assymetry of desire.

'To grow close is always to move away; no force of attraction exists without its force of repulsion.

'Distortions, enlargements, casual resemblances, noses like cities and cities composed of lingering scents: these are the paving stones of ordinary life.

'The speculative symmetries beloved of film-makers, of philosophers with a taste for irony, of novelists who rely on advances in technology to supply their psychology – these are the artifices of the devotees of endings.

'Your beginning is, if I may say so, one long ending; a sustained glissando; a painfully lingering fade to nothing: or, rather, to the mirror of what we already know.

'What is more certain than that Nostalgia and the photographer, fatally attracted to one another, forget the world and retreat into some purely bourgeois affair.

'But my motivation is different.

'My notion of telling a story may be likened to the charting of the little nooses of turning water constantly forming along the border of the foaming wake.

'Just as their nose-like whorls must be governed by physical laws belonging to the surrounding surface, so, the laws of physical attraction determining the lives of people must be found in the environment.'

'Your idea of composing a story is equally artificial, the controposto just as contorted and self-regarding.

'What are you going to say to me? That we have not met before? That if we have not met before, if I am not secretly related to
Nostalgia, there is no reason to meet now, there is no reason to
meet for the first time unless remotely we remember each other?'

'Your logic resembles that of a city where the inhabitants have
no choice but to run in the same grooves day-in, day-out.

' "If I repeat what I once said to Nostalgia, she will merely think,
as Nostalgia did, that I am departing from the truth ... And, if she
does not think this, she will not be another Nostalgia ...

' "If I treat her as Nostalgia she will take offence at being mistaken for someone else. She will have nothing more to do with me
and instead of leading me to Nostalgia she will become an
opportunity squandered, consigned to the might-have-been realm of
nostalgia ...

' "I must pretend she is not Nostalgia. If she is not to remain a
complete stranger to me, I must pretend she is a stranger ... to find
Nostalgia I must not yield to nostalgia. ...

'This is how you go on. It is no way of going on at all.'

✍

But nothing in L— is merely local. The force waves of Christopher and Nostalgia meeting, not meeting, bring together everything that has ever happened here; and rebounding from the space
they radiate to the city's furthest shores.

They flutter the flags on the Municipal Palace.

They cause a gauzy veil of cloud to throw up its hands and
evaporate.

The Piazza pigeons register them as turbulent undulations encountered when they descend to resume their cryptic stenography.

And rebounding from the surrounding walls and coming back
to them as faint whispers and lingering echoes, they remind Nostalgia and Christopher that there is no end of the stories that may
happen to them if they take a turn together ...

'Your nose, since you raise it ...'

'Father!'

'Resembles your mother's nose.'

'I wanted to find another way.'

'You have made a mistake, I said.'

'Do not panic, it will all come back in time.'

'Our city is exactly as you remembered it, a Baroque arrangement of fragments.'

'It occurs to me that this double spiral is a way of giving depth to the surface'

'The universal face – of which the celestial nose was the most prominent feature – expressed in its countenance every conceivable human feeling; and, to aid in its interpretation, the different feelings were located in different regions of the face.

'Once familiar with this temperamental diagram, it was possible to read a person's character in his face.

'A pronounced curve in the profile, like a road turning out of sight, signified a love of travelling; its absence, or a weaker curve, revealed a sedentary disposition and, when allied to a tendency to purse the lower lip like a portcullis, a pronounced affection for home.

'Those with a nose for it could distinguish the combative nose from the executive nose, the economical nose from the mystic nose.

'Let a woman cast the shadow of her profile on a wall and the skilled observer instantly knew whether she loved the motion of the sea, had a fear of heights or was easily led astray.'

'What do his "perambulating presences" amount to but the automata of his indecision?'

'Nostalgia!'

'Unless we begin as complete strangers, I do not see how it is possible that we shall ever find out anything about each other.'

'Nostalgia!'

'Christopher!'

'Nothing will be lost …'